Agricultural Development in Brazil

T0361876

In the last few decades, Brazilian agriculture has experienced a seismic transformation, and its contradictory facets have fed different and opposing narratives regarding recent changes. This book covers these changes, exploring the issues from several empirical and analytical angles, including the role of agriculture in the contemporary Brazilian economy, the dynamics of Brazilian agricultural value chains, environmental challenges and the processes of social differentiation.

Brazilian agriculture continues to be viewed in the international literature, either through the lenses of the past century – those of former problems relating to land use and land tenure – or apologetically. This collection of essays aims at updating the current interpretations, providing objective accounting of the main transformations, its determinants, results, contradictions and limitations. As it covers the most relevant traits of Brazilian agricultural and rural development, the book will provide the reader with an encompassing view of contemporary Brazilian agriculture, including the positive and negative sides of the so-called tropical agriculture revolution. It highlights the tremendous economic potential, as well as the continuing structural heterogeneity, concentration of production and marginalization of millions of small farmers.

Written in an engaging and accessible style, this book will be perfect for all those interested in learning about Brazilian agriculture. It will be of particular interest to undergraduate and graduate students of economic development, agricultural economics, rural sociology, comparative economic development, rural development and agricultural policies.

Antônio Márcio Buainain is senior lecturer of Economics at the Institute of Economics at the University of Campinas (Unicamp), in Campinas, Brazil. He is also a researcher at the National Institute of Science and Technology on Public Policy, Strategies and Development and at the Center for Agricultural and Environmental Economics, Unicamp. His research areas are agricultural and rural development, including extensive work on innovation in agriculture, agrarian reform, rural poverty and agricultural policies in Brazil and Latin America.

Rodrigo Lanna is associate professor at the Institute of Economics, University of Campinas (Unicamp), Brazil. He is also a researcher at the Center for Agricultural and Environmental Economics, Unicamp. His research has focused on agricultural economics and finance and his current work on agricultural finance includes price and volatility analysis, risk management and credit issues in agriculture.

Zander Navarro is a senior researcher at the Brazilian Corporation for Agricultural Research (Embrapa), Brazil. A sociologist specializing in "rural social processes", he was previously a research fellow at the Institute of Development Studies, UK from 2003 to 2009.

Routledge Studies in Agricultural Economics

Series Editor: Ashok K. Mishra
Arizona State University, USA

Public Policy in Agriculture
Impact on Labor Supply and Household Income
Edited by Ashok K. Mishra, Davide Viaggi and Sergio Gomez y Paloma

Agricultural Development in Brazil
The Rise of a Global Agro-food Power
Edited by Antônio Márcio Buainain, Rodrigo Lanna and Zander Navarro

For more information about this series, please visit: www.routledge.com/Routledge-Studies-in-Agricultural-Economics/book-series/RSAG

Agricultural Development in Brazil

The Rise of a Global Agro-food Power

Edited by Antônio Márcio Buainain, Rodrigo Lanna and Zander Navarro

Routledge
Taylor & Francis Group

LONDON AND NEW YORK

First published 2019 by Routledge

2 Park Square, Milton Park, Abingdon, Oxon, OX14 4RN
605 Third Avenue, New York, NY 10017

Routledge is an imprint of the Taylor & Francis Group, an informa business

First issued in paperback 2020

British Library Cataloguing-in-Publication Data
A catalogue record for this book is available from the British Library

Library of Congress Cataloging-in-Publication Data
Names: Buainain, Antônio Márcio, editor. | Lanna, Rodrigo, editor. |
Navarro, Zander, editor.
Title: Agricultural development in Brazil : the rise of a global agro-food power /
edited by Antônio M. Buainain, Rodrigo Lanna, and Zander Navarro.
Description: New York, NY : Routledge, 2019. |
Series: Routledge studies in agricultural economics |
Includes bibliographical references and index.
Identifiers: LCCN 2019003554 (print) | LCCN 2019015507 (ebook) |
ISBN 9781351029742 (Ebook) | ISBN 9781138492776 (hardback : alk. paper)
Subjects: LCSH: Agriculture–Economic aspects–Brazil. | Rural development–Brazil.
Classification: LCC HD1872 (ebook) | LCC HD1872 .A6536 2019 (print) |
DDC 338.10981–dc23
LC record available at https://lccn.loc.gov/2019003554

ISBN: 978-1-138-49277-6 (hbk)
ISBN: 978-0-367-72907-3 (pbk)

Typeset in Bembo
by Newgen Publishing UK

Contents

List of editors and contributors

Editors

Antônio Márcio Buainain, Associate Professor, Institute of Economics, University of Campinas (Unicamp), Campinas.

Rodrigo Lanna Franco da Silveira, Associate Professor, Institute of Economics, University of Campinas (Unicamp), Campinas.

Zander Navarro, Researcher, Brazilian Corporation for Agricultural Research (Embrapa), Brasília.

Contributors

Adriano Nogueira Zerbini, consultant in foreign trade and public affairs.

Alexandre Gori Maia, Associate Professor, Institute of Economics, University of Campinas (Unicamp), Campinas.

Alfredo Kingo Oyama Homma, Researcher, Brazilian Corporation for Agricultural Research (Embrapa), Belém.

Bastiaan Philip Reydon, Professor, Institute of Economics, University of Campinas (Unicamp), Campinas.

Carlos Augusto Mattos Santana, Researcher, Brazilian Corporation for Agricultural Research (Embrapa), Brasília.

Carolina Habib Ribeiro, Researcher in Energy Planning, University of Campinas (Unicamp), Campinas.

Geraldo Sant'Anna de Camargo Barros, Professor, University of São Paulo (USP), Piracicaba.

Hildo Meirelles de Souza Filho, Professor, Federal University of São Carlos (UFSCar), São Carlos.

Isabel Cleaver, Senior Analyst Asia–Brazil Agro Alliance (ABAA).

João Ricardo Ferreira de Lima, Researcher, Brazilian Corporation for Agricultural Research (Embrapa), Petrolina.

José Eustáquio Ribeiro Vieira Filho, Researcher, Research Institute for Applied Economics (IPEA), Brasília.

José Garcia Gasques, Researcher, Ministry of Agriculture, Livestock and Food Supply (MAPA), Brasília.

Junior Ruiz Garcia, Associate Professor, Department of Economics, Federal University of Paraná (UFPR), Curitiba.

Marcelo Pereira da Cunha, Assistant Professor, University of Campinas (Unicamp), Campinas.

Marcos Sawaya Jank, CEO of the Asia-Brazil Agro Alliance (ABAA).

Maria Sylvia Macchione Saes, Professor, University of São Paulo (USP), São Paulo.

Maria Thereza Macedo Pedroso, Researcher, Brazilian Corporation for Agricultural Research (Embrapa), Gama.

Marjorie Mendes Guarenghi, Researcher in Energy Planning, University of Campinas (Unicamp), Campinas.

Pedro Abel Vieira, Researcher, Brazilian Corporation for Agricultural Research (Embrapa), Brasília.

Abbreviations and acronyms

ABAA	Asia-Brazil Agro Alliance
ABC	Low Carbon Agriculture Program
ABCAR	Brazilian Association of Credit and Rural Technical Assistance
ABCZ	Brazilian Association of Zebu Breeders
ABIOVE	Brazilian Association of Vegetable Oil Industries
ACAR	Credit and Rural Technical Assistance Association
AGF	Federal Government Acquisition
ANDA	Brazilian Fertilizers Association
ANEC	National Association of Grain Exporters
ANFAVEA	Brazilian Automotive Vehicle Manufacturers Association
ANP	National Agency of Petroleum, Natural Gas and Biofuels
ASEAN	Association of Southeast Asian Nations
BACEN	Brazilian Central Bank
BNDES	National Bank for Economic and Social Development
CAR	Rural Environmental Registry
CDA	Agricultural Certificate of Deposit
CDAF	Direct Purchase from Family Agriculture
CDCA	Agribusiness Certificate of Credit
CDLAF	Local Direct Purchase from Family Agriculture
CECAFÉ	Brazilian Coffee Exporters Council
CEPEA	Center for Advanced Studies on Applied Economics
CFP	Production Financing Company
CGEE	Center for Management and Strategic Studies
CIDA	Inter-American Committee for Agricultural Development
CI-INCRA	INCRA Rural Property Registration (check for "INCRA" below)
CIPP	International Plant Protection Convention
CNIR	National Registry of Rural Properties
CODEVASF	São Francisco and Parnaíba Valley Development Company
CONAB	National Food Supply Company

CONSECANA	Council of Producers of Sugarcane, Sugar and Ethanol
CONSEPA	National Council of State Agencies for Agricultural Research
CONTAG	National Confederation of Rural Workers
COV	Sales Option Contract
CPR	Farmers Certificate
CPTPP	Comprehensive and Progressive Agreement for Trans-Pacific Partnership
CRA	Agribusiness Certificate Receivables
CTC	Sugarcane Technology Center
DET	Differential Export Taxes
DNOCS	National Department for Works to Combat Droughts
DNPEA	National Department of Research and Experimentation
EAP	Economically Active Population
EGF	Federal Government Loan
EMATER	State Enterprises for Technical Assistance and Rural Extension
EMBRAPA	Brazilian Corporation for Agricultural Research
EMBRATER	Brazilian Company for Technical Assistance and Rural Extension
EPE	Energy Research Office
ESALQ	Luiz de Queiroz College of Agriculture
EU	European Union
FAO	United Nations Food and Agriculture Organization
FGV	Getúlio Vargas Foundation
FIPE	Institute for Economic Research Foundation
FUNAI	National Indian Foundation
FUNDECITRUS	Citrus Defense Fund
GDP	Gross domestic product
GMOs	Genetically modified organisms
GTDN	Working Group for the Development of the Northeast
GVAP	Gross value of agricultural production
Ha	hectare (one hectare equals 2.47 acres)
HK	Hong Kong
IAA	Institute of Sugar and Alcohol
IAC	Agronomic Institute of Campinas
IAP	Rural Active Age Population
IBAMA	Brazilian Institute of the Environment
IBGE	Brazilian Institute of Statistics and Geography
IBRD	International Bank for Reconstruction and Development
ICMBio	Chico Mendes Institute for Biodiversity Conservation
ICMS	Tax on the Circulation of Goods and Services
ICO	International Coffee Organization
IFDM	Firjan Municipal Development Index

ILPF	Integrated Crop-Livestock-Forest
IMEA	Institute of Agricultural Economics of Mato Grosso
INCRA	National Institute for Colonization and Agrarian Reform
INDC	Intended Nationally Determined Contributions
INPC	National Consumer Price Index
INPE	National Institute of Spatial Research
IPCL	Incentive to Milk Production and Consumption
IPEA	Institute of Applied Economic Research
IPO	Initial public offerings
IPTU	Urban property tax
ISI	Import Substitution Industrialization
ITR	Tax on rural properties
LCA	Agribusiness Credit Note
MAPA	Ministry of Agriculture, Livestock and Food Supply
MDA	Ministry of Agrarian Development
MLA	Meat & Livestock Australia
MMA	Ministry of the Environment
MME	Ministry of Mines and Energy
MODERAGRO	Agricultural Modernization and Natural Resources Conservation Program
MODERFROTA	Modernization Program for Machinery Acquisition
MODERINFRA	Incentive Program for Irrigation and Storage
MST	Landless Movement
MTE	Ministry of Labor and Employment
NDCs	Nationally Determined Contributions
NRCS	National Rural Credit System
OCB	Organization of Brazilian Cooperatives
OECD	Organization for Economic Co-operation and Development
OEPAs	State organizations of agricultural research
OIE	World Organization for Animal Health
PAA	Food Acquisition Program
PCB	Brazilian Communist Party
PEP	Premium for Commercial Buyers Program
PEPRO	Equalizing Premium Paid to Producers
PGPAF	Family Farming Price Guarantee Program
PGPM	Guaranteed Minimum Price Policy
PGPM-Bio	Guaranteed Minimum Price Policy for Socio-biodiversity Products
PIN	National Integration Program
PLANAVEG	National Plan for the Recovery of Native Vegetation
PMDBBS	Project of Satellite Deforestation Monitoring of the Brazilian Biomes
PNAE	National Schools Food Program

PNATER	National Policy for Technical Assistance and Rural Extension
PNMC	National Policy on Climate Change
PNPB	National Program of Production and Use of Biodiesel
Polocentro	Program for the Development of the Cerrado
PPAs	Permanent Preservation Areas
PPCDAm	Action Plan for the Prevention and Control of Deforestation in the Legal Amazon
PPCerrado	Action Plan for the Prevention and Control of Deforestation and Forest Fires in the Cerrado
PROAGRO	Program of Guarantees for Agricultural Activities
PROALCOOL	Brazilian Alcohol Program
PRODES	Amazon Deforestation Monitoring
PRODUSA	Program for Sustainable Agriculture
PRODUSK	Japanese–Brazilian Cooperation Program for the Development of the Cerrados
PRONAF	Family Agriculture Strengthening Program
PROP	Private Sales Option Contracts
PROPFLORA	Program for Planting and Recovery of Commercial Forests
PSR	Endowment Program for Rural Insurance Premium
RC	Rural credit
RCEP	Regional Comprehensive Economic Partnership
R&D	Research and development
SDGs	Sustainable Development Goals
SERFAL	Extraordinary Office for Land Title Regularization in the Legal Amazon
SFAs	Agroforestry Systems
SIBER	Brazilian Rural Extension System
SIBRATER	Brazilian System of Technical Assistance and Rural Extension
SICAR	National Rural Environmental Registry
SIGEF	Land Management System
SINTER	National System of Territorial Information Management
SNCI	National Property Certification System
SNCR	National Rural Credit System
SNPA	National Agricultural Research System
SPU	Department of Heritage
STR	Rural Workers' Trade Union
SUASA	Unified System of Monitoring Agricultural Health
SUDENE	Superintendency for the Development of the Northeast
TFP	Total factor productivity
TRQs	Tariff rate quotas
UBRARIO	Brazilian Union of Biodiesel and Biojetfuel
UFV	Federal University of Viçosa

UN	United Nations
UNFCCC	United Nations Framework Convention on Climate Change
UNICA	Brazilian Sugarcane Industry Association
UNICAMP	University of Campinas
US	United States of America
USDA	United States Department of Agriculture
USP	University of São Paulo
VBC	Basic cost value
VEP	Premium for transporting agricultural products
VIGIAGRO	International Agricultural Surveillance System
WA	Agricultural and Livestock Warrant
ZAE	Agroecological Zoning of Sugarcane
ZARC	Agricultural and Climate Risk Zoning

Introduction

Antônio Márcio Buainain

Brazil has undergone major transformations over the last 50 years, particularly since the 1970s. From a rural economy, highly dependent upon exports of coffee beans and refined sugar to one of the largest industrial economies in the world; from a rural society, with approximately 65% of population living in rural areas in 1950, to a sophisticated unequal urban society, with roughly 90% of the population living in urban areas and over 60% in metropolitan areas in 2010. The country, with six different biomes and a bad international reputation regarding environment and high social inequality, is plagued with contradictions and structural heterogeneity across its vast territory (see Figures 0.1 and 0.2). However, to a large extent, the external views of Brazil have been emphasizing features that, in general, correspond to the past.

The Brazilian agricultural sector shows, to some extent, an accurate picture of contemporary Brazil. A modern agriculture based on advanced technology coexists with a traditional agriculture, which is still based on unsustainable use of natural resources, deforestation and social inequalities. Entrepreneur farmers operate side by side poor farmers, which are characterized by nineteenth century production practices. These last ones have been faced by a fiercer market competition, which imposes a rigid Darwinist selection of only the most fitted to produce according to highly demanding market criteria. In this context, the conventional role of agriculture, as a traditional supplier of capital, labor, food and raw materials to sustain the urban area, is being rapidly redefined. In this century, agribusiness is becoming one of the most dynamic and strategic axes of the national economy.

More recently, since the beginning of this century, Brazilian agriculture has been raising a lot of interest in the international community, for several reasons, either positive or negative. According to forecasts and studies from FAO, OCDE, UNCTAD and US Agriculture Department, Brazil is expected to become the most important food supplier to the international market until 2050. To some extent the world is relying in the Brazilian agriculture to avoid the emergence of a Malthusian scenario. Will Brazil stand up to these expectations or will the country disappoint the international community once more? On the other extreme, Brazilian agriculture is still singled out for its presumably negative impact on climate change due to deforestation, intensive cattle raising and use of agrochemicals as well as for social exclusion and even for condemned labor exploitation. While some of these claims may find basis on the pervasive contradictions still characterizing Brazilian agriculture, other may not correspond to the current state of affairs and may be political echo of the past, which nevertheless is still fuelling the academic, political and ideological debate on the patterns and future of Brazilian agriculture.

Despite the profound structural changes described in the various chapters of this book, the dominant interpretations regarding agriculture and rural development in Brazil continue to some extent to reflect the conditions prevailing in the 1950s, 1960s and 1970s. In that period, the agricultural sector was still mostly backward in terms of technology and social relations. Its growth was basically driven by an extensive and predatory development model, incorporation of land and cheap labour. Similarly, the contemporary debate on land use, resulting from an alliance between social movements that pursue causes linked to rural development and intellectuals who espouse a caricature of Marxism, reflects categories and conditions that no longer exist.

Indeed, an examination of appearances shows that several features of a bygone rural world can easily be identified in the present-day rural milieu: many large-scale properties with low productivity; millions of small-scale properties; rural poverty and poorly paid farm labourers; migration; and frequently grave social and environmental conflicts. One of the most distinctive characteristics of this backward-looking approach is the difficulty of understanding that although on the face of it these features have not changed, in actual fact they are intrinsically different. They are associated with novel processes and dynamics, which respond to different determinants.

The clearest example may be the unproductive large property or latifundium, which certainly persists. In the past, the dominant presence of unproductive land justified land reform policies designed to pursue two goals: a reduction in social inequality and the dynamization of agriculture and the domestic market. The absence of production, or very low productivity, was associated with absentee landowners, who retained the land as a source of income from the exploitation of landless labourers, or peasant farmers who were permitted to use it in the context of archaic relations such as sharecropping and tenant farming. Thus, lack of productivity reflected unfair social relations, backwardness, super-exploitation, as well as structural constraints such as limited services markets and high risks associated with investments for intensification of production. The continuing existence of unproductive large-scale properties, albeit as exceptions, basically reflects the lack of economic feasibility of producing under the specific conditions that prevail in certain localities. In the context of twenty-first century Brazilian agriculture, not even the most backward landowners would relinquish an opportunity to make money from their land. Even retaining landed property for speculative ends and as a hedge against inflation has lost relevance compared to the emergence of a dynamic financial market, which in recent decades has offered a safe and highly profitable haven for idle financial capital. Brazil has been a paradise for this capital and land is only exceptionally considered an investment for speculation or hedging, as it was in the past. In this context, most latifundia have been transformed to a considerable extent into large enterprises and/or modern productive farms.

The environmental question is another example. As evidenced in Chapter 8, there can be no doubt that the relations between agriculture and environmental management are conflict-ridden and full of contradictions. However, the environmental question is of an entirely different nature now compared with the past. Except in the case of illegal deforestation and criminal logging, present-day environmental pressures no longer arise from the forces of backwardness but rather from the intensification of production. Moreover, they do so in a context and within a governance framework that clearly point to an improvement in the way the problem is addressed.

However insufficient, Brazil now has effective laws and mechanisms for protecting the environment and governing the relations between agriculture and environmental management. These laws and mechanisms are recognized by all the main multilateral organizations and forums as being among the most advanced in the world. The Forest Code, which Congress passed in 2012 after ten years of intense debate among its members and with society, requires all properties of a size exceeding four 'rural modules'[1] to set aside at least 20% of their total area for permanent preservation of the natural plant cover (called the 'legal reserve'). In the Amazon biome, the proportion is 80%; in the Cerrado it ranges from 20% to 35%, depending on the location. Many properties no longer have any natural plant cover to protect, in which case landowners are allowed to purchase other properties' reserves in the same biome as offsets, or to execute environmental rehabilitation projects, which are creating a new market for native seedlings and seeds, as well as environmental management services. This does not mean deforestation has ceased to be a problem, but it can no longer be associated with growth in extensive and predatory agriculture. Indeed, the sector is saving land. Brazilian agriculture is estimated to have economized some 366 million hectares through rising total factor productivity between 1990 and 2015 (see Chapters 4 and 6) and to have reduced greenhouse gas emissions per ton of food produced by 4.5% annually thanks to the application of modern techniques.

The mismatch between interpretations and the reality of agriculture and rural development in Brazil has been a focus for fruitful debate, triggered by publication of an article entitled *Sete teses sobre o mundo rural brasileiro* (Buainain et al, 2013), in which new theses on the present state of Brazilian agriculture are provocatively counterposed against the dominant theses. To summarize extremely, the new theses postulate that: (i) at the end of the 1990s agricultural and rural development in Brazil entered a new phase in terms of production and social and economic relations and that this new dynamism is irreversible; (ii) innovations in agriculture have changed the dynamics of the sector completely and replaced the traditional determinants of competitiveness, with impacts on land use geography and on demographic and occupational patterns; (iii) the new phase is characterized by a two-track development model, in which increasing concentration of production coexists with growing differentiation and selection of producers; (iv) this evolution is gradually wiping out the past, relegating to history such previously burning issues as land reform, peasant oppression and archaic production relations, so dear to the Brazilian and Latin American scientific literature in this knowledge area; (v) the state's role has changed (or needs to change) to one of promoting sustainable development in harmony with the new institutional framework that is already in place and that extends to the social and environmental dimensions of agriculture as well as market demands for safe food products with defined origin etc.; (vi) the sector's current dynamics has activated a perverse trend that reinforces its structural heterogeneity and reduces the competitiveness of smallholdings, which in the past depended on family labour; (vii) the countryside is becoming depopulated in various parts of Brazil owing to the predominance of large-scale, high-tech, high-efficiency agriculture, which leaves no room for small farmers to survive.

The article with these theses gave rise to a book, *O Mundo Rural no Brasil do Século XXI* (Buainain et al, 2014).This compilation of papers by 51 authors with different methodological and theoretical orientations discusses the theses either by questioning them totally or partially on the basis of empirical evidence or by presenting new elements to enrich the analysis.The result is a reinterpretation of the rural world in twenty-first century Brazil, acknowledging the features that have persisted while highlighting both synchronically and diachronically the new elements introduced into the sector from the mid-1970s. It focuses on the new institutional framework, which is increasingly significant and on the market dynamics characterized by intensification of the innovation process, with steadily less room for those who cannot keep pace to survive. Initially the book was to have been translated so that it could be useful to speakers of other languages than Portuguese, but the project proved impracticable owing to the cost of translating its 1,182 pages. It was therefore reformulated to present a more direct, objective and up-to-date portrait of Brazilian agriculture and of Brazil's emergence as a global power in this market.

The present book is inspired by this debate in a certain sense. It also has an additional motivation, which derives from the conclusion that Brazilian agriculture continues to be viewed in the international literature either through lenses of the past century – those of former problems relating to land use and land tenure – or apologetically.The arguments in question are frequently biased by the positions of militant groups who pursue specific causes, ranging from environmental and food security concerns to advocacy for a peasantry whose existence is at least doubtful, among other issues.

Historically speaking, Brazilian agriculture expanded by occupying new territory and absorbing abundant and cheap labour that operated at the threshold of survival. Its productivity was extremely low, while its environmental costs were very high and at that time completely ignored. In the 1970s the state launched an ambitious package intended to modernize agriculture and agroindustry. To this end it deployed an array of financial, tax and regulatory incentives, as well as investing heavily in R&D. A national agricultural research system led by

EMBRAPA was established (see Chapters 3 and 6).These interventions, guided by a nationalist vision and by the import substitution paradigm, both of which were then dominant, produced intense, uneven and contradictory effects (see Chapters 1, 3, 6 and 8). As a result, it laid the foundations for changes that were to take place starting in the 1990s, in the context of both the institutional reforms then implemented in Brazil (monetary stabilization, trade liberalization, privatization, deregulation, an improved business environment and lower taxes on agricultural exports, among others – see Chapter 1) and the globalization process, in particular China's emergence as a major importer of soybeans (see Chapter 5).

This book addresses several facets of these changes. One is the affirmation of a new pattern of accumulation and new socio-productive dynamics, determined by the inclusion of agriculture in a process of Schumpeterian competition in which the market acts as a factor of coercion that forces players to comply with minimal institutional and economic standards. New rules have also been put in place – rules deriving from international agreements,[2] and on the other hand domestic rules banning child labour and forced labour and protecting workers' rights and the environment, among others.

Another facet relates to the new roles played by agriculture in the Brazilian economy and society, discussed in Chapter 1. Its traditional roles of supplying food and hard currency from exports have undoubtedly persisted, but its importance is much greater than can be inferred from its contribution to GDP (5.4% in 2017). A more appropriate indicator would be the contribution of so-called agribusiness to the Brazilian economy, estimated to have corresponded to about 20% of GDP in the 2010s. Agribusiness exports have earned about US$92 billion per year on average since 2010, accounting for a trade surplus of about US$76 billion (see Chapters 4 and 5).

Although this contribution is significant, it still does not accurately reflect the strategic importance of agriculture to the effective inclusion of several regions in the national economy, or its role as a basis for value chains that are strategic to that economy, including the industrial and service sectors. Indeed, in the past 50 years Brazil's productive territory has expanded into regions that were considered improper for agriculture until the mid-1960s (see Chapter 12). The frontier has been occupied mainly by migrants who were previously family farmers in the Southern and Northeast and were either driven out by a lack of options to survive in their places of origin or left voluntarily in search of new and better options. In these frontier areas, the migrants have succeeded in surmounting the constraints imposed by the limited supply of land back home. In 30 years, they have become the family or corporate entrepreneurs who in the early decades of the twenty-first century represent the most modern segment of Brazilian agriculture. This group is currently made up of highly productive medium and large producers operating at the technological frontier. Moreover, despite highly concentrated land tenure, social indicators for the new cities driven by the dynamism of agribusiness are better than the national average, a fact that at the very least raises questions about the polarized view which fails to recognize that despite contradictions this new agriculture has also been a bearer of social progress.

These themes are explored in various parts of this book, but mainly in Chapters 9 and 10, which analyses the dynamics of rural–urban migration and institutional changes with regard to labour relations. The impacts of these latter changes on the agricultural labour market and on the pattern of growth in the agricultural sector are also discussed. Migratory flows, both rural–rural and rural–urban, are part of the formation of Brazil. The novelty may be that the traditional drivers of migration, especially the lack of job opportunities in the countryside, have given way to factors of attraction. Young people above all are seduced by the advantages of urban life compared to living conditions in a rural environment that has been socially degraded by decades of abandonment, as is the rule in Brazil and are not interested in remaining in the rural milieu even if they have a job or a piece of land.

Demographic changes have had a significant impact on the agricultural labour market, which since the start of the 1990s has been governed by the ordinary labour laws, with severe sanctions for infringements by landowners and rural employers. Mechanization has been one of the responses to these changes, supported mainly by public funding mechanisms on special terms (see Chapter 3 on the ModernFrota Programme) and aggressive marketing by manufacturers of farm implements and machinery. However, in the context of the structural heterogeneity of Brazilian agriculture, mechanization is a partial response that only meets the needs of certain types of producer and production system (Chapter 6). It is difficult for the vast majority of small farmers to solve the problem of the dwindling supply of labour via mechanization (Chapter 11). This is mainly due to a lack of products and services suited to these producers, as well as factors that restrict access to innovation in general, such as tight credit, difficulties with technical assistance and maintenance and conditions that make investing economically unviable. In this context, it is worth noting the gap between those with and without access to innovation, reinforcing the perverse effects of structural heterogeneity and concentrated production, a topic explored particularly in Chapter 6.

Many of these changes revolve around the restructuring of Brazil's agri-industrial value chains, discussed in Chapter 4. These chains are becoming increasingly complex and, in many cases, have superseded the traditional organizational structures in which agriculture was a mere source of raw material and the rural milieu was a supplier of labour power. In the main agribusiness value chains, the relations between agriculture, industry and services are intense, involving competition and conflict, but also cooperation and harmonization of interests. These relations take various forms. A good example is the integration model used by the pork and poultry value chains, in which the producers, most of whom are family farmers, are contractors to the meatpacking conglomerates. Another example is the model used by the giant trading companies that operate in the grain and oilseed segment, based on financing and purchasing of crops in advance of the harvest. These operations make up for part of the working capital deficit and also serve to mitigate market risk for producers. This theme is also discussed in Chapter 3, which focuses on the role of public policy.

This entire set of transformations has not just resulted from the interplay of market forces. The state has also made a key contribution, helping to shape and dynamize Brazilian agriculture. From a historical perspective, agriculture has always played a strategic role in the Brazilian macroeconomy and this fact can lead to a mistaken reading of the role played by agriculture more recently. Under the predominant model in the past – industrialization via import substitution – agriculture was 'plundered' in the sense that its resources were transferred to supply the needs of the urban industrial sector. These transfers were operated by means of multiple mechanisms that severely penalized agriculture, from the exchange rate to food price controls. In return, agriculture enjoyed compensatory measures, which benefited few and reinforced the sector's structural heterogeneity and social inequalities, such as the exclusion of farm workers from protection by the labour laws, as well as permissiveness in land tenure and environmental management. In the modernization process that began in the late 1960s, subsidized credit was made available only to a small group of producers in a few regions.

As is widely known, these policies proved insufficient to ensure that agriculture would play a more positive role in Brazil's development. Price controls helped restrict food supply and led to frequent food, with economic, political and social effects. Restrictive trade policies designed to protect domestic agroindustry and improve market supply acted as a disincentive to exports, contributing to periodic balance-of-payments crises and proved ineffectual as a means of averting domestic supply problems and their inflationary effects. Chapter 1 analyses the changes in the relations between agriculture and the macroeconomy since the 1990s. In this period, when agriculture was placed in a more liberal context, it played a more sustainable and significant part in containing the endemic inflationary process that was corroding the economy and society in Brazil and in surmounting the balance-of-payments crises. Indeed, since then the sector has become a source of opportunities for investments that help drive the economy as a whole. Among the many opportunities, the standout is the biofuel segment, discussed in Chapter 7. Biofuel production was originally concentrated in two states of the Northeast region and in São Paulo but now takes place throughout the country, with significant economic, social and environmental impacts.

One of the most important dimensions of the changes discussed in this book is the process of 'deagrarianization' whereby Brazilian society has become steadily less rural in character and less economically dependent on agriculture. This thesis is presented early on in the book, in Chapter 2. To a large extent the discussions held in the second half of the twentieth century, as well as the agricultural policies implemented in the period, were shaped by the 'agrarian question'. Needless to say, one of the pillars of this question was the idea that a major land reform programme was needed to enable capitalism to develop in Brazil, guarantee food security and expand the domestic market for the industrial sector. On the other hand, public policy sought to respond via modernization to this same challenge and to promote a controlled land reform process involving the compulsory purchase of over 90 million hectares between 1985 and 2018, redistributing all this land to more than 1.4 million families of settlers (See Chapter 13). The results, which are not assessed in this book, are highly controversial. Some authors (Ramos, 2014) argue that the intervention is justified regardless of whether the families settled have overcome poverty and made a significant contribution, while others (Graziano Neto and Navarro, 2015) claim that land redistribution may have been justified in the past but is not so in the present either as social policy or as a measure to assure food security, let alone as a strategy to promote the nation's development.

Deagrarianization does not mean that rural poverty has vanished or that the changes have reduced the heterogeneity that characterizes the rural milieu, as stressed in several parts of this book, especially Chapter 11 on family farming. On the contrary, the discussions presented here note the dual or contradictory nature of development mentioned earlier, adding a new duality between, on one hand, innovative segments that respond to the demands and challenges posed by the market, combining private entrepreneurship with political lobbying and public support; and, on the other hand, the vast majority of producers, who are steadily lagging more and more behind, losing competitiveness and no longer able to rely on a state with the wherewithal to subsidize their reproduction, as can their European counterparts. The poorest only keep their heads above water thanks to social cash transfer programmes, which however important do no more than shore up bearable conditions of poverty. The oldest take succour from the pensions guaranteed by the 1988 Constitution, which are becoming less and less sustainable. The rest appear condemned to losing productive and social space. In this context, de-agrarianization means that the solutions to these problems lie not in the agrarian dimensions but in the possibility of educating viable rural producers to seize the opportunities created by development in general and training the young so they have the skills and qualifications needed to grasp the opportunities available outside agriculture, whether in the countryside or in the towns.

The consolidation of Brazilian agriculture and agribusiness as a global power, noted by multilateral organizations such as FAO, OECD and the World Bank, is no trivial task. It requires overcoming a number of obstacles that in the early years of the twenty-first century were circumvented thanks to an exceptional combination of circumstances in the international market, especially high prices due to the imbalance caused by China's emergence as a major world power. The challenges involved in surmounting these obstacles, discussed in Chapter 5, involve several dimensions, such as: (i) sustaining innovation, which is increasingly complex because it is no longer a matter merely of the productivity gains and cost savings, often achieved in the past at a high cost to the environment and to animal or human health, but entails above all innovating to respond to society's ever stronger and more imperative demands relating to environmental sustainability, food quality, employment relations and fairness; (ii)

Figure 0.1 Brazilian states and regions.

11 Rondônia
12 Acre
13 Amazonas
14 Roraima
15 Pará
16 Amapá
17 Tocantins
21 Maranhão
22 Piauí
23 Ceará
24 Rio Grande do Norte
25 Paraíba
26 Pernambuco
27 Alagoas
28 Sergipe
29 Bahia

31 Minas Gerais
32 Espírito Santo
33 Rio de Janeiro
35 São Paulo
41 Paraná
42 Santa Catarina
43 Rio Grande do Sul
50 Mato Grosso do Sul
51 Mato Grosso
52 Goiás
53 Distrito Federal

building the transportation infrastructure needed by as vast a country as Brazil, so that the areas occupied in the last 50 years can produce and so that the old areas can overcome the loss of competitiveness due to a lack of secondary roads, which are essential to the diversified production systems used by small and medium farmers; (iii) building the infrastructure required to support the spread of agriculture 4.0 and investing in the creation and diffusion of new technology to avert a fresh wave of social exclusion and economic concentration; (iv) settling environmental liabilities and forging ahead toward zero-carbon agriculture; (v) promoting the inclusion of viable family farmers in agribusiness value chains to combat the ongoing process of economic concentration and the sector's structural heterogeneity; (vi) developing and strengthening traditional and short production chains to add more value to the national economy and reduce the share of commodities in total output; (vii) addressing animal health problems so that Brazil complies with the standards required by the most demanding foreign markets and establishing reliable health risk management mechanisms to prevent a recurrence of the periodic crises that tarnish the

Figure 0.2 Brazilian biomes.

reputation of Brazilian agriculture and interrupt its exports; (viii) promoting access to international markets by means of bilateral and multilateral diplomatic and trade agreements; and (ix) promoting the reputation of Brazilian agriculture by objectively and scientifically raising international awareness of the positive changes undergone and good examples of the sustainable practices increasingly implemented by the sector.

Overall, the idea of the book is to present and discuss the transformations of Brazilian agriculture and rural areas, highlighting its contradictions, its strengths and weakness, its potentials and risks.

These different facets of Brazilian agriculture – the so-called agrarian transition – have fed different and not seldom opposite narratives regarding recent agrarian and rural changes, stemming from politically engaged analysis highlighting and generalizing the negative social and environmental impacts of modern agriculture while romanticizing the advantages of traditional small producers to the opposite analyses that oversee the social, economic and environmental contradictions of the recent transformations and the nowadays dominant productive systems. Chapter 14 deals with the main traits of intellectual trajectories about the Brazilian agrarian transition, in a 'desperately short' space to explore such a rich subject.

Chapters of the book cover most of this trajectory and explore several empirical and analytical angles, from its contemporary history and its corresponding structural changes; from the birth of the country's most relevant value chains and emerging technological density to its implications on the labour market; from environmental challenges to processes of social differentiation that are deepening and may thus transform rural areas into quasi-demographic deserts in the near future.

Notes

1 A rural module (MR) is roughly equivalent to a family subsistence farm. The actual area varies in different parts of Brazil.
2 Such as TRIPS and other trade accords overseen by the WTO; the Convention on Biological Diversity (CBD); the Cartagena Protocol on Biosafety; the Agriculture Framework Agreement; the Agreement on the Application of Sanitary and Phytosanitary Measures (SPS); and the Paris Agreement.

1 Agriculture, industry and the economy

From extensive farming to a global agro-food power

Geraldo Sant'Anna de Camargo Barros

1 Introduction

The debates on Brazil's transformation from a typical agro-exporting country to a modern and sustainable developed economy traditionally emphasized the requirements imposed by the urbanization process. The discussions focused prominently on the decisive role played by the domestic industrialization. The policy goal was to promote economic development based on capital formation in the industry anchored on surplus extracted from agriculture and on occasional foreign savings. An intricate and interdependent set of relations, including technological intensification and greater productivity based on an ever-growing trained and educated population – both urban and rural – was one of the basic premises of the desired path to development. The transformation presupposed the need to invest strongly in human capital in order to cope with the increasing complexities of the economic expansion at large. However, as argued below, limited progress was achieved in this relevant area.

The chapter discusses some aspects of the historical framework applied to the development of the Brazilian economy. It also addresses major obstacles to the process followed over time, especially since the 1930s, when several initiatives to promote the country's industrialization started. The structural transformation was consolidated at the turn of the 1970s. It will be argued that, despite the impressive results obtained, a series of macroeconomic and social challenges were not overcome. Moreover, the stated objective of pursuing an equitable pattern of development was only partially achieved. In particular, the undisputable social aim of building a robust educated society is still far from reality.

From a historical perspective, industrialization depends on savings, which in general originates from agriculture. In the case of Brazil, the main source of savings was, initially, the coffee sector, either through surplus collected from foreign trade or resulting from forced extraction imposed by public policies, e.g. fiscal and exchange rate measures.

Thanks to favourable climate and soil conditions, significant increases in the relative prices of coffee and sugar on the international market and a replacement of slave labour by European and Japanese immigrants, coffee production developed rapidly in São Paulo during the 1880–1930 period. However, after the economic crash of 1929 a different picture emerged. The repercussions of the crash on the international trade of agricultural commodities led to a crisis in the coffee sector. In this context, production incentives were given to promote crop and livestock production – as a result, sugarcane resumed its leadership decades later as a major productive sector.

Following those years, it became clear that industrialization and urbanization, already well advanced, would not be sustained without the support of an efficient agricultural sector. Therefore, in the 1970s major public investment was made in the transformation of agriculture. Until then, agricultural research was carried out by subnational institutes and universities. According to Alves (1979), although agricultural production increased between the 1930s and the mid-1970s, it did so at decreasing and insufficient rates to keep up with demand. Thus, supply gaps emerged causing price pressures to the detriment of the urban population. This situation worsened at the initial phase of the industrialization.

The industrial sector has frequently received government incentives, from the 1930s to the present – protectionist tariffs, overvalued exchange rates, tax and credit subsidies, etc. – and agriculture has traditionally been considered a source of resources – labour, savings, foreign currency, food and fibre, often at controlled prices. Nevertheless, since the 1960s agriculture has benefitted from subsidized credit and price support programmes.[1] The establishment of a national agricultural research system and the creation of rural extension institutions in the early 1970s contributed also to enhancing the sector's performance. A programme of land redistribution (land reform) and new labour legislation were also simultaneously introduced.

After decades of investment in agriculture and in the industry, a positive picture is observed, i.e., a strong and efficient agricultural sector producing ever-larger volumes at stable or even decreasing real prices. However, the same is not the case with the industry – the sector still shows low competitiveness and efficiency, and is unable to survive when protectionist measures are withdrawn. For many analysts, starting in the 1980s, a 'deindustrialization drive' has been under way in Brazil (Bacha and Bolle, 2013). Since then, the country has fallen into the middle-income trap, with a high degree of income concentration. In agriculture, larger and high technology farms (less than 10% of the total), generating three quarters of the sector's income, have been a stark contrast to the vast majority of farmers living in poverty, with little human capital and making small use of modern technology. Therefore, a major agricultural challenge remains: How can the gap between these two realities of Brazilian agriculture be reduced? The next sections of this chapter present the evolution of Brazilian agriculture in the 1930–2017 period, highlighting some of its links to industry and to the economy as a whole.

2 The development of an agro-exporting economy through industrialization: 1930–1960

Throughout the nineteenth century, the industrial revolution expanded its social and economic impact, particularly in Europe. From a global point of view, at that time Brazil was characterized as an agro-exporting economy. Gold mining was in decline and coffee production was just beginning to expand. From the middle of the century onwards, the building of railways with routes to the ports accelerated in response to the export flow needs of coffee producers. The initial phase of industrialization (wool, cotton, silk, iron and steel, as noted by Luz, 1978) did not prosper much in Brazil during that century. It always involved some form of protectionism, partly as a reflex of the fiscal policy, focused on taxes imposed on agricultural exports.

At the turn of the nineteenth century, the industrial sector still represented only 12% of Brazilian GDP (Bonelli, 2006). The state of São Paulo stood out due to its large coffee resources, which were used to finance the import of both capital goods and raw materials, as well as the recruitment of foreign labour through immigration (Suzigan, 1971). According to Versiani and Suzigan (1990), until the 1920s sectors such as textiles, clothing and shoes, food and beverages met the overall demand created by the coffee industry. These sectors consisted of small factories, most of them operated by middle-class immigrants (Cardoso, 1960).

The following decade saw the establishment of plants for the production of inputs such as pig iron, cement, capital goods tools and machinery, for use in the agro-industry. Suzigan (1988) argues that the role of the state in the industrialization process, however, was negligible until the end of the 1920s. By then, the industry already represented 16% of GDP while agriculture accounted for 38% of the total (Bonelli, 2006). These shares remained stable until the end of the 1950s. Apart from coffee – by far the main source of foreign exchange – there was practically no direct state intervention in agricultural prices (Brandão and Carvalho, 1991).

With the rise of Getúlio Vargas to the presidency of the country, after the revolution of 1930, the structure of power changed – from the old regional aristocracies towards a centralized militarized technocracy. A state-sponsored programme aimed at promoting industrialization (involving exchange rate control, fiscal subsidies and restrictions on imports) was forcefully imposed while somewhat maintaining incentives for the coffee sector, whose resources remained essential for the implementation of the programme.

Under Vargas a new institutional framework, compatible with the industrialization strategy, was developed. By the end of the 1950s, a broad system was in place; it included new labour rights, but at the same time increased the control over the decisions taken by workers and their unions. While addressing some issues related to the quality of life of the workers in preparation for the intended thrust towards industrialization, very little was done in terms of their productivity, as evidenced by their low educational level. In 1940, still 56% of the population was illiterate (Figure 1.1). The variable fell slowly to 51% in 1950 (Souza, 1999). Among the rural population, the illiteracy rate was 68% in 1950 (Ferraro, 2012).

Further to the above, in order to boost economic growth, an official credit programme to finance agricultural and industrial production started operating

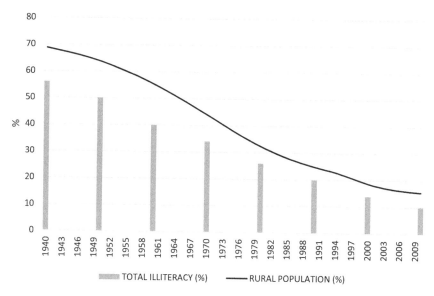

Figure 1.1 Evolution of rural population (%) and national illiteracy (%) in Brazil between 1940 and 2010.

in 1937 under the auspices of *Banco do Brasil* (Bank of Brazil). Moreover, state or 'mixed economy' companies were established in the areas of steel, minerals, engines, chemistry and electricity generation.

In the 1950s, public bodies and new regulations were created for the purpose of managing the exchange rate, licensing and financing foreign trade and establishing customs tariffs. During that decade, the automobile industry functioned as the main industrial driver, dragging behind heavy industry (steel, metallurgy, machinery and equipment).

As a result of the policies followed to promote the domestic industrialization, the sector continued to grow. Thanks to government actions that coordinated the use of national (public and private) with foreign savings, which were increasingly necessary considering the desired pace of investment, the industry share of GDP increased from 15% in 1930 to 20% in 1950. In contrast to this performance, the share of agriculture in GDP fell from 36% to 25% in the same period. Thus, part of the population soon faced serious food shortages. Malnutrition and hunger were predominant in some regions of the country, where 70% of the population still lived in rural areas (Castro, 1946;Vasconcelos, 2008). This situation forced the government to gradually turn its attention to agricultural production.

Initially, the government's reaction was to control the symptoms (high food prices) rather than focus on the causes – the low income of the population and the inefficiencies of the agricultural production structure. Therefore, marketing and food price control bodies were created, culminating with the establishment of the National Food Commission in 1951 (Silva, 1995). The second response, during the 1940s, was to implement a major territorial occupation programme known as the 'March to the West'. This initiative was adopted because food production in the Southern and Southeast regions, albeit on the rise, was not growing as steadily as the urban population demanded.

An enlightening analysis regarding the development of agriculture in the Southern, Southeast and Center-West of Brazil was developed by Chaddad (2016). In the Center-South, European immigrants were able to transform their socioeconomic conditions from tenants working on coffee plantations in São Paulo in the 1920s and become independent producers. From the late 1950s onwards, small farmers in the southernmost state of Rio Grande do Sul began to plant soybeans and other crops, using inputs that increased the fertility of the soil. In other places, such as in the states of Paraná and Santa Catarina, the production of milk, poultry, pigs and grain, was successfully developed by producers' cooperatives. Given the level of schooling and certain cultural and social facets of the producers, they have been organized into colonies and cooperatives since the 1920s.

According to Chaddad (2016), since the crisis of 1929 coffee production in Brazil was partially replaced by pastures and other crops. Cattle ranching, which had in turn been an important vehicle for territorial occupation in the colonial period, was boosted by the establishment of pastures in the 1920s and 1930s in areas formerly under forest, which made use of new varieties of grass from Africa (Wedekin, 2017). Slaughterhouses, funded by foreign (British and American) capital, were built in the Southern and Southeast regions, dominating beef exports, which were previously in the hands of Brazilian firms.

As industrialization advanced, the process frustrated those who had perceived it as a tool to raise labour incomes and reduce inequality and poverty. Agriculture's share of GDP shrank to 18% in the 1950s, whereas the contribution of the industry increased to 26% of the total (Figure 1.2.). Meanwhile, labour productivity in the industry was more than six times higher compared to agriculture (Menezes Filho et al., 2014). However, while agriculture employed 15.4 million people, the industry secured merely 1.8 million jobs (IBGE, 2006a). Thus, the most productive sector occupied a small part of the labour force, and the vast majority were excluded from the direct benefits of the industrializing effort.

Agriculture, despite registering a significant spatial expansion, faced several challenges in keeping up with the rapidly growing demand due to urbanization and industrialization. The 1940s saw a real increase of 35% in the price of food in the city of São Paulo. In the following decade a further price boost was observed, this time reaching 42%, according to surveys carried out by FIPE (Institute for Economic Research Foundation) and FGV (Getúlio Vargas Foundation). The food price increases had negative impacts on the living conditions of the population, especially on those families that moved quickly to urban areas but were unable to find employment in the industrial sector.[2] Given this situation, price controls – of both, food and industrial goods – were

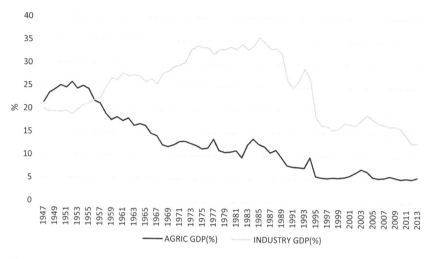

Figure 1.2 Shares of agriculture and industry in Brazil's GDP (%), 1947–2013.

reinforced. According to Oliveira (1984), domestic food price control, together with an overvalued exchange rate of the national currency, resulted in a high taxation on agriculture. The overvaluation was estimated at its highest in 1964, i.e. 42%; in 1974, it was still relatively high at 34%.

3 Preparing agriculture for industrialization and urbanization: 1960–1990

The 1960s and, in particular, the 1970s were very intense in terms of macro-economic and sectoral policies. The period was marked by remarkable rates of economic growth and became known as 'the Brazilian miracle'. Agriculture was required to supply food and raw materials to the urban areas; at the same time, agricultural production and conditions of life in the vast countryside also claimed for outside support given the historical shortcomings affecting them. Rocha (2013) shows that income concentration increased after 1960, resulting in poverty levels close to 70% of the population in 1970. In rural areas it was even higher – close to 80%. According to Neri (2012), the Gini index of income concentration in Brazil increased in the 1960–1970 period, from 0.535 to 0.581. The illiteracy level was 34% of the population on that occasion. In the 1960s, CEPAL concluded that industrialization had failed to bring the desired social progress (Bielschowsky, 2009). Thus, it recommended the adoption of an agrarian reform programme with the expectation that access to land would lead to greater efficiency in agriculture, and hence a reduction in the poverty level.

   As a result, and in response to the existing situation, the government began to implement mechanisms to deal with the so-called agrarian question, which involved labour relations and land use in the countryside. Laws that sought to regulate the rural labour market (already applied in cities since the 1940s), including social security, were enacted. Some laws also established a set of sophisticated procedures to implement land redistribution. Over the years, the effect of these measures was an increase in the wage rate, thus resulting in some cases in a replacement of labour by machines, whose costs were mitigated by subsidies granted to rural investment credit (Rezende, 2006). The sum of these effects, together with the possibility of exploring economies of scale, were a strong stimulus to the persistent increase in farm size, particularly in the case of large-scale rural establishments.

According to Alves and Pastore (1980), the agricultural policy was oriented to increasing production through land expansion and productivity growth. Land reform was restricted to specific cases in which the agrarian structure was incompatible with the goals required. In this regard, agricultural support programmes and policies were implemented, such as subsidized rural credit and minimum price and storage programmes. However, the provision of cheap credit tended to be concentrated in the hands of the largest rural producers. In general, the price policy failed because of the inefficiency of the government policies to act in the markets and to facilitate the physical movement of production between regions (Barros, 2000).

The 1960s and 1970s also saw the heyday of the 'March to the West', a spatial movement of occupation towards the formerly sparsely populated Center-West of Brazil, following the inauguration of the new capital, Brasília, located in the region. As a result, from 1960 to 1980, the cultivated area in Brazil doubled in size (Gasques et al., 2010a). During the 1970s, the population in that region grew 46%, while the Brazilian population expanded by almost half (26%). A number of government programmes were implemented covering a wide range of investments: transportation, storage facilities, electricity power, research, mechanization and soil fertilizers. In the Center-West, a number of farms was managed by producers who had migrated from the Southern and Southeast regions of the country to this new agricultural frontier. In general, they brought with them reasonable amount of capital due to the sale of more valuable lands in their region of origin. They were also self-assumed entrepreneurs, relying on human capital to assimilate new technologies and used to take decisions in more complex economic environments.

In the 1960s, the farmers that remained in the Southern began to grow soybeans with the use of inputs, which increased soil fertility and boosted productivity. Over time, cooperatives began to conduct research, provide technical assistance and to organize marketing. Different modalities of contract production were implemented. Vertical integration through processing was used since at least the 1950s for both, crop and animal products (Chaddad, 2016).

According to the same author (*Ibid.*), since 1970, sugarcane became an important crop in the state of São Paulo. In 1969, an association (Sugarcane Technology Center – CTC) was formed by producers to generate sugarcane varieties adapted to local climate and soil conditions. Since the mid-1970s, this activity received government support through the Brazilian Alcohol

Programme (PROALCOOL), an initiative that also fostered the generation of technology and provided credit at favourable conditions to advance ethanol production – see Chapter 7.

Boosted by severe frosts in Florida, the production of orange and its juice began to develop in the same period in the state of São Paulo, which became a major exporter. Like sugarcane, the orange sector also adopted the strategy of vertical integration and contract production. Since then, the sector has been working on genetic breeding and controlling pests and diseases through various mechanism, including the creation of FUNDECITRUS (Citrus Defense Fund), which is funded by orange growers and the juice industry (Chaddad, 2016).

According to Wedekin (2017), the beef industry experienced a stronger impetus in the 1970s in response to high meat prices. With the support of government credit, animal feed and livestock management, including sanitary aspects, were improved. The work conducted by the Brazilian Association of Zebu Breeders (ABCZ) resulted in great advances in the area of genetics. Meantime, in face of strong government interventions in the markets, foreign slaughterhouses became involved in mergers and acquisitions, but this competition eventually resulted in the dominance of the sector by domestic capital slaughterhouses. Similarly to what was observed with several crops, the migration of beef cattle to the Center-West accelerated in the 1980s.

In the same decade, public investment in agricultural research was firmly established, mainly through the creation of the Brazilian Corporation for Agricultural Research (Embrapa). This was followed shortly by the creation of the Brazilian Company for Technical Assistance and Rural Extension (Embrater), which was in charge of agglutinating several then uncoordinated subnational public rural extension services formerly set up in almost all states. Financially anchored on the Federal Government, Embrater stimulated the diffusion of new technologies that became available through the new agricultural research system formed around Embrapa (Alves et al., 2008). The adaptation of technologies for the production of grains and animal products was essential for the occupation of the Center-West. The intensive use of modern inputs and machines was the lever for persistent agricultural growth.

The surge in world commodity prices in the 1970s, especially in the agricultural sector, represented a great opportunity for Brazilian farmers. To take advantage of this opportunity, the total amount of subsidized rural credit grew almost fivefold in that decade – the credit volume for the Center-West alone expanded more than sevenfold. Real yearly interest rates on rural credit decreased from −1% in 1970 to −35% in 1980. The value of the subsidies through rural credit represented 20% of agriculture's GDP at its peak in 1980 (Shirota, 1988). Agricultural research was strongly encouraged – Embrapa's budget more than tripled between 1975 and 1980 (Alves and Oliveira, 2005).

Soybean production grew by 1,790% between 1965 and 1975, with an additional cumulative rate of 85% until 1985 (IBGE). From 1975 to 1985, the production of sugarcane increased 170%, orange production by 120% and coffee by 50%. The basis of this production growth was the intensified use of modern inputs. From 1975 to 1985, the total consumption of fertilizers more than doubled (Alves et al., 2008), as did the stock of tractors in agriculture (Bragagnolo and Barros, 2015). Meanwhile, the total area harvested with grains grew 50% (Gasques et al., 2010a). Cattle herds more than doubled (a rate of 111% growth) between 1960 and 1980, while pastureland increased 44%, all figures according to IBGE.

The production of typical crops consumed in the domestic market, however, grew at lower pace vis-à-vis the exported commodities: maize, 35%; rice, 16%; beans, 12%; cassava, −11%. The implementation of the agricultural policies produced an imbalance in the production of crops devoted to foreign markets (soybean, orange, sugarcane) and energy (sugarcane), to the detriment of those consumed in the domestic market (rice, beans and cassava, for example). Melo (1982) associated this result with the evolution of relative prices between these two groups of crops. According to this author, the products whose prices were predominantly determined in the external markets presented a better production performance. Higher agricultural exports meant lower domestic supply, which was a common interpretation at the time. As a result, stagnation in the *per capita* availability of calories and proteins was observed from the mid-1960s well into the 1980s, even with increased subsidized wheat imports. In terms of consumer costs, food became relatively more expensive than other items, which was especially harmful to the poorest families.

Overall, from 1967 to 1980, the Brazilian agriculture grew at the robust rate of 6.4% per year. Data available from 1975 show that by 1980 the total factor productivity (TFP) of agriculture had already grown by 25%, probably due to the impact of the research and extension work that was being carried out (Gasques et al., 2010b) – Figure 1.3. According to Bacha and Bonelli (2012), the TFP for Brazil as a whole was stagnant after a pattern of accelerated postwar growth until the 1970s. The positive growth of agriculture in the 1970s took place in spite of a transfer of 8% to 9% of the total income from the sector to the rest of the economy (Brandão, 1989). However, when including the subsidized rural credit in the calculation, agriculture received a net benefit equivalent of 5% to 6% of its total income.

Even under these favourable circumstances, agricultural growth in the 1967–1980 period was less than 60% of the industrial performance. Given the heterogeneous growth of the economy, agricultural relative prices (measured by the ratio of sectoral to the total GDP deflators), increased by 50% during the ten years to 1977. Fiscal and monetary uncontrolled policies and the intensification of the price indexation process meant that changes in relative prices led to higher annual rates of inflation, which jumped from 27% in 1968 to 92% in 1980. The attempt to contain real wage losses was evident in the aggravation of labour disputes.

In 1980, only 25% of the employed population worked in the industry, although 67% of the population lived in cities. Agriculture, accounting for 11% of GDP, hired 33% of the employed population. As a result of this situation, poverty levels in Brazil reached 43.2% of the population in 1981 (Barros et al.,

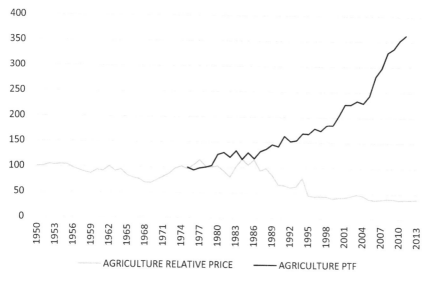

Figure 1.3 Relative prices (1950/2013) and total factor productivity of agriculture in Brazil, between 1975 and 2011.

2001), of which 26% were illiterate. The concentration of income measured by the Gini index increased from 0.581 to 0.589 between 1970 and 1980 (Neri, 2012).

All these tendencies and indicators lead to the conclusion that the priority given to industrialization focused exclusively on the formation of physical capital with little commitment to the human capital development. This resulted in an accelerated growth of the economy but left behind the majority of the population that was not integrated into the most productive sector of the economy.

According to Bonelli (2006), the Brazilian GDP grew at an average annual rate of 9% in the 1967–1980 period. The manufacturing industry grew at 11% per year (*Ibid.*). This was due to expansionary fiscal and monetary policies, state and private investments, fiscal incentives and tariff exemptions on equipment imports (*Ibid.*). The creation of state-owned companies reached record levels. During the military regime (1964 to 1985), 302 state enterprises were created, compared to 73 in the 1930–1964 period (Da Costa and Miano, 2013). The national industry was then able to produce, besides durable consumer goods, also basic inputs and capital goods. Brazil had achieved an industrial structure that resembled OECD countries, including the electro-electronic, metal-mechanical and chemical sectors. In addition, much of the resources mobilized were also allocated to develop infrastructure. A substantial contribution of external savings – direct investments and floating interest rate loans from commercial banks (irrigated by the so-called petrodollars) – was essential. This strategy would lead later – on the downside – to the accelerated growth of the external debt.

Bacha and Bonelli (2012), however, showed that the growth of Brazilian GDP fell severely after 1980 dropping from an average close to 7.5% per year in the 1970s to around 2.5% in the following years. They attributed this decline to the drastic reduction in the external savings influx and to the substantial increase in capital goods prices from 1980 up until 2010, a period when local production became more significant as a result of the import substitution process. The TFP in Brazil as a whole became stagnant from 1980 to the mid-2000s. Consequently, the GDP growth rate was 1.6% per year in the 1980s; agriculture grew at a 2.5% rate in the same period, while the industry remained stagnant.

During the 1980s, inflation accelerated as a result of uncontrolled fiscal and monetary policies and widespread social and economic practices, which indexed prices to rates of inflation. An ineffective sequence of heterodox economic plans to control inflation took place. The government interventions included freezing prices and currency changes, which resulted in disorganization of the economy and a very asymmetrical distribution of substantial losses and gains among different sectors of the economy.

Regarding agriculture, two important aspects marked the 1980s. On the one hand, its pattern of relative prices followed a downward trend that began after the commodity crisis of the mid-1970s (Figure 1.3). At the end of the 1980s, agricultural and livestock real prices faced by producers and consumers were between 40% and 60% lower than the 1975 values. Fortunately, the TFP of agriculture increased 32% in the same period (Gasques et al., 2010b) attenuating the impact of the fall in prices paid to producers (Figure 1.3). The increase in agricultural TFP also occurred on a global scale, particularly in other emerging countries such China and Indonesia (Fuglie, 2010). During the 1980s, total world agricultural output grew at 2% per year and 3.7% in Brazil. In the same decade, Brazilian soybean exports began to rival and ultimately surpassed coffee exports (Castro and Rossi Jr., 2000).

An additional facet of Brazilian agriculture was the severe string of cutbacks suffered by agricultural policies in the 1980s. The Proalcool programme was terminated in 1985. In addition, as a result of the worsening fiscal crisis, a 46% cut in public spending on agriculture funds took place between 1987 and 1989 (Barros, 2014). The cuts focused on price support and regulatory stocks, which fell 78% (Barros, 2000). When comparing a short period of two years, 1987 and 1989, agricultural policy experienced another setback – a drop in the rural credit volume by 35%.

By the end of the decade the industry had stagnated. Its share of GDP in 1990 dropped to 26.5% compared to 34% in 1980, indicating that a process of de-industrialization was in course (Bonelli, 2006). Agriculture had slightly increased its share of GDP to 10.5% in 1990. The Gini index of 0.61 pointed to the record of inequality for the available data (Neri, 2012) and 19.7% of the population was illiterate. For Rocha (2013), the poverty level was 30%. The urban population accounted for 76% of the total.

4 Agriculture generates expected benefits but industry is not competitive: 1990–2010

The 1990s was characterized by important macroeconomic achievements by Brazil. The most significant was the inflation control under the Real Plan enacted in 1994. After reaching almost 2,500% in 1993 the annual inflation rate dropped to 5.97% in 2000 as a result of the Plan. The adopted measures included the use of an ingenious mechanism of de-indexing, maintaining price flexibility in the markets, accompanied by very high interest rates and highly valued exchange rates. The implementation of the Plan inaugurated a period of continuous increases in fiscal taxation in order to compensate for the heavy inflationary taxation that no longer existed. According to Almeida (2014), the tax burden in Brazil increased from 25% of GDP to 36% in the 1993–2012 period. As a result, several productive difficulties remained, especially for less competitive activities. In addition to high interest rates and to an overvalued currency, poor infrastructure, bureaucracy and a high tax burden made up the so-called 'Brazil Cost' that continues to affect the macroeconomic performance of the country to date.

Throughout the 1990s, structural changes materialized after the implementation of several orthodox policies widely defended in the context of the so-called 'Washington consensus'. Protectionism was reduced, and regional trade agreements signed, such as that of Mercosur. The average import tariff imposed by Brazil of 32.1% in 1990 fell to 13.1% in 1995. A series of privatizations of state-owned enterprises and concessions of public services were carried out along with the creation of a number of regulatory agencies. Several state agencies operating price control mechanisms were extinguished. Embrater, the Brazilian agency in charge of rural extension, was also closed. A decision that would prove very harmful to small and poor farmers, particularly those in the Northeastern region of the country. Lopes et al. (2007) report several estimates of the support for agriculture in Brazil in different periods of time. Estimates by Schiff and Valdés (1992) indicates that the support for agriculture (sum of price and non-price transfers) was between 18% and 25% of its GDP from 1970 to 1983; Lopes et al (2007) report as well that that support fell to only 0.1% in the period from 1985 to 1992 according to Valdés (1996).[3] While agriculture adapted well to the imperatives posed by globalization, industry, however, suffered from a low competitive capacity and technological backwardness, demanding and obtaining continuous protection and financial and fiscal support (Milanez, 2007).

As pointed out by Chaddad (2016), an important change positively related to agriculture was the consolidation of the cooperative system in the 1990s, with the Organization of Brazilian Cooperatives (OCB) as the only representative of the system in Brazil. As a result, the cooperative system became self-regulated. Public resources were used to train managers to work in liberalized markets and in cooperative management. The provision of technical assistance, supply of inputs and collective marketing expanded, thus boosting productivity and profitability of the cooperative farmers. In the 1980s, the cooperatives in Paraná were pioneers in the implementation of the so-called no-till farming, which minimizes the impact of cultivation on the soil. In partnership with Embrapa, this technology was disseminated to other regions of the country. Vertically integrated value chains were developed by incorporating the supply of inputs and raw material processing.

Chaddad (2016) also demonstrates that with the end of the price control system, the sugarcane sector went through a significant consolidation process in the 1990s, with groups of sugar mills being controlled by organized groups. Vertical integration and coordination with farmers through long-term contracts were implemented. A collective decision-making body (CONSECANA – Council of Producers of Sugarcane, Sugar and Ethanol) was established to determine sugarcane prices (linked to sugar and ethanol prices) jointly with farmers and the industry. In the orange sector, improved production conditions in Florida had a negative effect on the market. Thus, there was a significant decrease in the number of domestic orange producers and a concentration in the industry.

In the case of the beef industry, Wedekin (2017) shows that it repeated the experiences of sugarcane and orange production and most slaughterhouses moved to the Center-West. The control of inflation brought about by the Real Plan transformed the beef production system. With high and uncontrolled inflation, live animals were formerly an asset conducive to speculation. However, with inflation under control, it was necessary to respond with technology and efficiency in both, livestock production and in the industry as a whole. Export possibilities provided further incentives to improve meat quality and safety. All of the adjustments were supported by the public sector.

An agricultural policy programme aimed especially to small producers was established in 1996, the Family Agriculture Strengthening Programme – PRONAF. Through this programme, the government has been providing credit, rural extension and fostering productive and commercial activities carried out by this type of farmers and their families. The price support policy to other farmers also changed. The indexation of minimum prices to rates of inflation was eliminated and the government gradually reduced its former menu of interventions. Overall, public expenditure on agriculture was reduced by 52% between 1995 and 2000 (Gasques and Bastos, 2009) – see Chapter 03. It is interesting to note that public spending on agrarian reform projects increased tenfold during the 1985–1995 period (Gasques et al., 2006). Even so, the Gini index of land ownership concentration was virtually the same in 1995 and 1985, i.e. 0.856. In 2006, the index increased to 0.872 (Souza and Silva, 2012).

In the 1990s, agriculture stood out prominently in relation to other sectors. It registered an average growth rate of 3.7% per year, while total GDP increased by 2.5%. Nevertheless, in 2000 the share of agriculture and of the industry in the Brazilian GDP were, respectively, 6% and 17%, i.e. almost half of those observed in 1985.

Agricultural TFP increased 42% in the 1990s (Gasques et al., 2006) compared to a 5% decline in the entire economy (Veloso, 2013). Fertilizers use in Brazil doubled (Anda, 2011) while its worldwide use remained stagnant (Bragagnolo and Barros, 2015). Agriculture employed between 15% and 17% of the country's labour force in the same decade (Buainain and Dedecca, 2008), close to half the figure that prevailed by the end of the 1970s – see Chapter 09.

Agricultural prices fell more than 38% in the 1990s. This drop was in line with the evolution of international food prices, which fell 18% in dollar terms plus the impact of a real appreciation of the domestic currency of about 20% (FGV, Cepea, IMF). Consumer prices were also relatively lower at the end of 2000. Specifically, in that year food inflation was 3.9% compared to a national inflation rate of 8.5%. The favourable evolution of agricultural production and consumer food prices facilitated the adoption of a series of income transfer programmes that were implemented throughout the decade to combat inequality and poverty. Since the Real Plan, the orientation of the minimum wage policy has been to effectively grant real increases. In this context, the income concentration as measured by the Gini index fell from 0.61 in 1993 to 0.59 in 1999. Over the same period, the poverty rate fell from 35% to 28.7%. These figures marked unprecedented social gains in Brazilian history. Rural poverty indicators, although still high, fell from 61.4% to 54.3% (Neri, 2011).

Regarding the external performance of agriculture, it should be mentioned that the dollar value of the sector's exports grew 75% in the 1990s (Figure 1.4). The value of soybean exports doubled, sugar exports quadrupled and beef exports tripled (Castro and Rossi Jr., 2000). Nevertheless, at the end of that decade, Brazil's total trade balance was in deficit given the 170% increase in imports (more than 80% of the value of these imports corresponded to the

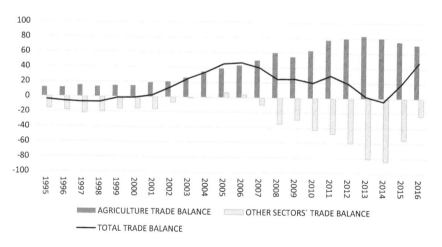

Figure 1.4 Trade balance of agriculture and other sectors in Brazil between 1995 and 2016 (US$ billion).

purchase of industrial products). The significant increase in agricultural exports occurred at the same time as the fall in the relative prices of the sector. Thus, growing exports did not lead to an increase in domestic real prices – a fear that came from the 1970s – but most likely prevented them from falling too far to discourage production growth.

At the end of the 1990s, a persistent overvalued exchange rate aggravated the external deficits. The country was therefore forced to devalue its currency and adopt a more flexible system. Without the exchange rate anchor, it became necessary to change the monetary policy to an inflation-targeting regime. Additionally, in a short time, a new law of fiscal responsibility was promulgated in order to establish a regime with greater control over the public accounts. As a result, the macroeconomic policy was restructured.

In the 2000s, the policy framework was similar to that of the previous decade. Under this context, agricultural exports in dollar terms increased 270% in the decade while total imports also increased by 270% in the same period. As a result, in 2010, Brazil had a trade surplus of US$ 20.1 billion, broken down into an industrial sector deficit of US$ 42.9 billion and a surplus of US$ 63 billion generated by agriculture. Industrial trade deficits offset by agricultural trade surpluses have been constantly observed since the mid-1990s.

Barros (2016) analysed the impact of the commodity boom (2003–2011) on the relative prices of agriculture. The author shows that much of the increase in dollar prices did not reach the Brazilian producers due to a strong appreciation of the national currency. From 2003 to 2011, the relative domestic prices of agriculture fell 21%. The growth in exports was not driven, therefore, by producer price increases, but by cost reductions as a result of improved productivity. Gasques et al. (2016a, 2016b, 2018) estimated that the TFP of Brazilian agriculture grew 48% in the decade, while that of the whole economy increased less than 5%.

Chaddad (2016) recalls that during the 1990s and 2000s important institutional changes were adopted – such as the Intellectual Property Act in 1996, the Law of Protection of Cultivars in 1997, the Seed Law (2003) and the Biosafety Law in 2005 – creating a more favourable context for private investment in agricultural science and technology, in particular in the field of genetically modified organisms (GMOs). Multinational companies started to acquire Brazilian seed companies and to establish partnership agreements with Embrapa. The participation of these new competitors changed the structure of the technology market, although Embrapa and other public institutes still play an important role. Between 1998 and 2012, the number of varieties and cultivars available to farmers in Brazil increased from 51 to 1,708. Moreover, the area under no-till farming increased from 1.4 million hectares to 25.5 million hectares between 1980 and 2007.

From an organizational point of view, it should be highlighted that in 2013 the Brazilian agriculture had 1,516 cooperatives with more than one million members (Chaddad, 2016). The 30 largest cooperatives accounted for 74% of wheat production, 57% of soybean, 48% of coffee, 44% of cotton, 43% of corn, 35% of rice and 30% of milk. In terms of meat production, currently more than 95% of swine and poultry production is produced under contract. In general, the contracting firms provide credit, technical assistance and inputs. They also stipulate the price of the product based on efficiency parameters. The industrial processors are now consolidated in oligopolies: the four largest companies process 88% of the poultry and swine.

The beef industry was also consolidated in the 2000s as a continuation of the process initiated after the Real Plan and with the support of the National Bank for Economic and Social Development (BNDES) in the form of credit and subscription of shares. A strong internationalization process of the industry has taken place since 2005. Between that year and 2015, seventeen acquisitions of foreign companies by Brazilian groups were carried out in Latin America, North America, Europe and Australia (Wedekin, 2017).

In the 2000s, the sugarcane sector was once again stimulated, this time with the introduction of flex-fuel vehicles (which could be fuelled with gasoline or ethanol in any proportion). The initiative increased substantially the demand for ethanol – see Chapter 07. In addition to the above, the industry underwent significant structural changes. Joint ventures were formed, and some firms were accepted into the stock markets with initial public offerings (IPO). At least thirteen multinational companies entered the ethanol market, including three oil companies. Regarding the orange sector, the industrial concentration reached its peak throughout the 2000s. The three largest companies hold 95% of the processing capacity. Four Brazilian companies acquired US companies and started operating in Florida.[4]

From 2003 to 2011, under the commodity boom, a substantial part of foreign revenues generated by exports was channelled into imports. During the 1995–2014 period, the overall volume of trade, both exports and imports, grew approximately 170% (World Bank, 2018a). This was possible because exports (as well as the inflow of currency through the balance of payments capital account that occurred as Brazil improved its risk assessment) generated cheap dollars (due to appreciation of the Brazilian currency) that made imports attractive. As a result, inflation control became easier even with a policy of real wage increases and with the expansion of public spending on income transfer programmes. In fact, these programmes were responsible for 70% of the increase in primary government spending from 2001 to 2010, estimated in 2.7% of the GDP (Orair and Gobetti, 2011).

The flow of foreign currencies through both, the trade balance and foreign investments in the country, was enough to eliminate the Brazilian external debt. Thus, about 200 billion dollars in reserves were accumulated at the end of 2008. According to Ipeadata and Cepea data, the share of agricultural-based exports in agribusiness GDP (including raw materials and processed agricultural products) increased from 10% in 1997 to 24% in 2016. An additional evidence of the relevance of Brazilian agribusinesses on international markets is that, in 2014, fifteen of the 40 major exporting companies in the country belonged to the agribusiness sector (Salomão, 2016).

During the 2000s, as agricultural GDP increased by 4% per year (compared to 3.6% for the economy as a whole), the Gini index of income concentration fell from 0.59 to 0.53. The poverty rate observed in the country was reduced from 28% of the population to 15%; in the rural area, the registered drop was from 54% of the rural population to 32% (Neri, 2012). In 2010, the rural population living in rural areas represented 16% of the total. One of the reasons for the reduction of the poverty incidence in the country was that the minimum wage increased 76% in real terms during the 2000–2010 period.[5] According to Neri (2012), the most important reduction in the poverty level occurred from 2003 onwards, when the commodity boom began. These so-called 'bonanza years' extended until 2011 – during this period the Brazilian economy experienced unexpected rates of rapid growth. The observed changes occurred and were feasible because inflation remained under control.

5 Conclusions

The industrialization in Brazil produced several major structural changes, among them, the total number of employed persons in the country doubled between 1980 and 2009 reaching approximately 89.4 million at the end of period (Horie, 2012). During those 29 years occupation in agriculture fell from 29% of the country total population to 16%; in the manufacturing industry the variation was very small, a drop from 15% to 14%; in the construction sector from 8.1% to 7.5%; and in the service sector from 47.9% to 61.5%. In the aggregated balance, the loss of occupation in agriculture was absorbed by the service sector. The Gini index of income inequality, which grew until 1990 declined afterwards, however, it remained relatively high (0.53).

According to Barros (2016), in 2012 agriculture and the industry, each employed around 15% of the labour force, construction employed close to 9% and services just over 60%. In 2005, labour productivity in the industry was four times that of agriculture, and in the service sector twice that of agriculture (Menezes Filho et al., 2014). Average years of schooling in 2009 were four years in agriculture, 7.8 in the industry, 9.5 in the service sector and 8.2 years in the economy as a whole. In agriculture, in 2010, 48% of the employees earned less than US$ 1,000 per year (equivalent to a monthly salary of 1/4 of the national minimum wage) and 90% earned less than US$ 8,000 yearly (two minimum wages). In the other sectors, at least 2/3 of those employed received less than US$ 8,000 per year. Less than 4% of those employed in any sector received more than US$ 36,000 per year. Thus, the major growth effort through modernization and industrialization over thirty years did not lead to the creation of good quality jobs neither a reasonable remuneration for the vast majority of the Brazilian workforce. This process, which began in 1980, has been characterized as a middle-income trap with high inequality. Brazil continues to grow slowly and the reduction in poverty and inequality is more attributable to agriculture performance than to industrialization.

The 2006 Agricultural Census shows the severity of income concentration in agriculture. Alves and Rocha (2010) estimated that 87% of the gross farm income is generated by only 460 thousand farms or 11.7% of the 4.4 million farms, while 3.9 million (88.3% of the total number of farms) generated only 13% of gross income. In the first group, 27,000 farms (0.6% of the total) were responsible for 51.2% of the gross income of Brazilian agriculture in that year.

This overview of the evolution of Brazil's agricultural sector and its relations to the broad processes of industrialization and urbanization makes it possible to conclude that investments in Brazilian agriculture provided significant returns to society as a whole. First, the remarkable expansion of food, fibre and renewable energy production led to an impressive fall in the cost of food, thus contributing to a fall in poverty and income inequality. In addition, the Brazilian agricultural exports have increased significantly. However, in rural areas in general (the rural Northeast in particular), the major challenge of fighting the remaining poverty and inequality still remains. In this context, it is essential to maintain the generation and use of technology in agriculture and to overcome the limitations of infrastructure, which are the necessary foundation for the continuous increase in productivity. Moreover, additional measures aimed at enhancing the social progress of the majority of the rural population must be taken urgently. In addition to income transfer programmes, rural extension services, education and other support policies in this segment of the farming sector need to be recovered and reactivated on a large scale. Regarding the structural challenges, new policy topics of discussion related to agriculture have been consolidated in relation to climate, environment and food quality. The performance of Brazilian agriculture over the last decades has proved to be a successful story, but problems of major importance have yet to be solved.

Notes

1 The incentives provided compensated, to a certain extent, the policies that usually penalized the sector, such as a strong overvaluation of the domestic currency.

2 The urbanization in Brazil grew from 31% of the population to 45% between 1940 and 1960 (IBGE).

3 According to OECD (2005), 'Brazil provides relatively little support to its farmers. Producer support, as measured by the PSE, accounted for 3% of the gross value of farm receipts in 2002–2004 – a rate comparable with that of New Zealand (2%) and Australia (4%), and far below the OECD average (30%)'.

4 For a comprehensive analysis of the changes in some of the main Brazilian agro-chains, see Chapter 4.

5 Barros (2010) showed that until the mid-1990s, nominal increases in the minimum wage were accompanied by equivalent increases in inflation, making it impossible to raise the real minimum wage.

2 Rural Brazil

The demise of its agrarian past, 1968–2018

Zander Navarro and Maria Thereza Macedo Pedroso

1 Introduction

Spanning a period of five decades, Brazil underwent a radical transformation of its countryside, moving from a commercially dominant, but stagnant coffee sector in the 1970s, to one of the most vibrant world food powerhouses. This chapter discusses some of the main processes and contexts of rural change that have surfaced over the years, in order to paint a picture of this seismic rupture with the past. Broadly analysed within this perspective, it has turned agricultural production upside down while failing to overcome controversial and enduring social asymmetries. This evolution constitutes an epochal change ignited by the military regime (1964–1985),[1] after a decisive thrust to modernize the highly unequal and export-driven rural structure that had prevailed for almost five centuries. Following this initial set of policies, a social behaviour led by productive ambitions became ingrained among a growing number of farmers, eventually building, albeit heterogeneously, a strong, flexible and sophisticated agro-food system that has successfully inserted itself as the commanding core of the whole economy. In historical terms, it has meant *a process of deagrarianization* that brushed aside not only most of the old-fashioned economic facets so typical of the past, but also social and even cultural aspects, which have been significantly reshaped over the years.

The interpretative axis of this essay proposes an *essentially empirical* analysis under which some of the characteristics of the Brazilian countryside are examined and a comparative focus over half a century is made in order to shed a light on the main changes. If these two-time extremes (1968 and 2018) are carefully considered, the eventual comparison will surely be surprising – because one will then observe some aspects that were radically transformed over time, almost as if they were two very different countries.

In 1970, an oversimplified picture of rural Brazil would refer to a very modest performance from the standpoint of total production, which was then determined by an extremely primitive technological foundation (please check Table 4.1 of Chapter 4). Commercial relations were relatively limited, both in terms of the still incipient domestic market and with foreign sales. As far as exports were concerned, Brazil notably maintained an organized trading structure with overseas markets centred on coffee, a core crop that expanded significantly in the second half of the nineteenth century, and to a much lesser degree, sugar, a commodity established in old colonial times. The third largest product worth mentioning was cocoa, though it never amounted to more than 4% of the total value of agricultural exports. The strong economic hegemony of coffee for almost a century (1870–1970) has been well documented by historians and experts alike, as the following reference illustrates:

> Summarizing the situation of the Second Empire [1840–1889] during which one of the principal products of colonial times, sugar, had declined, we might perhaps claim that the decline of the monarchy is [was] defined by the first coffee crisis, the cultivation of which had been badly affected by abolition. During the period of the Republic [after 1889], the commercial profits of our balance of trade came from coffee. It is building São Paulo, it is sustaining Brazil (…). Thus, up to the Revolution of 1930, and even beyond, coffee would be the mainstay of Brazil's economy (…) *General Coffee*, as they already called it.
>
> (Cruz Costa, 1967, p. 328, italicized in the original).

Brazil is an enormous country with a highly skewed land ownership structure since the onset of colonization. Its periods of growth in production always derived merely from the expansion of the cultivated area and, until recently, productivity was not an economic orientation that had motivated farmers. From 1948 to 1969, for example, 92% of gains in total production out of the main crops were exclusively due to the expansion of the area under cultivation (Patrick, 1975). It is surely for this reason that the central analytical framework of this book uses the 1970s as its starting point. It was during that decade that the formidable process of productive transformation was undertaken, after a backward and predominantly *agrarian* Brazil that had prevailed in the past. In fact, under the ironfisted military regime Brazil observed the first concerted and planned effort in its history to modernize agriculture (Kageyama and Silva, 1983).

From a social and political perspective, the former and initial agrarian context was even more retrograde as the vast majority of those living in rural communities had almost no rights of any nature (even if they already were in force in urban areas) and virtually all State policies and administrative structures were nonexistent out of urban contexts.[2] This was the case of the system of Justice. Conflicts in rural regions were invariably resolved through brute force. Very often it was through the coercive political resources mobilized by large landowners that disputes were settled and the forms of social protest employed by rural workers and small-scale farmers were peremptorily put down (Martins, 1981; Medeiros, 1989). According to José de Souza Martins, one of the leading scholars who studied agrarian change in Brazil:

> Never in the history of Brazil were large landowners so powerful in the use of private violence and never were the armed forces so weak in their

response, as during the military regime (…) the structurally basic alliance between capital and land, promoted by the military, weakened the effectiveness of social movements that could claim recognition and the expansion of social rights for the poorer populations.

(Martins, 1994, pp. 83, 92).

A vast majority of the rural population was extremely poor and, with no guarantee of access to a plot of land, resorting to out-migration seemed to be the only available alternative – to the cities or towards more remote regions where free land still existed. It is not surprising, therefore, that between 1950 and 1980, according to census statistics in comparison to the total population, migratory processes were the most intense in the history of the country. This movement of the population was particularly vigorous during the 1970s, when the equivalent of *a third of the total population* left the countryside seeking new forms of employment (Martine and Garcia, 1987, pp. 59–80).

In short, this half-century comparison illuminates that dismaying starting point: the fifth largest country in the world and usually ranked at eight to the ninth biggest economy, with abundant resources of water, energy and natural resources, found itself unable to feed its own people at that time. Rural regions exhibited deplorable indicators of economic and social backwardness on that occasion, including the absence of the most elementary human rights. Malnutrition and diseases plagued those regions and illiteracy was rampant. It was this structural base that actually reflected a history of unacceptable concentration of land ownership and wealth in general, in addition to historical processes that rooted a gloomy legacy – slavery, for example, which prevailed over four hundred years until the end of the nineteenth century.[3] In short, an agrarian past anchored on two main pillars: the abundance of land in the hands of a few and a large supply of labour with no rights.

Half a century later, these rural realities have not been entirely transformed, since numerous challenging tendencies or deplorable indicators still persist, particularly those of a social nature echoing the past. However, when examined as a totality, the rural milieu in Brazil cannot be compared nowadays with those of the past due to a series of differences that are profound and many of them became structural. The companion chapters of this book speak eloquently to this situation, analysing in detail various specific aspects of this truly historical transformation. Present-day Brazil emerges as one of the largest global producers of food, probably the only one with a robust agricultural sector capable of further expanding its presence in global markets. A few empirical facts illustrate this transition: as late as in 1970, agriculture in Brazil used no agrochemicals at all. Today, however, Brazil consumes somewhere between a sixth and a seventh of the global total of these inputs. In that same initial year, approximately 50,000 tractors were available, all of which imported and mainly concentrated in the coffee producing-areas of the state of São Paulo. Nowadays, an estimate 70,000 new tractors are sold *every year* (all manufactured in Brazil). Soybean production was not even registered in the 1970 agricultural census, as it was just starting to be planted, while today the country is on the verge of becoming the largest global producer of this commodity. Finally, the most conclusive of these illustrative indicators: when comparing the two extremes of time, the agriculture and livestock sectors in present-day Brazil produce 80 times more wealth (in terms of the real or deflated *gross value* of production), a remarkable result that has monetarily imbued the entire agro-food system, and indeed the economy as a whole.

Though not specifically the focus of this article, it is also at least revealing to comment in passing that this radical structural change in rural domains has also spread repercussions onto other dimensions of social, political or cultural life in Brazil. In literature, for example. Such was the case in many of the classic works that depicted the remote past, such as *Vidas secas*[4] (1938), by Graciliano Ramos, a book that reflects on the broad context of the droughts affecting the rural northeastern region. Perhaps another illustration, among many others, might be *Vila dos confins*[5] (1956). This book, by Mário Palmério, also introduces us the past rural life, concentrating on a description of electoral frauds typical of small towns – a masterpiece of so-called regional literature. The same topic was discussed in another classic, this time written by a social scientist, *Coronelismo, enxada and voto*[6] (1948), by Victor Nunes Leal, in which the author describes the then prevailing economic system and its recurrent pattern of electoral frauds. Both were anchored in the concentrated structure of land, argued the author, although a pattern slowly being undermined by urbanization and an emerging electoral competition, even if strict control of the votes in rural backlands would last at least until democratization, in 1985.

Among various other examples from that period *Grande sertão: veredas*[7] is perhaps the single most important literary book *of all times*. It is an extensive, richly multifaceted epic which has as its backdrop the vast rural region of the central hinterland of Brazil, or the *sertão*. Its author, Guimarães Rosa, offers his readers delightful descriptions of those vast regions and uncover complex modes of human interaction. That book is associated with another referential book of the time, *Os donos do poder*[8] (1958), by Raymundo Faoro, this time a sophisticated Weberian analysis about the history of patrimonialism in Brazil. It was an interpretation about the origins and consequences of unbridled concessions of land to state employees by the colonial Portuguese Crown, thus forming a powerful institution (and its corresponding social patterns) that would endure for the years to come.

These are brief economic and cultural illustrations typical of *agrarian Brazil* surfacing in past times. They could be repeated using various other examples, and indeed also other non-rural social contexts and are here cited merely to suggest that this was literature set in rural social spaces that *are fast disappearing*. At the present time, there are few Brazilian authors that still work inspired by these contexts, a fact that is a robust empirical indication of the social and economic changes analysed here.

The present chapter comments on this journey that moves from the agrarian Brazil of half a century ago to a present-day profoundly reshaped rural context – in all aspects of social life. As this chapter is not especially concerned with theoretical aspects, the second section offers a mere glimpse of some analytical elements that might explain this transition. In addition, it suggests various drivers of change to describe not just this passage towards a 'new world' but, in fact, to show that the rural Brazil of the past which strongly moulded the culture and social mentalities ingrained in the Brazilian *psyche* is gradually vanishing. Finally, in the third section a number of emerging trends are briefly listed. They will reconfirm this 'new rural setting' as *an essentially economic and productive space, though largely emptied of human interaction.* This reconfiguration of rural spaces has also signified the birth of a society which is increasingly oriented towards and dominated by urban imperatives, particularly with regard to economic and cultural processes.

2 Seven facts about the 'great transformation' in rural Brazil

There have been numerous *meaningful facts* (social, economic, technological) occurring in rural regions over recent decades that are worthy of extensive analytical discussion. These are not episodic facts but rather situations or trends that help to demonstrate the maturation of an *unprecedented* phase in Brazil's rural history, generating profound implications for the immediate future of the sector. This is the overall underlying rationale of this book, with various dimensions, themes and specific facts about this 'great transformation' being analysed in its various chapters. They are not necessarily related to exclusive national determinants spread throughout the country. Sometimes a specific change appears to be only regional when in reality it reflects a wider context that has also transformed, insofar as the web of relations linking agro-food chains and their economic possibilities is concerned. This is particularly the case after the late 1990s when a global nexus was established.[9] In other situations these changes are territorial movements that mirror the mobility of capital in search for greater profitability, an economic orientation that was still relatively unborn in Brazil's agrarian past. This section presents and discusses, albeit under limited lenses, *seven new major facts* that have been defining this process of trans-formation, not only in production itself but also affecting rural social life in general. They are facts extremely significant in some regions, less so in others, as might be expected in an economic arena that is so very large (geographically), mirroring its structural diversity (as discussed in Chapter 6).

What the factors discussed below have in common, however, is that *all of them are in the process of being materialized in rural regions*, with any differences merely being a question of depth and scope. When analysed together, these changes clearly point to an emerging phase of capitalist development in Brazil's countryside. In order to inscribe it under a more conceptual framework, it means a new stage of capital accumulation where 'land, which in the past was the principal source of wealth in the countryside, is gradually being supplanted by [new] forms of capital' (Buaiain, 2014, p. 213; Navarro, 2016). It is this assumption that allows us to assert, with empirical conviction, about *the end of an agrarian era* in rural Brazil, in face of tangible and irreversible impacts brought about by these factors that are restructuring the very essence of rural productive contexts and their modes of social life and human interaction.

The word 'agrarian' in the specialized sociological literature points out to processes of building rural social life and agricultural production. But it is particularly rooted in the past when there was a dominant and decisive role for two factors of production – land and labour. In addition, those were age-old times related to the dawn of agrarian capitalism when there were widespread conflicts opposing landowners and impoverished rural landless workers and petty producers. These conflicts were especially motivated by threats on their social reproduction when faced by unavailability of land. One of the most impressive references in this field is the legendary work by Jeffery Paige, *Agrarian Revolution* (1975), particularly its sophisticated 'theory of rural class conflict' (Paige, 1975, pp. 1–71), which discusses the concrete variations linking the forms of land tenure and their corresponding modes of labour mobilization. It is for this reason that the derived expression 'agrarian development' usually refers to interpretations about patterns of change in the rural life of some countries or regions in which this factor – labour – existed in massive figures representing the poor rural masses, whereas the other factor – land – was usually in the hands of a minority of owners. Unsurprisingly, under the rural trajectories of many countries, these were periods when themes coming out of the 'agrarian question' and its ensuing list of conflicts (not to mention the inevitable search for political possibilities to implement a programme of 'agrarian reform') occupied a heavy footprint in the literature on rural social processes.[10]

How to interpret this protracted transition?

A process of 'de-agrarianization' is inextricably associated to historical transformation of rural domains. As such, it can be studied under the most ambitious theories of agrarian change, for example, or under the lights of purely theoretical concepts, such as 'agrarian capitalism'. Not being able to uncover all these conceptual niceties in this chapter, we rely here on the excellent revision of these ideas proposed by a leading Mexican scholar, Hubert C. de Grammont, who scrutinized several articles and books that used the central notion of de-agrarianization or similar ideas (De Grammont, 2017). He called the attention, for example, for the best definition of this term, proposed by Deborah Bryceson:

> De-agrarianization is defined as a process of economic activity reorientation, occupational adjustment and spatial realignment of human settlement away from agrarian patterns. The most overt manifestations of this process are: a diminishing degree of rural household food and basic needs self-sufficiency, a decline in agricultural labor relative to non-agricultural labor in total national

labor expenditure, a decrease in agricultural output per capita in the national economy relative to non-agricultural output and a shrinking proportion of population residing in rural areas.

(Bryceson and Jamal, 1997, p. 5).

For the purposes of this chapter, perhaps it is sufficient to emphasize the commonest indicator used by economists. In this discipline, authors call attention to periods of economic expansion, when necessarily a growing number of value chains sprouting from the agricultural sector will mean, among other *empirical* consequences, the simultaneous expansion of non-agricultural employment (either in rural areas themselves or in urban contexts, but associated to these chains). In short, it means that there is a tendency of diminishing proportions of agricultural jobs in relation to the total labour employed in the whole agro-food sector and its web of specific value chains.

This is precisely what has happened in the Brazilian case in the period under analysis. In 2015, *for the first time ever*, the total of non-agricultural jobs in value chains of the sector was higher (11%) that the total employment created in direct agricultural jobs (10%), according to official data. Not to mention that if the 'agribusiness GDP' is taken into consideration, also for the first time the total gross value created by production itself was also supplanted by those remaining parts involved. While direct production responded for 30.5% of the total, services existing in the agro-food system accounted for 30.7%, inputs for 11.8% and processing for 27.0% (all statistics organized in Barros et al., 2015).

In Latin America, one relevant book containing fascinating research pieces about that initial period was *Land and Labor in Latin America. Essays on the Development of Agrarian Capitalism in the Nineteenth and Twentieth Centuries* (1978). This remarkable volume of 18 essays analysed rural patterns of development in several Latin American countries at a time in which a diversity of transitional processes were being fermented on existing *agrarian societies*. Notwithstanding the immense variation determined by other factors (e.g. climate, ecology, demographic structure, rural history, ethnic patterns and the structure of land tenure), the core process under analysis by most of the authors was the passing (in the language of the time) from one mode of production to another – ultimately, the expansion of agrarian capitalism. On the one hand, the drivers of the processes of change were centred on land disputes over its forms of ownership, and on the other, rural labour and its contractual relations, thus generating a heated debate about 'the agrarian question in Latin America' (Duncan et al., 1978). In the Brazilian academic circles this was a somewhat distinct literature dominated by Marxist authors, perhaps most notably the debate inspired by Caio Prado Júnior' work in the 1960s. The epicentre of this discussion was a fierce discussion about the nature of the social relations then prevailing in the rural regions of Brazil, that is, if they were capitalist or feudal (the main articles are to be found in Prado Jr., 1979). Regarding the central role of land to structure production and the organization of rural society, the main reference was *Quatro séculos de latifúndio*[11] by Alberto Passos Guimarães, originally published in 1968. But this was a debate that was gradually eroded away after the process of economic expansion developed in the 1970s, later to be known as 'the Brazilian miracle'.

At the onset of the period under analysis, there existed a high proportion of workers out of the total rural population – that is to say, an unlimited supply of labour – and, as such, labour costs would always be low. Productive changes thus favoured the intensive use of labour reflected in scandalous wages and non-existent workers' rights. In almost all regions the abundance of (privately owned) land was a powerful stimulus for the expansion of agriculture exclusively via the growth of planted area and highly extensive livestock activities. These situations made the pace of truly capitalist modernization in the countryside rather slow and erratic, maintaining low indicators of overall productivity. However, once a capitalist logic was ignited, those earlier structural ingredients gradually lost ground and a technology factor (or intensive production) slowly became the main engine of change and, gradually, would embody the driver of agricultural expansion encapsulated by a word turned into *the essence* of this economic sector: – productivity. In brief, what is being suggested in this chapter is precisely the transition from an 'agrarian Brazil' typical of the past to an '[essentially] agricultural rural Brazil', increasingly oriented by strictly economic and financial forces. Inspired by this historical change, among many other implications, the labour market shrank in line with mechanical intensification and land increasingly became a sparse factor of production. The productive factor we call 'land' came to be managed in a radically different way. It shifted from a pattern of extensive growth prevailing in the past to a relentless quest for 'vertical productivity', thus raising the output per unit of land, capital and labour.

As one of the most crucial aspects resulting from the aforementioned transition, technological intensification has been noted as a challenging characteristic because it is promoting even more acute social asymmetries throughout the Brazilian countryside. In the 1970s, social inequality in those regions was already appalling. On the one hand, in the face of one of the greatest skewed structures of land ownership in the world and, on the other, a vast throng of impoverished landless families and poor small-scale farmers. Recent economic growth, together with the dissemination of modern entrepreneurial practices among the layer of capitalist farmers increasingly integrated into global markets, further widened the economic gap opposing this minority and the rest of the rural population. Although the virtual absence of specific studies that investigates deeply this subject (that is, technological intensification and patterns of distribution of wealth), it is known from non-systematic evidence gathered in different rural regions that technology has been the most decisive variable to promote social inequality. This was precisely the case with the agricultural sector from the end of the 1990s onwards. Theoretical literature on the topic is relatively conclusive, suggesting that 'both technology and globalization, the latter enabled by technology, have had a major impact on capital's share of national income (…) and on the growing inequality in labour incomes and of wealth inequality' (Tyson and Spence, 2017, p. 171).

As a result, briefly presented in the summarized notes that follow, the first and most decisive factor of those seven to be cited is the incontrovertible and irreversible emergence of economic and financial imperatives as the driving force to animate the process of transformation. This force subordinates all other dimensions that had also enjoyed prominence in past decades. Empirical evidence of this new causal relation is abundant. For example, rural credit in former decades was totally dependent on public funds but shifted towards funding by private companies or the farmers' own capital. More recently, foreign investors and other sources of funding have been increasingly interested in Brazilian agriculture. The expansion of value chains has included powerful national and multinational companies and their investments have led to the appreciation of these firms in the stock exchange, as highlighted by Balestro and Lourenço (2014).[12] In fact, this economic sector has transformed itself into a *wealth producing machine*. As a result, it has continuously attracted more capital, both domestically and from foreign investors. In short, the domination of financial capital is directly mirrored in the unstoppable flow of money. But it can also be proved indirectly through various concrete manifestations, from the growth of the total cultivated area to the persistent effort to increase productivity. All of this empirical evidence is summed up by the entrepreneurial behaviour that has been dominating the expansion of these activities in the Brazilian agro-food system. In brief, an intensive, truly and irreversible capitalist *ethos* has been establishing itself in rural regions.

As discussed in detail in other parts of this book, the notable expansion in total factor productivity (TFP) is a second aspect that must be emphasized. The dominant presence of technology and innovation (or 'science' in general) is tangible evidence of not just the formation of a new generation of rural farmers nor merely a behaviour that is very different from the past. It also represents the reality of the domination of economic and financial drivers, since the growth of technology in agricultural production systems means higher costs, with a larger number of firms involved, an expanded role of the new chains of production, more investments and an eventual greater profitability for this industry as a whole. An economic sector driven by the relentless quest for TFP signifies, in practice, resolute efforts by rural entrepreneurs and the complete dominance of a strictly capitalist logic and, from a historical standpoint, this is a culmination of the transition nurtured in the 1970s, whose roots were hinted at by the authors of the abovementioned book compiled by Kenneth Duncan and colleagues.

Another aspect to be highlighted, which reiterates previous assertions, relates to the diminishing importance of economic accountability in this new model of accumulation of the factors land and labour *vis-à-vis* the emerging factor of production technology. This statistical turnaround was demonstrated by Alves and Souza (2015), who calculated the factors responsible for the rates of growth in the agricultural sector by comparing the last two censuses, compiled in 1995/1996 and in 2006. While the proportion of the factors labour (0.26 and 0.21) and land (0.15 and 0.09) fell in-between the two censuses, technology grew remarkably in this period, from 0.42 to 0.64 (Alves and Souza, 2015, p. 19). These are indicators that conclusively demonstrate the recent irrelevance of a national programme of land redistribution because the allocation of land to poor rural families does not really mean a promising opportunity to prosper but rather a quick fix for access to land without addressing rural poverty. In fact, these figures represent a definitive statistical evidence of *the end of the agrarian era*.

The fourth aspect we may emphasize is a 'new factor' due to the recent period being typical of expansive processes of economic growth that 'liberate the factors of production' (capital, labour) and endow them with greater mobility (or volatility). This is true either in terms of their quantitative levels or in relation to their territorial (spatial) mobility. In this case, as we cannot illustrate this factor with numerous specific examples, we will merely register what is currently evident from empirical observations collected in various rural regions. Firstly, there currently exists a broad mobility of rural salaried workers capable of traveling long distances in search for work that affords better pay. This is a break from the past when the means of transport did not exist, thus preventing such labour mobility. The movement of capital is even more flexible and intense, empirically known because of the spatial changes in land use and production that have materialized over the last fifty years. A new 'productive wave' has been emerging in the centre of Brazil: a huge geographical area that extends from the west of the São Francisco river in the state of Bahia, and embraces the states of Goiás, the largest part of Tocantins, practically the whole of Mato Grosso and of Mato Grosso do Sul, also extending westwards out to Rondônia (see map in the introductory chapter). This vast region is currently emerging as the most important from the point of view of agriculture and cattle ranching and will surely become the largest productive core in Brazil – and one of the most relevant in the world, as a matter of fact. Its emergence ultimately represents the effects of the mobility of capital, as it is the region that is gradually consolidating the forms of large-scale ownership, with a distinct entrepreneurial focus (Embrapa, 2018a, p. 44).

The fifth 'new fact' is of immense importance because of its multifaceted implications and its relation to the productive structure of the agro-food system in Brazil. This system is becoming increasingly diversified, flexible and sensitive to market signals, as well as showing growing signs of adaptive sophistication. The main evidence of this trend is its integration into global markets, a fact that has huge consequences for agricultural and livestock production. A recent study calls attention on this fact:

> [There is] one fact that seems increasingly crucial to an analysis of the historical relations between globalization and agriculture in Brazil. Whereas all previous cycles, except coffee, had only moderate effects on internal

economic and productive restructuring, the recent period has been substantially different. In the last 20–30 years, Brazilian agriculture has developed vigorously in economic, financial and technological terms, responding rapidly to incentives offered by global markets and with internal repercussions of enormous importance, not least in the social arena. Real food prices, for example, have fallen systematically in the domestic markets, reducing the cost of food for most of the population (…) the formation of large-scale production chains linked to agriculture has more broadly dynamized the economies of many regions, bolstering growth of the agro industrial sector and the whole array of services of many regions.

(Navarro and Buainain, 2017, p. 27).

There is a sixth dimension that needs to be brought into this analysis too. It is this dimension that provides evidence of the subordination of the countryside, production and even an array of social and cultural aspects conventionally associated to rural life, under the sway of dominant urban influences. This is also the resulting historical inversion contributing decisively to the burial of the agrarian past. A fascinating research topic would be to investigate the cultural industry that 'captured' most, if not all, versions of country music (*sertaneja*) and transformed it into one of the most potent initiatives of today's music scene in Brazil, completely controlled by urban interests. Another specific empirical facet, however, relates to the creation of new jobs linked to the agro-chains or, more generically, to the 'non-agricultural employment of agribusiness'. Barros et al. (2016) have used more recent data to demonstrate that these are burgeoning forms of employment, with the continuous modernization of the agro-foods system in Brazil and it is gradually leaving behind agricultural employment *per se* (Barros et al., 2016).[13]

Lastly, in conclusion, there is further telling evidence of a new era which is restructuring agricultural production and transforming rural social life. This evidence can be found in two typically 'agrarian' facts that were so conspicuous in the past. Firstly, the gradual disappearance of topics associated with the prior rural history of the country in the public agenda. Examples, such as agrarian reform and its associated conflicts, like the emergence of a social movement of landless rural workers (the MST) represent this trend. Not only was the Brazilian programme of land distribution dramatically curtailed in recent years but also the social demand for access to land has faded into obscurity and the MST consequently lost its *raison d'être* (Navarro, 2010).

Though rarely mentioned in the specialized literature, other empirical evidence speaks even more emphatically, when comparing different census data that illuminate the 'rural world' existing in 1970 with the most recent one, published in 2006. Consider, for example, the total number of rural establishments surveyed and the number of private landowners which rose from 59.5% in 1970 to 75.9% in 2006. The indicators about poor tenants and renters are even more revealing and decisive. They indicate that these forms of non-capitalist production fell from 20.0% to 6.9% in the same period. Lastly, when considering occupants in the same period, the numbers fell from 16.1% to 7.8% in 2006. These are data that demonstrate a persistent encroachment of poor rural families by an ever-growing movement to privatize appropriation of land. Those non-capitalist arrangements mushroomed in the past given the overabundance of labour, the existence of 'free lands' and migration towards new regions in the agricultural frontier. But they were increasingly surrounded by the advent of fatal economic determinants. It is evidence of the privatization of land resources and the advancement of a capitalist logic that at the time was capturing rural regions and, consequently, acting as the gravedigger of its agrarian past.

3 Medium-term trends

In the coming medium period (perhaps around the next two decades), what might be the main trends that are immediately identifiable based on the transition suggested in this chapter? There are probably six national macro-processes that when working simultaneously and one reinforcing another, will certainly confirm in that suggested period the *irreversible affirmation of a new pattern of capital accumulation*. These processes throughout the Brazilian countryside will thus have wide reaching social and economic implications. Once this new phase has taken firm roots through its main components, the agrarian face of the past will definitively cease to exist in the country's rural regions.

Schematically, these main trends would be:

(a) the definitive domination of financial capital on *all the essential processes* that determine the functioning of the national agro-food system, and not just on one or another specific part of production chains – from production itself and its technological organization in the farms to the distribution of the economic returns among all participants. It is a determination that presupposes a hierarchy of power and an active capacity of finance capital to exercise it in articulation and on behalf of some firms, either benefitting from a reduced government interference or instead through the power of this mode of capital and its agents to organize the technological, organizational and normative structure which best serves its interests. It is an empirical fact that has been increasingly characterizing operations in the sector, faced with new opportunities opened by globalization as well as its central role in the Brazilian economy;

(b) largely as a consequence of the first tendency mentioned above, a strong and so visible process of *social differentiation* is rapidly intensifying, sometimes also referred to as 'social exclusion' (thus highlighting its negative connotations). This means that the economic expansion of agriculture is developing an uneasy paradox in rural regions – a balance showing few winners and a lot of losers. Specifically, this economic and financial imperative, when linked to the demographic trends of recent decades (discussed in other parts of this book), is forcing a great number of families to leave the countryside. In this coming period of two decades, the rural regions of Brazil will likely undergo a process similar to that experienced by the United States rural history, where the number of farms fell by half between 1950 and 1970. Social policies such as the '*Bolsa Família*' programme (implemented after 2004)[14], when added to the post-Constitution welfare rights (such as rural pensions) are helping to retain mainly older couples in the countryside. It appears undoubtedly that by 2040, only two regions, the Northeast and the three states that comprise the Southern region, will still be exhibiting indicators of demographic density of any significance in their rural areas;

(c) discussed in detail in a separate chapter elsewhere, the structural diversity of rural Brazil is assuming a dramatic aspect, not just in economic terms but also from a social and cultural point of view. In the origins of the process of modernization here proposed as the zero-point – the 1970s – rural regions were already characterized by strong structural distinctions, with the rural northeast prominently standing out on account of its secular trajectory of poverty. During the five decades analysed in the book there emerged a vivid and deeper diversity opposing groups and social classes from region to region, among the complex network of the productive chains and also when comparing types of production. From this broad perspective, what appears as the most crucial question is *the demise of the rural Northeast*. It is here where an enormous area of Brazilian territory is characterized by the presence of the semiarid region at its heart, increasingly affected by climatic changes and economically unviability especially because of the scarcity of water. Would the rural northeast (particularly the semiarid region) be condemned in the years to come? This appears to be an ostensibly irreversible trend resulting from most empirical tendencies, mainly those of a demographic nature;

(d) technological modernization of various segments of agriculture has stimulated the materialization of diverse organizational forms characterized by *growing complexity* – sometimes elevating forms of management to the level of art. It is a trend likely to become even more difficult over time, demanding a sophisticated and specialized knowledge from farmers in order to deal with forms of organizing their businesses that will become more technically abstract and complex. This is a barrier that will also be increasingly extended to the trading and financial interactions in the entire group of agro-chains. It does not seem, therefore, too bold to insist that 'technology' and its endless intensification and complexity will become the principal conduit of wealth concentration, thus further selecting those farmers to be crowned as winners in this journey;

(e) given the former set of processes and trends the following question has been stressed with anxiety amongst scholars: what will be *the course of government action* in the coming years? As can be learned from Chapter 3, which provides a historical comparison of public policies, one of its conclusions is to insist that initiatives by the State directed towards rural regions have been erratic.

It is this action that corresponds to the macroeconomic vicissitudes and their variations experienced by the country in different junctures, but without a predefined strategy. This tendency is likely to deepen further in the coming years with State policies only refining their regulatory framework and capacities of enforcement. As a result, conventional policies instituted in the past to modernize the sector will be gradually reduced or minimized;

(f) as a final probable tendency in the near future, the polarity of '*the environment*' versus '*production*', an antinomy that has been conflictive since the 1970s, appears to be calming down. It is not possible to offer many details here, but two major causes explain this relatively pacific convergence in recent years. First, a growing number of farmers has improved their understanding about the value of their natural resources in order to produce profits and are consequently developing better management practices on their farms. Many of them, while controlling vast expanses of land, pursued in the past an economic orientation via the expansion of the cultivated area and had no serious concern about productivity. This is not the dominant orientation anymore and nowadays farmers have been preoccupied with environmental practices – not to appease urban pressures but to increase their own rates of profitability. The second cause that explains a possible pacification in the near future of environmental demands and productive aspirations involving agriculture in Brazil comes out of the new normative framework approved in the end of 2012, the so-called 'Forest Code'. After a fierce political and legislative battle, a compromise was reached and the Code was formally approved in the National Congress. Even if it has been criticized by both sides (environmental groups and organizations of farmers), the plain fact is that a new law is in force and, as such, daily routines in the countryside have been gradually adapting to its injunctions. Since there are not absurdities in the new Code, there is a tendency to soften this remaining space of conflict with the passing of time.

4 Conclusions

This chapter sought to demonstrate the existence of abundant evidence, both historical and empirical, of a transition that has taken place during the last half a century. Rural Brazil was profoundly transformed, from an agrarian rural of the past to an 'agricultural Brazil' of the present. The latter demonstrates the predominance of global economic and financial determinations, thus downplaying factors that dominated the past – land and labour. The implications of this passage in the country's rural history are radical, in all contexts, regions and social spheres, from the economy to the culture, from the nature of institutions to how public policies may function, from the broad political processes prevailing in former times influenced by choices taken by the rural populations to the emergence of an essentially urban Brazil.

If this is to be a definitive transition in the years to come, it will be a transformation that will close a chapter of almost five hundred years, opening the door to a distinct Brazil that is now heavily centred on urban life and its populations and aspirations, relegating the vast world of the hinterland and its former peculiarities to secondary importance. The social conscience of Brazilians, which used to be anchored in agrarian themes and rural language, cultural habits and customs as well as the idiosyncrasies of production, will be gradually relegated to the footnotes of history. This outcome means that in the near future industrial agriculture and the whole agro-food system will be a topic more circumscribed to debates of experts and firms in the sector.

Notes

1   The period of agricultural modernization referred to in literature, however, occurred between 1968 and 1981. In 1965, the 'National Rural Credit System' (SNCR) was enacted though the most significant results of which did emerge only with the harvest of 1967/68. The 1970s saw massive expansion, but at the end of this decade its pillars became untenable because the country could not recur on foreign savings anymore to finance economic growth. In the early 1980s, Brazil experienced a dramatic economic crisis, resulting from foreign debt and accelerating inflation, interrupting the economy's cycle of modernization. The so-called 'lost decade' of the 1980s was thus already in the making.

2   In Brazil, the national law of labor relations, known by the acronym CLT (inspired by Italian fascism), was signed in 1943. However, the minimum wage enshrined therein and also the majority of the rights assigned to salaried workers, were not afforded to rural workers. It was only in the 1970s, during the military dictatorship, that a fraction of these urban rights was also enacted in favour of the rural population. However, it was only with the 1988 Constitution that they were fully assigned to rural workers.

3   Apart from being the last country in Latin America to abolish slavery (1888), Brazil was solely responsible for half of all slaves forced to cross the Atlantic towards the Americas.

4   It was translated into English as *Barren Lives* (The University of Texas Press, 1971).

5   A fictional village set in the remote backlands.

6   Literally, it means 'The oligarchs, the hoe and the vote'.

7   Translated into English as *The Devil to Pay in the Backlands* (Knopf, 1963).

8   It means 'The owners of power'.

9   As is the case, for example, with sugarcane, a crop that currently occupies one quarter of the planted area in the state of São Paulo, the most productive of the federal states, but whose economy has a domestic impact not just in the functioning of the national agriculture, but even on several related economic sectors. In 1975, total production in the country was 91 million metric tons, which soared to 672 million metric tons by 2015.

10 Notwithstanding the fact that the programme of land redistribution in Brazil allocated almost 90 million hectares to (approximately) one million poor rural families, the Gini index measuring the concentration of land practically did not change in fifty years. According to the censuses, in 1975 the index was 0.855 while in 2006 it had changed marginally to 0.856, being one of the highest in the world (Hoffmann and Ney, 2010, p. 53).

11 Literally meaning 'Four centuries of latifundium'.

12 According to the authors,

an increase in the share of foreign capital was observed in Brazil's stock exchanges (…) rising from 24.1% in 2003 to 42.1% in 2013 (…) the most significant growth occurred in 2011, coinciding with a shift by the institutional investors towards financial assets linked to natural resources, particularly in the case of commodities.

(Balestro e Lourenço, 2014, p. 257)

13 Rural activities were the biggest employers throughout the history of Brazil, a cycle which ended in 2011. This is true, even when considering all job possibilities – salaried and other forms of occupation. From 2011 onwards, the services sector surpassed the total number of rural jobs and this gap is getting progressively wider.

14 A social welfare programme instituted by the Brazilian government. *Bolsa Família* provides financial aid to poor Brazilian families.

3 Agricultural development in Brazil

The role of agricultural policies

Carlos Augusto Mattos Santana and
José Garcia Gasques

1 Introduction

The Brazilian agriculture is frequently distinguished for showing a remarkable performance and playing a major role in global food supply. The domestic production of grains, meats, fibres, fruits and biofuel, among other products, registered an extraordinary growth in the last five decades, sustained mainly by productivity gains. The sector is a key contributor to global food security and the main pillar of repeated trade surplus achieved by the country.

Several factors have contributed to these achievements, among them, the agricultural policies implemented by different governments. The policies implemented did not always interpret correctly the observed transformations. They neither were invariability effective. However, in general, they followed a positive path.

Complex, sophisticated and wide-scope policies were adopted over time, for instance, the Agricultural Zoning Program established in 1996. It is one of the main policy tools used for the sustainable development of agriculture. It identifies the most suitable areas for the production of various crops. It also determines the technical procedures and requirements to grow specific crops, increase productivity, reduce risks and to protect the environment. It has successfully supported the implementation of rural insurance programmes and complemented other measures to expand agricultural production.

In parallel to effective policies as the one above, some unsolved gaps have been observed in the agricultural policy framework, for example, the fragility of the plant and animal health protection system – a source of risk and a threat to the sustainability of agriculture in the country. In addition, some policy measures have presented contradictions and contributed to destabilizing markets and crop production. In the mid-1980s, successive commodity price freezes, the use of regulatory stocks to control inflation, and the adoption of ad hoc market interventions introduced an institutional risk (Lopes, 1986). Moreover, on the production side, the indexation of financing, together with price controls, contributed to the accumulation of large farm debt by agricultural producers. Therefore, part of the positive effects of the subsidized credit system were cancelled or even reversed. Under such conditions, financing became a risk factor rather than an incentive to production.

Brazil's framework of agricultural policies of the 1960–2017 period is also characterized by major changes in the general orientation of the policies. Faced with the need to meet a growing domestic demand for food resulting from both, population increase and the process of import substitution industrialization (ISI), the government adopted in the mid-1960s a development strategy aimed at expanding agricultural and livestock production through agricultural modernization. The implementation of this strategy took place through a strong State intervention in agriculture, which was reduced after the mid-1980s due to the macroeconomic crisis of the decade. The economic instability experienced by the country in that period led the government to introduce deep reforms on its macro and sectoral policies, including in agriculture. Those changes resulted, among other things, in a marked reduction in State interventions in the sector and in a growing use of market instruments. In the 2000s, the general policy was to continue replacing the intervention measures through regulations and the adoption of new policies focused on social and environmental sustainability issues.

As highlighted above, the Brazilian agricultural policy changed during the 1960–2017 period in response to economic, political, social, international and environmental issues. A large and diverse number of measures was adopted; some produced positive results, others were not effective vis-à-vis its objectives. However, as corroborated by the positive performance of the sector along the years, the overall balance is favourable.

To analyse the set of agricultural policies followed by Brazil in the last five and a half decades is a great challenge that goes beyond the scope of the chapter. Therefore, the objectives here are limited only to examine the role of the agricultural policies that contributed most to the performance of the Brazilian agriculture in 1960–2017, and to assess the evolution of the State presence in the sector throughout this period. The analytical approach used to pursue these objectives consists in examining the role of the policies according to specific time intervals, which correspond to particular contexts and policy orientation that characterized the period.

2 The roots of agricultural modernization: 1960 to 1990

Brazil's agricultural policy framework presented two main characteristics in the 1960–1990 period (Buainain, 1999; Coelho, 2001). Between the 1960s and the mid-1980s, the nature of the policy instruments used characterized the period as highly interventionist. In contrast to this approach, in the second half of the 1980s, the severe macroeconomic imbalances of the time[1] led the government to initiate a major change on its policy orientation. Specifically, policy measures, which emphasize market forces as the main resource allocation mechanism were increasingly adopted.

The agricultural policies of the 1950s and 1960s reflected the well-known ISI development model, which advocates replacing foreign imports with domestic production[2] (Prebisch, 1964; Baer, 2008). In the context of the ISI, important roles were assigned to the agricultural sector. It was expected to contribute to the industrialization process through the purchase of agro-industrial inputs manufactured in the country. In addition, it should put an end to food supply crisis, free up labour for the urban sector, generate foreign exchange and contribute to reduced real wages in nascent industries through low food prices.

Notwithstanding the positive effect of land expansion on domestic agricultural production, food supply crisis occurred in Brazil in the early 1960s. In this context, amidst intense discussions[3] on structural reforms required to ensure a good performance of agriculture, the prevailed view advocated that the main problem was the technological backwardness of the sector. Therefore, the strategy to follow was the modernization of the sector, induced by strong State intervention in all relevant segments, from agricultural research to foreign trade.

In line with the above orientation, different agricultural policies were implemented in the 1960–1990 period. Among them, the following are distinguished for their particular importance in the modernization process of the Brazilian agriculture (Alves and Pastore, 1980; Coelho, 2001): rural credit; Guaranteed Minimum Price Policy (PGPM); agricultural research; and rural extension and technical assistance.[4] The adoption of these policies resulted in a selective modernization process of the sector, which favoured mainly the middle and large producers.

2.1 Rural credit (RC)

Rural credit was one of the main policy instruments used by the government to promote the modernization of agriculture, especially since 1965 when the National Rural Credit System (NRCS) was established. The main objectives of the System were: to stimulate capital formation in the sector; finance a substantial part of the direct costs of agricultural production and marketing; promote the adoption of technologies; and to strengthen the economic situation of producers, especially those of small and medium size.

According to Barros (1979), an implicit objective of the RC was to stimulate the demand for industrial goods produced in Brazil, that is, to contribute to the industrialization process through import substitution. Another implied objective was to partially compensate[5] the discrimination of some domestic policies against agriculture, especially the negative effects of price and exchange rate policies (Araújo and Meyer, 1979).

In the 1960s and 1970s the rural credit policy presented four main characteristics (Araújo and Meyer, 1979): negative interest rates charged on agricultural loans; provision of credit through the local banking system, instead of by specialized institutions set up for this purpose; legal requirement for banks to provide loans to farmers based on growing percentages of the total amount of checking deposits made in public and private banks; and relatively lower interest rates charged on small loans, supposedly those made to small farmers.[6] The RC

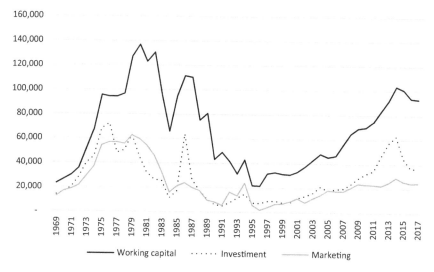

Figure 3.1 Brazil: Rural credit provided to farmers and cooperatives by purpose (values in millions of Reais of 2017). Source: BACEN (2018a).

was also characterized by providing financing for working capital, marketing and investment operations. These types of loans continue to exist until today.

During the 1969–1979 period, the total volume of credit granted to farmers and cooperatives expanded 400% in real terms[7] increasing from R$50 billion to R$253 billion (Figure 3.1).

Since the beginning of the 1980s, the rural credit policy underwent substantial changes due to three main factors: the policies to fight inflation; high external debt; and stagnant economic growth in the 1981–1983 period. The new orientation of the RC became more restrictive in terms of the total credit provided to the sector and with respect to the interest rate charged on the loans. Another change was a significant reduction in the implicit subsidies in the rural credit through the establishment of higher interest rates and indexing the loans to monetary adjustment.

The sources of rural credit also changed over time. Initially, most of the credit originated from bank deposits made by the population. However, with the acceleration of the inflationary process, the bank deposits reduced substantially. In this context, the Treasury became the main source of rural credit in the country. As a result of the new policy orientation, total rural credit fell sharply in real terms[8] dropping from R$ 210 billion in 1981 to R$ 31 billion in 1996 (Figure 3.1). Notwithstanding the observed reduction in the agricultural credit and on its implicit subsidies, there was no evidence that the performance of the sector was affected significantly (Gasques and Verde, 1990).

The explanation for this fact is that a set of incentives, predominantly resulting from the use of market-friendly policy instruments, began to emerge in agriculture. The loss of income transfers, via subsidized credit, induced farmers to reduce the average cost of farm activities. The focus of farmers' efforts were to increase productivity growth at the rural property via a moderate reduction of the cultivated area and a strong reduction in the use of labour.

The results of the rural credit policy implemented in the 1960s, 1970s and 1980s were contradictory. The policy was central to a significant change in the technological pattern of agriculture, to the consolidation of the domestic industry of inputs, machinery and equipment, and to the expansion of agricultural production and productivity. Nevertheless, the limited coverage[9] of the rural credit and the concentration of the resources in the centre-south region of Brazil on commercial crops[10] and on large and medium-size producers, caused social and economic distortions. There were also negative environmental effects, diversion of funds to other purposes and waste of financial resources associated with the almost unlimited supply of subsidized credit, particularly in the financing of mechanization and use of fertilizers (Pinto, 1980).

2.2 Guaranteed Minimum Price Policy (PGPM)

The PGPM was established in 1943 with the objectives of promoting the stabilization of agricultural prices and ensuring adequate income for producers[11] (CFP, 1989). From the mid-1960s to the present, it went through three phases.[12] Between 1966 and the end of the 1980s it was characterized by a strong intervention in marketing operations. In the 1990s, the PGPM left behind the interventionist approach giving growing priority to the use of market instruments. From the beginning of the 2000s onward, it focused part of its attention in supporting family farmers linking the minimum guaranteed price to the Food Acquisition Program[13] (PAA).

One of the main milestones of the PGPM in its early days was the enactment of Decree-Law n. 79 of December 12, 1966. It established that the Federal Government would pay a minimum guaranteed price to producers or their cooperatives for the sale of their products. The price applied also to processing industries, traders and exporters. The minimum prices, fixed in nominal terms by the National Monetary Council, were initially announced at least 60 days before the beginning of planting.

From 1960 to 1990, this policy was operated through two policy instruments: The Federal Government Loan (EGF) and the Federal Government Acquisition (AGF). The first involves the provision of credit to farmers based on the value of the crop stored,[14] and the second consists on the purchase of the production the farmer wishes to sell to the government. In both cases the resources received by the farmer is calculated according to the minimum guaranteed price established by the government.

Besides operating as a minimum guarantee price instrument through the purchase of production surpluses, the AGF contributes to stabilize the price faced by domestic consumers through regulatory stock building established in years of abundant supply (Oliveira, 1977). On the other hand, the EGF, by financing the storage of agricultural products, increase the bargaining power of producers at harvest time; at the same time, it contributes to the reduction of seasonal price fluctuation. Therefore, it favours a better allocation of resources. The advantage of the EGF in relation to the AGF is that the producer does not need to sell the production, he only pledges it as collateral for the loan received.

Substantial adjustments were made in the implementation of PGPM in the late 1970s, when serious macroeconomic problems pointed out earlier led the government to replace the rural credit by the PGPM as the main agricultural policy instrument (Coelho, 2001). In 1979, with the creation of the Basic Cost Value[15] (VBC), the minimum prices were no longer used as parameters in the calculation of the credit granted to producers. Giving this change, the minimum prices took on the role of stimulating sector production. Two years later, another major change occurred. The Base Price, which until then included an expected inflation rate, began to be adjusted based on the National Consumer Price Index (INPC).

Faced with the intensification of the inflationary process, the urgency of controlling the public deficit and the need to regulate the intervention in agricultural markets, the government introduced in 1988 specific rules for the automatic release of agricultural public stocks (Lopes, 1992). Specifically, it was decided that the government would participate in the marketing of rice, corn and edible beans by buying these products at the minimum price and selling their stocks when the market price reached the Intervention Price[16] set by the Production Financing Company (CFP). According to Lopes (1992), the advantage of this mechanism 'is that it allowed the government to intervene in the market, without disorganizing the private marketing, since the agents knew in advance the intervention rules'.

In the same direction of liberalizing the domestic markets, the exports and imports of cotton, soybeans and of basic food, including rice and corn, were liberalized in the late 1980s (CACEX Resolution n. 155).

The implementation of PGPM in the 1960s, 1970s and 1980s resulted in a growing withdrawal of large volumes of agricultural products from the market through EGF and AGF operations. According to the National Food Supply Company (CONAB), the volume of products stocked through EGFs expanded approximately 14 times in the 1968–1983 period, increasing from 961,000 tons to 13.5 million tons. In 1984 and 1985 the amount stored via EGF was reduced significantly, returning to the 1975–1979 levels, i.e., approximately seven million tons.

The volume marketed via AGF expanded substantially also during the 1968–85 period, particularly since the mid-1970s. The quantity purchased through AGF operations increased from 168,000 tons in 1968 to 8.8 million in 1985. As suggested by the above data, traditionally the EGF was used more than the AGF in marketing activities. Among other reasons, this was due to the conservative approach adopted by the government in setting the minimum price. Another factor is that, while the AGF is used in the purchase of production surpluses, the EGF is a financing instrument, which includes the option to sell the product.

In addition to the above aspects, the favourable relation between the minimum guaranteed prices and the production costs of agricultural products observed in the 1980s was an explanatory factor for the expansion of agriculture during this period[17] (Gasques and Verde, 1990). In contrast to this result, in the second half of 1980, the PGPM presented a low effectiveness in reaching the objective of stabilizing the prices faced by domestic consumers through the sales of regulatory stocks (Melo, 1991).

Regarding the implementation of the PGPM in the centre-west region of Brazil, Rezende (2002) argues that the policy sought to favour this region through minimum prices fixed in a 'spatially inconsistent' manner, that is, without properly considering the transportation costs between this region and main consumption centres. As a result, agricultural production increased; however, negative effects were also observed. For instance, the spatially inconsistent setting of minimum prices prevented the private marketing of grains between the centre-west and importing regions of Brazil. Therefore, the government had to be responsible alone for building stocks, as well as for the transportation, storage and sale of the products.

A second negative impact pointed out by Rezende was that the spatial inconsistency of minimum prices discouraged the formation of industrialization 'chains'. According to this author, the risk of policy change affected also the development of these chains. As shown in the next section, the change in the policy actually occurred in the 1990s.

2.3 Agricultural research

Driven by the goal of promoting increased agricultural productivity and influenced by the 'Green Revolution' and the works of scholars like Schultz's (1964), the Brazilian government made important reforms in the public system of agricultural research between 1960 and 1990. Among the changes introduced, the creation of the Brazilian Corporation for Agricultural Research (Embrapa), in December 1972, stands out as a turning point and a seminal measure in the history of agricultural research in the country.

With the birth of this institution, a new organizational structure for public agricultural research was established in Brazil. The responsibility for coordinating[18] and executing the researches efforts was transferred from the National Department of Research and Experimentation[19] (DNPEA) to Embrapa. In addition, the diffusion research model was replaced by the concentrated model. The latter is characterized by an emphasis on research aimed at finding solutions to practical issues and by making large investments in a limited number of products (Pastore et al., 1974). In addition to Embrapa's units, the system included integrated programmes developed in partnership with universities and state research institutes. State organizations of agricultural research (OEPAs) were also created as part of the system.

Historically, one of the most important actions undertaken by Embrapa was investment in human resources. The first initiative in this area occurred in 1975.

In that year, the organization financed graduate studies of approximately 500 researchers in the best universities in Brazil and especially abroad, in different areas of the agricultural sciences (Embrapa, 2002). This special attention to capacity building of its professionals has been maintained over the years. In 2017 approximately 86% of Embrapa's researchers had a PhD degree and 13% a science master.

Embrapa's budget grew exponentially in real terms between 1974 and 1982, increasing from R$ 212 million[20] to R$ 2.5 billion. Between 1982 and 2003 its financial resources fluctuated. They peaked in 1996 (R$ 2.8 billion) and fell successively until 2003. After that year they started to grow again reaching R$ 3.4 billion in 2017.

The technological assets generated by Embrapa contributed significantly to the extraordinary performance of Brazilian agriculture in the last five decades.[21] However, a significant number of producers were excluded from the agricultural modernization process due to their impossibility of using the available technologies (Alves and Rocha, 2010; Kageyama, 1990).

In addition to Embrapa's contributions, the Brazilian agriculture also benefited from the research activities developed by the OEPAs – a group of 16 state-owned institutions,[22] five of which in São Paulo. Notwithstanding their valuable contributions, they faced major financial difficulties, which affected their operations in the 1988–2006 period (CGEE, 2006). Therefore, in view of this situation, it was necessary for Embrapa to complement the work carried out by a number of OEPAs.

The third axis of the research policy was investment in federal and state universities, which played a relevant role in both, agricultural research and in the formation of quality human capital. The number of university courses in agricultural sciences expanded rapidly in Brazil since 1960. In 1981 the country had 39 agronomy courses, 26 in veterinary medicine and 12 in zootechny (Moreira and Teixeira, 2014). Nine years later, these numbers increased to 53, 32 and 16, respectively. Similar growth occurred with graduate courses in agricultural sciences. The first graduate courses in this field were held in 1961 at the Federal University of Viçosa and in 1970 at Luiz de Queiroz College of Agriculture (ESALQ). In 2012, a total of 588 graduate programmes in different areas of agricultural sciences were offered by Brazilian universities (Teixeira et al., 2013). Further to the above, it should be mentioned that the private sector has also contributed significantly to agricultural research in Brazil, especially in the last two decades.

2.4 Rural extension and technical assistance

The establishment of rural extension in Brazil has as a historical landmark the technical and financial cooperation between the Rockefeller Foundation and the government of Minas Gerais. As a result of this partnership, the Credit and Rural Technical Assistance Association (ACAR-MG) was created in 1948 in the state of Minas Gerais.[23] By the end of the 1960s, 21 ACARs had been established, comprising 1,025 municipalities and 138 regional offices (Olinger, 1996). All these units were non-profit civil entities operating in cooperation with the three levels of government (federal, state and municipal) and other institutions, including related to rural credit (Ribeiro, 1985). The 21 ACARs formed the Brazilian Rural Extension System[24] (SIBER), which was coordinated by the Brazilian Association of Credit and Rural Technical Assistance (ABCAR).

Inspired by the American experience, the ACAR activities were based on rural credit and technology, that is, transforming the 'traditional farm' through the diffusion of agricultural technologies enabled by supervised rural credit. The main target was the vast group of small farmers. The technical assistance and rural extension actions included improving agricultural activities, enhancing the wellbeing of rural families and strengthening the socioeconomic conditions of their communities.

As part of the modernization strategy adopted since the first half of the 1970s, the Federal Government created the Brazilian Company for Technical Assistance and Rural Extension (EMBRATER). Moreover, it promoted changes in the institutional organization of rural extension in Brazil. In this context, the ACARs were replaced by State Enterprises for Technical Assistance and Rural Extension (EMATER): that is, the ACARs were changed from non-profit civil entities into public institutions run by the states. The SIBER was transformed into the Brazilian System of Technical Assistance and Rural Extension (SIBRATER). It incorporated both, private and public technical assistance institutions.[25] Another change was the closing of ABCAR and the transfer of its coordinating function of the SIBER to EMBRATER. In addition to this responsibility, EMBRATER also had the role to provide financial support to the EMATERs. This was carried out through the transfer of federal and international resources managed by EMBRATER.

The operation of SIBRATER produced important results. The number of counties assisted expanded from 2,581 in the first half of the 1970s to 3,166 in 1983 (Ribeiro, 1985). The rural properties assisted also increased from 8% of the total in 1975 to 22% in 1983. During this same period, the number of muncipal offices expanded from 1,565 to 2,506 and the field staff more than doubled, increasing from 4,419 professionals to 9,754.

According to Olinger (1996), after a few years of operation the SIBRATER began gradually to lose its prestige and to provide limited technical assistance to farmers.[26] Parallel to this, the ten-year loans provided by the International Bank for Reconstruction and Development (IBRD) to finance EMBRATER's operating costs and investment expenditures were no longer renewed. In this context and in view of the negative effects of the macroeconomic crisis then experienced by Brazil, EMBRATER was extinguished in early 1990. As shown later in this chapter, the elements mentioned above, together with the serious financial situation of the states and hence of EMATER, resulted in the establishment of a new rural extension and technical assistance system in the country in the 1990s.

3 The 1990s: a decade of reform

According to Baumann (2000), the 1990s are considered the 'decade of reforms' in Brazil.[27] The period was marked by the adoption of heterodox macroeconomic policies that significantly influenced Brazil's agricultural policies. The approach followed changed from a strong State intervention in the sector to a paradigm guided by the use of market-friendly oriented-policies. They were inspired, to some extent, by international institutions such as the World Bank and the IMF.

The stable macroeconomic environment resulting from the adoption of the Real Plan in 1994, created favourable conditions for policy reforms, induced confidence on the part of Brazilian and foreign investors, and at the same time, eliminated significant gains obtained by the government and the banking sector from high inflation rates. The reforms followed three main axes (Dias and Amaral, 2000): liberalization of national agricultural markets; stabilization of domestic prices; and institutional changes aimed at improving the framework of public institutions and dismantling state monopolies in agriculture. In relation to trade, the reforms were oriented to eliminating the anti-export bias faced by agriculture. In this regard, the main policy measures included a gradual reduction of tariffs (particularly those applied to imports), cutting red tape applied to commercial operations and elimination of quotas, licenses and prohibitions to exports.

Among the agricultural products, greatest protection was given to sugar and milk with tariffs of 20% and to wheat. The tariff on wheat imports fell from 25% to 15% between 1991 and 1993. Cotton was left without tariff protection. Therefore, the sector suffered strong impacts from external competition. In this context, the domestic production of this product fell and many cotton producers and firms went bankrupt. In the case of imported chemical fertilizers, especially nitrogen, tariffs were reduced significantly. The opposite was observed with tractor imports, i.e., tariffs were imposed in order to protect the domestic industry against the poor economic environment created after the fall in investment credit (Buainain, 1999).

Parallel to the above, some reforms were introduced to accelerate foreign trade operations, particularly in 1991–1996 (Baumann, 2000). The implemented reforms included: compensatory measures to reduce the delay in the analysis of anti-dumping processes; removal of export taxes; elimination of quota systems and withdrawal of export licenses. Direct and indirect subsidies were also abolished, with the exception of those applied to free zones and to drawback system. The Tax on the Circulation of Goods and Services (ICMS) was withdrawn from exports in 1996 – it represented, on average, 12% of the value added (Dias and Amaral, 2000).

In addition to the aforementioned reforms, the government established in 1995 an agenda geared to change the instruments used in the implementation of the rural credit and the PGPM. Among other elements, the changes were influenced by the need to adjust the policy instruments to the fiscal reality and due to the impossibility of maintaining the level of public spending and sub-sidies in line with the requirements of the monetary stabilization programme. In addition to the strong reduction in the volume of credit granted to the sector (Figure 3.1), one of the most important measures was the restructuring of the large agricultural debt accumulated by producers during the macroeconomic instability period (late 1980 to mid-1990). Debt rescheduling was inevitable, given the need to renew the flow of liquidity in the sector.

According to Coelho (2001), the strategy followed by the govern-ment to restructure the NRCS in the 1990s also included the following measures: securitization of agricultural debt; de-indexation of financial charges in order to make them compatible with those observed in other countries; and promotion of private financing to reduce the role of official credit in the financing of productive activities. Moreover, reflecting the government's interest in modernizing the stock of machinery and agricultural implements the Modernization Program for Machinery Acquisition (MODERFROTA) was established in mid-1999. The programme grants investment credit at con-trolled interest rates.

With regard to the PGPM, the traditional instruments used in the imple-mentation of the policy, i.e., the AGF and EGF, were adjusted to the strategic orientation of reducing public intervention and encouraging the partici-pation of the private sector in agricultural marketing. Four policy measures stand out: (i) the creation of the EGF settlement price;[28] (ii) the elimination of the EGF with selling option (EGF/COV); (iii) the establishment of the Sales Option Contract(COV);[29] and (iv) the introduction of the Premium for Commercial Buyers Program (PEP).[30] The purposes of this last measure were to guarantee a reference price to agricultural producers and their cooperatives, to reduce part of the AGF operations and, consequently, to drop the building up of public stocks.

Further to the above, some measures were taken to rationalize the set of public institutions active in agriculture; for instance, the creation of the National Food Supply Company (CONAB) and the elimination of monopolies and state agencies in the sugar, alcohol, coffee and wheat sectors by transferring the marketing activities to private enterprises.

In another direction, in order to promote the inclusion of small farmers in the productive process of Brazilian agriculture, the Federal Government created in 1996 the Family Agriculture Strengthening Program – PRONAF[31] (Buainain et al., 2014). With this same purpose, the Ministry of Agrarian Development was established in early 2000. Among others, its functions included the promo-tion of the sustainable development of family farm agriculture.

The main instrument used by PRONAF to support family faming was the provision of subsidized credit for working capital and investment. The total volume of credit granted by the Program expanded three times in real terms in the 1999–2012 period increasing from R$ 7 billion to R$ 21.7 billion.[32] It is interesting to note that the participation of the working capital and investment credit in the total credit provided by PRONAF changed substantially in this period. Specifically, the share of working capital fell from 82% to 45% while that of investment increased from 18% to 55%.

3.1 Policy reforms and public spending

As mentioned above, the period prior to the 1990s was characterized by a strong State intervention in agriculture. Until 1987 the share of agricultural public spending in total Federal Government expenditure was high. However, after that year it declined sharply as a result of the fiscal crisis of the late 1980s, the monetary stabilization policy of the 1990s, and the reorientation of agricultural policies. In fact, the total value of agricultural spending persisted falling through the new century. It fell to the total of R$ 235 billion accumulated throughout the period 2000–2009 when compared to R$ 361 billion in the 1990s (Figure 3.2).

Among the implemented reforms, the ones that contributed most to reducing agricultural public spending in the 2000s were: reduction of agricultural subsidies; creation of new sources of rural credit; the use of marketing instruments with strong participation of the private sector; and the entry of new agents in agricultural financing. Another element, which contributed to reducing public spending on agriculture was a cut on the resources allocated to Agrarian Organization. Public expenditures on land policy, which includes agrarian reform and the settlement of landless families, registered a marked reduction after the year 2000, that is, they dropped from R$ 8.74 billion in 2007 to R$ 1.84 billion in 2017; in other words, they registered a real reduction of more than 79% during that period.

As a result of the policy adjustments and the downward trend in agricultural public spending, the level of protection granted to Brazilian agricultural producers (as measured by the Producer Support Estimate) was one of the lowest

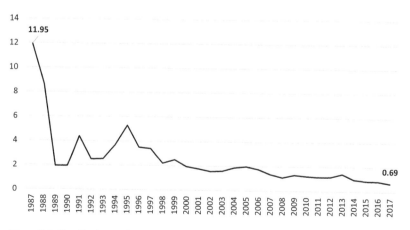

Figure 3.2 Brazil: Agricultural public spending share in total Government expenditure, 1987–2017 (percentage).

in the world in 2014–2016, i.e., approximately 4% in relation to agricultural production value (OECD, 2018).

3.2 Reform impacts

Foreign trade restrictions imposed by Brazil until the mid-1990s limited the domestic growth of agriculture. The exports of raw agricultural products were subject to quotas and the incidence of high taxes. Coffee, sugar and soybeans were heavily penalized by the trade policy in place until the early 1990s. Coffee taxation reached 40% of the exported value. The ad valorem tariff on sugar exports exceeded 50% until the early 1990s, preventing the industry to benefit from favourable international prices. Soybeans trade were subject to tariff and non-tariff restrictions.

After the policy reforms, notably since 1995, the discrimination against agricultural exports disappeared, thus, the sector exports boosted (Lopes and Lopes, 2010). Soybean production, which was virtually stagnant between 1984 and 1995, grew significantly after the removal of the export taxes. Therefore, Brazil started to occupy a prominent position among the world's largest exporters of this product.

Although the economic opening of the 1990s brought more competitiveness to the agricultural and processed food markets, it was the opening of the input markets that had the greatest impacts on agriculture. These markets, besides being less competitive, received much of the subsidies given during the previous decades. Thus, when exposed to a greater external competition, there was a strong improvement in their terms of trade. This fact, together with productivity increases, resulted in greater purchasing power with respect to agricultural inputs. This is the main explaining factor behind the growth of agriculture during the structural reform period (Lopes et al., 2007).

According to Dias and Amaral (2010), the effective stimulus received by farmers from trade opening can be evaluated through an index of profitability. Given this understanding, they constructed an index of purchasing power, which is calculated by the product of the terms of trade with productivity. The estimate obtained through this procedure indicates that between 1987 and 1998, the purchasing power of agriculture increased approximately 59% (Id., 248).

This good result in terms of productivity and improvement in the terms of trade enabled the high technology producers to find substitutes for the traditional rural credit system. Dias and Amaral (2010) argue that the beneficiary population of this form of capitalization was altered when compared to what was observed under the previous policy model, where the distribution of subsidized rural credit was the most important variable. Under the new system, producers with below-average productivity may have been gradually de-capitalized and possibly, expelled from the sector.

With regard to the impact of the policy reforms on agricultural employment, it is not certain that there has been a reduction in the number of people employed. According to Gasques et al. (2016a), when one considers the average number of persons employed in agriculture in the 1980s and 1990s, it is observed that there is a 9% increase. Therefore, there is no employment reduction in the period.

4 The 2000s: a relatively open model, less interventionist and based on sustainable productivity

The agricultural policies of the 2000s are different in relation to those of the previous periods. In the 1980s and 1990s the policies were predominantly focused on the short term with strong sectoral content. The policies of the 2000s are distinguished for incorporating long-term strategies and for relying more frequently on regulatory frameworks such as the Forest Code (Law N. 12,651 of 2012). Moreover, they are characterized by programmes oriented to stimulate innovation, for instance, the Program of Incentive to Technological Innovation in Agricultural Production (INOVAGRO). The policy framework of the 2000s is also notable for including sectoral plans such as the Low-Carbon Agriculture Program (ABC Program), which aims at reducing Green House Gas (GHG) emissions from agriculture and promoting the sustainable development of the sector.

The policies followed also reinforced the use of market instruments, improved measures introduced in the 1990s, such as PRONAF, and created new ones, like the Rural Insurance Subsidy Program. The policy framework of the 2000s is also distinguished for providing particular attention to environmental sustainability, biodiversity preservation, and to the consolidation of greater participation of the private sector in the financing of agriculture.

4.1 Environmental sustainability and biodiversity preservation

Since the late 1990s various policy measures were introduced to promote environmental sustainability and the preservation of the biodiversity, including the Agricultural Modernization and Natural Resources Conservation Program (MODERAGRO), the Incentive Program for Sustainable Agriculture (PRODUSA) and the Program for Planting and Recovery of Commercial Forests (PROPFLORA). These programmes provide special lines of credit for investments in sustainable production systems.

The Brazilian policies of the last 15 years in the area of environmental preservation also include the Forest Code, the Agricultural and Climate Risk Zoning (ZARC) for various crops and the Low-Carbon Agriculture Plan. The first of these instruments establishes rules to protect the vegetation in Permanent Preservation Areas and in Legal Reserve Areas. In order to monitor and control deforestation of native vegetation, the government established in 2012, the Rural Environmental Registry (CAR). It is an electronic instrument used by the Ministry of Environment to register georeferenced information of the rural property, such as areas of permanent protection, legal reserve areas, crop area and area with native vegetation. The information collected forms a strategic database used in the control, monitoring and combat of deforestation, as well as in the environmental and economic planning of rural properties.

The ZARC defines the counties recommended to grow specific products as well as, the appropriate soil type to be cultivated, the best planting period and the cultivars to be used. Given the relevance of this instrument for environmental sustainability and for the minimization of climatic risks, the government linked it to the provision of agricultural credit. Therefore, the access to credit is dependent on the mandatory use of the orientations provided by the Agricultural and Climate Risk Zoning.

The ABC programme in turn, is a policy instrument through which the government provides credit to producers for the following purposes: (i) to promote the reduction of deforestation through crop expansion in degraded areas or in process of recovery; (ii) to encourage the adoption of production systems that prioritize the recovery of degraded pastures, the use of non-tillage, the adoption of integrated farming systems, the planting of forests and the utilization of biological fixation of nitrogen; and (iii) to stimulate the use of plant residues. The Plan is one of the main instruments used by Brazil to achieve its Intended Nationally Determined Contributions (INDC) to the United Nations Framework Convention on Climate Change (UNFCCC).

As a complement to the initiatives above, in 2017 the government launched the National Plan for the Recovery of Native Vegetation (PLANAVEG). Among others, its objectives include to promote good agricultural practices, via credit provision, in order to recover native vegetation in 12 million hectares by 2030 (MMA, 2017). The Plan focus particularly on Permanent Preservation Areas, Legal Reserve and on degraded areas.

4.2 Rural credit

The rural credit policy of the 2000s consolidated the orientation followed since the 1990s, that is, it promoted the increasing use of private sources of agricultural finance and focused the use of public funds in specific programmes. In this regard, new instruments were created to stimulate urban investors, small savers and pension funds to finance production and marketing activities. These instruments include, among others, the Agribusiness Credit Note (LCA), the Agribusiness Certificate of Credit (CDCA) and the Agribusiness Certificate of Receivables (CRA).[33] According to Moraes (2018) the LCA accounted for approximately 15% of the resources invested in the 2017/2018 cropping year.

In addition to stimulating private financing expansion, the government continued to provide large amounts of credit for working capital, marketing and investment (Figure 3.1). Among the three types of credit granted, investment funds increased substantially as a result of a new feature of the rural credit policy of the 2000s. In order to support sector expansion, new lines of investment credit were established, for instance, the MODERFROTA and the Incentive Program for Irrigation and Storage (MODERINFRA).

An additional element of the rural credit policy of the 2000s is the intensification of debt rescheduling. The first debt restructuring took place in 1996 and 1999. However, as the problem persisted and became harder (due to plagues, diseases, increased production costs and appreciation of the Real), new debt-restructuring packages were adopted, for example, in 2001, 2005 and 2008. Despite the efforts made, rural debt has not been solved yet and continues to threat the sustainability of Brazilian agriculture.

4.3 Strengthening family farming

Attention to family farming continued to figure prominently among the agricultural policy priorities of the 2000s. Therefore, in 2003 the government established the Food Acquisition Program (PAA) with the objective of strengthening family farming and guarantee food access to vulnerable families. Through the PAA the government purchases agricultural products directly from family farmers. The products are purchased at 'reference prices', which are higher than the guaranteed minimum price. The products purchased are distributed to food insecure families and to target groups through specific mechanisms, for instance, the National Schools Food Program (PNAE), which benefits school children. Another part of the products is devoted forming a strategic stock required by law.

The implementation of the PAA has been carried out through five policy instruments: Direct Purchase from Family Agriculture (CDAF); Government purchase from family farmers with simultaneous donation (CPR Donation); Farmers Certificate Stock (CPR Stock); Incentive to Milk Production and Consumption (IPCL); and Local Direct Purchase from Family Agriculture (CDLAF).[34]

In order to continue supporting the development of family farming, the government also adopted the Crop Guarantee Program and the MODERFROTA PROGER. The first of these instruments works as a risk minimization mechanism. The MODERFROTA PROGER grants investment credit to family farmers for the acquisition of tractors, harvesters and agricultural machinery.

In addition to the above initiatives, the government has supported family farming through PRONAF More Food, the Guaranteed Minimum Price Policy for Socio-biodiversity Products (PGPM-Bio) and the National Policy for Technical Assistance and Rural Extension (PNATER).

Through the first of these instruments, the government provides resources for investments in productive infrastructure of family farm. The PGPM-Bio strengthens the socioeconomic conditions of extractivist communities and traditional population. Moreover, it promotes the conservation, preservation and sustainable use of natural resources. The PNATER in turn, was established as a response to the limited[35] technical assistance and rural extension services offered by the government to family agriculture. A characteristic of PNATER is the use of public and private institutions to provide technical assistance and rural extension services.

Public expenditure on technical assistance and rural extension in Brazil increased substantially in real terms after the adoption of PNATER. Specifically, it expanded from R$ 286 million[36] in 2003 to R$ 713 million in 2014 (Gasques, 2015). Part of these resources corresponded to technical assistance and rural extension activities carried out by state institutions.

4.4 Public support for marketing and income stability

As in the past, the PGPM of the 2000s sought to reduce price instability, support producer incomes and ensure an adequate balance and distribution of supply between producing regions and local consumption centres. However, new objectives were also included. They included: contribute to strengthening family agriculture through the PAA; avoid excessive formation of public stocks; and expand private sector participation in agricultural marketing. In line with these objectives, new policy instruments were introduced, such as: The Equalizing Premium Paid to Producer[37] (PEPRO), the Risk Premium for the Purchase of Agricultural Products arising from Private Sales Option Contracts[38] (PROP) and the '*Valor para Escoamento de Produto*'[39] – VEP (premium for transporting agricultural products).

The first of these instruments acts as a deficiency payment: that is, it pays the seller (producer or an agricultural cooperative) the difference between the minimum guarantee price and the price received for the sale of a product, so that the amount received reaches the minimum price. In addition to ensuring the receipt of the reference price, this instrument exempts the government from purchasing the product. Moreover, it allows the transfer of products from surplus regions to needed consumption centres.

Created in 2004, the PROP works in the same manner as the Sales Option Contract (COV), except that private agents take on the role of CONAB purchasing the products. The government pays these agents a risk premium if the market price falls below the price set in the COV. Therefore, in addition to acting as an instrument to reduce price risks, the PROP allows the government to transfer the purchase of products through the PGPM to private agents. The VEP, in turn, is an economic subsidy granted for transporting products marketed under the PGPM.

According to Gasques and Bastos (2014), during the 2005–2006 period the government spending with the PGPM increased in real terms from R$ 2 billion to R$ 3.5 billion. In the following two years it dropped reaching R$ 894 million in 2008. After this fall, the expenditures with the Program increased in 2009, totalling R$ 4.3 billion. The observed increases in 2006 and 2009 resulted from low market prices vis-à-vis the guaranteed price.

4.5 Agricultural risk reduction

The policies followed by Brazil in the years 2000 to minimize agricultural risks consisted in carrying out the implementation of the ZARC and the Program of Guarantees for Agricultural Activities (PROAGRO). The government introduced also other measures, such as the Endowment Program for Rural Insurance Premium (PSR). Through this programme, it pays part of the rural insurance premium owed by farmers; therefore, it promotes the access to private rural insurance and induces greater investment in the sector.

The utilization of private rural insurance grew significantly in Brazil between 2003 and 2017. Nevertheless, the breath of the activities has been limited due to several factors, for instance: budget constraints to subsidize the premium; fluctuation of resources employed; difficulties to regulate the disaster fund; and limitations to give legal certainty for insurance and reinsurance companies.

In addition to the above-mentioned instruments, two other risk minimization programmes began to be implemented in the years 2000, the Guarantee 'Safra' and the Guarantee Program for Agricultural Activities of Family Farming, also known as PROAGRO Plus. Both of these programmes are directed to farmers enrolled in PRONAF as beneficiaries. The first is focused mainly on producers located in the semiarid region of the country, the second has national coverage.

4.6 Policy results: highlights

One of the priorities of the government in the years 2000 was to continue promoting agriculture productivity growth. In this regard, substantial investments were made in public research institutions; for instance, in the 2000–2017 period, Embrapa's budget expanded 62% in real terms, increasing from R$ 2.1 billion to R$ 3.4 billion.[40] Among other things, this budgetary expansion enabled the institution to expand its network of research laboratories abroad (known as Labex), creating units in France, the Netherlands, England and South Korea.

The contributions of these labs include: the creation of state-of-the-art technological solutions such as nano-fibre production system for packaging application; the development of a vaccine against influenza A virus, also called swine influenza (H1N1); the use of Lidar technology[41] in a three-dimensional monitoring and evaluation of the Amazon forest; and the utilization of advanced methods and tools in researches related to carbon sequestration in the soil and greenhouse gas emissions.

The results of the Labex offices include also the establishment of a large multi-institutional network, the AgroNano. Created ten years ago, the Network has established itself as a consolidated research group. During approximately ten years, more than 50 projects were jointly implemented by the 62 research institutions which integrate the network.

As a result of the research efforts of different public and private institutions, the productivity of Brazilian agriculture has registered one of the highest growth rates in the world (Fugly et al., 2012). According to these authors, investments in research and sectoral policies were the main factors that put Brazil and China at the top of the list of countries with higher productivity levels.

It is interesting to note that the evolution of agricultural productivity in Brazil, measured in terms of Total Factor Productivity (TFP), registered a significant increase in the 1990s. After expanding at an annual average growth rate of 3% in 1975–1997, the TFP grew by 4.28% per year between 1997 and 2014. Estimates recently obtained by Gasques et al. (2016a and 2018) showed that the TFP continued to grow at an average rate of 4% per year in the period 2000–2016. According to these authors, a set of factors are associated with this presented performance of the TFP, among them, rural credit, the terms of trade and exports.[42]

Despite the above result and the positive effects of different policies followed by the government in the 2000s, other reforms are still needed to further improve the performance of Brazilian agriculture. In this regard, Figure 3.3 shows the average percentage of tariffs in force in several countries. As it can be seen, it suggests that, notwithstanding the various reforms made in Brazil's tariff system, there is still room to move forward in this area and further open up the economy.

A second result to be pointed out is that, according to Brandão et al. (2005), MODERFROTA, together with other factors, played an important role in supporting investment in agricultural mechanization. Since the creation of this programme in 2000, the domestic sales of wheel tractors grew 129%, increasing from 24,591 units in that year to 56,420 in 2010. The sales of harvesters registered a similar trend in that period, that is, it expanded from 3,780 units to 4,549. The increased investment in the purchase of these machines, especially of tractors, favoured the expansion of the planted area in Brazil. Moreover, the implementation of MODERINFRA and MODERAGRO contributed significantly to: investments in irrigation; recovery of degraded pastures; soil

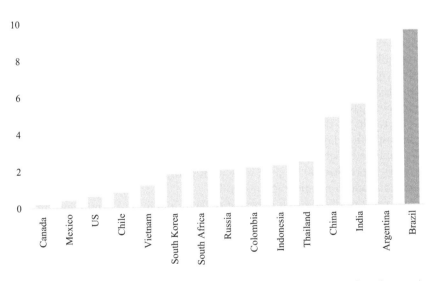

Figure 3.3 Average ad valorem import tariffs applied to all products by selected countries, 2015 or latest year available (in percentage). Source: World Bank (2018b).

fertilization; and investments in the production of fruit, milk, flowers, hogs, poultry and aquaculture.

According to the preliminary results of the recently released Agricultural Census, the purchase of tractors in Brazil increased from 820.70 thousand units in 2006 to 1.22 million in 2017, i.e. an expansion of approximately 50% during the period. The irrigated area also increased substantially; it totalled 6.9 million hectares in 2017 vis-à-vis 4.5 million in 2006. The same occurred with the utilization of agrochemicals. A total of 1,681,001 farms used this input in 2017, i.e. an increase of 20% in comparison to what was observed in 2006.

Regarding family farming, the credit granted by PRONAF in the 2000s, together with a greater provision of technical assistance services, contributed to boost small farmers' investment in agriculture, to increase food production and to expand income growth of local economies. The implementation of the PAA also brought significant benefits to family farming. Between 2003 and 2009, the purchase of agricultural products by the Program totalled R$ 2.7 billion and benefited 764 thousand families of small farmers (MDA, 2010). In addition, every year, about 7.5 million people received food free of charge through the programme.

In addition to the above results, the reorientation of the PGPM contributed to reduce government intervention in agriculture and to support family farming. Moreover, it increased private sector participation in agricultural marketing, and at the same time, directed public sector actions towards food security of vulnerable people.

5 Conclusions

The performance of Brazilian agriculture is a success case. The hands of the State, among others, were always present in this process, however, with different intensity over time. The historical reading of the country's agricultural policies in the last six and a half decades suggests some conclusions. First, the path of the implemented policies during this period, did not follow a preconceived scheme or a clear strategic view regarding the role of agriculture in national development. In reality, the policies were shaped by internal and external factors, among which the following stand out: the macroeconomic context of the Brazilian economy; and theoretical/practical influences resulting from international experiences and from schools of thought advocated by scholars, multilateral organizations and/or NGOs operating in various countries.

Regarding the conditioning factors of external nature, it can be mentioned, by way of illustration, the influence of agricultural modernization theories developed by Schultz (1964), Hayami and Ruttan (1985), and by Evenson and Kislev (1975). The American experiences with rural credit policies, support prices and rural extension also influenced the design of Brazil's policy framework.

A second conclusion, which in a certain extent is related to the previous one, is that the orientation of Brazilian agricultural policies in the analysed periods was broadly consistent with the prevailing macroeconomic context.

This, however, should not be understood as a favourable assessment of policy effectiveness. The policies followed produced positive and negative results. The assessment of what was achieved vis-à-vis the policy objectives goes beyond the scope of this chapter. Therefore, the purpose of the above conclusion is limited to indicating the attachment of the agricultural policies to the macroeconomic context.

It is also noted that the State intervention in the Brazilian agriculture decreased substantially over the years. In the 1960–1985 period, strong government intervention in the sector took place through policy instruments, which distorted the functioning of market forces. In contrast to this situation, since the mid-1980s, the loss of government capacity to continue assisting agriculture led the authorities to reduce the sectoral intervention through the adoption of market instruments. According to some analysts such as Baer (2008), Kageyama (1990) and others, the strong presence of the State in the Brazilian economy until the second half of the 1980s was considered necessary to accelerate national development.

An additional aspect that differentiates the Brazilian agricultural policies of the 1960–1985 period from those adopted in the following years is the fact that the interventions in the first of these periods were considered a planned effort (Buainain, 1999; De Janvry, 1983). The main objective of the policy framework was to promote structural changes considered necessary to set in motion the growth of agriculture. This planned nature of the policy set was abandoned since the 1980s, when the policies started to increasingly respond to short-term pressures from the sector and/or the macroeconomy.

Besides diminishing the intervention, the State also changed its role in the last decades, that is, it began to act mainly as a normative agent and a regulator of markets, sector activities and natural resource use, especially its conservation. This new role has been more noticeable in three main areas: animal and plant health protection; environmental quality; and rural work. Examples of public measures in these areas include the New Forest Code;[43] the Unified System of Monitoring Agricultural Health (SUASA), which seeks to ensure safer products to domestic and international consumers; the Animal and Plant Health Plan, which aims to modernize public services related to animal and plant health protection; the International Agricultural Surveillance System (VIGIAGRO); and the labour reform[44] of 2017, which establishes important norms to labour relations in agriculture.

Regarding the perspectives for Brazilian agricultural policies in the coming years, it is believed that they will hardly be guided by interventionist measures that contribute to distorting the functioning of markets. Strong fiscal constraints, coupled with the dispute over public resources from other sensitive areas such as education, health and public security, shall establish a new turning point with respect to State action. As a result, future agricultural policies are likely to present, among others, the following characteristics: greater private sector participation in rural credit financing and in the storage of agricultural products; increased public-private partnerships in agricultural research and rural technical assistance activities; smaller agricultural public institutions in terms of employees, due to greater pressures to reduce staff costs; larger number of measures related to rural insurance; continued support to market integration of producers who were left outside the agricultural modernization process, in particular the small producers; and stronger policy attention to environmental, social, labour, commercial and food safety issues.

Notes

1 Skyrocketing inflation, stagnation of GDP and external debt crisis, among others.
2 The ISI process began in Brazil in 1929 and continued until the end of the 1970s.
3 Different explanations were given as the main cause of the supply crisis, among which substantial losses in the marketing process (Smith, 1969). A second hypothesis pointed out the agrarian structure as the main factor, so the solution would be an agrarian reform (Cline, 1970). For Schuh (1974), the lack of investment in research, together with labour-saving industrialization and price policy for domestic and foreign markets, were the main explanatory factors. A fourth explanation resulted from Hayami and Ruttan's Theory of Induced Innovation, that is, the abundance of land and labor limited the modernization of agriculture and inspired policies that stimulated area expansion instead of promoting productivity growth (Pastore et al., 1974).
4 The agricultural policies adopted by Brazil between 1960 and 1990 included others besides those mentioned here. Given their relatively low importance for agricultural modernization, they will not be considered here.
5 The compensation was carried out through a subsidized credit.
6 This measure was based on the assumption that small farmers needed special incentives to engage in credit operations.
7 Expressed in Real of 2017.
8 Expressed in Real of 2017.
9 The coverage of the NRCS in the late 1970s encompassed only 20% of the rural properties (Pinto, 1980).
10 Mainly soybeans, coffee, sugarcane, cotton and wheat.
11 Initially the PGPM covered a few products such as rice, beans, corn, cotton, peanuts, soybeans and sunflowers. However, the number of products benefited from the policy increased over time. In 2014 they totalled 41 products.
12 In line with the organization of the chapter, the elements of the first phase will be presented here; those referring to the second and third phases will be addressed in the next sections.
13 This programme was created in 2003 with the objective of supporting family farming through the purchase of its products and the distribution of the strategic stocks to the population in greater social vulnerability.
14 Through the EGF the producer has the option to sell his product to the government or to a private agent.
15 The VBC was the value that corresponded to the total expenses incurred by farmers to grow a given crop in a specific region using a determined technological system (Colsera, 1993).
16 Since 1991 this price was replaced by the Stock Release Price (PLE). For an explanation of the criterion used to define this price see the Interministerial Order ('Portaria Interministerial') n° 657 of 10/07/1991.

17 This period was characterized by decreasing real prices and rural credit reduction.

18 This function was of a normative and programmatic nature.

19 The DNPEA was abolished in 1973.

20 This value and the following ones are expressed in Real of 2017.

21 Among the research results achieved, the following stand out: the development of technologies that transformed the acid and nutrient-poor soils of the savannahs in fertile and highly productive areas; biological nitrogen fixation in the soil; generation of soybean cultivars adapted to climatic conditions of different regions of Brazil; and development of several production systems for different products.

22 Data provided for 1980 by the National Council of State Agencies for Agricultural Research (CONSEPA).

23 According to Peixoto (2008), 'at least from the point of view of legislation, technical assistance and rural extension activities already existed as a legally established activity'.

24 This system was also known as ABCAR System.

25 Technical assistance was also provided by independent professionals who charged for their services. These professionals, as well as private technical assistance institutions, should be accredited in EMBRATER in order to carry out activities in an integrated way to SIBRATER (Olinger, 1996).

26 Among others, the following elements contributed to the deterioration of the SIBRATER (Olinger, 1996): lack of adjustment of technical and extension services to new requirements (more demanding markets; definition of priorities and strategies; renewed methods of action; etc.); excessive number of employees; political interference in the system operation; deficient evaluation of employee performance; limited availability of adequate means to work, especially transportation of extension workers.

27 As indicated earlier, some initial actions were introduced in the second half of the 1980s.

28 It corresponded to the difference between the minimum guaranteed price and the market price. It was established to support the producer's income, without forcing the government to carry stocks. The establishment of this price enabled the producers to sell their products in the market (at a price relatively lower than the minimum guaranteed price) and to receive the difference from the government.

29 The COV is similar to option contracts traded on commodity exchanges, with the government as buyer at the minimum price. It is used when the market price is below the minimum guaranteed price. The operation is carried out via auction. The Contract gives the producer and/or his cooperative the right – but not the obligation – to sell his product to the government at a future date at the minimum price.

30 The PEP is an economic subsidy granted to agents who purchase the government-nominated product directly from agricultural producers or cooperatives at the minimum price. According to the norms of the Program, those agents are responsible to transport the product from surplus regions to areas with scarcity.

31 The Decree 1,946 of June 20, 1996, which established the PRONAF, created the socio-economic category family farming, which was later institutionalized in 2006 through Law 11,326.

32 Values expressed in Reais of 2017.

33 For an explanation of these instruments see Ministry of Agriculture, Livestock and Food Supply, 2008.

34 For a detailed explanation of these instruments, see Almeida (2014).

35 This limited assistance resulted from the dismantling of EMBRATER and from the State's withdrawal from these services.

36 Expressed in Reais of 2014.

37 Created in 2005, the PEPRO works by paying the seller (producer or agricultural cooperative) the difference between the minimum price and the price received in the auction. In addition to ensuring the payment of the reference price to producers and cooperatives, this instrument exempts the government from the acquisition of the product and allows the transfer of products from producing regions to deficit consumption centres.

38 Created in 2004, the PROP works in the same way as the COV, except that private agents take on the role of CONAB by purchasing the products. The government pays these agents a risk premium if the market price falls below the price set in the COV. Thus, through the PROP, the government transfers the purchase of products through the PGPM to private agents.

39 This is an economic subsidy granted for transporting the products marketed through the PGPM.

40 Values expressed in Real of 2017.

41 It is a sophisticated technology based on the use of light and laser.

42 The impacts of these variables on the TFP were statistically significant.

43 Law n. 12,651, of May 25, 2012.

44 Law 13,467, of July 13, 2017.

4 The restructuring of Brazilian agri-chains

The role of value chains

Maria Sylvia Macchione Saes, Hildo Meirelles de Souza Filho and Rodrigo Lanna Franco da Silveira

1 Introduction

Around the end of the 1980s, the Brazilian agri-chains went through major changes caused by liberal agricultural policies and newly-imposed international food safety standards and environmental sustainability practices. In the domestic arena, the government abandoned old mechanisms of direct market intervention and also reduced subsidies as well as the crucial role it played in the diffusion of technologies via rural extension services. In the international trade arena, multilateral agreements were established and tariffs were reduced, although technical barriers related to food safety and the environment were raised by importing countries. Pressures exerted by importing companies for certifications and traceability increased significantly. An ample and complex set of food safety regulations regarding product quality was established. All these issues have resulted in major challenges for the actors in the agri-chains.

As a result, new governance and cooperation arrangements linking agribusiness players arose, many of which due to unintentional strategies to overcome sporadic crises or meet different demands of the markets. In other words, Brazilian input suppliers, farmers, processing companies, wholesalers and retailers swiftly acted in order to remain competitive. The structure of these new interactions between and within production sectors was largely associated to distinct levels of creativity and innovative capacity of those involved, articulating parts of or the whole value chain. For example, input manufacturers established closer relationships with farmers and processing companies to develop integrated technological packages and input retailers expanded their roles to offer credit and technical assistance to farmers. An illustration of this took place in the centre-west of the country. After the credit crisis that hit agriculture in the 1990s, various partnerships among all actors in the soybean industry emerged, in which farmers, suppliers and trade companies developed new contractual arrangements to finance the activity.

Relationships between processing companies and wholesalers also changed rapidly. Stronger ties, formal and informal, were established between processors, farmers, input suppliers and credit suppliers in order to increase efficiency and boost profitability both on the farms and in the processing plants. Contract farming, already present in certain specific segments (such as poultry, hog and tobacco), and usually carried out between large companies and small farmers, became an usual commercial tool. This multifaceted array of new arrangements proved to be decisive for Brazilian value chains in terms of their competitiveness in international trade given that transaction and logistics costs fell, and the quality and diversification of products rose. A notable example of this process can be seen in one of the most traditional chains in the country – coffee. Following the deregulation of the coffee sector after the end of the 1980s, new and complex contractual arrangements guided by product differentiation strategies were developed between coffee farmers and processing companies. This led to the emergence of different product categories, such as coffee with denomination of origin, organic varieties, quality certifications, and fair trade certification. A growing variety of contract types has been adopted in different agri-chains, such as milk, beef, orange, coffee, soybeans and seeds, from simple forward contracts to complex ones with detailed clauses for technical specifications, technical assistance, input supply and credit supply. As well as closer relationships with independent farmers, many processing companies have also adopted partial vertical integration – this is the case of beef, orange juice and sugar and ethanol, for example.

This movement was not restricted to the production link of the agri-chains. Large supermarket chains created supplier development programmes, with their own certifications and traceability, in response to supply-related problems caused by inconsistencies in product quality and delivery. In joining these supply chains and certification and traceability programmes, a large number of small and medium-sized producers of fruit, vegetables and legumes raised technology and quality standards. Many wholesalers went from being mere speculators and providers of logistical services, such as transport and storage, to adopting quality control functions.

Considering these broad issues introduced here, the objective of this chapter is to analyse changes in some of the main Brazilian agri-chains, investigating how they were able to react positively to changes in the institutional and competitive contexts in both domestic and international markets. Particular attention will be given to the new ways in which the transactions linking farmers, input suppliers and processors are coordinated. It is understood that the new forms of coordination were fundamental to maintaining systematic competitiveness in these agri-chains (Ménard et al., 2014).

2 The expansion of the Brazilian agribusiness

The importance of agriculture and livestock production in Brazil is widely known, having been analysed in a number of studies (OECD and FAO, 2015; Chaddad, 2016). Despite only 5% of the country's gross domestic product (GDP) comes directly from activities that take place on farms, the agri-food system as a whole is a key strategic sector for the economy given its importance for the domestic supply of food, exports, job-creation, new forms of income and occupation of areas of national territory, among many other positive impacts. The sector has greater importance considering the range of activities carried out by various links of their value chains countrywide. Brazil is one of the world's leaders in the production and export of different agricultural products, such as soybean, maize, orange, coffee, sugar, cotton, beef and chicken. Taking into account the agri-chain activities (from input production to retailer services), agribusiness is responsible for around 20% of Brazilian GDP (Cepea, 2018) and approximately 45% of national exports (Mapa, 2018a).

Table 4.1 summarizes the evolution of some economic indicators related to Brazilian agribusiness between the 1960s and 2010s. The expansion of agriculture and livestock production in the country has been remarkable – the value of agricultural production increased around 42% per decade in this period. Input suppliers accompanied this tendency – while the consumption of fertilizers doubled, on average, every decade, the sale of tractors increased approximately 40% in the same timescale, with a significant increase in the power and the technological level.

In the 1960s, Brazil was a marginal player on the international market, with exports at around US$ 1.3 billion per year, of which almost 60% was concentrated in coffee. In the 2010s, exports enjoyed an average revenue of US$ 77.3 billion. In addition, Brazil consolidated its leadership in the international market of a number of agricultural products but mainly from exports from the soybean, maize, coffee, sugarcane, forest products and beef industries (80% of the export value of the sector). The exports of agri-chains of soybean and beef alone increased more than six-fold between the 1990s and 2010s.

The growth in total production was even more notable from the 2000s onwards. At that time, while there was a significant increase in the demand for fertilizers and equipment, a fall in the use of labor was observed, notwithstanding a major expansion in the area of crops planted in the centre-west region of the country (Gasques et al., 2016a). The total factor productivity (TFP) significantly increased during this time (Table 4.2). In the 1980s and 1990s, the average annual increase in TFP of agriculture varied between 2% and 3%, and in the following period it jumped to 4% per year.

Three key and highly positive impacts characterized these revealing trends of growth. Firstly, the expansion was largely determined by increased productivity, notably adopted in large-scale contexts of the diffusion of innovation with an extensive use of inputs.[1] Secondly, the increased growth in internal and external demand for food resulted in the diversification of production and an increase in processing activities and value creation. The domestic market grew due to urbanization, the increase in life expectancy and monetary stability – the latter observed from the mid-1990s onwards. The external market grew as a result of the sudden increase in Chinese demand for food.[2] Thirdly, considering major changes in the institutional and competitive environments, actors in the main agri-chains constructed new forms of transaction

Table 4.1 Overview of the Brazilian agriculture, from the 1960s to the 2010s.

Variable		Average value per year						Decade average growth rate (%)
		1960s	1970s	1980s	1990s	2000s	2010s[a]	
General information	Agriculture: gross production value (constant 2004–2006 million US$)[b]	16,051	22,321	32,993	44,267	69,068	92,926	42.08
	Export Value: crops and livestock products (US$ million)[b]	1,299	4,769	9,040	12,078	31,263	76,066	125.70
	Agricultural land: arable and permanent crops (1,000 ha)[b]	34,116	47,416	54,348	62,220	73,203	83,316	19.55
	Rural population (1,000 persons)[b]	40,955	42,375	41,019	36,443	31,963	29,576	-6.30
Agriculture	Grain (1,000 metric tons)[c]	N/A	44,396	57,625	74,567	123,685	191,901	44.19
	Soybean (1,000 metric tons)[b]	532	7,311	16,377	23,911	49,299	81,667	173.65
	Corn (1,000 metric tons)[b]	11,141	15,691	22,391	29,873	43,988	70,240	44.52
	Seed cotton (1,000 metric tons)[b]	1,633	1,838	2,032	1,427	3,039	4,016	19.72
	Sugarcane (1,000 metric tons)[b]	70,291	101,568	219,431	296,319	463,300	742,245	60.22
	Orange (1,000 metric tons)[b]	2,281	5,785	13,335	20,009	18,280	17,857	50.91
	Coffee (1,000 bags of 60 kg)[b]	26,773	19,190	25,297	22,858	38,310	47,811	12.30

(continued)

Table 4.1 (Cont.)

Variable		Average value per year							Decade average growth rate (%)
		1960s	1970s	1980s	1990s	2000s	2010s[a]	
Livestock	Live cattle stock (1,000 heads)[b]	64,092	93,053	129,620	157,555	195,209	213,030	27.15
	Chicken stock (1,000 heads)[b]	160,513	292,547	479,643	690,354	1,004,240	1,285,503	51.60
	Pork stock (1,000 heads)[b]	27,734	33,599	32,620	32,752	34,152	38,783	6.94
	Meat production – cattle (1,000 metric tons)[b]	1,500	2,216	3,462	5,331	8,042	9,366	44.24
	Meat production – chicken (1,000 metric tons)[b]	209	599	1,634	3,735	8,084	12,166	125.41
	Meat production – pork (1,000 metric tons)[b]	627	789	920	1,726	2,897	3,261	39.07
	Exports: meat and meat preparations (US$ million)[b]	33	217	781	1,286	7,172	15,077	240.43
Input	Fertilizer consumption (1,000 metric tons)[d]	367	2,175	3,353	4,638	8,752	12,956	103.93
	Domestic wholesale of wheels tractors (units)[c]	8,279	40,753	34,803	21,689	30,261	49,442	42.96

Notes: [a] Average value obtained between 2000 and 2016;
Source: [b] FAOSTAT (2018); [c] Conab (2018a); [d] CepalStat (2018); [c] Anfavea (2018).

Table 4.2 Average growth rate (% per year) of products, inputs and productivity in Brazilian agriculture and livestock production between 1975 and 2014

Variable	1975–2014	1975–1979	1980–1989	1990–1999	2000–2009	2000–2014
Product index	3.83	4.35	3.38	3.02	5.18	4.51
Input index	0.29	1.14	1.08	0.03	1.17	0.46
Labour index	-0.35	0.07	0.62	-0.25	-0.03	-0.77
Land index	-0.01	0.76	0.30	-0.33	-0.22	-0.18
Capital index	0.66	0.32	0.15	0.62	1.43	1.42
Total factor productivity	3.53	3.18	2.28	2.98	3.96	4.03
Labour productivity	4.20	4.29	2.74	3.28	5.22	5.32
Land productivity	3.85	3.57	3.07	3.36	5.41	4.70
Capital productivity	3.15	4.02	3.23	2.39	3.70	3.04

Source: Gasques et al. (2016a).

coordination to preserve the competitiveness of the value chains. On the one hand, it was necessary to overcome, or at least manage, market failures, at a time when the state was progressively restricting its actions in certain areas (such as credit, price and production risks, R&D and supply of information) (Zylberstajn, 2014). On the other hand, all economic agents involved were increasingly faced with a competitive environment characterized by growing market concentration in different commodity chains, increasing participation of foreign companies as well as intensification of the technological base. This scenario was also characterized by growing demand for higher quality and greater diversity of food, food safety and socioenvironmental sustainability. In summary, the major changes in the institutional and competitive environments triggered the restructuring of organizational arrangements of agri-chains in order to deal with issues ranging from productive efficiency to socio-environmental responsibility within production.

In face of these adversities (market, climatic and/or institutional) and the large socioeconomic and environmental diversity in existing agricultural contexts, various types of governance were constructed by agri-chain agents. Positive results from previous experiences contributed to consolidating certain practices using a mimetic isomorphism process. For example, to solve problems of erosion in the state of Paraná, local cooperatives provided incentives to employ no-till farming among members, a model that rapidly diffused throughout the country (Machado-da-Silva and Graeff, 2008). Another example to solve the problem of insufficient credit for farmers was the introduction by input suppliers and trading companies of new forward contracts to increase farmers' access to financial resources. These contracts became known as '*gaveta*' (literally, 'drawer') contracts given that they were signed by the different parties and then kept in their private domains, thus avoiding any of the legal controls established in Brazil's financial regulation. From this experience the Brazilian government created the *Cédula de Produto Rural* (Farmers Certificate – CPR), a regulated financial bond that enables sales when the farmer is paid in advance. This new mechanism became an important instrument in the expansion of agricultural credit.

Under this myriad of solutions, a highly heterogeneous productive structure was gradually materialized, comprising groups of small family farms (supported or not by cooperatives), strictly coordinated agri-chains (vertical integration), large and medium-sized farms coordinated by processing companies and input suppliers, contract farming, etc. (Figure 4.1). In general, the structure of each coordination mechanism was influenced by regional histories related to factors such as the agrarian structure, producer profiles and availability of infrastructure.

The southern region is mainly characterized by small and diversified (grains, beef cattle, poultry, hog production and dairy) farms, settled by European immigrants, and supported primarily by farmer cooperatives or associations. Some agri-chains in this region, such as those of poultry, pork meat and tobacco, are strictly coordinated with contract farming arrangements and vertical integration. In the poultry chain, for example, processors maintain ownership of

Figure 4.1 Main agricultural regions in Brazil.

some strategic stages, such as feed factories, slaughterhouses, by-product processing facilities and product distribution centres.

In the Southeast, particularly in Sao Paulo, strictly coordinated chains stand out, such as those of sugar, ethanol, paper/cellulose, coffee and oranges, with large processing companies predominating. Chaddad (2016, p. 15) observes, 'in addition to vertical integration, these large companies have contracts with farmers upstream and form complex collaborative ventures downstream in the supply chain'.

Finally, in the centre-west and northeast, small farms, with very low technological standards, coexist with large and modern farms. Maize, soybean and cotton are the main crops. Hog and poultry production, on a larger scale than those in the Southern, are also important. High-yielding varieties of agricultural crops were developed by EMBRAPA (The Brazilian Corporation for Agricultural Research) for the *cerrados* (Brazilian savannas), so that large-scale production in large farms became economically viable. Large farmers developed sophisticated contractual arrangements with trading companies and input suppliers (Chaddad, 2016).

3 New forms of coordination and governance in Brazilian agri-chains: recent experiences

This section explores three examples of Brazilian value chains that developed different coordination mechanisms. The first one is the coffee chain. For approximately two centuries, Brazil has been a traditional exporter of this commodity, which has been produced on farms of different sizes, technologies and organizational structures that have changed over time. The second is the orange chain, in which domestic companies consolidated themselves as major suppliers on the international market of juice. The third one analyses the case of soybean, the main agricultural product exported from Brazil.

3.1 The coffee chain

Brazil has been the number one producer and world exporter of coffee since the eighteenth century. The share of Brazilian coffee in world exports was over 50% until the 1950s, but fell to around 20% in the mid-1980s (ICO, 2018). This fall can be explained by the nearly century-long regulation policy of the market, which ended in 1989 (Bacha, 1992). It was aimed at increasing revenue from a product with inelastic demand, but eventually turned Brazil into a residual supplier on the international market.[3] In a market with low barriers to entry, overpricing attracted new competitors. The coffee industry experienced robust growth in various countries. Vietnam stood out, producing 29.5 million of 60kg bags in 2017 compared to 1.3 million in 1990 (ICO, 2018). Brazil would see also a decline in its international competitiveness due to commercial practices that hampered implementing quality improvement.[4]

New opportunities for Brazilian coffee emerged with market deregulation and continuous growth in global consumption, partly as a result of the boom in coffee shops (and the popularization of the *espresso*) and a rise in Eastern European and Asian consumers. International buyers soon recognized Brazil as a strategic supplier and adopted organizational arrangements to stimulate the adoption of innovations that raised the quality level. As an example, an Italian coffee roasting company, Illycaffé, has been purchasing green coffee from Brazilian farmers using an incentive system, the Illycaffé quality award. The system favours best practices in production, drying and harvesting and became the benchmark for the creation of quality awards in many producing regions (Saes, 2010).

Three main factors also influenced the increase in quality, with a consequent effect on Brazil's share in the international market. The first factor is the geo-graphical dislocation of production. Coffee production increased in new areas, migrating to regions less subject to frost and with more adequate physical features to produce better coffees, such as in the southern regions of the state of Minas Gerais, where 60% of Brazilian coffee is now produced (Conab, 2018a). The second was the adoption of new production technologies, such as fertirrigation, and new techniques, such as mechanic harvesting and 'cherry pulping'.[5] These methods make it possible to dry the grains evenly, with greater control over the final quality of the product. Improving processes allowed regions that were less apt to produce higher quality coffees to replace their previous productive structures. The third factor regards certification, fostered by accrediting organizations that certify suppliers and buyers of high-quality coffees, including sustainable coffees and those with geographical denomination (Moreira et al., 2011).

This new competitive and institutional context was one of the crucial reasons for the increase of the Brazilian production and exports, with the rise in Brazil's share in the international market. From 2010 to 2017, the Brazilian exports accounted for 29% of the world total, followed by Vietnam (17%) and Colombia (10%) (ICO, 2018). In 2017, around 17% of coffee (5.1 million bags) exported by Brazil were accrued different types of certification (Cecafé, 2017). In line with the global trends, increasing number of coffee shops and value adding incentives caused an expansion in domestic demand, which increased drastically from 8.5 million bags in 1990 to 20.5 million in 2017 (ICO, 2018). It is relevant to note that the country is the second largest world consumer of coffee.

In terms of organizational structures, the coffee chain in Brazil involves diverse actors, with complex relationships (Figure 4.2). The first link in the chain (I) involves the input suppliers, such as machines and equipment, seedlings, pesticides and fertilizers. These inputs are bought by the primary coffee produ-cers (II), largely intermediated by cooperatives or firms, that diffuse new tech-nologies. After the harvest, coffee beans can be sent to three different links in the chain (III, IV,V), either alternatively or concomitantly, where the product is processed (roasted, ground and soluble) and then sold. In addition to exporting green coffee, Brazil holds an important position on the market of soluble coffee, albeit with significant competitive difficulties due to a rise in strong competitors. Finally, different retail methods are used to reach the final consumer (VI).

During the former regulated period, most transactions between the coffee players were heavily influenced by state regulations. Coordination exerted by

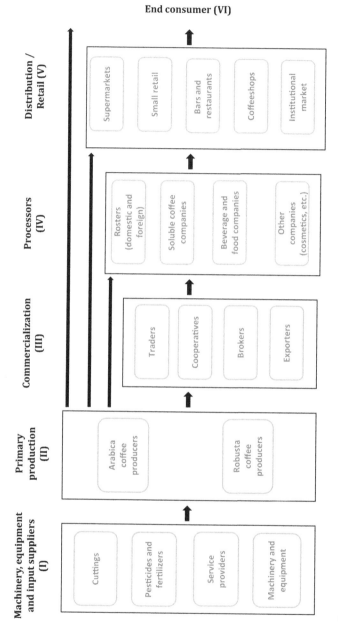

Figure 4.2 Coffee agri-chain. Source: Adapted from Saes & Farina (1999).

government was incompatible with creating and exploring market opportunities. The deregulation process and the rise in high quality coffee markets ensue the emergence of new and innovative ways to organize the chain in order to meet different demands. This was also made possible given the vast variety of producing areas and producers. Coffee production in Brazil is carried out by more than 300,000 producers (land use is around 2.22 million hectares). Their properties are predominantly smaller than ten hectares and are spread among approximately 1,900 municipalities (IBGE, 2006b).

Each region has a specifically organized chain, formed over time, primarily in accordance with the agrarian structure and edaphoclimatic conditions. The enormous diversity in climates, relief, altitude and latitudes has made it possible to increase coffee supply with greater product differentiation. The southern and centre-west regions of the Minas Gerais state are largely made up of small family farmers that sell their product via cooperatives. Cooxupé, which is said to be the largest coffee cooperative in the world (with around 13,000 members) is based in this region (Chaddad and Boland, 2009). These cooperatives are structured in such a way that they help not only to market coffee but also to offering inputs, credit and technical assistance to the producers. They have also encouraged the diffusion of quality standards and certifications, such as Nespresso AAA™, C.A.F.E Practices, 4C, Rainforest Alliance and UTZ. These strategies eventually turned the state of Minas Gerais into the largest exporter of coffee in the world. In addition to several cooperatives, commercialization of coffee also takes place via wholesalers, trading companies, national roasting companies and processers of soluble coffee, among other participants in coffee chains. Many producers use more than one channel depending on actual prices and other advantages offered by buyers. In the regions where coffee production is relatively recent (for instance, the *cerrados* of the Minas Gerais and Bahia states), large farms are predominant, and production is generally negotiated directly with international buyers (Chaddad, 2016).

Traditional coffees and high-quality coffees make up two strategic groups with distinct types of governance. Traditional types of coffees focus on price/cost and the majority of producers carry out transactions with intermediaries – brokers, cooperatives and exporters who then resell to processing companies. Large producers in this group sell directly to processing companies. These transactions are most similar to the spot market, with conventional price variations and careful monitoring of costs of production playing a crucial role in securing profits and positions in the market. Investments in production technology boosted yield over a period of 15 years (2005 to 2017) – from 15 to 25 bags/hectare (Conab, 2018a). Coffees with higher quality attributes and sustainability certifications have higher added value. They are traded by means of different types of long-term and/or relational contracts in order to guarantee a regular supply of coffee with the desired attributes. These are the cases of coffee originating from the *cerrado* of Minas Gerais or beans produced in the Alta Mogiana (in São Paulo state), organic coffees, fair trade and gourmet (Ménard et al., 2014). In some cases, vertical integration has been adopted, where the company produces 'farm coffee' in the so-called strictly coordinated systems (Saes, 2010).

The coffee chain is thus characterized by the coexistence of multiple governance structures. On the one hand, horizontal types of governances, based on collective initiatives promoted primarily by cooperatives or associations aim to alleviate common difficulties (investment in certification and quality, along with access to the market, and technical assistance), and focus on specific strategies. On the other hand, more coordinated systems have led to modes of governances that enable the construction of complex relationships that explicitly recognize suppliers and buyers. These arrangements make it possible for the country to meet the needs of the most demanding markets. However, Brazil is a major exporter of green coffee, with marginal share in the international market of roasted and ground, given the barriers to entry.

3.2 Orange chain

Citrus fruits are grown throughout Brazil, but 70% of the national production of fruits and more than 90% of orange juice are located in the state of Sao Paulo. This regional concentration is due to specific conditions from a favourable ecosystem to the technical support initially provided by the local government and to the installation of processing plants to export the juice. As a result, at the end of the 1980s Brazil became the main world producer of oranges (Neves et al., 2010). In 2017, Brazil accounted for 78% of global exports of orange juice, with the main destinations being the European Union, the United States and the Asian market (USDA, 2018a).

Figure 4.3 presents the main links of the chain. The first link (I) comprises a vast number of firms supplying agrochemicals, soil fertilizers, foliar nutrients, machines, various equipment, irrigation systems and seedlings. On several occasions, orange orchards in Brazil and Florida fell victim to greening and citrus canker diseases. The corresponding demand for pesticides was supplied by firms in this link. In the second link, several varieties of orange are planted by farmers with the objective of staggering the harvest, increasing technical and economic efficiency in the next links, as well as reducing climatic risks (drought or excess rains) and disease in the orchards.

Oranges are grown on farms of independent producers as well as on large-sized farms of companies that export orange juice. It is estimated that in the 2012/2013 harvest, the largest processing companies obtained around 50% of their requirement from their own orchards (Boteon et al., 2013). The rest came from independent farmers, but their numbers have reduced significantly over time. Production costs in the field increased due to the rise in pests and disease, as well as the governmental imposition to eradicate contaminated trees. The harvested area also fell from 913,000 hectares in 1990 to 659,000 hectares in 2016 (IBGE, 2018b). Despite the reduction in the number of producers and the planted area, orange production did not fall significantly. The diffusion of new techniques, such as high-density planting, and the development of more

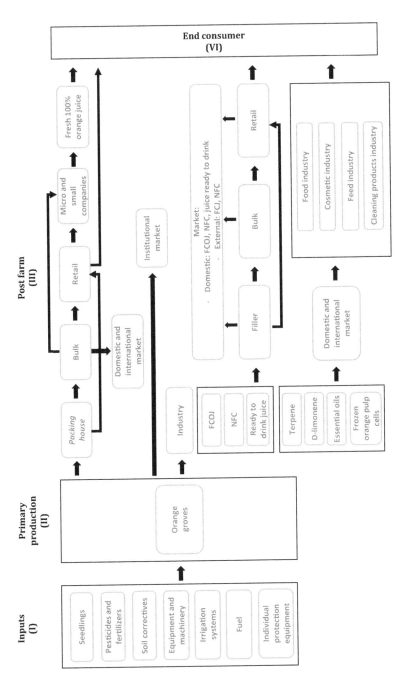

Figure 4.3 Citrus agri-chain.

productive disease-resistant varieties increased general productivity. High-density planting minimized the impacts of land appreciation in São Paulo, as well as the production losses that accompanied the removal of infected plants.

The processing link (III) is predominantly made up of a small number of large companies that produce juice for exporting. The majority of the processing plants are located close to the orchards in the state of São Paulo and have access to good transport logistics including their own container terminals at the Santos port. These companies are world leaders on the orange juice market, also owning processing plants in Florida and container terminals in Europe, the USA and Asia.

In addition to orange juice, the industrial process generates other products and by-products, such as essential oil from the peel, aromatic oils, limonene or citrus terpene, pulp and dried orange pulp, juice extracted from the pulp, comminuted citrus base, pectin and alcohol. They are sold to other national and international sectors of the manufacturing industry, such as beverages, cosmetics, perfumes, animal feed, paint, etc. (Rossi, 2017).

Until the mid-1960s, transactions between citrus companies and processing companies took on characteristics of typical spot markets, i.e. informal and based on a verbal agreement. Commercialization agreements between citrus farmers and processing companies became more formalized in the mid-1980s with the adoption of a standard contract. In this type of contract, the government, via the Brazilian Bank (*Banco do Brasil*), inspected and determined a value of the whole orchard based on the flowering of the trees or when the fruits are in the initial stages of formation. Therefore, the price was defined before the harvest and remained constant. In this type of contract, processing companies were able to determine the technological standards to be adopted by farmers, as well as take on the tasks of picking and transporting the fruits. This arrangement enabled processing companies to obtain fruits of higher quality that met growing international demands, as well as increase the efficiency on processing plants. The way in which the prices have been fixed, however, has been contested by farmers. Orchard production estimates were largely imprecise and there was visible asymmetry of information in terms of juice prices and costs of the industrial process, thus generating conflict among farmers and processing companies.

The end of standard contracts in 1995 imposed by the state marked the beginning of a period in which free and direct negotiation between farmers and processing companies took over. Different arrangements regarding the purchase and sale of oranges emerged. Three types of contracts came to predominate: short-term contracts, long-term contracts and toll processing contracts. In the majority of short-term contracts, price and volume are agreed before the harvest. In long-term contacts, prices and volumes are agreed either before or after harvest, comprising various specifications. The majority of these contracts are extended over three harvests and negotiated with medium and large-sized producers, as well as with groups of producers that make up pools to obtain economies of scale and better prices (Rossi, 2017). Finally, toll processing contracts are less common. In this type of contract, citrus farmers – alone or in groups – lease part of a processing plant to produce the juice themselves. The process is carried out by the processing company; however, the sale of the juice is carried out by the farmers themselves.

The production of the companies' orchards compared to the total production of orange (backward vertical integration) also increased significantly. According to analysts, there are at least four reasons for adopting this strategy: (i) the need to produce oranges that meet niches of quality in the frozen orange-juice market; (ii) the need to stagger production in order to improve control of the logistics and processing flows; (iii) the assumption that integrated farms could provide better quality oranges, at lower costs; and (iv) to obtain bargaining power in the negotiations with independent farmers (Figueiredo et al., 2013).

Although new arrangements were created for orange transactions, they were not enough to resolve conflicts in the chain. Following farmers' reports of abuse of market power, the Brazilian antitrust agency developed an operation that apprehended documents in the offices of the main processing companies and at the homes of their directors in 2006. The agency concluded the case in 2017, confirming the existence of a cartel and anti-competitive practices. The companies admitted fault and signed an agreement. During this litigation, several processing companies left the market, and a number of mergers and acquisitions took place with the approval of the antitrust agency. The three largest companies in the sector were capable of purchasing more than 80% of orange production in the leading regions of the country in 2011 (Figueiredo et al., 2013).

Despite the fact that the orange juice chain reached international levels of competitiveness, its experience of self-regulation after the government ceased to be decision-maker and regulator did not reduce conflicts surrounding distribution. Many farmers left the market due to buyers abuse of bargaining position. Net economic results have been largely accumulated by just a few processing companies. There has been a systematic fall in the number of independent producers, notably small and medium-sized, with a rise in backward integration, with negative impacts on the distribution of income among the main players in the chain and on economic development within producing regions.

3.3 Soybean chain

From the 1970s onwards, Brazil's soybean production increased eight-fold (Conab, 2018a). The cultivation of this crop on frontier areas of the tropical ecosystem (notably the centre-west), which were previously considered unviable for agricultural production, grew significantly. While Brazilian production was close to 12 million bags (with 83% of this production located in the Southern) by the end of the 1970s, in the mid-2010s the number of bags harvested increased to 100 million tons (with 46% of this production now located in the centre-west) – Table 4.3. The centre-west, northeast and northern regions of the country, where production was low in the initial period eventually came to account for around two thirds of the total output. On the one hand, this growth

Table 4.3 Evolution of soybean production and area planted across Brazilian regions between the 1970s and 2010s.

Area	Average value per year					Share 2010s
	1970s[a]	1980s	1990s	2000s	2010s[b]	
Production (1,000 tons)						
Northern	–	25	61	1,039	3,715	4.1
Northeast	1	172	1,151	3,594	7,227	7.9
Central-West	1,017	4,963	10,345	25,881	42,486	46.4
Southeast	1,021	1,710	2,362	4,033	6,262	6.8
Southern	9,701	10,020	11,403	18,860	31,817	34.8
Total	11,740	16,890	25,322	53,407	91,508	100.0
Area (1,000 hectares)						
Northern	–	15	29	382	1.275	4.2
Northeast	0	145	561	1,409	2,644	8.8
Central-West	703	2,606	4,204	9,123	13,673	45.3
Southeast	641	907	1,088	1,531	2,030	6.7
Southern	6,565	6,139	5,622	7,902	10,564	35.0
Total	7,909	9,811	11,504	20,347	30,186	100.0

Notes: [a]Average value obtained between 1976 and 1979; [b]Average value obtained between 2010 and 2018.
Source: Conab (2018a).

is explained by the expansion of the cultivated area, which increased fourfold. Again, the centre-west stands out with the total cropping area increasing from 9% to 45% between 1970s and the 2010s. On the other hand, yield doubled in the period to more than three tons per hectare with the adoption of new varieties and new management techniques, along with the intensification of mechanization.

The expansion of soybean production, from areas with a subtropical (the Southern) to a tropical (Central-North) climate, occurred under a new dynamic of production usually characterized by: i) harvesting two crops per year (particularly corn-soybean and cotton-soybean) (Mattos and Silveira, 2018); ii) the intensive use of capital and gradual reduction in the use of labour; iii) farmers' dependence on subsidized credit in the face of large investments in inputs and services, which increased financial risk; iv) farmers with high level of managerial skills, from production to marketing (Buainain et al., 2014).

Montoya et al. (2017) estimated that the GDP of the soybean chain doubled between 2001 and 2017, after the occupation of these new territories, reaching around R$100 billion in the second half of the 2010s and providing employment for 3.8 million people in the country. In 2017, Brazil produced a third of worldwide production. Revenue from exports increased by around 10% per year between 1997 and 2017, reaching an average annual value of US$27 billion in the 2010s (an average of 60 million tons per year).

The soybean agri-chain is made up of agricultural input companies, farmers, buyers of the product (wholesalers, cooperatives, trading companies, processors, among others), distributers and final consumers (Figure 4.4). One notable characteristic of this sector is its organizational diversity, particularly regarding the size and organizational characteristics of the farms. While in southern Brazil small and medium-sized family farms are predominant, the centre-west boasts mostly large-scale cooperative farms with monocropping systems anchored on professional forms of management (Chaddad, 2016).

Changes in the competitive and institutional contexts have significantly impacted transaction governance in this sector. New types of financing and commercialization have emerged during the last two decades. On the one hand, the private sector has taken on a relevant role in providing credit to farmers after credit subsidies fell in the 1980s, particularly in the agricultural frontiers, where capital-intensive farming was largely adopted. On the other hand, input companies and buyers have developed new types of contracts with farmers, establishing new arrangements to trade soya and finance the activity (Stages III and IV – Figure 4.4). This was a reaction to the growing competition and market concentration in the input (I) and grain processing (III) links, along with farmers' (II) need for financial resources.

Greater use of these new contractual arrangements did appear in the 1990s, with the increase in soybean production in the centre-west. Soybean farmers and input companies developed a contract, known as the '*troca-troca*' (literally, 'exchange-exchange'), in which trading companies supply the farmer with soybean inputs, and the payment is made not in cash but in bags of soybean after the harvest. Alternatively, trading companies or grain crushers provide financial resources in advance for farmers, an arrangement known as 'soja verde' ('green soybean') contracts, in which the payment is made after harvest in the form of bags of soybean (Leme and Zylberstajn, 2008). Since the items of these contracts are defined by the counterparts, different arrangements are observed, with distinct forms of payment and price fixing. An example is the 'harvest term' sale, in which the manufacturer (or distributer) of the inputs sells seeds, pesticides and fertilizers (i.e. the 'technological package') to the farmers, and the payment is made six months after the grains are traded.

Throughout the 1990s and 2000s, new contractual mechanisms multiplied, broadening the types of financing and commercialization available in the country. One example of this process is the creation of the Cédula de Produto Rural (CPR), a bond issued by rural producers, farmers' associations and cooperatives in order to obtain financing for production. Traded on the exchange or over-the-counter markets, the CPR anticipates the supply of resources to farmers. The Physical CPR establishes the future delivery of the commodity as payment, while the cash settlement or Financial CPR establishes a cash payment, whose value depends on prices and other contractual conditions.[6]

More complex contractual arrangements also exist. One example of this is the barter operation, commonly used in the center-west among soybean and

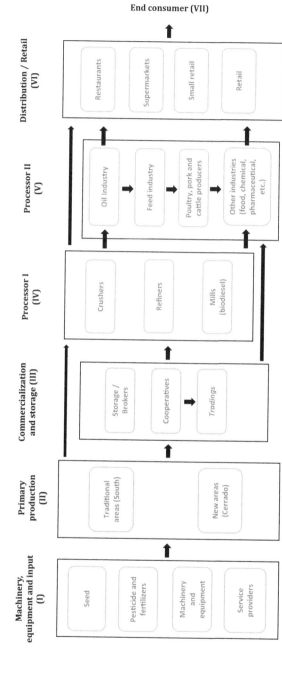

Figure 4.4 Soybean agri-chain. Source: Adapted from Lazzarini & Nunes (1998).

winter corn producers. This operation is carried out in two main stages: (i) the farmer purchases inputs from suppliers before planting, and, as a form of payment, agrees to provide part of his production to a trading company (exporter or processor) – in general, the farmer issues a CPR as collateral to sustain this transaction; ii) after the harvest, the farmer delivers the grain to the trading company, which is both traded as a commodity and used to pay the input company. This operation has been common practice between large grain trading companies (such as ADM, Bunge, Cargill and Louis Dreyfus), input companies (such as Bayer, Basf, Pioneer, Monsanto and Syngenta) and even agricultural equipment companies (such as New Holland and Agco Corp.). Given mounting restrictions in credit supply in the form of government subsidies, Banco do Brasil – the government bank and main operator of agricultural credit policy in Brazil – also takes part in barter operations. In this contractual arrangement, the bank provides credit resources to the input company that sells the technological package (inputs) to the farmer. The farmer issues a CPR as a guarantee of payment that will be made to the bank after the product is sold. The credit risk is transferred from the input company to the bank.

These new contractual arrangements come with a number of advantages for farmers. First, they reduce the liquidity risk, given the increase in the number of sources of credit (Silva, 2012). To illustrate this point, in the main soybean producing state in Brazil (Mato Grosso do Sul), financial resources were obtained primarily from credit provided by processors (44%) and farmer's own capital (32%), between 2005 and 2017. Government rural credit policy supplied just 13% of financial resources, and 11% were loans obtained from private banks (Imea, 2017). Second, the contracts of some of these mechanisms, in addition to financing the activity, can be considered as hedging instruments for price and exchange rate. (Leme and Zylbersztajn, 2008).

However, as previously highlighted, this new dynamic of production on agricultural frontiers ensues the need to increase investment in capital, services and inputs. In short, there is a new rationale demanding financial resources. As a result, both the business's financial leverage and the risk escalate. The intrinsic nature of the risk was clearly presented when comparing the potential opportunities to potential threats in the context of the growing financialization of agribusiness.[7] The increase in the chain's competitiveness resulted in greater opportunities to increase profits. However, the farmers were also more vulnerable, given that they were more exposed to volatility (particularly of interest rates and exchange rates). In summary, as emphasized by Buainain et al (2014, p. 226), 'competitiveness requires investment and a greater inclusion of farmers into financial markets, which increases their vulnerability because of higher leverage'. Two disadvantages of these new forms of financing involving the private sector can be verified: higher interest rates and short-term payment conditions. In addition, the new arrangements increase the margins of players located downstream and upstream in the chain, particularly the margins of large companies that operate simultaneously as input suppliers (mainly fertilizers) and as grain buyers (Silva, 2012).

4 Conclusions

This chapter showed how the players of Brazilian agri-chains reorganized their markets and created new tools to access credit, technological innovations and, most decisively, the international market. Private and governmental actors were able to change their relations according to changes in the institutional and competitive environments from the 1980s onward. The role of new forms of coordination to improve the competitiveness of these chains was highlighted. Brazilian participation in world exports increased significantly during this period.

Plurality and diversity are notable characteristics of these new structures. Various arrangements were created to accommodate regional and socio-economic differences, in which small family farms and large-scale farms were incorporated into the new setting, according to their competitive advantages. However, such changes did not come without tensions. In the frontier regions, for example, new producing areas emerged at the cost of deforestation, land conflicts and land concentration.

A greater understanding of how the markets in these agri-chains really operate is imperative. The massive asymmetry of market power between farmers, or their organizations, and the majority of input suppliers and product buyers, as well as between processors and large retailers must also be taken into consideration. Farmers embraced strategies conceived by their input suppliers (adoption of technologies) and by buyers of their products (demand oriented). It also cannot be denied that centralized forms of coordination and the growing control of the markets by just a few large companies enabled the increase of competitiveness, generating gains for most players, including farmers and consumers. However, the centralization of decisions and increase in asymmetries continue generating significant conflicts, with implications for current public policies and the general pattern of economic development.

Notes

1 Public and private investments in agricultural R&D grew enough to sustain the country's level of competitiveness. Innovations made it possible to combat pests and diseases with greater efficiency, to cultivate two crops in the same area of land in the same year (e.g. soybean-maize and soybean-cotton), and to add new agricultural land in the Center-West, North and North-eastern regions (Gasques et al., 2016a; Chaddad, 2016).

2 Exports to China grew more than 40 times from the end of the 1990s to the second half of the 2010s, with average annual exports reaching US$23 billion. As a result, the share of Chinese imports expanded from around 2% to 25% in this period.

3 Given the importance of coffee for the Brazilian economy in the past, the Brazilian government implemented agreements in which other producing countries would share the cost of policies for price stability in the international market. These attempts did not work and Brazil assumed sole responsibility of the strategy. Brazilian exports fell while exports from other competitors increased.

4 Guaranteed price support schemes for farmers reflected the government's concerns surrounding coffee production. In some occasions, prices of different quality grains were the same, destroying the incentive function of the price mechanism (Saes, 2010).

5   In Brazil, coffee is traditionally dried naturally. The harvesting and washing of the grains is shortly followed by spreading the grains out on sunny areas. With this old technique, green grains can be mixed with ripe ones and the grains are subject to fermentation. At the cherry pulping phase, however, the skins are removed from the ripe grains separately with less chance of fermenting, albeit at a higher cost.

6   In the mid-2000s, in order to diversify the ways in which agribusiness could obtain resources from the private sector, financial institutions launched five new negotiation bills – The CDA (Agricultural Certificate of Deposit), WA (Agricultural and Livestock Warrant), LCA (Agribusiness Credit Note), CDCA (Agribusiness Certificate of Credit) and CRA (Agribusiness Certificate Receivable). These bills are backed by agricultural products (the CDA and WA) or direct credit (the LCA, CDCA and CRA). Thus, both farmers and processors have greater access to more lines of credit. For example, large multinational companies such as Bayer, Syngenta, Monsanto and Bunge, have obtained resources via the emission of CRA.

7   Three factors characterize the intensification of the Brazilian agribusiness financialization process: i) increasing importance of capital markets for industrial companies and national retailers; ii) increasing importance of processors as credit providers (using contracts such as CPR and barter operations); iii) higher presence of institutional investors in commodity derivative markets, in order to boost profitability and diversify portfolios (Balestro and Lourenço, 2014).

5 Global competitiveness of the Brazilian agri-food sector

Strategies and policies

Marcos Sawaya Jank, Adriano Nogueira Zerbini and Isabel Cleaver

1 Introduction

Brazilian agribusiness has been transformed significantly in the last few decades, leveraged by exports that increased from US$21 billion in 2000 to US$96 billion in 2017. In addition to gains in yields and improvements in sustainable practices, both the scale and complexity of agricultural production chains have greatly increased.

Brazil evolved from being primarily an exporter of typical tropical products that made up the country's colonial history, such as coffee, sugar and cocoa, to a dominant exporter with a global role in several important production chains centred at food, beverages, fibre and bioenergy industries in the beginning of the twenty-first century.

On the one hand, a tropical technological revolution occurred in agriculture, which allowed the production of crops in regions that were previously underproductive (e.g. the Brazilian Center-West) and prompted the migration of producers and gains-in-scale of various strategic agribusinesses. On the other hand, economic growth – particularly in emerging countries – and the expansion of international trade along food chain products since the 1990s led to an equivalent increase in world demand for these products.

This 'marriage' between an increase in the country's total production and an expansion in global demand has positioned Brazil as one of the largest global players in the trade of grains, oilseeds, animal proteins, sugar, ethanol and forest products. The poultry industry and its production chain serve as a revealing illustration.

Until recently, Brazilian exports of poultry increased according to world demand. Markets opened often unilaterally, without any pre-defined strategy or major initiatives by the Brazilian government or the private sector. Nonetheless, Brazilian chicken export volumes increased by roughly 15% per year between 2000 and 2012 and by nearly 20% in US Dollars during the same period. If such an increase in exports was the result of wide access to markets – as competing exporters such as Thailand and Europe faced problems with avian influenza and therefore lost their markets to Brazil – the structural competitiveness of this industry also made Brazilian chickens-as-commodities more attractive in terms of cost and quality.

However, since 2012 this growth has significantly slowed. We will see throughout this chapter that despite the country's notorious competitive cost, Brazilian meat exports have been losing international market share in the past few years. Furthermore, while the Brazilian share of world meat trade has fallen, that of grains and oilseeds has risen. Both grains and meats are part of the same production chain as soybeans and corn are both primary feedstocks in the production of poultry and hogs. Therefore, Brazil has been losing export shares of commodities with higher value-added and gaining share in the market of raw materials for this product (i.e. feed). So, why is this occurring and what could be done?

In conjunction with a persistent expansion in global demand, Brazil's competitors (i.e. the United States, Argentina, Canada, Thailand and the European Union) have also increased their exports in the past decades. Additionally, many countries (both developed markets such as the European Union and emerging markets such as China, India and Indonesia) use sophisticated protectionist practices to restrict access to their domestic markets, particularly for value-added products. This competitive scenario *vis-à-vis* other exporting countries, in addition to the expansion of protectionism in strategic markets, has demanded not only greater cost reductions from Brazil, but also the drafting of complex and well-designed strategies uniting both the government and the private sector to maintain and expand access and share in relevant markets.

In this context, this chapter explores possible interpretations of this scenario, discussing proposals and tools that could allow Brazil to compete in a more promising manner with other large agribusiness players on the world market, using concrete strategies and tools that are similar (or even better) to those of Brazil's competitors.

2 The recent dynamic of the international integration of Brazilian agribusiness

Global trade in agricultural products is concentrated in 13 regions and countries: the European Union, the United States, China, Brazil, Canada, Japan, South Korea, Mexico, India, Indonesia, Australia, Argentina and Russia. Of this group, eleven countries were responsible for nearly half of world agricultural trade in 2017. The European Union and the United States are the largest agricultural importers and exporters, with a total trade of US$350 billion (EU) and US$330 billion (US) in 2017. Brazil has increased its participation in international trade and is currently the third-largest exporter of agricultural products, with nearly 6% of total market share (Figure 5.1).

In 2017, China tied with Brazil for the position of third-largest exporter of agricultural products. Both countries maintained high annual growth rates during the period of 2006 to 2017, with 6% and 8% annual growth respectively. However, one should note that among the five largest world agricultural exporters (EU, US, China, Brazil and Canada), only Brazil has no significant presence in the list of largest agricultural importers. In fact, Brazil holds a negligible share of world agricultural imports.

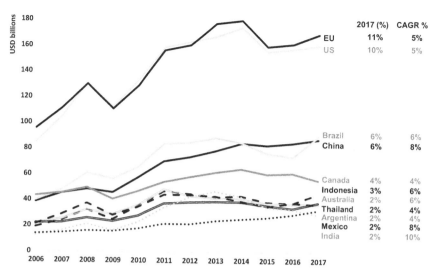

Figure 5.1 Top agri-food exporters in the world (value). 2017 (%) refers to the countries' share of total world exports in 2017; CAGR (%) is the Compound Annual Growth Rate between 2006 and 2017. Sources: USDA (2018b) and UN Comtrade Data (2018a).

In relation exclusively to agribusiness imports, only China and India gained ground during the period and both enjoyed greater market shares. China increased its agricultural imports from US$40 billion in 2006 to US$148 billion in 2017. Its share of world imports increased from 4% to nearly 10%, making it the largest world importer among the major players in the world. China's imports during the period of 2006 to 2017 increased at an annual rate of 12%, unlike the modest growth experienced by the European Union (2% annual average import growth), by the United States (5% annual growth) and by Japan (1% annual growth) during the same period. As a result, China saw its import share move closer to that of the European Union and double in relation to that of Japan. Considering the combined imports of China and Hong Kong (since a significant portion of the agricultural exports that arrive in Hong Kong has China as their final destination), the performance of the combined two is even more remarkable, exceeding the United States to become the second-largest world importer.

The strong presence of Brazil in exports and of China in imports of agricultural products becomes visible when we observe the largest world trade surpluses and deficits in this area. Brazil currently maintains the largest agricultural trade surplus, US$72 billion in 2017. Meanwhile, China, due to its sharp growth in imports, became the country with the second-highest trade deficit in the world (US$61 billion), only after Japan, whose deficit totals reached US$71 billion in the same year (Figure 5.2). If we consider China and Hong Kong combined, the two assume the largest agricultural trade deficit in the world, with US$78 in

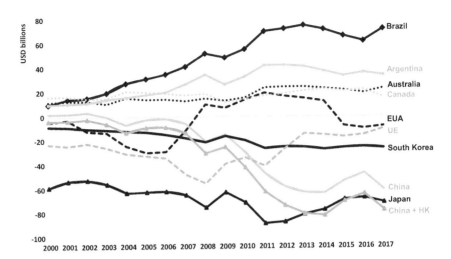

Figure 5.2 World agri-food trade balance: major surpluses and deficits. Figures for "China + HK" may occur double counting. Sources: USDA (2018b) and UN Comtrade Data (2018a).

2017. The large agricultural surplus in Brazil allowed the country to reach equilibrium in its balance of payments, avoiding an economic crisis.

As previously mentioned, despite Brazil being a very relevant agricultural exporter, the country still holds a considerably small share of the global imports value. While importing is fundamental to being able to export – and the agricultural sector is no exception – Brazil's agricultural exports (in value) are nearly seven times the size of its imports. If we analyse the case of China and Hong Kong as a contrasting example, while their joint exports have doubled in the last ten years, their joint trade deficit – sustained by an annual increase in imports of 15% since 2000 – facilitates market access negotiations. Since China is the third-largest world food importer and the fourth-largest exporter of agricultural products, its power in world agricultural trade negotiations is insurmountable. The US and Europe hold similar clout in international discussions. There is an obvious learning here: Brazil must allow a substantial growth in its imports to expand its bargaining power during trade negotiations within the world food system.

Today Asia is a crucial market not only globally, but also with respect to Brazil. The import growth trend of agricultural products in Asia, driven by China, radically changed the geography of Brazil's agricultural exports in the recent period. Asia is already the largest agricultural destination for Brazilian agricultural exports, representing 48% of the country's total in 2017. Within Asia, China remains the main destination, receiving 30% of Brazilian agricultural exports in 2017. However, countries such as Indonesia, Malaysia and Vietnam are gradually becoming important destinations for products such as soybeans, sugar and corn (Figure 5.3).

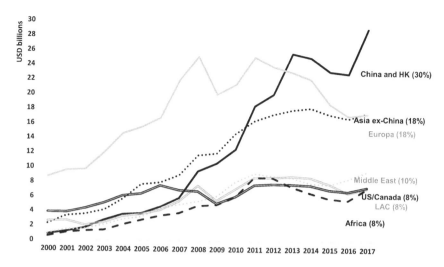

Figure 5.3 Brazil: agri-food exports by destination (value).
Note: LAC – Latin America Countries.

Traditional Brazilian trading partners, such as the European Union, the United States, Canada and Latin America lost share to Asia, the Middle East and Africa as destinations for Brazilian exports. The growth of exports to such emerging markets has been driven by increases in population size and urbanization rates and by economic growth and changes in dietary habits (e.g. the substitution of vegetable proteins for animal protein) in those countries.

Current Brazilian exports are concentrated in four large groups: (1) soybeans, (2) meats and leather, (3) sugar and ethanol and (4) forest products, which together accounted for 77% of total exports in 2017 (Figure 5.4). These four segments demonstrate the greater dynamism of emerging markets in Asia, Africa and the Middle East. The exports of the soybean complex (grains, oil and meal) are concentrated and robust, representing 33% of total export values. Asia was responsible for the import of US$25 billion in 2017 and China alone accounted for US$20 billion of this total, representing 80% of Brazilian exports of the soybean complex in that year. With respect to meat and leather, Asia comprises 40% of Brazilian exports and the Middle East also accounts for a sizeable share of Brazilian exports (20%), due to the increase in poultry exports to the region. Within the sugar and ethanol sector, the main export destinations are Africa (30% of exports) and a range of Asian countries including Indonesia, Bangladesh, India and Malaysia (totalling 30% of exports). They are followed by the Middle East, which is responsible for 20% of Brazilian exports from the sector. In the case of corn and cotton, Asia is responsible for 50% of exports, due to the region's concentration of textile production and growing corn consumption as animal feed. The Middle East and Africa, combined, are responsible for 20% of exports. As for other sectors, the traditional markets of Europe and

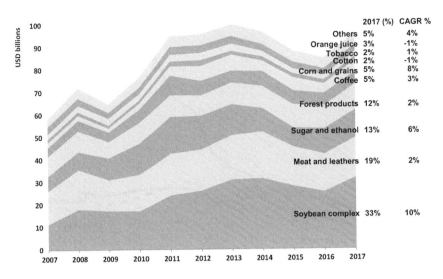

Figure 5.4 Brazil: agricultural exports by product (value).

the Americas continue to dominate Brazilian exports of forest products, coffee, tobacco, fruit, juices and dairy products.

The four large product groups listed earlier (i.e. the soybean complex, meat and leather, sugar and ethanol and forest products), that have emerging markets as their primary destination, are also the most concentrated groups. Only seven countries dominate world exports for these production chains: Brazil, Argentina, Paraguay, Uruguay, the United States, Australia and Thailand. The competition for products derived from soybeans, corn and cotton are notably concentrated, with these countries responsible for more than 70% of world exports. In the case of meat exports, the market share of these seven countries totals nearly 50%.

New markets – within the less-developed countries of Asia and Africa – have enormous demand growth potential as a function of the currently low per capita consumption of certain products. For example, the per capita consumption of meat in Asia and Africa is three to four times less than that in Brazil and in developed countries and is growing at a rate of 1.1% to 1.8% per year. In the case of least developed countries, per capita meat consumption is roughly nine times less than that of Brazil and developed countries (Table 5.1). Brazil, therefore, has an opportunity to further direct exports to these regions, taking advantage of demand growth and creating better conditions for competition with other players in the industry.

When we look at Brazil's export shares of the main products here discussed, the need for reforms in the country's export structure is straightforward, particularly when focusing on exports of value-added products, such as animal proteins. If we take a closer look at the current situation in the meat sector, we

Table 5.1 Per capita meat consumption in 2016

	Total meat		Beef		Pork		Chicken	
	Per capita consumption (kg)	Annual Growth	Per capita consumption (kg)	Annual Growth	Per capita consumption (kg)	Annual Growth	Per capita consumption (kg)	Annual Growth
Brazil	99	1.6%	37	−1.2%	15	2.4%	46	2.2%
Developing Countries	93	−0.2%	23	−1.2%	35	−0.2%	35	1.0%
World	41	0.8%	9	−0.4%	16	0.6%	15	1.9%
Less-Developed Countries	11	1.7%	5	−0.2%	2	2.7%	4	3.9%
Africa	24	1.1%	11	−0.2%	3	1.9%	11	2.4%
Asia	32	1.8%	5	1.8%	17	1.3%	10	2.8%

Source: OECD/FAO (2018).

Note: Annual logarithmic growth rate between 2005 and 2016.

find that while Brazil is a large and efficient producer of chicken, pork and beef and faces a very favourable situation of increasing world demand, it is not able to translate such favourable conditions into an increase in global export share. Due to the intense competition from other countries that are better organized to support exports – such as Australia, the United States, Thailand and Canada – Brazil's capacity to enter new markets has been restricted.

However, Brazil is gaining 1% to 2% of additional market share annually in global exports of sugar, soybeans, coffee and cellulose. In corn and cotton, Brazil's market share increases more than 10% per year, which is in fact a spectacular rate of growth even if departing from an initial low export volume. With respect to chicken, pork and beef, Brazil unfortunately lost its export market share (–1% to –2% per year), due to problems with competitiveness, market access and product image. Brazil must improve its export structure to become more competitive – particularly in segments with higher value added – and thus decrease its export dependence on basic commodities.

3 Market access and differentiation challenges

3.1 Soybean complex

The soybean complex (soybeans, soybean meal and soybean oil) is the main item in the export agenda of Brazilian agribusiness. In 2017, Brazil exported products of the soybean complex to 87 countries, primarily in the form of raw grains. The access of soybeans in the world market is broad and diversified, thanks primarily to strong global demand growth for the product – particularly in China and the rest of Asia. However, even in these markets, exports face many restrictions with respect to exporting soybean meal and oil (products with higher value-added following soybean processing). The primary restrictions encountered in exporting these products are the following: i) tariff escalation; ii) Differential Export Taxes (DET) practiced, for example, by Argentina; and iii) difficulties to approve biotechnology events (new varieties using GMOs). Tariff escalation is the restriction that affects exports of the soybean complex the most, because they close the doors to goods with higher value. This is particularly the case of China. China buys soybeans to crush locally, restricting their purchases of soybean meal and oil.

3.2 Poultry

In 2017, Brazil exported chicken to 141 countries. The region that is most open to chicken exports is the Middle East. In contrast, Brazilian chicken continues to face significant market access barriers in the United States, Europe and Asia. The main factors restricting market access in these three regions are: i) slow processing plant licensing; ii) operational difficulties such as rejection of cargoes, port delays, records and signatures; iii) tariffs, import quotas and escalating tariffs; iv) sanitary restrictions (i.e. avian influenza, salmonella, listeria); and v) religious restrictions (related to Halal production/processing).

One of the most successful cases of Brazil's poultry exports occurs in the Middle East. Brazilian companies were able to adapt their production structure to meet Halal demands and processes (rites of production based on precepts of the Islamic religion) imposed by Muslim countries. On one hand, Brazilian fact made Brazil a fundamental partner in the food security of countries in the region. On the other hand, the experience of exporting to the Middle East, beginning in 1970, was crucial for Brazil to expand its chicken exports to other markets. Today, Brazil is the world's largest chicken exporter, serving more than 140 countries on seven continents. However, in other markets – as is the case in Europe, Russia and a large part of Asia, including China – these exports continue to face restrictions in the form of technical, sanitary and bureaucratic barriers to trade, which in turn restrict imports to protect domestic production.

In the case of Europe, for example, the variety of tools used to restrict poultry imports is large and ranges from restrictive import tariffs and quotas to microbiological criteria that discriminate against imported products in favour of local products, as in the case of salmonella. The pressure by local producers on European authorities is strong and if not confronted in a rational way, can lead to losing markets in the European Union, despite the significantly lower production costs of chicken in Brazil versus in Europe.

In most countries, while the import of animal feedstuffs (soybeans and corn) is generally unrestricted, imports on animal proteins (poultry, pork and beef) faces several barriers. This is one way for countries to maintain self-sufficient policies and encourage domestic production.

3.3 Pork

Out of the previously discussed products, pork exports represent the least volume and face major market access barriers. In 2017, Brazilian pork was exported to 72 countries, mostly to Russia, Hong Kong, South America and a few countries in Africa.

The primary trade restrictions that Brazilian pork exports face are: i) religious prohibition (e.g. prohibition of pork consumption within Islamic countries); ii) slow plant licensing process; iii) tariffs and tariff quotas; iv) sanitary restrictions (e.g. foot-and-mouth disease/vaccination); and v) technical restrictions (e.g. ractopamine use, a beta-agonist growth catalyst promoter).

The three greatest difficulties for worldwide pork exports are religious restrictions that prohibit pork consumption for a large portion of the world population, the pressures against pork imports in Europe and China and sanitary restrictions such as foot-and-mouth disease. These three factors make it very difficult for Brazil to increase its exports for this segment and diversify its markets.

However, pork remains the most-consumed meat in the world, with average annual global consumption of 16 kg/capita, compared with an average annual consumption of chicken (15 kg/capita) and beef (9 kg/capita) (Table 5.1). This significant global pork consumption is a function of being the preferred meat of the Chinese population, who consumes an average of 34 kg/capita of pork annually. China is the world's largest pork producer, producing roughly 54 million tons of the meat annually or half of the world's supply of this protein.

3.4 Beef

The export of Brazilian beef reached 133 countries in 2017. While the global market for beef is slightly more open, significant import restrictions remain in Asia, in addition to a strong competition in the region primarily from Australia, the United States and India.

The main restrictions encountered for beef exports are: i) the plant licensing process; ii) sanitary restrictions (e.g. foot-and-mouth disease, spongiform encephalopathy-BSE); iii) bureaucratic restrictions (e.g. rejection of cargoes, port delays, records, signatures); iv) technical restrictions (e.g. traceability); v) religious restrictions (e.g. Halal processes); and vi) import quotas.

One of the greatest barriers for beef exports is the issue of market access, where a solution depends on joint efforts by the industry and the government. Brazilian exports manage to enter markets in Africa, the Middle East and Europe (under tariff quotas in the case of Europe). However, Asia presents a tough challenge in terms of export growth, as exports to the region continue to confront either closed or very restrictive markets.

When we compare beef exports to Asia, it is remarkable the success of Australia to gain access to those markets and grow in the region. In addition to being completely covered in terms of trade agreements in Asia (through preferential agreements and free trade agreements), Australia also benefits from an impressive trade support structure set up by the government and private sector entities such as *Meat & Livestock Australia* (MLA). Australia's entire export structure consists of simplicity, rationality and efficiency: from the structure of the factory floor to the constant and proactive presence of the government and the private sector in target markets.

The main Asian markets closed to Brazilian beef are Japan, South Korea, Indonesia, Thailand and Vietnam. These countries alone imported 1.2 million tons of beef in 2016 (US$6.6 billion). If we consider the average Brazilian share of 13% of world beef exports, opening markets to Brazilian product in these five countries alone could generate an annual increase of US$870 million in Brazilian beef exports.

An additional challenge to Brazilian beef exports is the lack of differentiation of Brazilian beef. Brazil has not yet managed to promote the image of its higher value-added products.

4 Strategic vision and public and private policy recommendations

The transformations that have taken place in Brazilian agribusiness in the last decades have not been small (see Chapters 1 and 4). In addition to yield gains provided by the technological advance in different links of agricultural chains, production scale and complexity have increased significantly. Production chains have become increasingly complex. This process has additionally been driven in the last decade by the economic growth of emerging economies, which have gained worldwide prominence in terms of demand for agricultural products.

Until recently, persistent increases in world demand were enough to foster the expansion of Brazilian exports. However, this model has been reaching its limits, particularly in a world where protectionism and nationalism have gradually gained strength in detriment to trade liberalization and multilateralism and in turn increased the risk of rupture of Brazilian agricultural production chains. As noted earlier, the world market is far from being completely open to Brazilian agricultural products, particularly in the case of animal proteins, sugar and ethanol. In reality, markets have opened and closed in a selective manner, based on increasingly more sophisticated criteria, particularly in the field of non-tariff trade barriers. In addition, Brazil's competitors (the US, the European Union, China, Canada, Australia and others) have been using several tools to significantly increase the competitiveness of their similar products. Such tools have included the signing of bilateral and regional trade agreements, significant institutional representation abroad, the expansion of the work of export promotion agencies, image campaigns and technical-commercial cooperation programmes.

Based on those empirical evidence presented, five actions could be envisaged for both the government and the private sector in order to boost Brazil's share in global agricultural trade. They are briefly discussed below.

4.1 Strategic vision

With exports of US$96 billion in 2017 (45% of Brazil's total exports) to more than 200 countries, agribusiness is by far the most globalized sector of the Brazilian economy. These exports have increased nearly fivefold since 2000, thanks to both demand growth in developing countries and lower relative costs of Brazilian agribusiness.

This is a scenario that might not repeat itself as easily going into the future. In fact, Brazil increased its market share for commodities such as soybeans, corn, cotton and cellulose, with little or no government influence. But the country has lost ground where it has encountered tariff, sanitary, technical or trade remedy restrictions, in products such as soybean by-products, ethanol, meat, dairy products and fruits. And these barriers do not include trade discrimination suffered by Brazilian exports as a function of non-existing relevant trade agreements signed during the period.

Therefore, it is crucial that Brazil adopts a more strategic position in both the short and long-term role of agriculture and its relationship with other countries. Until recently agricultural products were simply 'bought' by importers for delivery in the ports. Today, growth in Brazilian exports is a much greater challenge, including qualitative new facets. In this context, what is the strategy? Which countries should be strategic partners? Which sectors and production chains are strategic for Brazil? Which type of partnership does Brazil want to build? What are our priorities in trade negotiations, in attracting investment, in technical cooperation with other countries?

For Brazilian agriculture, the risk is to return to an era of 'managed trade', in which geopolitical interests, threats and bargaining have more influence than the comparative advantages of countries. In a competitive scenario, Brazilian agriculture would be central in the world. In a 'managed trade' environment, success depends on exogenous variables and demands greater internal coordination.

Thorough studies are necessary to help define priorities and strategies, while avoiding decisions that only benefit the most vocal groups. More priority must be given to the themes of attracting investment and strategic partnership with China, both of which require a long-term vision, a strong team of experts and solid guidelines.

Meanwhile, the private sector should cease to act in the wake of government and assume more prominence abroad. In an environment dominated by geopolitics and managed trade, companies need to strengthen the structure of their entities to address issues of common interest abroad. In addition, one of the greatest challenges of agribusiness is the lack of organization and representation abroad. Exports are supported by a series of institutional agents and programmes that need to be coordinated, aligned and work in cooperation. Although Brazilian agricultural products are exported to more than two hundred countries, the physical presence of Brazil abroad remains precarious and insufficient.

If Brazil traditionally gained market share through lower-costs, today the key to winning market share is systematic organization involving companies, associations and better public-private sector coordination. In a world where protectionist waves occur simultaneously with an increase in demand not only for food but also for other agricultural products, a vision that places agriculture as a strategic asset of the country becomes necessary. Brazil can and must present itself as a strategic partner in policies of food security and in supplying relevant markets – particularly emerging markets, which have been driving demand for agricultural products. This vision should be shaped in conjunction with the institutions involved in agricultural exports – whether public institutions (ministries, government agencies and their representation abroad) or private entities (sectoral associations, industry federations) – that ought to act in coordination, join forces and make the process more fluid.

4.2 Market access

Market access is the most crucial issue for consolidating a new growth cycle for Brazilian agribusiness. In the past, the main restrictions for market access were high import tariffs, prohibitive quotas and competition using domestic subsidies. Today, the most pervasive barriers are of non-tariff origin: sanitary, technical or bureaucratic restrictions.

As Brazilian agricultural production has long exceeded the needs of the domestic market, Brazil must act on three fronts:

a) Trade negotiations: to maintain the access that Brazil has already achieved on the world market, the country must return to trade negotiations with strategic countries and trade blocks. The government must implement a new trade policy based on impact studies that demonstrate the trade-offs of implementing various strategies. The government should also define which trade negotiations are strategic for Brazil, by defining priorities. Multilateral and bilateral agreements are essential for the implementation of an international trade strategy.

In the case of agriculture, Asia deserves special attention. An agreement with the Association of Southeast Asian Nations (ASEAN) appears to be an issue of great importance. The economic block of the ten nations of Southeast Asia totals nearly 650 million inhabitants and has gained relevance in the global trade of agricultural products, while maintaining an impressive range of trade agreements with partners such as China, Japan, South Korea, India, Australia and New Zealand. In addition, ASEAN has promoted the Regional Comprehensive Economic Partnership (RCEP), an initiative that seeks widespread multilateral integration among its members and its partners with which the trade block already holds trade agreements.

Entering into the Comprehensive and Progressive Agreement for Trans-Pacific Partnership (CPTPP) should also be among Brazil's objectives and could be accomplished via the Pacific Alliance, a trade block formed by Colombia, Peru, Costa Rica and Chile that aims to integrate these economies with those of Asia.

Although agribusiness products remain a source of discord, concluding trade negotiations between the European Union and Mercosur would bring greater stability to trade with the European block. Even a revision or improvement of Mercosur is necessary for greater regulatory convergence, which would minimize the frequent obstructions of agricultural products at the borders between countries within the block.

b) Strategic partnerships: in addition to trade agreements, Brazil should also focus on widespread strategic agricultural partnerships with China and the United States – central players not only to world supply, but also to the world demand for agricultural products. Such partnerships would seek integration in the value chains of these countries, which in turn would stabilize trade flows and generate synergies and efficiency gains for all involved.

Brazil's most important partnership by far is with China, who is currently the largest customer of and investor in Brazilian agriculture. Brazil should focus on diversifying its exports to this country away from soybeans, on attracting investment and acting in a more strategic and coordinated way within government and in conjunction with the private sector. A strategic partnership with the US would also be fundamental.

In general, such trade agreements and strategic partnerships should also incorporate an effort for regulatory convergence, to prevent technical and/ or sanitary barriers. In addition, tools that generate high costs and operational complexities, such as Tariff Rate Quotas (TRQs) should be avoided in favour of a simpler and transparent system based on import tariffs.

Furthermore, Brazil should participate more actively of international bodies that define international technical standards, such as the *Codex Alimentarius* of the Food and Agriculture Organization of the United Nations (FAO), the World Organization for Animal Health (OIE) and the International Plant Protection Convention (CIPP). These international organizations frequently establish standards that wrongfully end up being used as barriers to agricultural product trade.

c) **Opening doors to imports:** greater market access also requires greater bargaining power by Brazil. This could be accomplished by a more modern vision of international trade, opening the Brazilian market to the import of agricultural products that the country does not currently import. In reality, Brazil holds a negligible share of world agricultural imports. As mentioned earlier, of the world's five largest agricultural *exporters* (EU, US, China, Brazil and Canada), Brazil is the only one that does not also make the list of the largest agricultural *importers*. This condition weakens Brazil's position at the negotiating table. Despite having a negative impact on the agricultural trade balance in the short term, a greater role in world agricultural trade through increased imports would allow the country to open relevant markets and expand its trade balance in the long term. Wheat, cocoa, coffee, bananas, coconut, shrimp, dairy products and fish are examples of products for which the country's localized protection prevents large volumes of potential exports.

4.3 Differentiation and product image

Among the largest global agricultural exporters, Brazil is the least well known. Rarely have people abroad heard of the Brazilian tropical revolution that caused a drastic increase of agricultural yields.

In general, Brazil is associated with images of deforestation, excessive use of agricultural inputs, social conflicts and even slave labour. Achievements in the area of sustainability, including the Forest Code (*Código Florestal*), the vast vegetation cover maintained on private properties, the instruments of low–carbon agriculture, the low water footprint and the clean energy matrix, are usually neglected and unknown abroad.

If in Europe the debate about sustainability is intense and nearly always critical of Brazil, in other regions of the planet, the country is invisible through the absence of assertive messages. In Asia, for example, the theme of sustainability is less relevant than concerns over food safety, quality and traceability – an area where our competitors heavily invest in their image. These themes, in addition to sustainability, are those that most demand the building of Brazil's reputation and image.

4.4 Productivity and competitiveness

The fourth point to be improved upon is the competitiveness of agricultural production chains. Brazil continues to be competitive in the field, with increasing yields and low costs. However, when an agricultural product enters the stage of processing, its competitive edge from the farm begins to be lost. High costs of energy, packaging, labour, capital and the complexity of the tax system are elements in which Brazil is less competitive than many of its peers.

This becomes clear in the production chain for poultry and hogs, for example. In this case, grains (feed) and the animal production are competitive. As animals enter processing facilities, the above elements begin to corrode gains from the farms. The logistics from a product leaving the processing plant to arriving to the final consumer also cost more than a similar journey in most of the countries that are Brazil's competitors. In the end, total meat production costs in Brazil have become very much closer to those of the country's competitors. Therefore, a thorough 'x-ray' of the competitiveness of Brazil's main agricultural production chains is necessary to identify links of this chain that have potential for efficiency gains. As we have seen in this chapter, cost is not currently the only factor in the competitiveness of agricultural products on the world market, but the factor continues to be a precious competitive advantage of certain Brazilian products and must be preserved.

Investment continues to be fundamental for agriculture not to lose its competitiveness. Therefore, Brazil must establish a stable regulatory framework to attract international investment – particularly in infrastructure – and expand the interaction between public and private research along the different links of production chains. The private sector, meanwhile, must initiate a new cycle of innovation aimed at increasing competitiveness and sustainability in inputs, agricultural production, processing and distribution. The private sector must improve sanitary and quality controls for issues such as BSE (known as 'mad cow'), foot-and-mouth disease, avian influenza, salmonella, swine fever and others and must make use of geo-technologies, big data and information management and precision agriculture tools such as drones and automation.

4.5 Regulatory reform

Brazilian agricultural exports have increased fivefold since 2000, but the regulatory structure surrounding the country's exports has not accompanied the process in its operational, financial, regulatory and manpower terms.

Therefore, Brazil's primary challenges are:

a) **Legislation:** which is far behind schedule and needs to be modernized and simplified. Certain regulatory framework in the area of animal health dates to the 1930s. The Brazilian normative framework is more complex and intricated that of its competitors.

b) **Inspection:** which needs to be more efficient and less costly. Brazil must definitively implement new regulation that transfers to industry the responsibility of sanitary compliance in processes and final products, with periodical checks defined by risk analysis and the application of exemplary penalties in cases of noncompliance. It is essential to have a process of constant and mandatory inspections by enforcement agents. It is not recommended that the same compliance agent inspect the same industrial plant for a long period of time. In addition, it is necessary to place several professionals in key locations such as in Brasilia and working overseas. Another major challenge is to improve the structure of people and equipment to avoid the entry of pests and diseases into a continental country that has 15,700 km of borders with ten countries.

c) **Responsiveness:** despite the great advances in the digitalization of processes and the expansion of the network of Brazilian agricultural attachés in strategic countries, one still observes deficiencies on both government and the private sector. Disagreements in the exchange of information with other countries and poorly completed and badly translated technical questionnaires remain frequent.

5 Conclusions

The agriculture sector is a crucially important and a precious strategic asset for Brazil. However, global agricultural product trade is full of barriers and restrictions that generate threats and instability in production chains.

In a scenario of increasing protectionism and disputes in different areas of the planet – particularly in developed economies – a strategic and structured vision of the integration of Brazilian agriculture in the world is increasingly important. This strategic vision must involve the primary stakeholders – both public and private – of agribusiness: embassies, ministries, sectoral associations and private companies.

This strategy must be accompanied by information flows and agile processes between agents. In addition, tools equivalent to those of our competitors such as the United States, the European Union and Canada (e.g. image promotion, presence in strategic markets, advocacy) should be widely used, under the threat of Brazil losing share in important markets. In this sense, Brazil does not need to 'reinvent the wheel'; instead, it is enough to map and incorporate what Brazil's competitors do best.

The United States is a benchmark in organizing and leading coalitions and in its capacity for advocacy and awareness. Australia's regulatory system functions with great efficiency. Europe is a reference in added value products, branding and in promoting product image, while China has enormous power in bargaining through negotiations and uses this power with efficiency and within a long-term strategy.

For all of this to work, Brazil must modernize its regulatory framework for agribusiness, including not only updating standards (sanitary and production) but also improving the adequacy of institutions, which must act in a coordinated way with common objectives. Efficiency gains in the various links of production chains, product differentiation and adding value to products are additionally important conditions for maintaining the edge of Brazilian agriculture.

6 Innovation and development of Brazilian agriculture

Research, technology and institutions

José Eustáquio Ribeiro Vieira Filho

1 Introduction

The previous chapters have dealt with some of the facets of Brazilian agriculture, emphasizing the fast growth of agricultural production and agricultural productivity, the role played by the reorientation of public policies following the macroeconomic stabilization in the 1990s and, in particular, by the emergence of China as a net food importer. Notwithstanding the changes, the historical structural heterogeneity of Brazilian agriculture has remained.

While Brazil is richly endowed with a vast territory, innovation is unequivocally behind the rapid growth of production and productivity as well as the maintenance of structural heterogeneity.

Looking 50 years back, it is clear that the creation of Embrapa (the Brazilian Corporation for Agricultural Research) and the reorganization of the National System of Agricultural Research, early in the 1970s, are landmarks of the modernization of Brazilian agriculture.[1]

Over the last 50 years, additional land has been incorporated into the productive process, particularly in the Center-West region and, since the late 1990s, in the area known as Matopiba (acronym that includes the states of Maranhão, Tocantins, Piauí and Bahia, located in the Cerrado biome – see Figures 0.1 and 0.2 in the introductory chapter), probably the last agricultural productive frontier available for occupation. The occupation of the frontier was made possible by the combination of technologies adapted for tropical conditions and economic incentives for investments and innovation. The incorporation of new land was accompanied by the intensification of production, fundamentally based on a continuous and swift hike in total factor productivity, obtained through investments in research and development (R&D) and by the consolidation of a modern system of agriculture-focused innovation. Gasques et al. (2018) showed that productivity improvements accounted for 76.40% of total output growth between 1975 and 2016.

However, as mentioned by Alves and Rocha (2010) and Vieira Filho and Fornazier (2016), this process of modernization has been marked by sharp heterogeneity, with the exclusion of a large number of producers and by an unprecedented process of wealth concentration. In this context, the lack of access to technology has been the main explanation to increasing inequalities (Vieira Filho and Fishlow, 2017).

The purpose of this chapter is to explore the role of innovation in fostering the growth of Brazilian agriculture. On the one hand, the innovation process has promoted a fast-growing expansion in the Brazilian agricultural production, including several cultures. On the other, this process has caused increasing heterogeneity and increasing inequality amongst farmers of different regions. These topics are investigated in the next sections.

2 National system of innovation and growth of Brazilian agriculture

The Brazilian agricultural activity has changed drastically since the 1960s, when the country was a net importer of food and experienced successive food crisis with pervasive economic, social and political impacts. The Brazilian agricultural exports were highly concentred in few products, such as coffee and sugar. Since the 1990s, soybean – until then produced mainly in temperate regions – has become an important product both for export and the domestic market, especially as popular edible oil and as input for the expansion of animal protein and dairy products value chains. Brazil became the top exporter of poultry meat and several other primary products (see Chapter 5). The increasing integration of crops and livestock, or the role of supply chains, became much more complex than it was in the past. In addition, economies of scope and scale have fostered productive integration in various value chains, such as sugarcane and soybean, which have become bioenergy producers (see Chapters 4 and 7).

Over the past 50 years, the intensive use of science and technology resulted in dramatic productivity gains (Gasques et al., 2012a). Induced innovation[2] founded on local institutional change was essential for the consolidation of Brazil as one of the world's largest food exporters. The Brazilian Green Revolution was more than a transfer of external technology to local farmers. As mentioned by Vieira Filho and Fishlow (2017), Brazil was one of the few developing countries that incorporated external knowledge from international research centres and succeed in adapting it to its local tropical conditions. Endogenous institutional changes were essential to promote R&D to the tropical Brazilian environment.

The initial modernization drive of Brazilian agriculture was mostly supported by technological packages developed to suit the prevailing production and environmental conditions in Europe and in the US (see Chapter 8). The response was dismaying and, in the beginning of the 1970s, the government decided to invest in local research and rural extension services, in addition to expanding rural credit to support the investments required to modernize Brazilian agriculture (see Chapter 3). The recurrent domestic food crisis was a real issue, with relevant economic, social and political consequences, standing as an acute problem that undermined the country's development effort. Food scarcity caused chronic inflationary problem, unleashing labour unrest, pressures to increase wages and political instability. In addition, social unrest and union strikes strengthened social movements opposing the military rule and were met with tougher repressive measures which fed political instability and contributed to deteriorate the business environment. In 1973, Embrapa was created to foster research and innovation in agriculture and, especially, to occupy the Cerrado biome in the Center-West region.

The adoption of a new technology and its diffusion process depend on the technological regime[3] and on the learning networks within every productive organization. The Brazilian national research model was designed to deliver applied knowledge for productive agents, whereas technical assistance and extension services were responsible for the technological diffusion amongst farmers. In this context, Embrapa has been playing a relevant role, with an organization model characterized by decentralized research centres specialized in different crops, themes and regions, dealing with and responding to local realities. The division of responsibilities were clear: while Embrapa and the agricultural research institutions should provide technology, rural extension services – supported by financial agents – should disseminate the new technology to farmers. Adoption and diffusion were connected processes and dependent on the successful interrelated functioning of research, technical assistance and rural credit.

In 1992, the Brazilian government formally established the National Agricultural Research System (SNPA). Embrapa and its units, the State Organizations of Agricultural Research (OEPAs), universities, local research institutes and public and private organizations linked to the agricultural research activity represented the entire system. The SNPA designed guidelines and strategies for agricultural research policies. This system should help to eliminate overlapping and inefficient allocation of resources by planning the national research, but in practice it has rarely functioned as a system.

Table 6.1 presents the regional distribution of OEPAs, which should articulate regional demands with the national interests within the SNPA in principal. The OEPAs are composed of 21 different entities. Amongst 26 Brazilian states, 16 have agricultural research institutions, mostly concentrated in the Center-West, Southeast and Southern. In 2015, there were almost 1,800 researchers, carrying out 2,100 research and development projects in 230 labs and 215 experimental stations.

Table 6.1 State organizations of agricultural research (OEPAs) by Brazilian regions

Northern and Center-West	Northeast	Southeast	Southern
Agência Rural	EBDA	Apta	Epagri
Empaer-MT	Emdagro	Epamig	Fepagro
Idaterra-MS	Emepa	Incaper	Iapar
Unitins	Emparn	Pesagro-Rio	
	IPA		

Source: Vieira Filho (2012).

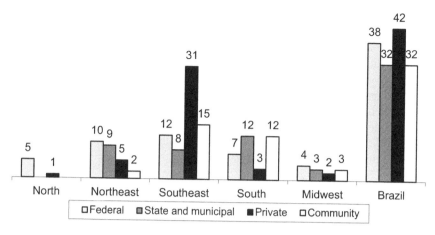

Figure 6.1 Higher education institutions linked to the SNPA by Brazilian regions.

Higher education agricultural institutions are also important players in the SNPA (Figure 6.1). Amongst the 144 institutions, 38 are maintained by the federal government, 32 by state governments and municipal administrations, 42 by the private sector and 32 are communitarian. Seventy per cent are located in the Southeast and Southern regions of Brazil, although many of them – particularly the federal institutions – have a broader regional reach. The high participation of private and communitarian institutions is particularly noteworthy.

As theorized by Lundvall (1992), institutional development stimulates public knowledge and technological opportunities. This idea was formalized through the concept of 'national system of innovation', in which public and private research institutions play essential roles to generate knowledge required to improve innovation. Innovation in the agricultural sector is highly dependent on the interplay of private-public institutions and on the institutional framework. Research expenditures in this field, such as the development of a new seed variety, are usually very high and incentives for R&D depend on top-down institutional strategies and public regulations.

Embrapa is a successful case of institutional innovation (Alves, 2010). It is a public organization that operates at the national level through spatially decentralized but specialized research units. From the very beginning, Embrapa attracted talented researchers and invested in the capacitation of its team in some of the best education and research institutions in the USA and Europe, particularly in France, England and the Netherlands. In fact, in the mid-1970s, Embrapa stablished a huge post-graduation programme to improve the quality of human resources and research projects. Complementarily, the corporation created an international capacitation programme, promoting the interaction between national and foreign researchers as well as its own research units and renowned international labs. Since then, the share of Ph.D. researchers has increased continuously. In 2017, there were more than two thousand Ph.D. scientists in the corporation, representing 83% of its scientific team.

Embrapa's research strategy takes as granted that modern agriculture is based on science and technology. However, given the particular features of agricultural production as highly dependent on nature and environmental conditions, technology has to fit local settings. For this reason, the definition of agriculture as a supplier-dominated sector, sustained by Pavitt (1984), with its corollary that technical change in developing countries would have to be imported, is not a realistic one. In agriculture, the knowledge of combining different productive factors improves non-embodied productivity, a feature which is not unique but that is particularly important to agriculture.

3 Cluster of innovations and land-sparing effect in Brazilian agriculture

Embapa's research plans have focused on three main fields: i) improvement of degraded tropical soils, ii) plant breeding and genetic engineering and iii) integrated management practices. Vieira Filho and Fishlow (2017) conceptualized the work of Embrapa as clusters of innovations, divided into innovation blocks, that have allowed the transformation of Brazilian agricultural production since the 1970s. The main blocks of innovation are: soil liming techniques, the 'tropicalization' of plant varieties, biological nitrogen fixation, no-tillage systems, pasture breeding, diffusion of genetically modified organisms (GMOs) and mechanization. The cultural background of migrant farmers from the Southern to the Center-West and Northeast regions has played a relevant role in the diffusion of new modern technology developed/adapted by Embrapa and other local agricultural R&D institutions. Experienced family farmers, long familiarized with market transactions and with mechanized grain production, met appropriate conditions to expand their production in the frontier regions.

Until the 1960s, the Cerrado biome was considered inappropriate for agriculture due to its soil characteristics, lack of infrastructure, land tenure policy and crop selection, amongst others. With the use of agricultural liming techniques and the introduction of tropical resistant seed varieties, the Cerrado became the most important agricultural frontier in Brazil. Since the 1970s, more than 40 million hectares have been incorporated into production. The Center-West has become a strategic region in the production of grains and livestock and its share of the gross value of total Brazilian agricultural production has increased from 6% to 30% over this period.

Scientific research carried out locally was fundamental to developing seed varieties tolerant to tropical conditions, the so-called 'tropicalization' of crops. In the case of soybean, in addition to improvements in productivity, new varieties have shortened the life cycle of the plant (Libera, 2016), enabling two harvests per year in several regions in the country. In 1976, farmers started planting corn after the first soybean crop. At that time, the second harvest was a residual one, called '*safrinha*', or small harvest (winter crop), planted only in the states of Paraná and São Paulo. In 2001, the *safrinha* was not representative and accounted for 12% of total production (or 3.9 million tons). Over time, the winter corn crop spread to the states of Mato Grosso do Sul, Goiás, Mato Grosso and Minas Gerais. Since 2011, its production, in tons of grains, is higher than the first harvest. In 2017, the winter corn crop reached around 65% (or 55 million tons) of total corn production (Mattos and Silveira, 2018).

The introduction of biological nitrogen fixation concurred to increase yields per hectare and, in addition, allowed significant reduction in the use of nitrogen fertilizers, whose supply in the Brazilian market is almost entirely dependent on imports. This technology played a key role in the occupation of the Cerrados – whose poorly fertile soils demand high levels of fertilizer. It also allowed for a significant reduction in costs of production, which contributed to increasing the competitiveness of Brazilian agricultural production, particularly of grains and sugarcane. According to Embrapa (2018b), '(…) considering the 27.7 million hectares used for soybean crops in Brazil, the savings from not using nitrogen fertilizers total about US$ 10.3 billion per year'. Moreover, biological nitrogen fixation offers environmental benefits, such as the rehabilitation of degraded areas.

Another innovation was the introduction of a no-tillage cropping system, which leaves organic material from the previous harvest on the soil – then working as a natural fertilizer –, protects against wind and rain erosion of topsoil and acts as a cover against weed growth. No-tillage was originally introduced in 1973, in 180 hectares in the Southern of Brazil. Its adoption spread rapidly during the 1990s and, in the 1995 crop season, around 3.8 million hectares used the system. In 2012, no-tillage was applied to roughly 31.8 million hectares, representing more than half of the total cropped area. In the case of soybeans, in the same year the adoption of no-tillage exceeded 90% of the total planted area.

Until recently, Brazilian cattle ranching was a semi-extensive activity and animals were raised and fed with pasture. Poor quality of pastures was a key determinant of low productivity for the Brazilian cattle meat chain. In the 1980s Embrapa, launched a pasture improvement programme, crossbreeding an African grass called *Brachiaria* with native grasses, which resulted in new pasture varieties with nutritional content three times higher than most native and African species (Correa and Schmidt, 2014). At the same time, with the support of local research institutions and private organizations, cattle ranchers, invested in the genetic improvement of the herd, with crosses of breeds of Indian origin – especially Nelore – with European ones. The combination of pastures with higher nutritional capacity with animals of improved genetic characteristics resulted in the reduction of both the time of rearing and fattening and the improvement of quality of the meat produced in Brazil. Slaughter time was reduced from four to less than two years (around 18 and 20 months) and, in 2015, Brazil became the second largest exporter of beef in the world.

Since the 1990s, the use of biotechnology has grown worldwide. In Brazil, GMOs were first introduced in 1997, unlawfully. Not until 2003 did the use of genetically modified soybeans become legalized in the country. Afterward,

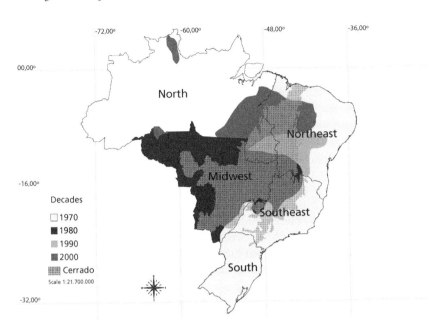

Figure 6.2 Expansion of the Brazilian agricultural frontier over time.

cotton and corn GMO varieties were introduced, respectively in 2005 and 2008. Following legalization, the adoption of GMOs spread quickly amongst Brazilian farmers. In 2014, the share of soybean, corn and cotton GMO seeds was 93, 83 and 67%, respectively. While multinational seed companies dominate the supply of GMO seeds, the role of Embrapa is still relevant as a primary source of genetical material to support the GMO technology. According to Vieira Filho and Vieira (2013), the average percentage share of Embrapa in all registered seeds was relevant: soybean (29.3%), corn (86.3%) and cotton (46.7%).

The set of innovations introduced since the 1970s have enabled the rapid occupation of the frontier in the Cerrado areas (Figure 6.2). With the opening of new areas, the price of land dropped and the opportunity cost of investments in tractors and harvesters became favourable as rates of interested were kept bellow market levels. In addition, geographic and locational characteristics – large plateaus far from relevant markets – favoured and required large scale production through mechanization.

Knowledge and technology developed by national research centres were fundamental to the occupation of the Cerrado biome. As mentioned by Vieira Filho and Fishlow (2017, p.72),

> [T]he Cerrado covers an area of 204 million hectares, nearly 24% of Brazil's surface. It is 34% larger than the Corn Belt region in the United States, represents 73% of Argentina's territory and is 3.7 times the size of France.

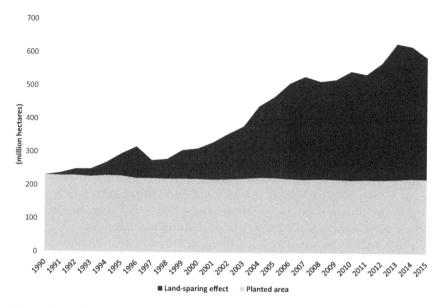

Figure 6.3 Total land-sparing effect (agriculture + livestock) in Brazil from 1990 to 2015.

As already mentioned, the experience of farmers from the Southern was crucial for the rapid diffusion of new technology as well as for the accumulation of knowledge through both learning-by-doing processes and the interaction with R&D institutions and private companies.

One of the most striking features of the expansion of Brazilian agriculture since the 1990s is the land-sparing effect, measured by Vieira Filho (2018). The land-sparing effect indicates the amount of land saved by the use of technology over time (Figure 6.3). Keeping average technological level used in 1990 constant, the amount of land needed to produce the output indeed produced during the 1990–2015 period was estimated at approximately 590 million hectares. However, during this period, the total planted area was roughly 224 million hectares. By subtraction, the total land-sparing effect in farming production (land which would be used with 1990s technology minus actually planted area) is nearly 366 million hectares. The land-sparing effect, only food crops, was estimated at 41 million hectares. In other words, through the use of technology, Brazilian agricultural production expanded and at the same time saved around 43% of the Brazilian surface.

4 Structural heterogeneity and the lack of absorptive capacity

Even though Brazilian agricultural production has increased significantly over time, there is still an enormous gap between regions and producers. As indicated by Alves and Rocha (2010) and Vieira Filho and Fornazier (2016), the agricultural growth co-evolved with structural heterogeneity and dualities. This structural heterogeneity manifests at macro and microeconomic levels. At the macro level, heterogeneity may take the form of differences in infrastructure and institutions, such as silos, ports, highways, railways and airports, energy supply, telecommunication network and so on. Institutions are also relevant, particularly financial and marketing organizations and the presence and effectiveness of public institutions from schools to police. At the micro level, farmers have different absorptive capacities, which is not determined only by the individual capacity to understand and interpret new knowledge but also to actual conditions to appropriate and use available technology –which is also highly determined by the macro heterogeneity.

Table 6.2 explores the evolution of the regional production of selected products from 1975 to 2015. In this period, Center-West production increased its share in all crops, except for coffee. For soybean and corn, in 2015, the Center-West accounted for almost half of all national production.

The Southeast increased its shares of sugarcane and coffee. Nonetheless, the share of soybean and corn decreased by contrast. Despite the fact that orange production faced a small decline, the Southeast still maintained a large regional share, almost 80% of the total national production. The Southern region lost share in all crops, except for sugarcane. Even so, by analysing yield performance, the Southern presented better yields when compared to the national average.

In general, the Northeast region has lagged behind in the modernization process – with the exception of the Cerrado and the irrigated areas in the semiarid area. For instance, its share in national sugarcane production fell from more than 37% in 1975 to roughly 8% in 2015. Conversely, the share of some selected crops has increased, particularly soybean and cotton. In fact, following the introduction of soybean production in the northeastern Cerrados and the occupation of the Matopiba frontier, the share of the Northeast in total soybean production grew from none to 8.6%.

The share of the agricultural production of the Northern region has remained low in the national context, in spite of the growth of production in irrigated areas (see Chapter 12 more details regarding the agricultural sector in the Northeast, Northern and Center-West regions). As regarding the yields, the Center-West, Southeast and Southern performed better than the Northern and Northeast regions. In addition to responding to the institutional infrastructure, it is clear that yields vary considerably according to crop and regional climate conditions.

As the agricultural production increased in the Center-West and Matopiba, logistic and infrastructure bottlenecks hindered the growth potential. Notwithstanding, the core of the Brazilian agricultural production moved from the Southern and Southwest to the Center-West and Northeast regions, right in the heart of Brazil. In 2015, the production of soybean and corn reached 183 million tons, while exports totalled 99 million tons. Dividing Brazil into two arcs, North and South, 58% of production came from the North arc, but approximately 80% of this output was channelled to markets through infrastructure located in the South arc. Considering both the continental size of Brazil

Table 6.2 Regional production and agricultural yields by selected crops (1975, 1995 and 2015)

Regions	Crops	Production (In thousand tons)			Regional share (%)			Yield (kg per hectare)			Regional yield per national yield		
		1975	1995	2015	1975	1995	2015	1975	1995	2015	1975	1995	2015
Northern	Sugarcane	458	725	4,371	0.5	0.2	0.6	29,616	51,296	73,231	0.6	0.8	1.0
	Corn	116	949	2,315	0.7	2.6	2.7	1,072	1,553	3,750	0.7	0.6	0.7
	Soybean	0	47	4,275	0.0	0.2	4.4	–	1,920	2,978	0.0	0.9	1.0
	Coffee	1	191	90	0.0	10.3	3.4	682	1,243	1,074	0.6	1.3	0.8
	Orange	159	1,746	308	0.5	1.8	1.8	87,411	88,347	15,550	1.1	0.8	0.6
Northeast	Sugarcane	34,228	60,659	61,546	37.4	20.0	8.2	44,680	48,662	59,285	1.0	0.7	0.8
	Corn	1,614	2,438	5,866	9.9	6.7	6.9	646	798	2,518	0.4	0.3	0.5
	Soybean	1	1,256	8,386	0.0	4.9	8.6	937	2,198	2,924	0.6	1.0	1.0
	Coffee	46	102	212	1.8	5.5	8.0	600	855	1,242	0.5	0.9	0.9
	Orange	2,386	7,764	1,799	7.6	7.8	10.6	79,487	80,187	13,511	1.0	0.7	0.5
Center-West	Sugarcane	911	19,577	136,108	1.0	6.4	18.1	38,946	70,295	77,104	0.8	1.1	1.0
	Corn	1,613	6,236	41,122	9.9	17.2	48.2	1,817	3,438	6,120	1.2	1.3	1.1
	Soybean	346	10,008	43,944	3.5	39.0	45.1	1,385	2,208	3,000	0.8	1.0	1.0
	Coffee	28	26	28	1.1	1.4	1.1	975	1,112	975	0.8	1.1	0.7
	Orange	290	734	173	0.9	0.7	1.0	69,767	80,782	19,686	0.9	0.7	0.8

(continued)

Table 6.2 (Cont.)

Regions	Crops	Production (In thousand tons)			Regional share (%)			Yield (kg per hectare)			Regional yield per national yield		
		1975	1995	2015	1975	1995	2015	1975	1995	2015	1975	1995	2015
Southeast	Sugarcane	51,895	201,052	499,678	56.7	66.2	66.6	48,962	73,685	75,771	1.1	1.1	1.0
	Corn	4,683	8,070	11,565	28.7	22.3	13.6	1,580	2,851	5,661	1.0	1.1	1.0
	Soybean	766	2,385	5,930	7.7	9.3	6.1	1,639	2,109	2,798	1.0	1.0	0.9
	Coffee	1,242	1,521	2,238	48.8	81.7	84.5	1,066	989	1,356	0.9	1.0	1.0
	Orange	25,782	84,864	13,357	81.7	85.6	78.9	77,532	123,534	28,803	1.0	1.1	1.2
Southern	Sugarcane	4,033	21,687	48,587	4.4	7.1	6.5	38,621	74,417	74,323	0.8	1.1	1.0
	Corn	8,308	18,575	24,417	50.9	51.2	28.6	1,890	3,294	6,604	1.3	1.3	1.2
	Soybean	8,781	11,987	34,930	88.8	46.7	35.8	1,719	2,212	3,144	1.0	1.0	1.0
	Coffee	1,227	20	80	48.2	1.1	3.0	1,300	552	1,803	1.1	0.6	1.3
	Orange	2,949	4,076	1,303	9.3	4.1	7.7	85,066	93,145	24,422	1.1	0.8	1.0
Brazil	Sugarcane	91,525	303,699	750,290	100	100	100	46,477	66,614	74,203	1	1	1
	Corn	16,335	36,267	85,285	100	100	100	1,505	2,600	5,536	1	1	1
	Soybean	9,893	25,683	97,465	100	100	100	1,699	2,199	3,029	1	1	1
	Coffee	2,545	1,860	2,648	100	100	100	1,148	994	1,339	1	1	1
	Orange	31,566	99,186	16,940	100	100	100	78,290	115,814	24,955	1	1	1

Source: IBGE (2018a).

and river and rail transport deficits, it is clear that logistics infrastructure is one of the most salient determinants of structural heterogeneity in Brazilian agriculture.

As shown by Alves and Rocha (2010), most producers, particularly small farmers in the poorer Northeast and Northern regions, have a rather low absorptive capacity and, consequently, have not benefited from technology efficiency gains. Only a small number of farms were able to innovate and benefit from productivity gains, thus reproducing the structural heterogeneity and a new divide in Brazilian agriculture between those which have innovated and those which have lagged behind. Both groups include small and large farmers, producing either for the external or domestic market. Access and size of land, traditionally pointed as determinants of social divide in rural areas, have become a secondary point. The capacity to innovate has taken the main role in shaping the dynamics of Brazilian agriculture and farmers' competitiveness.

Table 6.3 shows that the production is highly concentrated in a relatively small number of farms. Indeed, only 9.5% of farms (middle and high income) accounted for roughly 85% of the annual gross production value. On the opposite side, 90.5% of farms (extreme poverty and low income) accounted for only 15% of production. In the group of extremely poor farms, 69.6% of exploitations contributed to less than 4% of production. Variations between regions and crops legitimate the structural heterogeneity hypothesis and indicate the difficulties for widespread diffusion of technology amongst farmers.

The income inequality is high in the Northern and Northeast regions while Center-West and Southeast regions show better income distribution – Table 6.4, albeit far from what could be perceived as equality. In general terms, the Southern region –where family farming is predominant – presents the best economic indicators, thus contesting the common-sense idea that large farms perform better than small family farms. Large-scale production is largely dominant in the Center-West region, where only 2.2% of farms account for more than 64% of the annual gross production value.

The middle and high-income farms, roughly 439,000 farm units, accounted for 84% of the annual gross production. Absorptive capacity becomes a secondary matter here. For these groups, the real issues are consistent macroeconomic

Table 6.3 Farm revenue distribution by income groups in Brazil (2006)

Income groups by minimum wage equivalent	Minimum wage equivalent[a]	Number of farms (in thousands)	%	Annual gross production value (billions of Reais)	%
Extreme poverty	(0 a 2]	3.242	69.6	6.5	3.9
Low income	(2 a 10]	960	20.9	18.5	11.1
Middle income	(10 a 200]	416	9.0	59.9	35.9
High income	>200	23	0.5	81.7	49.0
	Total – Brazil	4.641	100.0	166.7	100.0

Source: Vieira Filho (2012).

a Minimum Wage Equivalent = Gross production value per month/ Monthly minimum wage.

Table 6.4 Farm revenue distribution by income groups regionally (2006)

Regions	Minimum wage equivalent	Income groups by minimum wage equivalent	Farms (%)	Annual gross production value (%)
Northern	(0 a 2]	Extreme poverty	69.3	8.7
	(2 a 10]	Low income	23.0	17.4
	(10 a 200]	Meddle income	7.4	43.1
	>200	High income	0.3	30.9
Northeast	(0 a 2]	Extreme poverty	87.2	9.9
	(2 a 10]	Low income	9.5	12.6
	(10 a 200]	Meddle income	3.2	29.0
	>200	High income	0.1	48.5
Center-West	(0 a 2]	Extreme poverty	52.3	1.3
	(2 a 10]	Low income	28.1	4.9
	(10 a 200]	Meddle income	17.4	29.6
	>200	High income	2.2	64.2
Southeast	(0 a 2]	Extreme poverty	56.5	2.1
	(2 a 10]	Low income	27.9	8.1
	(10 a 200]	Meddle income	14.7	32.2
	>200	High income	0.9	57.6
Southern	(0 a 2]	Extreme poverty	45.3	2.9
	(2 a 10]	Low income	37.9	16.1
	(10 a 200]	Meddle income	16.2	47.6
	>200	High income	0.6	33.4

Source: Vieira Filho (2014).

conditions, secure property rights, stable contracts and adequate rules regarding environment, labour relations, among others. The political battlefields for these farmers and firms are competitiveness, export promotion, agricultural insurance, logistics and improvement in infrastructure rather than public rural credit, technical assistance of even public R&D.

The extreme-poverty group represented around 3.2 million farm units – mostly, if not all, small plots, the so-called *minufúndio* – producing for self-subsistence or providing eventual surplus to local markets. The vast majority of these farms were excluded from the innovation process and have at most benefited from social policies and the special credit for family farmers, which to many is also a disguised type of income transfer. Extreme-poverty farms are concentrated in the Northeast (60% of the total), while the Center-West shows the lowest percentage of extreme poverty, approximately 4%.

Finally, 960,000 farms are classified as low-income grouts, which could benefit from agricultural policies – particularly rural credit, technical assistance and public R&D – and from an increase in absorptive capacity.

Table 6.5 presents demographic and economic data disaggregated by region, which provide an idea of regional differences in absorptive capacity in rural areas. The most populated regions are the Northeast and the Southeast, accounting for 70% of the Brazilian population. The highest urbanization

Table 6.5 Demographic and economic indicators by region (2010)

Indicators	Regions					
	Northern	*Northeast*	*Center-West*	*Southeast*	*Southern*	*Brazil*
Population (millions)	16	53	14	80	27	190
Urbanization rate (%)	74	73	89	93	85	83
Extreme poverty (%)	9	60	4	14	13	100
Illiterate and uneducated (%)	38	59	21	23	11	39
Basic education (%)	55	36	60	59	76	51
No technical assistance (%)[a]	85	92	70	69	52	78

Source: Vieira Filho and Fishlow (2017).

a Data from the 2006 Agricultural Census.

rates are found in the most developed areas, the Southeast, Center-West and Southern. The Northeast and Northern regions have the lowest urbanization rates, whose percentage is lower than the national average. Extreme poverty is highly concentrated in the Northeast.

When the last demographic census was carried out, in 2010, 9.6% of the Brazilian population over 15 years of age was still illiterate, a clear progress from previous censuses but remains below the Unesco literacy goals. The Northeast presented the worst regional indicator, with 19.1% of its population of the same age span being illiterate. The percentage of basic education was also low compared to national levels, with 59.1% of its population over ten years of age being either uneducated or having not completed basic education. These low education levels arguably limit the absorptive capacity of rural population and hinder the adoption of innovation (Vieira Filho and Silveira, 2012).

Provision of technical assistance is a proven instrument to promote innovation amongst farmers. However, in 2006, 78% of farm units did not receive any technical support and only 22% reported having received some technical assistance, whose quality cannot be evaluated. Regional data show that Northeast farmers are far away from the technological frontier and that more than 90% of them did not receive technical assistance. Even in the Southern, more than half of the farmers did not receive productive orientation.

5 Conclusions

This chapter presented two important observations. The first concerns the enormous growth of agricultural productivity due mainly to the innovative drive sustained by domestic investments in R&D, in which Embrapa played a key role. The second refers to agricultural growth with inequality. Indeed, amid noticeable productive progress, a significant group of farmers lagged behind mostly because of structural heterogeneity and low innovation capacity.

The cluster of technological innovations developed domestically was essential for the growth and transformation of Brazilian agriculture. From this set of technologies, a few stand out: agricultural liming techniques, crop 'tropicalization', biological nitrogen fixation, no-tillage systems, pasture breeding, the diffusion of biotechnologies and mechanization. Migration of farmers from the Southern to the Northern also played an important role in the diffusion of knowledge. However, nearly 80% of the farmers did not benefit, or benefited only little, from the so-called Brazilian green revolution – the tropicalization of grain production technology.

Although total factor productivity has grown significantly, there is differential growth amongst agricultural regions in Brazil. In the future, public policies should play a crucial role for the reduction of structural heterogeneity in Brazilian agriculture. Extension services and educational policies are essential to promote economic growth and improve the absorptive capacity of lagging viable farm units.

The example of Embrapa shows that a well-defined problem must be solved with specific targets and goals. At the time of its creation, the problem was the recurrent food crisis. The answer was to invest in R&D and provide incentives and conditions for innovation. The challenges, at the end of the second decade of the twenty-first century, have shifted to securing fully sustainable agricultural development, i.e., inclusive growth with environmental protection.

Notes

1 Although Embrapa is always pointed out as the one responsible for the so-called tropical agriculture revolution, this view is not entirely correct. Even before the creation of Embrapa, Brazil had already developed a significant capacity on agricultural research, embodied in several specialized research institutes and in agricultural universities spread in the main regions. The Agronomic Institute of Campinas (IAC) was founded in 1887 and played an important role in the coffee cycle and, later, in the modernization of agriculture in the state of São Paulo. In 1901, the Luiz de Queiroz College of Agriculture (ESALQ) was established to assist farmers and industrial agricultural entrepreneurs in the adoption of new technologies and has been a benchmark for agriculture research in Brazil and Latin America. In 1927, the Federal University of Viçosa (UFV), in Minas Gerais, was created to support the agricultural development of the dairy industry. In 1940, the Federal State created the National Service of Agricultural Research (SNPA), which encompassed several state institutions. Nonetheless, most of these initiatives were designed for regional purposes or to solve specific local crop problems. Embrapa was created as a national strategy to promote the modernization of Brazilian agriculture, illustrating the importance of a national and integrated strategy for science and innovation.

2 As pointed by Hayami and Ruttan (1985), induced technological innovation follows multiple paths of technical change in agriculture. The constraints imposed on agricultural development by an inelastic supply of land and labour may be offset by advances in biological and mechanical technologies. A change in factor prices guides the bias of innovation in order to save scarce resources. According to Dosi (1984), the institutional environment can shape and define paradigms and technological trajectories.

3 As deeply studied by Malerba and Orsenigo (1996), technology associates itself with the technological regime, which sets innovative standards according to opportunity conditions, appropriateness, accumulation and the nature of knowledge transmission.

7 Bioenergy and biofuels in Brazil

Marcelo Pereira da Cunha, Carolina Habib Ribeiro and Marjorie Mendes Guarenghi

1 Introduction

Incentives to produce and consume biofuels in Brazil have been originally driven by the potential availability of various alternative sources. These fuels (i) contribute to diversifying the country's energy matrix, thus minimizing the dependence on fossil fuel imports and (ii) present low negative impacts on the sustainability of production chains, with a focus on reducing greenhouse gas emissions.

In Brazil, the main biofuels produced are ethanol from sugarcane and biodiesel from soybeans. In 2017, Brazil held a prominent position as the second largest producer of ethanol in the world – responsible for 20% of global production – and the third largest producer of biodiesel, after the United States and Germany. In the same year, ethanol production just exceeded 28 million m^3 while biodiesel production stood at 4.3 million m^3 (ANP, 2018). Considering the national energy matrix, ethanol and biodiesel account for around 17% and 3% of total consumption in the Brazilian transport sector, respectively (EPE, 2018).

Ethanol is consumed either as anhydrous ethanol (ethanol added to gasoline) or as hydrous ethanol, which is primarily used in *flex* vehicles (vehicles that can run either on ethanol or gasoline). Biodiesel is only available in service stations as a blend with diesel. In 2018, the mandatory percentage of ethanol added to gasoline was 27.5% and the available biodiesel blend was B10, equivalent to a minimum percentage of 10% biodiesel. Approved legislation anticipates the availability of the B15 blend by 2023.

A brief overview on how the production of ethanol and biodiesel evolved in history is required in order to understand the current status achieved by Brazil in these fields. It must include the varied modes of State interventions and also several technological advances that ultimately enabled the dominance of large-scale production. These developments have caused economic, social, and environmental impacts, including issues related to land use and agricultural development. In this context, this chapter explores the trajectories and the impacts of sugarcane and soybean as the main sources of raw material of ethanol and biodiesel, respectively, in Brazil.

2 Ethanol

2.1 A short history of Brazilian sugarcane ethanol

Sugarcane production was born with the very formation of the country. The first sugarcane mill was built in 1532, in the southward village of Sao Vicente and shortly after expanded to the Northeastern coast. In 2018, there were around 400 plants mills in several regions of the country (Novacana, 2018) that produced sugar and ethanol for the internal and external markets, in addition to its use as bioelectricity. The sector's evolution has historically been strongly influenced by government policies, actions that ultimately determined the location of the sugarcane plantations and plants – and an effort that successfully made inroads through international markets. More recently, government measures also played a role in the expansion to the Center-West region and in the expansion of bioenergy.

Despite ethanol use being especially highlighted by the Pro-Alcohol (*Pró-Álcool*) programme in the 1970s, its history goes further back. In 1925, Ford tested a vehicle that travelled around Brazil on pure ethanol trying to encourage the substitution of gasoline derived from petrol (BNDES and CGEE, 2008). In 1931, the use of ethanol as an automobile fuel was made official when it was established the forced addition of a minimum of 5% of alcohol to imported gasoline. Government intervention, then evident in the sugarcane agroindustry through compulsory export quotas, was consolidated in 1933 (Decree No. 22,789), via the creation of the Institute of Sugar and Alcohol (IAA). The IAA was responsible for establishing and controlling production quotas, by fixing prices and financing the construction of distilleries joined to sugar plants.

Also, in 1933, another decree made it mandatory to add anhydrous ethanol to the gasoline. However, the real boost to substituting gasoline for ethanol took place in 1975, when the federal government established the National Alcohol Program (*Pró-Álcool*). The main objective of the programme was to reduce the country's dependency on imported oil. In 1973, more than 80% of Brazilian oil was imported and, as a result of the first oil crisis, prices rose from US\$2.70/barrel to US\$11.50/barrel (Leite et al., 2009). The Pro-Alcohol programme was therefore introduced as a political and economic response in order to reduce distortions threatening the balance of trade (Moreira and Goldemberg, 1999).

In addition, the fall in sugar prices on the international market worsened the trade deficit and caused an increase in the available surplus sugar for the domestic market, with negative effects on the production chain and public finances – the IAA was legally obliged to absorb the surplus at the minimum price established. Thus, *Pró-Álcool* was not only an answer to the energy crisis but to the impasses experienced by the sugar-alcohol sector itself. The economy was therefore the almost single driving factor and the environmental variable gradually emerged as a decisive dimension.

The Pro-Alcohol programme was characterized by two phases. The initial one, in 1975, following the 1973 oil crisis, was represented by the mandatory addition of anhydrous ethanol to gasoline and by the provision of subsidies to the sugar-energy sector. In 1979, after the second oil crisis, the programme entered into a new moment, which lasted until 1990. This second phase was characterized by fiscal incentives and tax exemptions benefitting the production of ethanol and cars run on pure ethanol (E100). All service stations were required to sell hydrous ethanol and guarantee a price of 65% of the price of gasoline. At the end of that period, due to the fall in oil prices and also a recovery of sugar prices in international markets, the incentive to produce ethanol diminished, resulting in drastic shortage of E100 in service stations around 1989. Due to a loss of social confidence, there was a significant fall in sales of ethanol-only cars and the production of new ethanol-only cars in relation to the total produced nearly collapsed – from 85% in 1985 to 11% in 1990 (CGEE, 2009).

During that period, deregulation of the sector began with the closure of the IAA in 1990 and the privatization of the production and commercialization of the sugar-energy sector. The production of hydrous ethanol fell due to the suspension of subsidies, while at the same time the production of anhydrous ethanol increased with the new stipulated addition of anhydrous ethanol to gasoline, from 20% to 24%. The law also imposed a reduction in pollutants emitted by automotive vehicles, mirroring an issue already being discussed within society (BNDES and CGEE, 2008).

The Pro-Alcohol caused profound impacts on Brazilian agriculture. In the first phase of the programme, the rise in alcohol production took place as a result of the absorption of surplus sugar, thus operating as a regulator of sugar production. In the second phase, however, spreading through the 1990s, the growth of production resulted in the incorporation of sugarcane cultivation in new areas, the majority initially adjacent to the already established plants in Sao Paulo state, in the Northeast, and, on a smaller scale, in the Center-West. This expansion took place over the 2000s, largely due to the launch in 2003 of flexible-fuel vehicles, which run on both gasoline and hydrous ethanol. These vehicles, together with favourable prices of ethanol at service stations, increased the sales of hydrous ethanol (BNDES and CGEE, 2008).

The period from 2003 to 2009 observed a major expansion of the sugar-energy sector. The launch of flex-fuel cars and the economic growth primarily due to domestic consumption – largely of cars – skyrocketed the demand for alcohol fuel. Globally, high oil prices and the intensified debate surrounding climate changes led to a favourable environment for new initiatives based on substituting fossil fuels. Brazil launched ethanol to the rest of the world as an already tested alternative – one that was technologically and economically viable and had a high environmental 'value'.

2.2 The expansion of sugarcane and ethanol production

In 2017, sugarcane was the third largest crop considering the total planted area in Brazil, behind soybean and corn. The area occupied by sugarcane, in Brazil, reached 10.2 million hectares, the equivalent of 6.5% of the total planted area with temporary and permanent crops (IBGE, 2018b). Figure 7.1 presents the spatial distribution of the Brazilian municipalities with more than one thousand hectares cultivated with sugarcane in 1974 and 2016.

The growth in the land use for sugarcane took place predominantly in the Brazilian Central-South region, especially between 1975 and 2010, with an intensification from 2003 onwards (Figure 7.2). The state of São Paulo stands out as the main sugar and ethanol producer in the country (IBGE, 2018a). Sugarcane production in this state rose from 38.3 million tons in 1975 to 357 million tons in 2018. In the 2016/2017 harvest, the state produced 13.2 billion litres of ethanol, around 48% of the country's biofuel production (UNICA, 2018).

Starting in 2008, sugarcane production expanded in some parts of the Center-West region, especially in the states of Minas Gerais, Mato Grosso do Sul and Goiás. Sheer expanses of land suitable for growing sugarcane are available in these states, while the availability of land in São Paulo gradually became more limited (Adami et al., 2012).

In addition to the expansion of the cultivated area of sugarcane, this activity experienced an increase in productivity. Improvements in sugarcane cultivation practices, logistics and processing pushed up revenues resulting from cane and ethanol production per ton of processed cane. According to Lago et al. (2012), the productivity of ethanol in litres per hectare increased 25% between 1975 and 2008. In the same time period, the cost of production of both sugarcane and ethanol fell by a record 70%. Indicators of productivity jumped from 46.8 tons of cane/hectare to 77.5t/ha, while the industrial gain went from 59.2 to 80.4 litres of ethanol/ton of cane. These productivity gains, both at the agricultural and industrial phases, in addition to boosting the sugar-energy sector profits, also contributed to alleviate the pressure on land use and competition for land between food and energy crops in Brazil, as well as reducing the need to expand sugarcane plantations.

This positive outlook, which included exports of ethanol from Brazil to the United States and optimism in the sugar-energy sector, culminated in an increase in investments. The sector received large funds to finance its growth, which resulted in major debt. In the same vein, the financial crisis in the United States rapidly impacted the rest of the world after 2008, in such a way that in 2009 there was a major effect in liquidity in the financial market, with a direct impact on the sugar-energy sector.

After years of sustained growth, the sugar-energy sector began to suffer financial and productive difficulties in the wake of the 2008 crisis. The international slump that hit the majority of companies, many of them already on course of

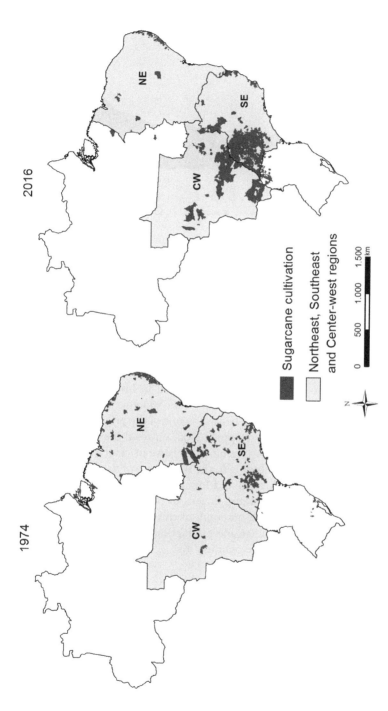

Figure 7.1 Brazilian municipalities with over 1,000 hectares of sugarcane crops in 1974 and 2016.

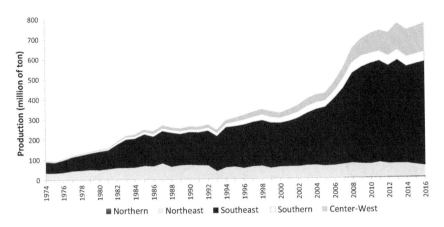

Figure 7.2 Total production of sugarcane in Brazil between 1974–2016 (millions of tons).

ambitious externally-financed expansion projects, led to severe unavailability of financial resources. On the other hand, climatic problems in 2009 and 2010 restricted the quantity of available raw material and jeopardized, to an even greater extent, the liquidity of companies. As a result, the productivity of the 2011/2012 harvest was seriously affected by poor recuperation of sugarcane plantations, difficulties in agrochemical treatments and a negligible increase in new planted areas. Moreover, discovery of pre-salt oil reserves led the Brazilian government actually to abandon the priority that had been given in previous years to the development of biofuel as one of the strategic axes of the economy. In practical terms the government began to control the price of gasoline (price freeze) after 2010, followed by scrapping a tax on fossil fuels that had secured ethanol's competitive margin. As a result, the relative price of gasoline compared to the ethanol one rose, contributing to the worsening of the crisis in the sector. With the high cost of production and low price of ethanol at the consumer level, companies went into debt and dozens of plants have closed or filed for bankruptcy in recent years. The outcome of this was the stagnation (or even reduction in some years), of sugarcane production after 2010, especially in the states located in the center of the country.

2.3 The dynamics of land use

Changes in land use have been discussed at length when concerning the expansion of crops to obtain biofuels that might reduce carbon emissions. The two ways in which land can be made available to produce raw-materials for biofuels, without negative impacts on other types of agricultural production, are: (i) using land that is otherwise unoccupied by agriculture (e.g. pastures), or (ii) intensifying the production on land where crops are already grown, thus maintaining at least stable yields of the existing crops. In both cases, there are changes in land use. On the one hand, we can observe the direct land use change – DLUC, which emerges from the actual pattern of production of biofuel, when the changes take place in the same location as the biofuel crop. On the other hand, we have the indirect land use change (ILUC), when the production of biofuel provokes changes in the use of the land in another location, such as, for example, moving rural activities to another region. Such changes can cause an increase in the environmental impacts related to the production of biofuel, including GHG emissions (Bertzky et al., 2011).

The expansion of sugarcane in the Center-South region (Goiás, Mato Grosso do Sul, Minas Gerais, Paraná and São Paulo states) largely took place on former pasturelands. Based on mapping land use, with satellite images from 2000 to 2010, Adami et al. (2012) estimated the direct effects on the change of land use due to sugarcane crop expansion in those states. The results highlight that, during this period, 69.8% of the expansion of sugarcane in these states took place on pastureland 25% on annual crops, 3.4% on land where sugarcane crops were already grown (corresponding to areas of recovering sugarcane plantations), 1.3% on citrus crops (only in the state of Sao Paulo) and 0.6% on native forest areas.

Thus, the sugarcane expansion for biofuel production in the Brazilian forest areas is of lesser importance. The dynamic of deforestation is complex in Brazil and the estimated indirect effects on land use due to bioenergy expansion require detailed studies. A repeated hypothesis, for example, is that sugarcane is indirectly related to the high levels of deforestation in the Amazon, due to the potential relocation of pastures and annual crops to newer forest areas. However, studies indicated that this hypothesis is overly simplified (Walter et al., 2014). Based on satellite images and an economic model of partial equilibrium, Moreira et al. (2012) estimated that the deforestation caused indirectly by the expansion of sugarcane between 2005 and 2008 was 7.6%, corresponding to roughly 180,000 hectares, compared to total deforestation of 2,395 million hectares due to other reasons. This relatively insignificant indirect effect can be related to the large quantity of land available for sugarcane expansion outside the Amazon region, the continuous improvement in yields of other crops, as well as the intensified use of pastures for cattle breeding.

According to Leite et al. (2009), greater levels of efficiency of land use through cattle breeding, for example from 1.0 head/ha to 1.3–1.5 heads/ha, would make 50 to 70 million hectares of land immediately available, a total area that is currently bigger than the estimated necessary to produce ethanol. Similar results were obtained by Alkimim et al. (2015) who evaluated the agricultural potential of pastures as an alternative to sugarcane expansion, thus preventing greater environmental losses, such as deforestation. The country's total area of pastures with high and moderate agricultural potentials to produce sugarcane equalled 50 million hectares, an area that is five times greater than that currently used. These pasturelands are predominantly located in the main regions of sugarcane expansion: Minas Gerais, São Paulo, Mato Grosso do Sul, Mato Grosso and Paraná states.

In order to determine scenarios for expansion and sustainable production of sugarcane, the ZAE (Agroecological Zoning of Sugarcane) was established in 2009. Created by Embrapa (The Brazilian Corporation for Agricultural Research), the objective of this zoning was to provide technical information to formulate public policies related to sugarcane activity (Manzatto et al., 2009). Geo-referenced information on climate capacity, soil capacity and land use was gathered, excluding areas located in the Amazon and Pantanal biomes, and in the upper Paraguay River basin, along with areas of environmental protection. These regions are environmentally protected under several restrictions concerning land use. The only areas considered suitable were those with potential use of intensive and semi-intensive agricultural production, temporary and annual crops and pastureland. As a result, it was estimated that 64.7 million hectares could be made suitable for new sugarcane plantations, with mechanized harvesting and strictly forbidden use of burning. More than 57% of this area was then occupied by pastureland (in 2012), a figure that clearly points how viable is to expand sugarcane crops without destroying native vegetation or competing against food crops (Manzatto et al., 2009). The classification of the national territory in terms of suitability – or not – for sugarcane production, according to ZAE, resulted in Decree No. 6,961 (2009). It established national rules regarding operations to finance the sugar-energy sector, such as the concession of rural and agroindustry credit for the production and industrialization of sugarcane, sugar and biofuels.

3 Biodiesel

3.1 A brief history of biodiesel production

Since the mid-2000s, the production of biodiesel has risen markedly in Brazil. In a decade, it increased more than fivefold, from 736 m^3 in 2005 to 4.3 million m^3 in 2016 (ANP, 2018). The use of biodiesel contributed to reduce the dependency on oil and diesel imports, minimizing the exposure to higher levels of international oil prices. In addition, there are many environmental benefits – biodiesel is biodegradable and advantageous in terms of reducing greenhouse gases and has low level of sulphur. Furthermore, the production of biodiesel is also viewed as being able to create jobs, generate income and therefore improve the quality of life in rural areas.

In general, biodiesel is obtained from crops with a low productivity of vegetable oil per hectare, thus requiring investment to increase competitiveness. A government policy to subsidize the production of these crops is fundamental in guaranteeing the development and success of biodiesel production.

Following the oil crises typical of the 1970s and 1980s, the government proposed programmes to extract oil from oleaginous crops and created the 'Production of Vegetable Oils for Energetic Purposes Plan' (*Pró-Óleo*). The objectives of this initiative were (i) to generate surplus vegetable oil, aiming at reducing production costs, in order to obtain a blend of 30% in fossil fuel around 1990 and (ii) completely substitute diesel in the long term (PNA, 2006). However, given the low price of diesel fuel compared to the costs of vegetable oil, projects attuned to this last goal was temporarily abandoned. It was only by the turn of the century, with the rise in the production of biodiesel in Europe and the concern surrounding the dependence on fossil fuels as the main energy sources, that Brazil turned its attention back to diesel alternatives, providing incentives for research that focused on using vegetable oil for the production of biofuel (Nogueira et al., 2016).

In 2005, the PNPB (National Program of Production and Use of Biodiesel) was launched and biodiesel was concretely made part of the Brazil's energy matrix. The objective of the PNPB was to promote technically and economically sustainable production and the use of biodiesel, encouraging social inclusion and promote regional development via employment and income generation. The programme also aimed at guaranteeing competitive prices, quality and the supply of biofuel, apart from stimulating the growth of different sources of oleaginous plants in different regions.

Rules were then introduced for the gradual addition of biodiesel to diesel. It started with the addition of 2% of biodiesel to diesel (B2), available across the country, in 2005. Three years later, the B2 blend became mandatory and the B4 and B5 blends were pre-established for 2009 and 2013. However, pressures from biofuel producers brought forward to 2010 the introduction of a minimum percentage of a 5% blend of biodiesel to diesel. Under a sequence of cumulative additions, the B10 blend was in place in March 2018 (Ubrabio, 2018) and a predicted blend at 15% is expected for 2020. As a result of these series of measures, production went up from approximately 700,000 litres in 2005 to 2.4 billion litres in 2010 and 4.3 billion litres in 2017 (ANP, 2018). From 2005 to 2015, however, the installed production capacity grew by around 18% per year, resulting in an average idle capacity of biodiesel production of 40% in recent years (Nogueira et al., 2016). Furthermore, the PNPB was important in guaranteeing competitive prices of biodiesel, via a reduction in taxes on gross revenue (Law 11.116/2005).

3.2 Family farmers in the production of raw-materials for biodiesel

In addition to the subsidies offered and the mandatory blends of biofuel in diesel, the government developed mechanisms to encourage the inclusion of family farmers in the production of oleaginous raw materials. These initiatives aimed to generate income, employment and social inclusion, primarily in the regions of frequent low economic growth, such as the Northeast. The 'Social Fuel Stamp' was then established, consisting of a set of requirements destined to biodiesel producers, with the objective of training family farmers and stipulating a minimum purchase of raw-materials from family farmers of 50% in the Northeast and semiarid regions, 30% in the Southeast and Southern and 10% in the Northern and Center-West. Producers' adhesion to the programme was stimulated by the fact that only plants certified have permission to participate in the largest auction lots promoted by the ANP, which can make up 80% of the mandatory biodiesel in the country.

However, this initiative was not successful. Contrary to what the programme initially envisaged, the supply of raw materials by family farmers to the production of biodiesel has been negligible. It was estimated that 400,000 farmers would be involved in the production of biodiesel by 2005, but the number of family farmers involved was less than 20% of this preliminary estimate ten years later.

Initial analyses on the PNPB showed difficulties for family farmers to get involved in biodiesel production, particularly those in the Northeast, because of lack of both education and the technical requirements (Garcia, 2007). According to evidence collected by the Federal Government, out of 70,255 families supplying raw-materials, just 3.1% were located in the Northern and Northeast and the large majority (90%) was located in the Southern (MDA, 2016). This asymmetry, in fact, is not surprising given the much better organization of family farmers in the Southern. Table 7.1 presents the participation of the family farmer in terms of the volume of raw material supplied to biodiesel production according to each region in 2016. The Northern and Northeast regions represented little over 1% of this supply, highlighting that the programme actually failed in terms of the social and regional inclusion and income distribution that had been expected.

Most probably, one of the main reasons to justify the failure of the programme to stimulate development in the Northeast was the strong incentive to use *Ricinus communis* (castor oil plant) as a feedstock for biodiesel production. This crop was a priority choice because it was a labour-intensive crop, highly resistant to dry weather and implied in low planting costs. However, several limitations indicated that this plant could not be used as one of the main raw materials for biodiesel. The restrictions included low productivity, inadequate agricultural management, technological restrictions not only in the processing process but also in the *Ricinus communis* biodiesel itself, poor technical assistance and difficulties in accessing rural credit. Therefore, the use of this plant in biodiesel production is still non-existent to date.

In the first decade of this century, Petrobras, one of the producers of biodiesel, invested in research and development strategies, creating a research network that involved universities and public research institutions. Its focus was the production of oleaginous alternatives to soybean especially for family farmers. However, the strategies adopted by Petrobras Biofuel were unable to concretely include these groups of farmers, particularly those from the Northeast and semiarid regions, into the production structures of biodiesel (Sampaio, 2017).

On the other hand, Brazilian biodiesel production has relied heavily on the soybean chain, a crop with advantages in terms of technical and productive performance when compared to the other oleaginous sources considered in the programme. The major contribution from family farmers in the Southern for the PNPB (Table 7.1) is not only due to the greater number of family farms in this region, but also because of the greater ability to manage their agricultural

Table 7.1 Volume of raw material supplied by family farmers in Brazil under the Social Fuel Stamp programme in 2016 per region (thousand tons).

Region	Volume (10^3 t)	Percentage (%)
Northern	3.25	0.1
Northeast	31.88	1.0
Southeast	85.09	2.6
Center-west	480.16	14.5
Southern	2,717.4	81.9

Source: MDA (2016).

output through cooperatives, making the purchase more attractive for processing industries (MDA, 2016).

3.3 Soybean as the main source in the production of biodiesel

Biodiesel can be produced from a reaction between vegetable oils or animal fats and alcohol. The commonest transformation process of oils in biodiesel is transesterification. This is a simple and efficient process, in which a combined mixture of 100kg of vegetable oil and 10kg of alcohol results around 100kg of biodiesel, as well as glycerine as a by-product (Knothe et al., 2006). Different raw materials are used for biodiesel production, such as soybeans, palm, canola, sunflower, cottonseed, castor, among others.

There are over 100 types of oleaginous plants that can be used to produce biodiesel in Brazil (Souza et al., 2017). The potential of the diverse oleaginous plants varies according to the region. Palm oil is found in the Northern, while in the Northeast, Ricinus (castor oil), babassu and jatropha predominate. In the Center-West states, the sources are soybean, cottonseed and jatropha and in the Southeast, *Acrocomia aculeata* (macaw palm), jatropha, cottonseed, peanut and sunflower. Finally, in the Southern, these sources are anchored on soybean, sunflower and cottonseed. However, by far the main raw material used to produce Brazilian biodiesel is soybean. Figure 7.3 presents the main raw materials used in the production of Brazilian biodiesel in 2017. The use of soy oil stands out, responsible for around 75% of the total production of biodiesel in the country. The second main raw material is bovine fat, produced largely in the Center-West (Ubrabio, 2018).

In relation to land use, soybean occupies the largest planted area in Brazil, covering almost 35 million hectares, resulting in a production of 119 million tons in 2017/18 harvest. In the same period, the biggest producer was Mato Grosso, with 32 million tons (accounting for 27% of the national production), followed by Paraná and Rio Grande do Sul, with 19 and 17 million tons of soybean, respectively (Conab, 2018a). In this context, the states of Mato Grosso and Rio Grande do Sul presented in 2018 the highest concentration of firms producing biodiesel – 17 and nine, respectively. There were 51 Brazilian biodiesel

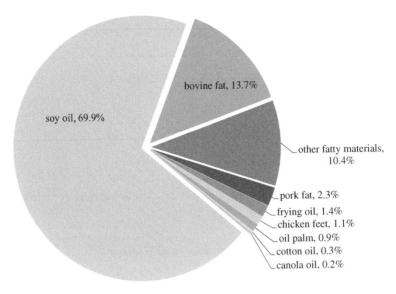

Figure 7.3 Raw materials used in the production of Brazilian biodiesel in 2017.

producers authorized by the ANP (National Regulatory Agency) in 2018. Their locations and capacities are given in Figure 7.4.

3.4 Soybean production and the dynamics of land use

The vast cultivated area of soybean is largely used, apart from grains, to produce soybean meal, used primarily in animal feeds. The use of soy as a raw material to obtain biofuels arose as an opportunity to profit from a co-product, thus adding new economic value to the soybean supply chain.

As with the case of sugarcane, the growth of soybean planted area can cause direct and indirect changes to land use. Lapola et al. (2010) used a spatial model to estimate the direct and indirect impacts on land use as a result of the expansion of biodiesel from soybean in Brazil. The simulation was carried out considering an increase of four billion litres in biofuel production between 2003 and 2020. To meet this demand, the authors estimated an additional area of 165,300 km² (57,200 km² for sugarcane and 108,100 for soybean crops). Considering the potential direct effects, results indicated that 88% of this additional area (145,700 km²) took place in areas previously used as rangelands; 14,300 km² on annual crops; and direct deforestation totalled 1,800 km² of forest areas and 2,000 km² of woody savanna. However, the authors also pointed to an estimated indirect impact on forest areas of 70,000 km², since the soybean expansion on pastures may dislocate cattle-breeding activities to forested areas. (Lapola et al., 2010, p. 3389).

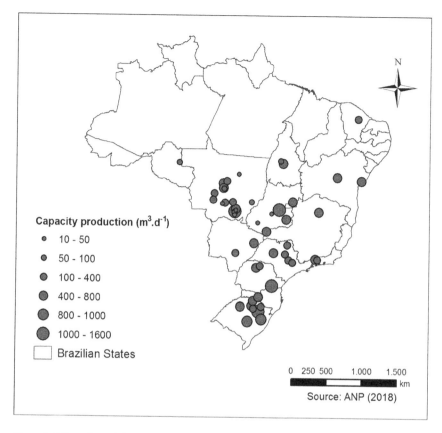

Figure 7.4 Location of the Brazilian biodiesel producers authorized by the ANP in 2018 and respective production capacities.

Soybean production has increased its importance in this century, primarily in the north of the state of Mato Grosso. This expansion occupied land that was previously home to natural ecosystems in the Amazon and Cerrado biomes (Lathuillière et al., 2017). In addition to soybean, cattle raising was also an important propelling factor in deforestation, provoking direct and indirect changes in land use. The rate of deforestation did however fall significantly after the implementation of the 'Action Plan to Prevent and Control Deforestation in the Amazon', in 2004 (Gollnow, 2014).

The objective of this Plan was to diminish deforestation by carrying out several measures, driven by four main themes: (i) agrarian and land ownership organization; (ii) environmental monitoring and control; (iii) stimulation of sustainable productive activities; and (iv) normative economic tools. These actions resulted in a significant fall in the rate of deforestation in the Amazon region, from 27,772 km^2 (2004) to 5,012 km^2 in 2014 (INPE, 2018a). The reduction in the state of Mato Grosso was even more significant, from 11,814 km^2 to 1,075 km^2 in the same time period. In recent years, however, the area of deforestation in this state rose again, reaching 1,561 km^2 (INPE, 2018b).

Another measure in place to combat deforestation is the so-called 'soybean moratorium', an agreement between the Brazilian Association of Vegetable Oil Industries (Abiove) and the National Association of Grain Exporters (ANEC). It is meant to forbid trade or finance soy grown on deforested land in the Amazon. This is an agreement monitored by the National Institute of Spatial Research (INPE) in 89 municipalities After July 2008, less than 2% of soy expansion occurred in deforested areas, even considering the fourfold increase in the area of soy plantations in the Amazon biome – from 1.14 million hectares in the 2006/07 harvest, to 4.48 million hectares in 2016/17 (around 13% of soybean planted area in Brazil) (Verdi, 2018).

3.5 RenovaBio – the new national biofuels policy

With the signing of the Paris Agreement in 2015, Brazil agreed to comply with targets established in its Nationally Determined Contributions (NDCs) to reduce GHG emissions by 37% of the 2005 levels in 2025 and by 43% in 2030, in addition to decarbonizing the fuel sector. In order to reach these goals, one of the mechanisms adopted by the government was the creation of the National Biofuels Policy (RenovaBio), in December 2017.

The objective of RenovaBio is to promote the expansion of biofuel production in Brazil, based on market scenarios and on the environmental, economic and social sustainability. The policy aims to recognize the strategic role of all types of biofuels in the energy matrix, as well as their importance to energy security and the reduction of GHG emissions. Targets to reduce emissions within 10 years will be thus established, making it possible to estimate the quantity of fuels necessary (both fossil and renewable), with greater quantitative precision regarding the demand and also better planning on the part of the producers. Such targets to reduce emissions must be met by various fuel economic agents involved in the distribution chain. In addition to the targets set, each biofuel producer is required to be certified and receive a rating related to their highest and lowest capacity to reduce GHG emissions (this rating reflects the complete lifecycle of the production of the fuel) (MME, 2018).

This policy also envisions the creation of a new financial asset, the Decarbonization Credit (CBIO), that will be traded on the stock market and will represent the reductions in CO_{2eq} emissions relative to the lifecycle of biofuel production and the decarbonization targets imposed on distributors.

In reaction to the new policy, The Ministry of Mines and Energy (MME, 2018) predicted an increase in production from a total of 30 billion litres of ethanol in 2017 to 50 billion in 2030, coupled with an expanded planted area of sugarcane by three million hectares. This expansion, however, must not take place on native vegetation, since the policy classifies all ethanol produced from deforested land ineligible, as of the date of its issuance (December 2017). Thus, it is necessary to substitute existing crops or occupy degraded land or expand into pasturelands. The production of second-generation biofuels, such as ethanol from straw and sugarcane pulp, has also an important role to increase the returns on biofuels (in litres) by planted area of sugarcane. The use of second-generation fuels can minimize the potential direct and indirect effects on changes in land use.

The RenovaBio policy also has a direct impact on the production of biodiesel and, as a result, affects soybean land use. The Ministry of Mines and Energy estimates that the production of biodiesel will more than triple, from four billion litres in 2017 to 13 billion litres in 2030. To reach this goal, it is necessary to expand the soybean planted area by seven million hectares (MME 2018). However, according to a study carried out by three biodiesel associations (The Brazilian Association of Vegetable Oil Industries, The Association of Brazilian Biodiesel Producers and The Brazilian Union of Biodiesel and Biokerosene), an even larger area of around 12 million hectares would be made available for sustainable occupation. This figure is derived from the approximately 145 million hectares of pastureland that are under-utilization or degraded; this area would allow for a part to be converted into cropland, as well as the possibility of intensifying cattle raising, with greater production of cattle per area and thus more land available for plantation. Native plant ecosystems, therefore, would not be affected (Trigueirinho et al., 2016).

The RenovaBio policy is also interested in diversifying the inputs for biofuel production, using crops of greater yield per hectare, which could lead to a decrease in the final price of the product thus increasing competitiveness. Along these lines, there are expectations of a greater participation derived from palm oil, a raw material currently used in 0.9% of biodiesel production in Brazil. The policy also considers palm oil as an alternative that could strengthen one of the pillars of the programme (family farming) given its high labor-intensity and high productivity. In addition, it could help improve degraded land in the so-called 'arc of deforestation' in the Amazon region.

4 Conclusions

The implementation of government policies to encourage the production of biofuels was fundamental to boost the production and consumption of ethanol and biodiesel in Brazil, as well as consolidating the participation of these energy sources in the country's energy matrix. As a result of new energy policies based on renewable sources, a rise in the production of biofuels over the coming years in Brazil can be safely predicted. This is not only because of the need to consolidate alternative energy sources with fossil biofuels in the transport sector, but also due to the worldwide pressure and concern surrounding the effects of (and on) climate changes.

Based on all of the information here presented, it is clear that Brazil has a major advantage in this market due to its vast territory. This favourable context also arises from the possibility of increasing production by occupying under-used or degraded areas and thus contributing to a reduction in greenhouse gases.

In addition, the use of land for energy sources does not compete with food crops; from the two main raw materials presented – sugarcane and soybean – as well as the biofuels ethanol and biodiesel, food co-products, such as sugar and bran, are also produced.

Despite the existent threat on deforestation to the Amazon, stronger and more sensible measures are recently being taken. Public policies are driving the development of biomass as an energy source in such a way that international agreements are complied with and thus aim to mitigate the effects of climate changes.

8 Agriculture and the environment

A conflictive and ambiguous antinomy in recent Brazilian development

Antônio Márcio Buainain and Junior Ruiz Garcia

1 Introduction

The history of agricultural development embodies a conflictive and ambiguous relationship with the environment. Agriculture has modified ecosystems, using both predatory and unsustainable methods as well as sustainable practices which have minimized environmental impacts. The history of Brazilian agriculture is no different. Over five centuries, the growth of Brazilian agriculture was based on the incorporation of new land and labor and on environmental degradation. This does not mean, however, that agricultural practices have always been predatory and unsustainable.

Itinerant farming has proven to be sustainable for centuries; the abundance of land and the rate of growth were compatible with both the availability of natural resources and their resilience and restoration capacity. The existent tension did not translate into contradictions and negative impacts to the point of threatening the overall sustainability of the system. It should be noted that, in general, extensive growth lead to the supply of food for the domestic market and export commodities. In general, productivity was very low and determined by the natural fertility of the new land and climatic conditions, which periodically led to food shortages, particularly in the Northeast semiarid region. However, this rather functional role was eroded *pari passu* with the acceleration of urban–industrial growth, particularly after the so-called heavy industrialization in the 1950s. The increasing economic pressures on the agricultural sector exacerbated social and economic unbalances, the rate of deforestation increased faster than the restoration capacity and the intensification of rural exodus exceeded the absorption capacity in urban areas.

Despite technological advances – praised as the main determinant of Brazil's upsurge as an important food player on the international scene –, agricultural development in Brazil has also resulted in controversial environmental trends that, in addition to potential negative impacts on global climate change, may pose threats to the long-term sustainability of the Brazilian food system itself. Modern agriculture has been driven by an economic logic which fosters the intensification of production, which increases the potential for undesirable environmental impacts. However, since the end of the last century, agri-food systems have not been able to avoid sustainability issues. In addition, the current institutional framework has been increasingly demanding growth with sustainability and inclusiveness, also considering environmental aspects. The truth is that amid contradictions, agricultural production and agribusiness are becoming more sustainable and greener.

Amid intense environmental conflicts, Brazilian agriculture is undoubtedly becoming greener. However, progress is slow and actual changes still localized. Competitive tropical agricultural production still relies on the intensive use of agrochemicals whose sustainability is greatly questioned. This chapter seeks to explore these conflictive and ambiguous relations between modern agriculture and the environment in Brazil.

2 Brazilian agriculture: a brief historical perspective

The formation of Brazilian agriculture is marked by an extensive production growth pattern of production – the incorporation of new land and labor with resultant environmental degradation (McNeill, 1986). Across four centuries, the growth of extensive agriculture erased large forest areas from the map and left behind degraded soils. However, it also contributed to occupying Brazilian territory and shaping Brazilian society. For centuries, agriculture has supplied foodstuff and raw materials to the domestic market and been the main source of foreign exchange and revenue for the public sector (Cano, 1998).

The abundance of land allowed agriculture to maintain levels of profitability and sustainability, in a functional productive system: abandoned land was re-occupied by small subsistence and food producers, herd and/or left for the restoration of secondary forests and soil fertility. The increase in production was slow, productivity depended fundamentally on natural fertility and climatic variations. Thus, until the end of the 1950s, the Brazilian agrarian and agricultural structure had not undergone major changes: additional land and labor were the sources of the expansion of production; food production expanded into marginalized areas or in the pioneering frontiers opened up by small farmers who occupied virgin lands on the borders up to the arrival of mid and large-scale farmers, who took possession of lands by legal means and/or violence and set up commercial establishments. Several foodstuffs were imported, particularly grains.

This apparent functionality was disrupted by the rapid urban-industrial development which took place from the 1950s onwards (Baer, 1984). By the mid-1960s it was no longer possible to meet the increased demand for food, foreign exchange and labor generated by the ongoing industrialization process. As a result, successive domestic supply crises occurred, causing inflation and distributive conflicts in cities (Baer, 1984). On the other hand, social tensions in the countryside were translated into demands for structural reforms, among which radical agrarian reform stood out (Cano, 1998).

3 The environmental and social degradation of agricultural modernization in Brazil

The modernization of Brazilian agriculture, which began in the 1950s with the diffusion of tractors and the use of fertilizers (IBGE, 2018b), was based on the package later embodied in the so-called Green Revolution: mechanization; intensive use of agrochemicals; genetic improvement; adoption of new management practices (Pingali, 2012); monoculture; increase in production scale.

This process was accelerated in the 1970s, driven by agriculture-specific public policies and actions (see Chapter 03). This early modernization set the basis for structural transformations (Buainain et al., 2014) which placed Brazilian agriculture, from the beginning of the twenty-first century, as a major agricultural producer and protagonist in the world market (FAOSTAT, 2018). The introduction of the technological package specific to temperate-climate agriculture resulted in increased production from the 1960s onwards. However, its diffusion in the Brazilian context, characterized by a tropical and subtropical climate, skewed land distribution and backward social and productive structures, generated strong negative social and environmental pressures thus partially countervailing its positive results (Albuquerque and Silva, 2008a, 2008b; Evenson and Gollin, 2003).

Modernization intensified the country's structural heterogeneity (Helfand, 1999), giving rise to the thesis sustained by Buainain et al. (2014) on the bipolar development of Brazilian agriculture, which replaces the traditional bipolarity of traditional agrarian structure, between small and large producers. On the one hand, there is a reduced group of highly dynamic producers, applying advanced technology and inserted into global value chains; and on the other, a large majority of producers which for various reasons was lagged behind the modernization process and are increasingly marginalized (see Chapter 11). According to data from the 2006 Agricultural Census, the 10% richest agricultural holdings – including small, medium and large – made up 85% of the gross production value, while almost two-thirds of the holdings – more than three million – accounted for just under 4% (Alves and Rocha, 2010). Therefore, one of the most significant results of modernization has been the marginalization of millions of producers, which poses an immense social cost on society.

Environmental impacts are associated with both modernization and the marginalization of small producers (Martinelli et al., 2010). In the Caatinga biome (see Figure 0.2 in Introduction), for example, a region that houses around two million farmers in a state of poverty (Buainain and Garcia, 2015), deforestation (IBAMA, 2018a) and desertification (Souza and Oyama, 2011) are driven mainly by the domestic use of firewood and the sale of coal. In the North Amazon region, poverty is an important vector of environmental degradation, particularly considering the extent of cutting and burning agriculture. In other areas, deforestation has been caused by land grabbing and 'modernization', either for the implementation of livestock or new crop areas.

The expansion of the so-called modern agricultural and animal-raising models – supported by mechanization and the indiscriminate use of agrochemicals – accelerated the occupation of the frontier zones, intensified deforestation, particularly in the Cerrado biome and on the edges of the Amazon rainforest (IBAMA, 2018a; INPE, 2018a), as well as caused negative environmental impacts, from soil compaction and loss through erosion to soil and water contamination (Evenson & Gollin, 2003).

Environmental issues were not on the Brazilian agenda in the 1960s and 1970s and public policy contributed decisively to negative environmental impacts. On the one hand, the military regime, which only fell in 1984, launched several programmes of territorial occupation, in particular of the Amazon (Amazon biome) and Central-West (Cerrado biome) frontiers, among which the following stand out: the National Integration Program (Programa Nacional de Integração – PIN), the Polocentro (Program for the Development of the Cerrado) and the Produsk (Japanese-Brazilian Cooperation programme for the development of the Cerrados). All of these programmes were co-financed by international institutions, particularly the World Bank and the Japanese Development Bank (Botelho, 2016; Cattaneo, 2002). On the other hand, agricultural policy and development programmes used subsidized rural credit and tax grants, with conditioned access to the adoption of the technological package, such as the use of machinery, fertilizers and even deforestation for planting pasture (Buainain et al., 2014; Seguy and Bouzinac, 1998) (see Chapter 03).

These mechanisms resulted in two negative consequences: on the one hand, the excessive use of machinery and agrochemical inputs, whose costs were reduced by up to 80% due to subsidies associated with inflation; on the other, a size bias, since small producers had neither access to the financial system nor generated tax credits to be discounted (Helfand, 2001). It should also be noted that the political environment shaped by military authoritarian ruling did not favour compliance with the then current legislation at times in which such legislation hindered the military government's modernizing project. This explains, at least partly, why environmental, land and labor legislation were rarely applied.

The modernization process, in its early stage, resulted in a huge socio-environmental cost, albeit bearable by society. On the one hand, there was the Brazilian Miracle. The economy was growing at rates above 7% per year (World Bank, 2018a) and the rural population displaced by mechanization and land concentration was readily reabsorbed in the cities and expanding frontier areas; on the other hand, the availability of land, subsidized credit and the adoption of the imported technological package produced immediate positive effects on the growth of production and masked the problems of sustainability until the end of 1970s, when erosion became a real threat. In summary, the state played a double role to play: it subsidized both environmental degradation and measures to correct and or delay the negative effects of modernization on production and productivity (Buainain et al., 2014).

There are no data on deforestation for the period, but between 1960 and 1980, the Brazilian farming area increased by 81 million hectares, from 151 million to 232 million; in the Center-West region, the expansion went from 81.7 million hectares in 1970 to 113 million in 1980 (IBGE, 2018a). Pastures – an important vector of vegetation to cover degradation (Dias-Filho, 2016) – increased by 52 million hectares, from 122 to 174 million, with an occupancy of only 0.68 bovine livestock per hectare (IBGE, 2018a). Between 1960 and 1980, the number of tractors increased by 789%, from 61,000 to 545,000 units – from one tractor per 468 hectares to one per 105 hectares (IBGE, 2018a). Tractors were mainly used for soil preparation, leaving the soil uncovered and vulnerable to tropical rain and wind during part of the year. The increased erosion associated with deforestation, mechanization and cultivation practices may have been the first catalyst of the unsustainable technological package that was spreading rapidly throughout the country.

According to the Agronomic Institute of Campinas (IAC), erosion reached 25 ton/ha/year in the 1970s (Romeiro and Abrantes, 1981). In the state of Paraná, the second largest grain producer in the country at that time, levels reached 187 ton/ha/year, i.e., more than 1 cm of soil was lost per year. During this time, the Paraná Integrated Program for Soil Conservation set the maximum acceptable loss at 25 ton/ha/year, which was twice as high as the levels admissible by the Soil Survey Staff and the Soil Conservation Service, at between three and 12 ton/ha/year (Romeiro and Abrantes, 1981).

The environmental impact was significant, especially in the states of São Paulo, Paraná, Santa Catarina and Rio Grande do Sul (see Figure 0.1 in Introduction), the main agricultural regions in the 1970s/80s. In order to contain the loss of yields, the use of nitrogen, phosphate and potassic fertilizers was increased, reaching 4.2 million tons in 1980 (IBGE, 2018a) and showing an increase of 954% between 1960 and 1980. However, the impact on yield was limited. Productivity gain was only 11% for rice and null for beans between 1960 and 1980 (IBGE, 2018a) and the increase in production was a direct result of the increased harvested area. In the case of coffee and sugarcane – export products – the yield fell by 14% in the period (IBGE, 2018a).

At best, the increase in the use of fertilizers neutralized the negative effects of erosion on average yields. However, it led to another serious environmental problem: chemical pollution and increased resistance of pests in the tropical environment. A study conducted by Paschoal (1979) showed a strong correlation between the intensification of pesticide use and the increase in pests. Between 1958 and 1973, the number of pests rose sharply from 193 to 593, while pesticide consumption grew by 403% between 1964 and 1978, going from 16,000 to 81,000 tons (Romeiro and Abrantes, 1981). It is worth highlighting that the increase in the use of pesticides coincides with the intensification of production and changes in the Brazilian agricultural geography, which moved from the south of the country, where a more temperate climate is found, to the Cerrado regions of the Midwest, where there is a tropical climate.

4 The 'tropicalization' of Brazilian agriculture

In view of the significant environmental impacts associated with modernization, the sustainability of the temperate agriculture model was put in check and the environmental issue was slowly introduced onto the agenda of public policies and agricultural research during the 1970s (Romeiro, 2014). Erosion was perceived as the main problem, as it was threatening production in the most productive areas in the country. Thus, erosion control became an urgent issue for many organizations in the National Agricultural Research System (SNPA). New technologies were introduced to overcome the problem, such as terracing, no-till farming and use of contour levels (Albuquerque and Silva, 2008a, 2008b). These practices were set as a requirement for accessing highly subsidized public rural credit.

As a result of the reduction in public funding and subsidies from the end of the 1980s (Santana et al., 2014), the adoption of soil conservation practices, whose positive results were already evident, gained new momentum, contributing to the viability of crops. In this sense, irrespective of social awareness of environmental issues, the adoption of more conservationist practices was driven by farmers' economic and financial calculus rather than by sudden environmental awareness. It is estimated that, in the 1981/82 harvest, only 230,000 hectares were cultivated using the minimum cultivation technique, reaching 32 million hectares in 2017 (FEBRAPDP, 2018).

The introduction of these conservationist practices and the use of enhanced seeds, which are more compatible with local soil and climate conditions, contributed to accelerating the occupation of the Center-West border. Together these techniques form the core of what became known as the tropicalization of Brazilian agriculture.[1] The result was a significant increase in the harvested area, in the production and productivity of main crops[2] between 1980 and 2017 (IBGE, 2018a): soybean acreage went from 8.8 million to 34 million hectares (in the Center-West, from 1.1 million to 15 million); sugarcane, from 2.6 million acreage to ten million (in the Center-West, from 41,000 to 1.8 million); and corn from 11.5 million to 17 million (in the Center-West, from one million to 8.3 million hectares).

The output of this acreage expansion was potentialized by the significant productivity gains registered between 1980 and 2017 (IBGE, 2018a): for rice (297%, 6,200 kg/ha), cotton (290%, 4,100 kg/ha), corn (216%, 5,600 kg/ ha), wheat (164%, 2,300 kg/ha), beans (156%, 1,000 kg/ha), soybean (96%, 3,400 kg/ha) and coffee (71%, 1,500 kg/ha). The national production of grains (rice, beans, corn, soybean and wheat) also grew, from 50 million to 232 million tons in the period, a growth of 365%. The Center-West Cerrados, practically absent from the agricultural map until then, went on to account for 44% of the national grain production and 18% of sugarcane in 2017. Thus, tropicalization enabled a new, more sustainable cycle of expansion for Brazilian agriculture.

The modernization of livestock farming from the 1970s onwards was also an important vector of agricultural transformations, albeit a source of intense social conflicts, environmental degradation and greenhouse gas emissions. Transformations in livestock farming gave rise to a strongly heterogeneous segment, with the coexistence of both an extensive and predatory system, with low production indicators and an intensive system, responsible for the 'genetic revolution' that placed Brazil as a major exporter of high quality beef (Dias-Filho, 2016).

However, both the tropicalization and the new expansion cycle also contributed to the worsening of other environmental problems, as serious and worrying as erosion. Firstly, the occupation of the new frontier in the Center-West and Northern regions provoked the deforestation of native forests in both the Cerrado and Amazon biomes. In both the Cerrado, deforestation was associated with the implementation of technology-intensive systems; in the Amazon, with the appropriation of unused public land due to the implementation of extensive livestock farming and largely illegal logging activities. According to data from Mapbiomas (2018), between 1985 and 2017, the total deforested area in the Cerrado totalled 22 million hectares; the area occupied by the agricultural sector totalled 86 million hectares. According to data from INPE (2018a), the total deforested area in the Amazon between 1988 and 2017 reached 42 million hectares.

In addition to deforestation, the intensification of agricultural production systems which allows up to three harvests per year in some regions and the increase in the production scale have exacerbated certain conflicts between agriculture and the environment, which have a varied impact on local life across producing regions: scarce water resources; waste disposal issues, such as poultry and swine waste, sugarcane bagasse and sugar and ethanol vinasse; chemical contamination; loss of biodiversity and 'local' climate change, with alterations in rainy seasons and temperature increases.

In 2014, producers used 14 million tons of fertilizers, going from 69 kg/ha in 1992 to 184 kg/ha, an increase of 165% (IBGE, 2018a). Consumption of active ingredients (pesticides) per planted area rose from 3.2 kg/ha in 2000 to 6.7 kg/ha in 2014 (109%) (IBGE, 2018a), reaching 453,000 tons (IBAMA, 2018b). The increase in the 2000s is also associated with new plant varieties with higher genetic potential – transgenics. Pesticide use also gave rise to the problems of packaging disposal and contamination of workers and communities surrounding rural areas (Carneiro et al., 2015). Hence, chemical pollution in the air, soil and water still remains a serious problem. The efficacy of using agrochemicals however also increased due to improvements in the genetics of plant varieties, soil conservation, the biological control of pests and diseases and advances in precision agriculture (Romeiro, 2014).

5 The 'Greening' of Brazilian agriculture: challenges and solutions

The growing perception of the negative social and environmental impacts of agricultural modernization, in addition to the diffusion and strengthening of civil society organizations defending conservationist and environmentalist agendas in an atmosphere of political openness and re-democratization, have intensified pressures and discussions related to sustainable development (World Commission on Environment and Development, 1987). Introduced initially by the World Bank and FAO, the debate on sustainable development has caused changes to agendas on agricultural and public policies in general. This process was reflected in the construction of an institutional framework linked to sustainable development and human rights, in which some of the basic precepts were included in the Federal Constitution of 1988 and in a set of rules, programmes and policies (Table 8.1) aimed at promoting the adoption of more sustainable technologies; environmental sustainability, including the control and punishment of practices contrary to environmental legislation; greater market demand for respect towards environmental and social issues; among others.

Table 8.1 also reveals the complexity and comprehensiveness of the relations between agriculture and the environment. In addition, it shows that the country has long built an institutional structure to regulate and guide decisions

Table 8.1 Brazil's basic environmental legislation related to agriculture

Subject Matter	Legislation
Forestry Code of 1965	Law no. 4.771/1965
Wildlife Protection	Decree no. 5.197/1967
National Environmental Policy	Law no. 6.938/1981
Environmental Protection Areas	Law no. 6.902/1981
Chapter VI – On the Environment	Federal Constitution of 1988
Coastal Management	Law no. 7.661/1988
National Environmental Fund	Law no. 7.797/1989
Regulation of the Use of Agrochemicals	Law no. 7.802/1989
Creation of the Brazilian Institute of the Environment – IBAMA	Law no. 7.735/1989
Concerning the Agricultural Policy	Law no. 8.171/1991
National Water Resources Policy	Law no. 9.433/1997
Protection of Plant Varieties	Law no. 9.456/1997
Environmental Crimes	Law no. 9.605/1998
National Policy on Environmental Education	Law no. 9.795/1999
Creation of the National Water Agency	Law no. 9.984/2000
National System of Units of Conservation	Law no. 9.985/2000
Regulation of Genetic Heritage	PM★ no. 2.186–16/2001
National Policy on Biodiversity	Decree no. 4.339/2002
Regulation of Genetically Modified Organisms	Law no. 11.105/2005
Public Forest Management	Law no. 11.284/2006
Atlantic Forest Protection	Law no. 11.428/2006
National Policy on Climate Change	Law no. 12.187/2009
National Climate Change Fund	Law no. 12.114/2009
National Policy on Solid Waste	Law no. 12.305/2010
Forestry Code of 2012	Law no. 12.651/2012

Source: Authors.

★Provisional Measure.

on agriculture that impact environmental quality. However, this institutionality is partly dormant and putting it into practice poses a huge challenge for society. Legislation was, for a long time, ignored by farmers, government and society and was only taken more seriously from the 2000s onwards, due to pressure from organized society and increasingly severe inspections carried out by public institutions, which under democratic ruling, gained certain operational autonomy to carry out their mandate, such as IBAMA and public prosecutors. The performance and effectiveness of these institutions were enhanced by improvements to the regulatory framework, the allocation of budget resources to fund regular operation and the introduction of new technologies, such as satellite monitoring.

As the legislation was taken more seriously, conflicts between the various actors became more acute. These conflicts cannot be reduced to two extreme positions – conserving versus squandering. The conflicts involve different and legitimate conceptions about the very meaning of sustainability, the actual limits of conservation and the use of natural resources, local and regional development issues and how to tackle climate change. These challenges were materialized in the Sustainable Development Goals (SDGs), but the paths to reach the goals are not entirely clear nor conflict-free.

The approval of the Agricultural Policy Law in 1991 meant an inflection point in the modernization strategy that had marked the previous period. Among its objectives was the protection of the environment and sustainable use and recovery of natural resources. In addition, agroecological zoning was introduced – the adoption of the zoning and its recommended production systems have become a necessary condition for farmer to be eligible to receive credit support. This law changed the very understanding of modernization, which under the previous paradigm was measured by the use of machinery and chemicals. Agricultural policy began to increasingly incorporate incentives for sustainable development, initially considered by farmers and their representative entities as restrictions to production and economic freedom. Restrictions and incentives would become the axis of disputes along the 2010s, which culminated in the approval of the Forestry Code, in 2012, following a decade of intense and conflicting debates amongst stakeholders.

The fight against deforestation reached priority status by the mid-1990s and several measures were implemented, such as satellite monitoring performed by INPE's Program for Amazon Deforestation Monitoring (PRODES); The Action Plan for the Prevention and Control of Deforestation in the Legal Amazon (PPCDAm), adopted in 2004, which includes not only control but also incentives for the sustainable management of the Legal Amazon forest (Mello et al., 2017); a pact signed between Abiove (the Brazilian Association of Vegetable Oil Industries) and ANEC (the National Association of Grain Exporters) not to acquire soybean from areas of the Amazon biome that had been deforested after 2006, known as the Soybean Moratorium; the Meat Moratorium, an agreement signed by the main meat producers and supermarket chains to no longer slaughter and sell meat of animals from illegally deforested areas of the

Amazon; and the expansion of protected areas by 50 million hectares (Mello et al., 2017). The 2017 overview of the PPCDAm pointed out positive results, such as the reduction of the annual deforestation rate from 29,100 km² in 1995 and 27,800 km² in 2004 to 6,900 km² in 2017 (INPE, 2018a).

The rapid occupation of the Cerrado biome was not subjected to the same control as the Amazon and concerns with the deforestation of the Cerrado and its consequences for the main watershed basins of the country were only manifested more clearly in the 2000s.[3] The main initiatives are the Project of Satellite Deforestation Monitoring of the Brazilian Biomes (Pmdbbs), created in 2007 (IBAMA, 2018a) and the Action Plan for the Prevention and Control of Deforestation and Forest Fires in the Cerrado (PPCerrado), created in 2010, which seeks to promote a reduction in the annual rates of deforestation and degradation, the incidence of wildfires and burning (MMA, 2011). The initial results appear relevant: between 2001 and 2004, the annual deforestation rate averaged 30,000 km² and fell to 10,000 km² per year from 2010 on. It is unclear, however, whether this decrease is due to public policy actions, including environmental inspection, or to a slowdown caused by market movements (MMA, 2016).

Deforestation control is an important axis of the sustainable development strategy of Brazilian agriculture and since the turning of the century the deforestation rates indeed registered a significant reduction. However, there are no signs of recovery of degraded vegetation, including in the Atlantic Forest, the most degraded biome in Brazil (SOSMA, 2018). Also, in spite of the measures to control deforestation, the country is far from the 'zero illegal deforestation' target set by national policy.

Another axis is the Low Carbon Agriculture Program (ABC, in Portuguese), created in 2010 (Decree no. 7.390/2010), which seeks to stimulate sustainable agricultural growth and to convert Brazilian agriculture into a green activity from the point of view of environmental impacts. The ABC programme stimulates the introduction of 'green' productive systems, agricultural practices and sustainable natural resource management, with the objective of reducing emissions and increasing the capacity of $CO2$ fixation in vegetation and soil[4] (MAPA, 2018b). It has national coverage, with a term set to end in 2020 and receives an estimated contribution of R$197 billion, of which R$157 billion is allocated to rural credit.[5] The ABC consists of seven programmes: Recovery of Degraded Pastures; Integrated Crop-Livestock-Forest (ILPF) and Agroforestry Systems (SAFs); No-till System; Biological Nitrogen Fixation; Planted Forests; Treatment of Animal Waste; Adaptation to Climate Change (MAPA, 2018b). Initial results of the ABC are modest: between 2010 and 2017, there were 30,300 contracts, with a total disbursement of R$14.4 billion, just 9% of the total budgeted resources (R$157 billion) (MAPA, 2018b). This performance is far from the ambitious targets set by the ABC programme which may be a result of the design and operational flaws hindering its smooth implementation. The main flaw in the design is the dissociation of the loans from the subsidies needed to reduce the private burden of non-profitable investments required for the adoption of low-carbon agriculture. There were also complaints from farmers and their representatives regarding the paperwork required to apply for loans, the length of time to process applications and the non-approval of some items of the requests, thus rendering the projects incomplete and even unviable. In addition to these problems, the macroeconomic scenery of the Brazilian economy since 2012 was far from favourable to increasing indebtedness to fund law-carbon agriculture projects.

The ABC programme and all other actions to combat deforestation are linked to the National Policy on Climate Change (PNMC), adopted in 2009, which could be considered the main public initiative to encourage the adoption of more conservationist practices in agriculture. This initiative is an attempt to improve the relationship between agriculture and the environment, which reinforces the commitments undertaken by Brazil at the UN framework conventions on climate change (UN, 2018b). This new scenario may contribute to the progress of several domestic agendas regarding sustainability and to accelerate the transition to greener farming, which irrespective of progress is still more a mirage than a reality.

The new Forestry Code was approved in 2012 (Law no. 12.651/2012) (Brancalion et al., 2016; Soares-Filho et al., 2014), in a process that revealed the tensions between agriculture, the environment and society itself. Although contested by environmentalists and farmers, this institutional milestone represents progress in relation to the previous framework and brings important mechanisms to regulate the tensions. First and foremost, it is a realistic piece of legislation that emphasizes which laws are applicable as well as defining effective monitoring and control mechanisms and implementing severe sanctions against transgressions. The code determines the preservation of permanent natural vegetation (PNV) and legal reserves in all rural private holdings, with the exception of small holdings with up to four tax modules. The preservation areas vary amongst the biomes: 20% in the Cerrado biome, 35% in the Cerrado in states comprising the Legal Amazon and 80% in the Amazon biome (Brancalion et al., 2016; Brasil, 2012b). Some studies indicate a reduction in the protected area in relation to the Forestry Code of 1965 (Silva et al., 2017; Soares-Filho et al., 2014); the opposing argument is that the previous code was never applied and was completely unrealistic 45 years after its approval. An open strain refers to financing recovery and the compensation for environmental services generated by private areas of conservation (Wang, Poe, and Wolf, 2017).[6]

One of the most important mechanisms for the enforcement of the code is the Rural Environmental Registry (CAR), which seeks to promote the integration of information, on each rural holding, regarding Permanent Preservation Areas (PPAs), Legal Reserves, native forest remnants and consolidated areas (Brasil, 2012b) (Box 1). The CAR is monitored by satellite images and a special unit was set up at Embrapa, called Embrapa Territorial, to monitor farmer compliance with the rules.

Box 1 The Rural Environmental Registry (CAR)

The CAR is a georeferenced record of information regarding the perimeter of rural properties, areas of social and public interest and environmental areas in accordance with the new Forestry Code. To assist in the execution of the CAR, the National System of Rural Environmental Registry, SICAR, was created (Brasil, 2012a).

The CAR newsletter, with general data updated up until March 31, 2018, indicated the registration of 4,915,221 rural properties, totalling 439 million hectares (MMA, 2018). The area of the Sustainable Use Conservation Unit, in which use by traditional populations is allowed, totalled 31 million hectares in 22,500 properties (MMA, 2018). An analysis carried out by Embrapa Territorial from SICAR data as of 2017 indicates that 177 million hectares would be destined to the preservation and maintenance of native vegetation in rural properties (Embrapa, 2018a) and the legal reserve area to be regularized is comprised of 162 million hectares in 3.8 million rural properties.

CAR data indicate that over 1.4 million rural properties need to restore four million hectares of PPA. These figures indicate that there is still an important environmental liability to be regularized. Finally, more than two million producers adhered to the Environmental Regularization Program (PRA), reaching an area of 256 million hectares (Brasil, 2018).

This new trajectory of Brazilian agriculture in the current context of climate change can contribute to increased sustainability in agriculture. The use of technologies based on ecological principles is increasing amongst farmers. These technologies have the potential to reconcile environmental pressures with the national commitments made with the world community regarding climate change and the need to foster agricultural production. The social and environmental demand should lead to the emergence of a new technological paradigm, comprising agriculture based on ecosystem services (Romeiro, 2014) or on the dynamics of ecosystems.

6 Conclusions

An analysis of historical events highlights the important contribution agriculture has made to the development of Brazilian society and economy. However, with it has come a significant environmental and social cost, whose reproduction is unacceptable and unfeasible in the context of the twenty-first century, marked by the challenge of global climate change. In a slow and contradictory process, under pressure from civil society and markets, the government, rural producers and leaders are quickly internalizing the environmental dimension in their decision-making structures. The results, however limited and somewhat contradictory, indicate the embryo of change towards more sustainable, greener agriculture.

Despite the advances in production and productivity, deforestation remains a central environmental problem and challenge in Brazil. Progress has been erratic, with reductions and increases in the pace of the rate of deforestation, according to a set of factors that seem to involve both market conditions and monitoring actions by the state. In addition, deforestation contributes to greenhouse gas emissions, damages the country's international image and may affect the business flow of the agrobusiness sector, one of the most dynamic sectors in the twenty-first century.

Despite the contradictory and ambiguous development of Brazilian agriculture, there has been noticeable progress in the environmental quality of productive systems, albeit still limited in terms of ensuring long-term sustainability. Finally, it is noteworthy that the challenges have been identified and much of the technical and institutional solutions have been put forth. What else, therefore, must Brazil do to promote the transition to sustainable, environmentally balanced and inclusive agriculture?

Notes

1   The creation of the Brazilian Agricultural Research Corporation (Embrapa) and the strengthening of the National Agricultural Research System were fundamental for the generation of technology specific to Brazilian conditions. In particular, the expansion to the Cerrado, a flat area with soil considered to be unfit for agriculture due to its acidity, was made possible by the tropicalization of the Green Revolution technology with the adoption of acidity correction techniques; the selection of varieties adapted to tropical conditions; nitrogen incorporation into the soil; minimum cultivation, among others.
2   Including herbaceous cotton, rice, coffee, sugarcane, beans, corn, soybean and wheat.
3   The Cerrado is known as the 'cradle' of water in Brazil.
4   The Decree no. 7.390/2010 forecasts the voluntary reduction assumed in the National Policy on Climate Change to vary from 1.17 billion tons of CO_2eq to 1.26 billion tons of CO_2eq by 2020, with the agricultural sector contributing with the reduction of 22.5% of these emissions (MAPA, 2018b).
5   The ABC plan has a specific credit line, the ABC Program of the Central Bank of Brazil (Motion no. 3.896/2010).
6   Some controversial points of the new Forestry Code include the reduction of the Permanent Preservation Area (PPA), a pardon for the producers who deforested land up to 22 July 2008 and compensation of legal reserves in other areas outside the property, among others (Brancalion et al., 2016).

9 Rural Brazil

A social and economic space without farmers?

Alexandre Gori Maia

1 Introduction

Until recently, the growth of Brazilian agriculture was centrally based on the sheer abundance and relative cheapness of labour and land. These historical trends allowed for a pattern of growth based on expanded cultivation and low growth in productivity. However, this was a pattern that underwent significant changes in recent times, driven simultaneously by demographic, social and economic factors. The rural population in Brazil is being sharply reduced, imposing serious constraints on agricultural production, especially among medium- and small-holder farmers who cannot easily replace labour by investments in technologies to boost productivity.

Studies in Brazil have investigated how endemic poverty and the highly concentrated structure of land ownership were key factors determining rural exodus in the country. But this is just one side of the history, because migrants usually tend also to act, at least partially, according to a subjective plan focused on an economic rationality, based on expectations of better wages and life opportunities in urban areas. As a result, out-migration in Brazil has been intense in both the more developed and in the less developed rural areas. These flows tend to be highly selective and are more restricted to the better educated women and youngest members of rural families.

Most rural migrants have moved to the larger metropolitan cities and a minority to the new borders of the agricultural frontier in the Northern and the Centre-West regions. Since the 1980s, however, recurrent economic crises have hampered the opportunities of employment and social mobility in the cities. In parallel, the process of technological advances in agriculture that took place in this period has reduced the total demand for low skilled workers in economically dynamic rural destinations and undermined the few opportunities of stability for small impoverished farmers through intensive competition.

Under such relevant socioeconomic constraints, important social policies have been implemented in an attempt to partly offset the high levels of rural poverty and social inequality among rural families. The Constitution of 1998 guaranteed a system of social protection that were gradually and under different approaches materialized in the 1990s and 2000s. The most visible cases are the rural pension system and various cash transfer programmes – most of them later embodied under *Bolsa Família*. It is a monthly stipend offered to poor families that varies according to the number of children in the family. These social policies have affected the demand for labour formerly offered by small farms, mainly because they have affected the labour supply of mothers and the elderly (Carvalho Filho, 2008; Mattos and Ponczek, 2009; Tavares, 2010). Demographic factors have gradually also undermined the pool of rural labour, mainly because fertility rate dropped sharply in both urban and rural areas. The total fertility rates started to fall dramatically in the 1970s, from a peak of 6.0 births per woman to a level below the replacement rate in less than three decades.

In this context, the objective of this chapter is to explore how this set of economic, social and demographic factors has reconfigured a 'new rural society' in Brazil, thus compromising the long-term perspectives of family farming, which is still labour intensive in the less developed rural areas. We also summarize the main determinants of the recent process of rural out-migration in Brazil.

2 The dynamics or rural out-migration

Despite conceptual difficulties and controversies to empirically designate the spaces and contours of rural and urban areas (Veiga, 2001), studies have highlighted *prima facie* the fast transition from a rural to an urban society in Brazil. The official estimates of the Brazilian Institute of Statistics and Geography (IBGE) indicate that the share of the rural population plummeted from 55% in 1960 to 32% in 1980 and to 15% in 2010 (IBGE, 2016). Martine et al. (1988) used a distinct delimitation of 'the urban', which considers only those municipalities with 20,000 inhabitants or more and indicated a similar trend between 1960 and 1980: from 67% to 48%. These percentages mean rural losses of 1.28 million per year during the 1960s and 1.56 million in the 1970s. In the 1980s, Perz (2000) pointed that almost 16 million people left rural areas to live in urban areas, which represent an annual loss of 1.6 million persons. These migratory tendencies continued at a slower pace in the 2000s. Maia and Buainain (2015) suggested that the number of rural residents reduced by more six million people between 1991 and 2010, although the number of rural households was kept almost constant.

In fact, according to the IBGE's official estimates, the total number of rural households remained close to 8 million between 1991 and 2010 (Table 9.1). But the average number of household members plummeted from 4.7 to 3.7, a reduction higher than 20% in two decades. In part, this fact can be attributed to lower fertility rates. But rural–urban migration also played an important role and the number of household members diminished at the same pace in all regions – one household member, on average, in the period. In other words, it means that the process of rural out-migration cannot be exclusively attributed to endemic poverty in most rural regions. The rural population is observing a swift reduction also in the more developed regions, particularly in the Southern and Southeast regions.

Table 9.1 Brazil and its macro regions – average members per rural private household

Year	1991			2000			2010		
	Rural Household (1,000s)	% (Rural + Urban)	People / Rural Household	Rural Household (1,000s)	% (Rural + Urban)	People / Rural Household	Rural Household (1,000s)	% (Rural + Urban)	People / Rural Household
Brazil	7,577	21.8	4.7	7,460	16.7	4.3	8,097	14.1	3.7
Northern	764	39.1	5.4	771	27.4	5.0	963	24.2	4.4
Northeast	3,355	37.2	5.0	3,259	28.6	4.5	3,723	24.9	3.8
Southeast	1,689	10.7	4.4	1,745	8.6	4.0	1,660	6.6	3.4
Southern	1,358	23.8	4.2	1,280	17.8	3.7	1,276	14.4	3.2
Center-West	411	18.3	4.3	406	12.9	3.8	475	11.0	3.3

Source: IBGE (2018a).

The transition from a rural to a predominantly urbanized country is not surprising and reproduces the process of spatial reconfiguration that took place in several societies and is recently being observed too in many developing countries, like China and Mexico (see, for example, Hare, 1999; Villarreal and Hamilton, 2012). But few countries in the world observed a transition so rapid in such a short period of time. For example, in Mexico, where socioeconomic development is similar to that of Brazil, the rural population decreased in a slower pace, even with the overwhelming outflow of rural migrants to the United States. According to official estimates provided by the World Bank (World Bank, 2017), the rural population in Mexico decreased from 49% in 1960 to 22% in 2010, which represents a reduction that is 13 percentage points lower than that observed in Brazil over the same five decades (from 55% to 15%). Still in the same period, the rural population of Argentina, where the process of agricultural growth is somewhat similar to that of Brazil, the shift has been even slower, from 26% to 9%.

In spite of such fast transition from a rural to an urban society, Brazil still maintains one of the largest rural populations in the world, almost 30 million people according to the IBGE (2016), a contingent that is larger than the total population of most Latin American countries. The flows of rural out-migrants lost strength slightly in the last decades due to several socioeconomic factors (to be discussed below), but the phenomenon of rural population movements is still meaningful in the country. According to Maia (2016), 2.3 million residents left their homes in rural areas to live in urban localities between 2005 and 2010, 600,000 less when compared to total figures of those leaving the countryside from 1986 and 1991. On average, roughly 500,000 rural residents left rural localities per year in the 2000s, against 600,000 in the 1980s.

3 Economic push and pull factors

Levels of extreme poverty associated with land concentration in rural areas have historically being pointed by several authors as the main determinant causing rural–urban migration in Brazil (Furtado, 1989). Levels of poverty have been reduced consistently in the last decades, a factor that may have contributed to attenuate the dynamics of rural migratory movements in Brazil. According to official estimates, the percentage of individuals technically considered to be poor in Brazil fell from 43% in 1976 to 13% in 2014[1] (IPEA, 2018). Despite these improvements, levels of poverty and extreme poverty are extremely high in Brazil as yet. The official estimates indicate that more than 16 million Brazilian lived in extreme poverty conditions in 2010 (with a monthly income lower than R$70, equivalent to US$40),[2] a group that comprises approximately 8.5% of the Brazilian population (IBGE, 2016). Rural poverty decreased consistently since the mid-1990s (Rocha, 2006), but the rates are nearly twice than those observed in urban areas (Helfand et al., 2009). In 2010, almost half of the social group under extreme poor conditions lived in rural areas, although the rural population was just 16% of the total (IBGE, 2016).

Poverty in rural areas, however, is not the sole cause of migration, because the gap of opportunities between origin and destination also matters. The traditional models of migration highlight how migrants are not only motivated by push factors related to the existing underdevelopment in their original localities, but also by pull factors related to the attractions of the localities of destination (Lee, 1966; Todaro, 1969). Rural out-migrants move to more dynamic urban centres in order to minimize their risks and to maximize household incomes. This natural process of choices made by migrants, as a general social behaviour that appears to be universal, implies that the differences between origin and destination are so important as the social conditions that prevail in the origin. And those asymmetries also explain why rural–urban migration continues as a permanent demographic process in more developed rural areas.

Among the main push factors related to the process of rural–urban migration in Brazil, we can highlight the precarious conditions of work and social assistance in rural areas, such as education and health services. Employment opportunities in rural areas are mostly in informal and low-paying activities. In addition, these opportunities demand low-skills and provide low social status (Maia, 2013). In turn, pull factors in urban destinations are related to higher paying jobs and easier access to a series of social services, such as education, health and nursery.

Under these historical facts, a social principle has been imposed over time: the largest the rural–urban gap, the largest scope and depth of rural–urban migration. Rural poverty has been particularly high in rural areas of the Northeast region, the less developed and the main net exporter of rural out-migrants in the country. Internal migratory cycles have historically been a way out of rural poverty in these areas. They are mainly destined to the larger metropolitan areas, notably São Paulo and Rio de Janeiro and to the new borders of agricultural expansion in the Northern and the Center-West regions (Cunha and Baeninger, 2001; Perz, 2000; Veiga, 2000). As a result, in face of the lack of proper national planning these spatial movements have created a semi-chaos in the biggest cities because of insufficient infrastructure and low quality of life (Martine et al., 1988).

The influx of rural migrants was mainly affected by profound economic changes witnessed in the 1980s, when the debt crisis introduced a long period of low and erratic growth. In those years, Brazil implemented a variety of economic reforms as a way to control hyperinflation, attract foreign investments and induce economic development. But ineffective or misguided implementation of these economic reforms resulted in unsatisfactory economic performance and additional difficulties to improve socioeconomic conditions (Maia and Menezes, 2014). The eventual success of economic stabilization only came with the *Plano Real* in 1994.

The largest industrialized urban centres were especially affected by the economic crises that hit the country in the 1980s and early-1990s, when unemployment reached 9% of the metropolitan labour force (IBGE, 2016). In parallel, a robust process of modernization took place in rural areas in the 1980s, reducing drastically the demand for rural workers in the Northern and Centre-West regions, the new frontiers of agricultural development (Mueller and Martine, 1997; Perz, 2000). In the 1990s, the Center-West, for example, experienced the formation of several highly productive farms. Later on, the process of agricultural expansion moved to the north, towards the Amazon region, where soya farming and cattle ranching are growing rapidly in its southern border, based on intense use of mechanization, large-scale farming and deforestation of the Amazon forest.

In the late-1990s, Brazil also witnessed a turnaround in its economic rate of growth, which also affected the internal migratory trends (Baeninger, 2012). Relevant consequences of this new economic moment in the late 1990s and the 2000s were the substantial increase in the average real levels of income and concomitant reductions in unemployment, inequality and poverty rates (Arbache, 2011). The poorest regions grew faster, benefited by the boom of agricultural commodities and several social policies targeting the poorest families. The Northeast region continues to be a net exporter of migrants, but a significant number of emigrants has returned to their original households. Lower levels of regional inequality, new opportunities of employment in smaller to medium towns, as well as high costs of living in larger metropolitan centres have contributed to these new migratory patterns (Oliveira and Jannuzzi, 2005).

But these same metropolitan areas, however, where better jobs may be found, continue to attract most of the rural out-migrants. The most emblematic case is São Paulo, the biggest city in the country (located in the Southeast) that has historically attracted the largest number of internal rural migrants in Brazil. Between 2005 and 2010, 88,000 rural migrants arrived in São Paulo city.[3] Goiânia, the main capital in the Centre-West region, at the heart of the new frontier of agricultural development, has also become an important destination of rural out-migrants; 46,000 between 2005 and 2010. Brasília, the federal district, comes next, with 42,000 rural migrants. The city was founded in 1960 and its population is still growing fast, attracted by one of the highest per capita incomes, sustained by the employment in the public sector. The capitals of the states of Minas Gerais (Belo Horizonte) and Rio de Janeiro (Rio de Janeiro) have lost the economic capacities of the past but are still important destinations of rural migrants: 32,000 arrived in Belo Horizonte between those years and 25,000 moved towards Rio de Janeiro.

Mainly as a result of demographic tendencies – reduced numbers of young rural residents (Maia and Sakamoto, 2016) – and also economic factors – lower regional indicators of inequality (Barros et al., 2007) – the percentage of rural out-migration decreased substantially between 1991 and 2010, from 13.4% to 9.0%, which means a reduction of almost 300,000 individuals. The dynamics of in-migration towards São Paulo and other state capitals, such as Curitiba (Paraná) and Belo Horizonte, helps to explain to a large extent this reduction. Only in São Paulo, the number of rural in-migrants was reduced by 47,000 in the period, which is 16% of the total net influx reduction in Brazil.

4 Demographic bonus and ageing

As a result of diminishing child mortality coupled with high fertility rates, the Brazilian population grew rapidly in the second half of the twentieth century, reaching 170 million in 2000. But the population boom was shorter than expected. The total fertility rate started to fall sharply in the 1970s, falling from 6.0 births per woman to below the replacement rate in less than three decades (Camarano, 2014). If the country observed a very favourable age structure in the 1990s, characterized by a prominent share of the working age population, in the 2000s the proportion of elderly started growing faster than expected, thus imposing serious constraints to the continuity of economic growth and forcing a change in many social policies.

Most commonly, in a first moment, demographic changes tend to occur more intensively among the richest and urban families (Maia and Sakamoto, 2016). In later stages, these demographic changes tend to spread throughout the social fabric. In 1970, the average number of live births per adult women was 3.1 larger in rural than in urban areas (7.7 in rural areas and 4.6 in urban areas). This meant a bigger supply of rural labour force in the sequential adult generations. But the demographic change affected rural areas more intensively in the 1980s and 1990s. In 2010, the fertility rate in rural areas was almost similar to that of urban areas (2.5 in rural areas and 1.8 in urban areas). As a result, from now on spatial movements in small number of rural dwellers to urban areas will make much more difference.

A particular consequence of the drop of fertility rates is the population ageing. The proportion of children between zero and 14 years fell from 38% to 25% between 1981 and 2011 (Maia and Sakamoto, 2016). At the same time, the share of persons with 60 years or older rose from 6% to 10% out of the total population. The ageing population tends to generate more challenging impacts in rural areas, where fertility rates diminish faster and the young members tend to move to urban areas. A main consequence in the middle term hits the reproduction of the labour force. In the 1980s, there were almost two young children (between zero and 14 years) to substitute each aged adult (between 25 and 49) in the labour force. In the 2010s, this relation was just only one per one. In other words, if labour productivity does not increase dramatically, Brazil will be condemned to observe stagnant economic growth in the next decades. Productivity has grown steadily in agriculture, but not in the same pace among most rural families (Almeida et al., 2008). Medium and small farms tend to be the main affected ones in middle term by demographic changes.

Maia and Sakamoto (2016) also highlighted other crucial facets of this fast demographic change in Brazil. The sharp drop in the proportion of couples with children and the parallel rise observed among couples without children, apart from single-headed families, in both rural and urban areas, are mostly indicative of a significant decline in fertility rates and of an ageing population. The higher proportion of families headed by older adults is remarkable; they are more likely to live alone or as couples without children. The conventional (average) rural family, which in 1991 was characterized by a couple with two children, nowadays is characterized by a couple of adults of elderly with only a child in school age (Maia and Buainain, 2015). Based on the trends observed in the last decades, this young child will probably attain a secondary school diploma and migrate to an urban area.

5 Institutions and social policies

Important social policies implemented in recent decades in rural areas may have also affected the demographic pattern of the rural population. Pressed by public opinion and landless organized movements, the Brazilian government was impelled to implement several land reform programmes in the 1990s and 2000s (Graziano Neto and Navarro, 2015). In the whole period, the country had one of the largest land reform programmes of the world, with approximately one million families settled in more than 9,000 projects allocated on 88 million hectares (INCRA, 2015). In addition to impoverished rural families, the reform benefited also many former rural out-migrants who had been living in urban areas for some while under poverty conditions (Graziano Neto and Navarro, 2015).

Although some land reform projects achieved socioeconomic improvements (Heredia et al., 2002), they were mostly ineffective in attenuating the high levels of inequality in the distribution of land, production results and access to technology (Graziano Neto, 2016). According to the Agricultural Census 2006, only 500,000 farms (11.4% of the total 4.4 million) were responsible for 86.6% of the total value of agricultural production, while other 2.9 million (66% of the total) accounted for only 3.3% of the total value (Buainain et al., 2014, p. 927). The current structure of agricultural production, based on a strong specialization and concentration of production in the most modernized regions, has employed relatively less workers and has shown to be scarcely social-inclusive, causing strong asymmetries in rural areas (Buainain et al., 2014, p. 623; Mueller and Martine, 1997).

Small farmers nowadays face enormous difficulties to compete with the highly productive large farms of the Southern and Center-West regions. The productivity gains of the Brazilian agriculture reduced the relative prices of agricultural products and the value added by unit of production (Navarro and Campos, 2013). As a result of technological changes, the actual management of farms is increasingly demanding a complex set of abilities and the operation of technologies that are hardly attained by most farmers. The cost of labour also raised, driven by the rise in real terms of the minimum wage and the lower supply of unskilled labour force in rural areas (Sakamoto and Maia, 2012). Most small farmers cannot afford to hire a permanent worker and the supply of family labour is reducing sharply.

Important social policies have also been implemented to partly offset the high levels of rural poverty and social inequality in Brazil, which might have indirectly affected the likelihood of migration. The *Programa Bolsa Família* (PBF) is one the largest cash transfer programmes in the world and has provided a small provision of income for more than 11 million families living in extreme poverty (Soares et al., 2016). In 2010, the criteria for eligibility to the PBF were:[4] (i) per capita income lower than R$70 per month (equivalent nowadays to US$40); or (ii) per capita income lower than R$140 (US$80) and at least one child 17 years or younger enrolled in school (which is a conditionality). The benefit is paid primarily to the mother and the value varies between R$68 (US$38) to R$ 126 (US$74), depending on the number of children in the family.

The Constitution of 1988 also guaranteed a non-contributory pension for all rural workers aged 65 years or more, or 60 years for women (Oliveira et al., 1997). Demographic changes and a more relaxed criterion to be eligible for a rural pension skyrocketed the number of beneficiaries. In the early 2000s, nearly four million Brazilians received a rural pension and the average income of their families was almost twice as high as that of non-beneficiaries (Beltrão et al., 2005). The benefit of a rural pension corresponds to the federal minimum wage, which was R$510 per month in 2010 (approximately US$280 dollars). This is a reasonable amount of money for most rural families, especially for those living in the poorest areas (Maia, 2010).

The impacts of social policies on rural migration are not well known. In some extent, one can expect that a lower deprivation of income in poorer households can stimulate the migration of young members, as a strategy to produce more sources of income and reduce risk. In developing countries, offering cash to poor households has shown to encourage geographical movements in order to raise income, largely because men are able to work more hours each day (Bryan et al., 2014). On the other hand, cash transfers and rural pensions have played an important role reducing poverty in rural areas.

6 The selectivity of rural migration

There is a growing concern in the literature about migratory issues on the positive selectivity of migrants, meaning decisions by the highly skilled individuals who have a greater propensity to migrate. Traditional models of migration assume that migrants will be positively selected when they respond to pull factors and this means that they are especially attracted by better opportunities of employment and quality of life in receiving localities (Lee, 1966).

Unsurprisingly, the young rural members are more likely to migrate to urban areas in search of better employment and income opportunities. For example, according to Maia and Buainain (2015), only 60% of the rural population aged 16 years in 2000 were still living in rural areas in 2010. But the flow of rural migrants ceases in the strata from 40 and 50 years and higher levels of age. This is so because rural workers stabilize in his agricultural activity after this age (whatever its economic situation) and actually lose the stimulus to migrate to the urban areas. But this behaviour also occurs because most of them are convinced about the immense difficulties of finding employment in urban areas after a certain age in life.

A direct consequence of the selective abandonment by young people is the changing ageing of the rural population. In rural areas, the young population aged 17 years or less decreased from 16.8 million in 1991 to 10.4 million in 2010; the adult population (defined as those aged 18 to 64 years) stopped growing (close to 17 million in the three decades); and the elderly population (65 years or more) grew slightly – from 1.6 million in 1991 to 2.2 million in 2010 (Maia and Buainain, 2015). In urban areas, the ageing process was less intense, as the adult population still grew at an accelerated rate. Although this pattern means a lower dependence ratio of school-age youth in the short term, could mean the commitment of the process of succession of the family farming in Brazil over the long term.

Rural women are more likely to move to urban areas. In most rural social spaces, the male population is higher than the female population for all age groups. On average, there were 1,101 men for every 1,000 women in rural areas in 2010 (Maia and Buainain, 2015). Several factors help us to explain this process of masculinization of the rural population. First, the changes observed in agricultural activities, such as the intensive use of technology and wage labour. In addition to reducing labour requirements, these changes favoured the hiring of permanent or temporary male labour, contributing to increase gender segregation in agricultural activities.

Second, the permanent lack of infrastructure and social services in rural areas, which makes harder for young women to live and work. These difficulties are rooted in the socially established prejudice prevailing in the country that attributes to women a series of domestic responsibilities, such as caring for children, elderly and domestic activities. Women are also more likely than men to search for health assistance, which is precarious and almost absent in rural areas (Arruda et al., 2018).

Third, we can also consider the cultural tradition of inheritance among rural family farms, which usually excludes women from the potential inheritance of property and, ultimately, land. This social practice, in fact, is illegal but customs and various cultural arrangements eventually block fair and equal access to women when succession comes to the table and those in charge must take decisions about inheritance. With little prospect of establishing themselves professionally within the family production unit, many young women leave the rural residence in search of better economic opportunities in the cities.

Finally, we must also to consider that women reach higher levels of education than men in Brazil. While many rural men are often forced to drop out of school to engage in the farming activities, especially in the most impoverished areas, women attain higher levels of education and are more likely to migrate and obtain a job in the service sector of urban areas.

7 Conclusions

The IBGE shows that roughly 30 million persons were still living in rural areas in the 2010s. But few studies in Brazil have carefully analysed the challenges and prospects of low density, remote and natural-resource dependent rural communities. Independently of how is conceptualized rural localities, the fact is that the total rural population is reducing sharply as a result of declining fertility rates and a persistent and still relevant process of rural–urban migration in Brazil.

Social policies targeted to the poorest rural families have played important role reducing extreme poverty in the countryside. But rural residents continue to leave rural areas. First, because family farming activities that are still strongly labour-intensive face serious difficulties in a competitive and dynamic agricultural sector that emerged in Brazil. Second, because metropolitan and urban areas in the country exert strong attraction to rural out-migrants. The youngest and more skilled rural residents are attracted by better opportunities in the labour market and in social life in general, such as an easier access to health assistance and education for their children in urban areas.

Overall, the agricultural production in the country has not been remarkably affected by demographic changes in rural areas, because a modern sector has effectively adapted to the use of new technologies. Nonetheless, the demographic dynamics in rural areas impose serious doubts about the sustainability of small family farming in the long run, especially for those located in the poorest regions of the country. Since such demographic tendencies will probably persist in the short and middle run, more effective policies are needed to attenuate the impacts of an imminent 'agriculture without farmers' in the country. First, by implementing effective strategies that could increase labour productivity among family farmers in a context of short supply of labour force. Second, by providing better education and technical skills for young rural residents, who can deliberately choose between either staying or leaving the rural to search for a better life in urban areas.

Notes

1 The poverty line considered by IPEA is twice the value of the extreme poverty, which is the value to attain a basket of food containing the minimum amount of calories recommended by the Food and Agriculture Organization and the World Health Organization (IPEA, 2018).
2 Considering an exchange rate of 1.8 R$/US$ from July 1st 2010.
3 This number does not take account of the population of urban migrants that arrive in even larger absolute number than rural migrants.
4 Considering an exchange rate of 1.8 R$/US$ from 1 July 2010.

10 Employment and forms of occupation in rural Brazil

From minifundio-latifundio to regulated rural labour market

Junior Ruiz Garcia and Alexandre Gori Maia

1 Introduction

In association with the productive innovations and technological tendencies discussed in the other chapters of this book, the rural labour relations and rural labour market have also undergone profound transformations since the early 1990s. These changes are mainly associated with the modernization of agricultural production as well as with the progressive enforcement of Constitutional rights and labour legislation.

Rural labour institutional framework is quite recent in Brazil. Just as an example, the first labour legislation for the sector was only enacted by the military regime in the 1970s (Brazilian Law 5,889 signed in 1973). It was a limited set of legal imperatives which was only changed by the Constitution of 1988, which extended labour rights to all irrespective to the sector. While the extension of general labour laws to all without considering the specificities of rural labour relations may have corrected an unacceptable negative discrimination against the rural population in general terms, it also introduced distortions which have accelerated the changes in rural labour markets. In particular, it has increased the costs of transaction of rural employment and it has significantly incentivized mechanization and the consequent reduction of rural workers hired by non-family farming.

Brazilian agricultural production has grown consistently (IBGE, 2018a), mainly as a result of productivity gains (Arias et al., 2017; Gasques et al., 2018; USDA, 2018b). This performance is a result of deep changes in agricultural production related to intensification of mechanization, expansion of agrochemicals and biotechnology, expansion of land use and crop substitution. On the other hand, structural constraints have been brought to light, such as the inappropriate regulatory framework regarding rural labour relations, environmental issues, use of agrochemicals and even trade. The intensification and concentration of agricultural production have ignited an intense process of social selection among farmers and deepened social inequalities in the rural labour market (Alves and Rocha, 2010). According to Alves et al. (2012), almost 90% of the total value added in the Brazilian agricultural production originated from roughly 10% of the most productive farms, after evidence collected by the 2006 Census.

Since the 1970s, the number of farms has remained around five million, but the number of farming workers has persistently declined (IBGE, 2018a). Despite this fact, the harvested area of temporary crops almost doubled between the 1970s and the 2010s (IBGE, 2018a) and production systems have radically changed in terms of technology adoption and management.

According to Maia and Menezes (2014), agriculture has been the only sector in Brazil presenting consistent increases in labour productivity: the value added per hour of labour almost double between 1981 and 2009, from 2.5 to 4.8 US$/hour. Nonetheless, the value added of agricultural activities is still, on average, very low in Brazil: almost seven times lower than in the United States. The country has been experiencing huge levels of regional inequality and the agricultural sector presents a substantial capacity of technological absorption in its less developed areas.

These recent transformations of the agricultural production brought a set of structural changes to the rural labour market. The sector was predominantly informal until the 1990s. The number of formal employees surpassed the number of informal employees for the first time in the 2000s (Maia and Sakamoto, 2014). Nonetheless, the largest share of rural workers are yet self-employed farmers, unpaid workers or farmers producing for the self-subsistence. The rural labour market is also characterized by huge heterogeneities. While formal employees linked to the modern value chains have benefited from a set of institutional rights guaranteed by the labour legislation, the country has yet more than three million families engaged in subsistence activities (Buainain and Dedecca, 2008).

In general, the agriculture in Brazil underwent profound technological and social transformations in the last decades. Modern capitalist labour relations are increasingly common in high-tech agriculture, but still restricted to the most developed southern states or expanding in most regions of the Centre-West. Meanwhile, persistent forms of low-skilled and informal occupations remain associated with small family production in the Northern and Northeast regions (Buainain and Garcia, 2015). As a general trend, the number of farming occupations have consistently diminished.

This chapter discusses some of the main reasons and implications of changes in the rural labour market in Brazil. In addition to present a brief overview of the Brazilian rural labour market in the 2000s, the chapter analyses the main institutional changes that has been occurring in this market.

2 The changes in the occupation in rural sector: from abundance to scarcity

Agriculture has played an important role in the Brazilian economy and society, especially in terms of economic development, employment and income generation. It has also functioned as a regulation valve for rural exodus, expelling people to urban areas and providing alternatives for rural occupation in the frontier areas with varying intensity in different periods. (Buainain and

Garcia, 2015). Conversely, the Brazilian agriculture sector presents high levels of inequality amongst regions, types of producers and production systems. While some productive systems are linked to the most modern value chains, most holdings still present low technical efficiency, mainly as a result of poor management practices and lack of technologies (Alves et al., 2012; Buainain and Garcia, 2015). The heterogeneity in the Brazilian agriculture also impacts on the rural labour market, which presents remarkable asymmetries in terms of employment opportunities and wages.

The modernization process, based in the introduction of the 'green revolution' package, has contributed to important structural changes in the rural labour market (Müller, 1989; Pingali, 2012). The process accelerated from the 1960s onwards and brought changes in the methods of production and management practices which intensified the transition from an agriculture with low total factor productivity (TFP), based on the intensive use of low skilled labourers, to a highly efficient agriculture, strongly supported by workers with special skills to operate machineries and the manipulate genetically improved seeds (Müller, 1989). However, this process has been mainly restricted to some activities in the most developed regions: Southeast, Southern and Centre-West.

The technological modernization had also important impacts on the demand for labour. In the cotton harvesting, for example, each machine replaces between 80 and 150 workers; in the coffee production, it can replace up to 160 people; in sugarcane and beans between 100 and 120 people (Balsadi et al., 2002). On the one hand, such substitution of labour per machines reduces the opportunities of employment for the low skilled rural migrants from the less developed regions of the country. On the other hand, agriculture production in Brazil has been able to grow consistently without the threats imposed by the declining rural population.

Despite remarkable growth in the agricultural production, the number of people employed in farms declined slightly: from 17.5 million in 1970 to 15 million in 2017 (IBGE, 2018a). In the same period, the ratio of area of agriculture and livestock per employed persons rose from 16.7 hectares per person to 23.3 hectares. In addition, the number of tractors increased from 165,900 in 1970 to 734,000 in 2017, changing the ratio of one tractor by 1,773 to 477 hectares (IBGE, 2018a, 2006b). According to Gasques et al. (2018), between 1975 and 2016, the TFP grew by 226% (3.1% per year) and the labour productivity grew by 346% (3.79% per year). The new productive structure has required new professions skills, creating new opportunities of employment in rural areas that were initially restricted to the urban economy, such as mechanics and technicians.

Technological changes brought new pressures to the Brazilian rural labour market, which was not yet prepared to respond to this sharp development. In addition to the absolute shortage of labour, most of the workers who remained in the sector lacked basic skills to meet the new production criteria. The intensive use of technology, in terms of both mechanization and decision-making capacity, requires qualification and autonomy. In the modern agriculture, rural workers must act as both operators of machineries and managers of the production systems.

Changes implemented in the agricultural policy in the 1990s had also direct impacts on production and labour market. Farmers were subjected to more intense international competition, characterized by the high subsidies of the developed countries. Some farmers successfully adapted to the new scenario, introducing modern management tools and concepts, intensifying mechanization and increasing total productivity. Others, mainly family farmers in the poorest regions, lagged behind in this dynamic process of innovation. Some of them migrated to urban areas, while others remained confined producing mainly for self-subsistence.

In parallel to significative increase in agricultural labour productivity, the rural population is declining sharply. In this respect, the perception of abundant supply of rural workers in Brazil was no longer valid in the 2000s. The false perception of unlimited supply has been to some extend influenced by the huge heterogeneity of the Brazilian agriculture. Basically 50% of the rural labour force in the country is concentrated in the poorest Northeast region, where labour-intensive production for self-subsistence is still prevailing over the capital-intensive agricultural production. However, the demographic dynamics observed in the recent period has significantly changed the availability of rural labour force. The main factors were discussed in the Chapter 9, such as declining fertility rate and migration in rural areas.

The perception of abundance of rural labour force has also been influenced by changes in the relative synchronization of productive cycles. Due to increasing seasonality of the modern agriculture, the demand for labour is not constant over time. The flow of seasonal workers is still high, centred basically on the NE-CO-SE axis (Northeast-Central-West-Southeast). And, until recently, there was no social protection system in the country to guarantee the survival of these workers in the off season (Buainain et al., 2014). Moreover, as a result of seasonality, many rural workers remained unemployed during certain periods of the agricultural calendar. The recent extension of urban legislation to the rural sector has still been deficient, not yet fully adapted to the characteristics of the agricultural sector. While it provides protection for those employed, it introduced clear incentives to mechanization and to the reduction in demand for seasonal labour.

3 The dynamics of employment and wages in agriculture

Figure 10.1 shows that, in general, the number of Brazilian farms has remained constant during the past 50 years in Brazil. However, two relevant points must be considered. First, between 1985 and 1995, the number of farms in Brazil reduced by almost 1 million. One of the reasons to explain the sharp decline in number of farms in the 1990s is agriculture productivity, which has grown consistently in Brazil since the second half of the 1980s (Gasques et al., 2018). Second, the number of farms has grown more consistently in the Southeast,

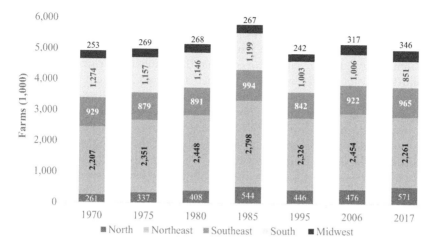

Figure 10.1 Number of farms in Brazil according to geographical region.

Centre-West and Northern regions, the frontier zones. Between 1995 and 2017 the number of farms increased by more 350,000 in the Southeast, Centre-West and Northern regions. In Southeast and Centre-West regions, agriculture is characterized by the adoption of high levels of technology and the production of high value-added crops, such as soy, corn and sugarcane. In the Northern region, modern agriculture has advanced mainly in the borders of the Amazon rainforest. Conversely, the number of farms has reduced in the most traditional regions of family farming, Southern and Northeast regions. The number of farms reduced by almost 220,000 in these regions between 1995 and 2017.

Despite small changes in the regional distribution of farmers in Brazil, there are no remarkable structural changes in the composition of small and large farms. For example, the number of small farms with less than 10 ha fluctuated between 2.4 million in 1995 (50%) and 3.1 million in 1985 (53%) (IBGE, 2006b). The number of large farms with more than 1,000 ha increased slightly from 37,000 in 1970 (0.75%) to 51,000 in 2017 (1%). The Northeast region concentrates the largest share of small farms with less than 10 ha (1.5 million, or 59%) (IBGE, 2018c). Despite the public efforts to promote land settlements in Northeast region, the number of small farmers reduced by more than 60,000 between 1995 and 2017. This negative trend is probably linked to the outflow of rural migrants: the region is the main net exporter of rural migrants in Brazil.

The number of small farms is also falling in the Southern region, from 380,000 in 1995 to 340,000 in 2017. This region presents one of the best indicators of human development in the country and has also been historically linked to small family farming. In this sense, the reduction in the number of small farms cannot merely be attributed to rural poverty, because it is happening simultaneously in the least and most developed regions of family farm in Brazil.

The reduction seems to be more a general trend linked to the dynamics of agriculture in Brazil. The fact is that many young farmers from the Southern region may have migrated to nearby urban areas or to Centre- West or Northern regions where they have access to more land and can practice modern agriculture in medium and large farms. For example, the number of farms between 10 ha and 100 ha increased by 120,000 between 1995 and 2017 and the number of farms with more than 1,000 ha increased by 3,000 (IBGE, 2018c, 2006b).

One main consequence of the tenuous increase in the share of large farms is an expected growing inequality in the distribution of land in Brazil. One easy way to analyze this trend is through the share of the total area accrued by the small (10 ha or less) and large farms (1,000 ha or more). The overall trend has been a growing asymmetry in the distribution of land between small and large farms. The share of the total area accrued by small farms reduced slightly from 3.1% in 1970 to 2.3% in 2017, while the share accrued by large farms increased from 39.5% to 47.5% in the same period (IBGE, 2018c, 2006b). The share of the total area accrued by intermediate groups of land size also reduced slightly: from 20.4% to 18.2% among farms with 10–100 ha and from 37.0% to 32% among farms with 100–1,000 ha. But this does not mean large farms are advancing over former small and middle farms. There is no information to back up such affirmation. The most likely scenario is that large farms are advancing over new areas of the territory, especially because the number of small and middle farms has remained practically constant for the last 40 decades (IBGE, 2018c).

In fact, the growing inequality in the distribution of land is exclusively related to the dynamics in the Centre-West region, the new frontier of agricultural development. In this region, the share of land accrued by the large farms grew dramatically between the 1970s and 1980s. Since then it remained mainly constant, close to 70%. In the most consolidated agriculture areas, Northeast, Southern and Southeast regions, the share of land accrued by the large farms remained close to 30% since the 1970s. In turn, the inequality in the distribution of land reduced remarkably in the Northern region between the 1970s and the 1980s, period that coincides with the largest inflows of migrants in this region. Since then, the share of land accrued by the large farms remained practically constant, close to 50%.

One consequence of productivity gains in agriculture is that the number of farm workers will decline if the total agricultural production does not grow enough to compensate for the substitution of jobs per technology. In fact, the number of farm workers reached a peak in 1985, 23.4 million workers (IBGE, 2018b), when labour productivity started growing more consistently (Gasques et al., 2018). Since then, the number of workers has declined continuously, reaching 15 million people in 2017 (see Figure 10.2) (IBGE, 2018a).

But this does not mean that growing labour productivity is expelling traditional farming workers from rural areas. Relation does not necessarily mean causation. The supply of rural workers has reduced consistently in the most traditional areas of agriculture in Brazil since the 1960s. First, because of a

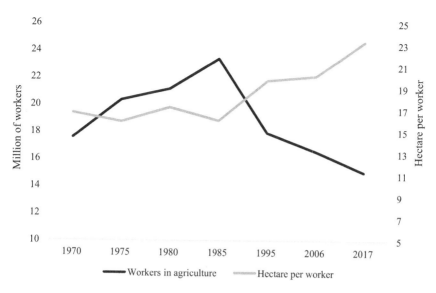

Figure 10.2 Evolution of workers in the Brazilian agricultural activity between 1970 and 2017.

persistent rural exodus, which has reduced slowly over the last decades, but it is still meaningful. Second as a result of a sharp decline in the fertility rate in rural areas since the 1980s. The problem is that demand for labour in the frontier areas, occupied basically by large holdings, using large-scale production systems, is not enough to absorb rural workers which cannot find occupation in the most traditional rural areas. But these are parallel phenomena, rather than one as a consequence of other. On the one hand, the number of small farms that are not able to produce in an increasingly competitive market is growing. These holding are freeing family labour from the obligations to stay and help the parents in the family holdings. On the other hand, the attraction exerted by better employment and income opportunities in urban centres is increasing, especially amongst the young population, including in the most developed rural regions where the youth have better education opportunities.

The most remarkable change in the farm occupational structure is the growing number of formal employees (Maia and Sakamoto, 2014): 1.1 million in 1992 (6%) to 1.4 million in 2012 (11%). In other words, the share of formal employees almost doubled in two decades. Nonetheless, the farm occupational structure in Brazil is yet largely characterized by the self-employment and self-subsistence production: 28% of self-employed farmers, 11% of unpaid workers and 27% of workers in the production for self-subsistence in 2012.

The wage structure has also undergone important changes over the last decades. Some important factors to understand the dynamics of wages in agriculture are: i) the steady valuation of the minimum wage, the reference for the remuneration of the majority of the agricultural jobs; ii) changes in the structure of occupations, especially the increasing participation of formal jobs in agriculture, discussed above; iii) the growth of labour productivity, especially in the regions where the modern agriculture is more present. The impacts are different amongst the regions, depending, among other factors, on the composition of the occupational structure (participation of employees, for example), the stage of agricultural development and the level of socioeconomic development of the rural areas.

The valuation of the minimum wage has played an important role in the dynamics of the average wages among low skilled occupational groups in Brazil. The value of the minimum wage almost doubled between the 1990s and the 2010s. And the labour legislation in Brazil requires that any employee with a formal job must receive at least a minimum wage. Informality in agriculture is still very high but has declined remarkably in the last decades. In 2012, informal employees represented 18% of the total rural workers (including employers, self-employed and unpaid family workers) and 59% of the total number of employees (only among formal and informal employees) (Maia and Sakamoto, 2014). In 1992, these numbers were respectively 20% and 75%. As a result of the declining informality in agriculture and the increasing minimum wage rate, average wages in rural areas have increased. Although it has happened at the cost of increasing wage gaps between formal and informal employees.

The substantial gains of productivity in agriculture should also be considered, since the relation between wages and productivity is unquestionable in the long term. A fair proxy to analyze productivity in agriculture is the average crop yield, which can be given by the total production per harvested area. The average yields of the main commodities have grown remarkably since the 1970s (FAOSTAT, 2018). The most noticeable cases are the productions of corn, soybean and sugarcane, which grew roughly 4 times between 1970 and 2017 (FAOSTAT, 2018) (see Chapter 4, Table 4.1). These are the main crops of modern agriculture in the South, Southeast and Centre-West regions.

These improvements are largely concentrated in few crops and groups of farmers. On the one hand, there are substantial gains of productivity in those crops practiced using high levels of technology in the most developed areas of agricultural production. On the other hand, a stagnation of the productivity is verified in the main crops practiced by family farming in the less developed areas of agricultural production. These parallel phenomena will undoubtedly result in a deeper gap of revenue and wages between these two groups of famers.

Finally, it should also be emphasized the persistence of huge inequalities between the agricultural and non-agricultural activities. In 2014, the average income of all farm jobs was only R$884 (US$375 – average exchange rate in 2014), equivalent to 51% of the national average, estimated at R$1,737 (US$738) (Ipeadata, 2018). Labour income is a great stimulus for the displacement of rural residents towards urban areas, whose objective is to obtain better income and public services. This panorama reinforces the persistent downward trend of the rural population.

4 Institutional changes in the rural labour market

The Brazilian government practically ignored the agricultural labour market during most of the twentieth century (Buainain and Dedecca, 2008). The focus was in the process of industrialization taking place in the country and the emergence of a new blue-collar middle class in urban areas. The informality and lack of social benefits remained as common characteristics of the rural labour force for several decades. But the quality of jobs in agriculture improved substantially in the 2000s, mainly as a result of the growth triggered by the commodity boom and the expansion of social benefits guaranteed by the Constitution of 1988.

The Constitution of 1988 equalized the rights between urban and rural workers. Although this equality is yet hardly verified, the impacts on the agricultural labour market were noticeable. The Constitution brought innovations in terms of social rights, such as the formalization of rural work, with emphasis on the institutionalization of night-time supplementation, limitations on housing and food discounts in rural property, social security, unemployment insurance, public health system, maternity leave and paternity (Krein and Stravinsk, 2008). However, the full implementation of these regulation in the rural labour market is still challenging. Especially because the rural labour market presents some important peculiarities that are not observed in the urban economy.

The labour legislation tried to consider, as far as possible, the inherent aspects of the agricultural sector. For example, the nocturnal supplement is 25% in the rural area for activities carried out between 9 pm to 5 am in the crop and from 8 pm to 4 am in the cattle raising, superior to the urban area, which is 20%, where the period comprises the work performed from 10 pm to 5 am. But the implementation of agricultural labour relations became a source of growing conflicts, associated with the inadequacy and/or imprecision of legal terms, which ultimately translate into high transaction costs and perhaps stimulating the introduction of labour saving innovations. Not to mention behaviours that are at the limit of legality, bringing to the surface situations of insecurity and imposing heavy burden for the rural worker.

Other important bottleneck to fully implement the labour legislation in the rural labour force is the large number of unpaid and seasonal (temporary) workers. Temporary jobs remain present in the sector, even in highly capitalized segments, because mechanization cannot replace labour in all stages of production. In addition, the low level of organization of unskilled temporary workers reduces the bargaining power of this group, undermining the perspectives of wage gains. The labour relations originally developed for the urban labour force have gradually been extended to rural workers. But this new institutional context puts a series of restrictions on the usual practices of temporary work. As a result, new contracting modalities have been adopted in the sector, such as labour cooperatives and professional associations (Staduto et al., 2004).

Labour cooperatives have been used by rural workers to increase their bargaining power in the negotiations and to improve remuneration and working conditions. Cooperatives have also contributed to alleviate the conflicts between workers and employers, ensuring labour rights and better remuneration. Cooperatives also contribute to the reduction of transaction costs by facilitating hiring for the employer. This modality of contracting has been used by many orange producers in the state of São Paulo (Alves and Almeida, 2000), as well as in the sugarcane and coffee productions. However, due to the frauds verified by the Public Prosecutor's Office in the creation and contracting of cooperatives, enforcement actions have reduced the use of this modality of hiring temporary work in agriculture (Staduto et al., 2004).

In recent years, the Labour Court and the Public Prosecutor's Office in Brazil have played important roles in guaranteeing the basic rights of rural workers, since non-compliance with the labour legislation is still very high. The inspections carried out by these institutions have focused on cases of informality, child and even slave labour. For example, between 2003 and 2013, the Labour Ministry operations to curb slave labour in the country surveyed 2,800 farms, redeploying 39,500 workers and paying R$79.5 million (US$36.8 million) in workers' compensation (MTE, 2018).

There are still many shortcomings and precariousness in labour relations in the rural labour market in Brazil, but the institutional progresses carried out by the Constitution of 1988 have significantly altered the issues discussed in this chapter. The set of actions and changes in progress may contribute to ensuring the supply of labour in agriculture, even changing the geography of the rural labour market in the country.

5 Conclusions

In this chapter the main changes that affected the agricultural production and rural labour market in Brazil has been analysed. First, it was highlighted that the premise of the abundant and unlimited supply of rural labour force is no longer valid since the beginning of the 2000s. Part of the reduction of the rural labour force can be attributed to demographic dynamics, such as reduction in fertility rate and rural exodus. However, institutional and technological changes have also played important roles. The adoption of modern technologies largely reduced the demand for labour in agriculture activities in the most developed regions of the country while the development of the urban labour market has raised the opportunity costs of staying in the rural areas.

Changes in the rural labour market were not homogenous among the regions or social groups. Although the number of farm workers has declined in the whole country, the number of farms has grown more consistently in the regions where (i) agriculture is characterized by the adoption of high levels of technology and the production of high value-added crops (Southeast and Centre-West) and (ii) modern agriculture has progressed (Northern and Northeast), mainly in the borders of the Amazon rainforest and Northeastern Cerrados. In parallel, the number of small farms has reduced more remarkably in the Northeast and Southern regions.

A remarkable change in the rural labour market is the improvement of the Brazilian social protection mechanisms, especially the formalization of the agricultural work. One main benefit is that workers subjected to formal relations and protected by the labour legislation had substantial improvements in the average wages. One second benefit is that all rural workers have now access to the social security system, independent of the contribution made to the system. Nonetheless, there are still many shortcomings in terms of labour relations in the rural labour market to be overcome in Brazil. For example, the asymmetry of benefits guaranteed by the labour legislation, which does not reach a substantial share of informal and self-employed small farmers.

11 The fate of family farming under the new pattern of agrarian development in Brazil

Carlos Guanziroli, Antônio Márcio Buainain,
Gabriela Benatti and Vahid Shaikhzadeh Vahdat

1 Introduction

The overall transformations explored by this book exerted direct or indirect influence on the various producers that conform the Brazilian agriculture. This chapter dedicates special attention to the influence of these transformations on the so-called family farmers. This heterogeneous group, formed mainly by small producers largely marginalized by the modernization process of the Brazilian agriculture, conquered their own status in the 1990s, when it became a beneficiary of public policies aimed at integrating them into the markets and the value chains of agribusiness. These efforts resulted in important advances, however, many of the structural challenges persist.

The debate that involves the issue of family farming is extensive and multi-disciplinary, starting with the conceptual question itself. Some theoretical approaches prioritize economic aspects related to the way that family units deal with the factors of production, land, work and capital, discussing their economic significance and productive contribution.

On the other hand, there are approaches that maintain economic issues as a background, highlighting the cultural, political and identity aspects that characterize this social group. In addition, several approaches express the importance of this activity from the standpoint of socioeconomic development and different proposals are presented to overcome the challenges (such as access to public policies, technical assistance, technologies, markets, income generation, etc.). This chapter will not have these discussions as the central axis but will focus on the explanation of this group of producers' internal diversity and the transformations that they have undergone in Brazil.

2 An agrarian structure and a polarized debate

The agrarian structure in Brazil is historically characterized by a high concentration of land ownership and intense social inequalities. Despite the implementation of an agrarian reform programme, which between 1980 and 2016 distributed 89,847 million hectares (ha) to 1,348,484 settlers (INCRA, 2016, 2017), the land concentration has been maintained over the last decades (see

Chapter 13). The Gini index, that measures inequality in land distribution, shows that the process of land concentration in Brazil did not recede over time: in 1985, the Gini was 0.858, going to 0.857 in 1996, 0.856 in 2006 and 0.86 in 2017. Regionally, the land issue is quite differentiated, but remained equally stable over time (IBGE, 2006a).

From the structural point of view, the Brazilian agricultural census of 2017 (IBGE, 2018c) identified that the large properties, with an area exceeding 1,000 hectares, totalling about 1% of the total rural establishments in Brazil, concentrate 47.5% of the total rural area of the country. The establishments with an area of less than 10 ha, the small properties, represent about 50.9% of the total establishments in the country, but occupy about 2.3% of the total area of rural establishments. The historical series recorded by agricultural censuses (1985, 1996, 2006 and 2017) confirms that the concentration was not reversed – Table 11.1.

As regards the gross value of agricultural production (GVAP), Alves and Rocha (2010), based on the agricultural census of 2006, pointed out that only 30.000 agricultural establishments accounted for half of the total production value. It is important to note that the group of more productive establishments also includes family farmers, responsible, in 2006, for 36.11% of the gross agricultural production value.

This polarization, revealed by the simple and direct correlation between the number of producers and participation in production, is different from those that historically marked the debates and analysis on the agrarian structure and rural development of Brazil: latifundium × minifundium; small × large producer; subsistence producer × commercial producer; peasant × capitalist; and more recently, family farming × agribusiness (Silva, 1999a; Lamarche, 1993; Wanderley, 1999). The 'new' polarization separates a small group of producers, which have high production capacity, integrated by large, medium and small establishments, owned by family farmers, employers and companies, scattered throughout the country, from other group, which have been in the margins of the processes of dynamization of Brazilian agriculture since the 1970s. However, even this new polarization minimizes the effective high complexity, heterogeneity and inequality that characterize the Brazilian rural environment.

Table 11.1 Land distribution by total area groups in Brazil

Total area Groups	1985	1996	2006	2017
Less than 10 ha	2.7%	2.2%	2.4%	2.3%
From 10 ha to less than 100 ha	18.6%	17.7%	19.1%	18.2%
From 100 ha to less than 1000 ha	35.1%	34.9%	34.2%	32.0%
1,000 ha and more	43.7%	45.1%	44.4%	47.5%
Total area (ha)	**374,924,421**	**353,611,246**	**329,941,393**	**350,253,329**

Source: IBGE (2006b).

3 The recognition of the Brazilian family farming as target of development initiatives

Until the first half of the twentieth century, the Brazilian agricultural production grew through the expansion of the agricultural frontier in fertile lands. However, from the second half of the 1950s, the acceleration of the industrialization process and urbanization put into check the extensive model – which was no longer able to maintain domestic supply and generate a flow of currencies needed to finance capital accumulation – and led to the adoption of a set of policies to promote technological modernization (Santana et al., 2014). This process gained momentum especially from the decade of 1970 onwards (see Chapters 1 and 3).

The modernization process favoured medium and large rural producers and relegated the vast majority of family farmers, which until mid-1990s were called in different ways, such as smallholder, small producers, subsistence farmers, huskers, settlers, peasants or low-income farmers. These producers, always mentioned in public policies, stayed at the margins of the modernization initiatives and had no benefits from generous credit incentives, minimum prices support programmes and commercialization policies.

Democratization of the country in the 1980s and the Federal Constitution enacted in 1988 are institutional milestones in the Brazilian history, also for rural areas. With the strengthening of rural workers unions, who gathered the employees and mainly small producers and the social movements in general, small farmers who were excluded from the national agenda began to express their demands. Still in the 1980s, the Agrarian Reform programme was relaunched. Among the claims, the 'National Fight Days' and the 'Scream of the earth Brazil' were highlighted. In the context of an internal economic crisis, from the second half of the 1980s to the 1990s, these movements evolved and strengthened, calling for specific policies for small producers. In addition to the social movements, in 1994, a study carried out by the Food and Agriculture Organization (FAO) and the National Institute for Colonization and Agrarian Reform (INCRA) provided a first delimitation of the family farm sector. The definition of group the universe of rural holdings in Brazil which fulfil two basic criteria: family management and the majority participation of the family's work.[1] This study identified the actual economic and productive conditions of family farmers' holdings, analysing their main productive systems, technological level, capitalization level and insertion in the agricultural markets and value chains (FAO/INCRA, 1994). In 1996, the family farming category was legally recognized in Brazil as a subject of public policy.

The FAO-INCRA study recognized the heterogeneity of Brazilian family farming and the consequent need for different solutions for different producer groups. The existing differentiation is related to several dimensions, such as education, professional experience, access to resources, technologies, capital, etc., in addition to the structural differentiation related to organization and access to land. The grouping of family farmers considered the level of agricultural income generated and not the size of the holdings. Thus, producers were divided into three groups: A, the consolidated family farmers, with higher capitalization level and income above the poverty levels; B, those in transition; and C, the peripheral group. The focus of agricultural policies should be in the transitional group, since the potential of this group to develop and become part of the consolidated group. The peripheral group, in turn, should be the focus of more general policies for socioeconomic development, such as health and education.

The study also revealed that family farmers were responsible for 37.9% of the gross value of national agricultural production (FAO/INCRA, 1994). In addition, this work revealed that the higher the income level of farmers, the better the indicators, such as access to technologies, electricity, technical assistance, use of fertilizers and corrective. In this sense, the best results were concentrated in group A.

This work, which had new versions in 1996, 2000 and 2010, laid the foundations in Brazil on the theoretical conceptualization of family farming and marked a rupture with the widespread notion that regarded family farming as marginal farmers, mostly archaic and mainly focused on subsistence production. The family farming emerged as a group with an important economic and social contribution, either as a food producer or as a labour employer. It was highlighted also its role in occupying productively part of the rural space which has been marginalized by the traditional rural development model, that is, the interior of the countryside.

Guided by the findings and proposals of the FAO/INCRA study, the federal government began to develop a project focused on family farmers. In 1996, under strong political pressure from the National Rural Workers Confederation (CONTAG), the Federal Government launched the National Program for Strengthening Family Farming (PRONAF), with the main goal of promoting the sustainable development of this group, mainly from the granting of credit. This programme was innovative and boosted by the institutionalization of Brazilian family farming category as a relevant political actor. Thus, received legal recognition and became a beneficiary of public policies.[2]

According to Buainain et al. (2013) and Guanziroli (2007), the objective of the delimitation proposed by the FAO/INCRA, that supported the creation of PRONAF, was to promote small producers, recognizing them as family producers who have their own economic and social dynamics, but not to separate them from the whole of agriculture. However, since the creation of PRONAF, family farming has become a centre of strong polarization and political dispute, opposing family farming to agribusiness, which ignores that a relevant group of family farmers is integrated into the value chains of agribusiness, including grain, meats, dairy, fruits and vegetables (Caume, 2009).

This polarization between family farmers and agribusiness was reflected even at institutional level: between 2000 and 2016, two ministries coexisted to deal with issues related to agriculture, the Ministry of Agriculture, Livestock and Food Supply (MAPA), responsible for non-familiar agriculture and the Ministry of Agrarian Development (MDA),[3] aimed at family farming. Both played important roles but rarely acted in a coordinated and harmonic way, thus contributing to sustain the polarization (Figueiredo and Limongi, 2007; Sabourin, 2007). The goals of the government and agricultural policy instruments were also separated into two different sectoral annual plans, the so-called 'Harvest Plans', one for family farming and one for non-family farming.

In the international context, there is no single definition on family farming, although some general parameters are used to guide the delimitation of the concept, at least for public policy purposes. In most cases, the fundamental condition to consider a holding as familiar is the direct management the family. This is the central parameter for the definition of family farming in the United States, for example, which includes from small to large holdings, irrespective to the level of income (Lowder et al., 2014). In light of the declaration for the International Year of Family Farming by the UN -2014-, FAO defined the activity as the means of organizing agriculture, forestry, fisheries and pastoral production managed by a family and that is predominantly dependent on family labour. In family farm holdings, economic, social, environmental and cultural functions are combined (FAO, 2014).

In Brazil, the family farming category was defined by the Law number 11,326, enacted in 2006, which sets the guidelines for the protection and promotion of rural family enterprises. This law also defined the limits of family farming entitled to access public policy specially designed for family farming, using four parameters: i) predominance of family labour; ii) size of the productive unit of families can't exceed four fiscal modules – which defines a small rural property in Brazil; iii) predominance of income from agricultural activities carried out by the family in the rural plot; and iv) management of the holding by the family (Brasil, 2006).[4]

4 From recognition to the access of different dimensions of public policies

The PRONAF was created in a context in which family farmers faced major difficulties in financing their process (Guanziroli, 2007), exacerbated by stringent fiscal policy adopted in the aftermath of the monetary stabilization Real Plan of 1994. Family farmers also faced difficulties to improve their productive capacity through the adoption of technological innovations and were strongly hit by the fall in food prices following trade liberalization in a context of overvaluation of the national currency, the Real. To overcome these bottlenecks, the programme sought to stimulate productive investment and provide families with working capital, considering the differentiation among family farmers and the need for special support for the most vulnerable groups. Lower income families would have access to credit with lower interest rates and better access conditions. The interest rates operated by the programme were always below those operated by the market.

The segmentation of the groups changed over time. At the beginning of the programme there were categories from A to C and, in 2000 and 2004, groups D and E were created. Later, in 2009, the groups D and E were unified in a single group to facilitate the operationalization (Bianchini, 2015). In 2018, for the purpose of access to credit, family farming is segmented into three groups (BACEN, 2018b), according to the annual gross income level. Group A is composed by the family farmers settled by the Agrarian Reform programme or who accessed the National Land Credit programme and is focused on investment credit. Group B includes low-income family farmers, who access microcredit. Group A/C, same audience as Group A, is focused on financing working capital. Besides group segmentation, the programme created, throughout the years, several subgroups defined by gender, age, main activity and purpose of financing, such as the Agroecology Pronaf, Eco Pronaf, Woman Pronaf, Youth Pronaf, Agroindustry Pronaf, among others (Brasil, 2014b). These sub-lines, which operate all under the same financial conditions of the non-specific credit lines to family farming, were introduced more in response to political pressures and to strengthen the programme from a political point of view rather than to offer special conditions suitable for each case or to facilitate the operationalization of this initiative (Benatti, 2018).

The creation of MDA and PRONAF has enabled the consolidation and the development of other policies to support family farming and meet different dimensions of the producers' needs. The first example is the Food Acquisition Program (PAA), an initiative launched in 2003 to guarantee a share of the market to family farmers and at the same time to supply food to the most vulnerable populations. Notwithstanding the lack of objective impact evaluations of PAA, it has been taken as example by international organizations, including FAO, which recommended its adoption to developing countries, particularly in Latin American and Africa. At its peak, in 2012, PAA commercialized 297,600 tons of food, produced by 128,800 producers organized in cooperatives and associations. The Northern and Northeast regions, the poorest in the country, accounted for 56% of the resources accessed in 2017 (Conab, 2013, 2018b).

The second example was the creation in 2004 of the Guarantee of the Agricultural Activity for Family Farming Program (PROAGRO Mais), an insurance service focused on family farming. The programme exempts small producers hit by negative climate events, pests and diseases, of financial obligations relating to the payment of rural credit. Between 2006 and 2016, the amount of resources applied in this policy increased at the average rate of 8.9% per year. Maize, soybean and sugarcane crops concentrate the most of insurance contracts, benefiting in general family farmers who are more capitalized and integrated into dynamic markets. But the coverage is still low. In 2017, only 24% of the agricultural areas were insured (Brasil, 2017).

Another important example is the Family Farming Price Guarantee Program (PGPAF), established in December 2006. This initiative indexes the debts of family farmers to PRONAF to a guarantee price equal to or near the cost of production. The guarantee price is based on the variable cost that includes remuneration of family labour, management of the production unit and costs incurred to access inputs and services. Almost 50 are covered by the policy, including chestnuts and native fruits, such as açaí, in addition to milk and sheep and goat raising (Brasil, 2014b, 2016a).

A fourth example is the National School Feeding Program (PNAE), which focuses on the acquisition of food for public schools. In 2009, it was instituted that 30% of the total resources for the purchase of food must be spent acquiring products from family farmers. This programme represents an important market to family farmers and a regular income flow that according to anecdotal information strengthened productive inclusion and generation of employment in rural areas. In 2016, the value of products purchased from family farming was around US$200 hundred million, covering 26 states of the Federation (Brasil, 2016b).

These policies contributed to the strengthening of family farming without, however, reducing the existing heterogeneity (see Chapter 6). However, many challenges still need to be faced. Credit, the main instrument of policy (via PRONAF), cannot adequately respond to the developing needs of a widely heterogeneous group such as the family farmers. In addition, even amongst those which could benefit from credit, access is still limited, especially to carry out long-term investments. The availability of agricultural credit in Brazil, mostly, is destined for financing operating expenses. However, investment–oriented credit and infrastructure credit are important for the development of a large segment of family farmers facing severe shortage of resources (Araújo and Vieira Filho, 2018; Buainain and Garcia, 2013).

The lack of organization (cooperative or associative) of many family farmers hinders access to public policies. In addition, the qualification of the technicians responsible for assisting family farmers is weak and their performance is insufficient to attend the demands from the sector. And there are flaws in the design of the programmes that limits their positive impacts. The purchase of food from family farms to attend school meals programmes faces several obstacles, from the difficulties to match the school menu with the supply by family farms to the low purchase ceiling from each family farmer, which often doesn't ensure the generation of the minimum level of income required to lift the family above the poverty line. Moreover, the effectiveness of the public policies is seriously undermined by the difficulties faced by the Federal Government to coordinate the various policies under responsibilities of different agencies, operating at different levels of government (federal, state and municipal) and regions.

5 The transformations of Brazilian family farming

Family farmers, as social actors and part of the agrarian structure could not rest immune from the transformations that have been occurring in the rural world over the years. Over the past decades, Brazilian family farming has experienced noticeable progress, yet highly concentrated in the better-off stratum and insufficient to revert the dual track development trend which

Table 11.2 Percentage participation of the production value of family farming in Brazil, 1996 and 2006

Product	1996	2006
Livestock	23.64	16.65
Dairy Products	52.05	60.53
Pigs	58.46	52.45
Poultry	39.86	30.34
Rice	30.87	39.19
Sugarcane	9.55	10.24
Onions	72.37	69.59
Beans	67.23	76.57
Tobacco	97.18	95.67
Cassava	83.88	93.17
Corn	48.57	51.90
Soybean	31.62	23.60
Wheat	46.04	36.38
Banana	57.58	62.40
Coffee	25.47	29.67
Orange	26.96	25.25
Grape	47.02	53.63

Source: Guanziroli et al. (2012).

Note: The methodology followed by the authors for calculating the data is the FAO/INCRA (2000) methodology, the details of which are contained in the text cited.

marginalizes the great majority of small family farmers. Guanziroli et al. (2012) indicate that the number of family farmers grew in the decade between 1996 and 2006 Agricultural Census, ranging from 4,139,000 to 4,551,855, which represents 87.95% of the total agricultural holdings in 2006.

Family farmers were also responsible for producing some essential foods for the country's population, in some cases contributing to more than 90% of domestic production – Table 11.2.[5]

The gross value of agricultural production of family farmers in 2006 corresponded to 36.11% of total agricultural production, a slight drop in relation to 1996 (37.91%). This production was carried out in 32% of the total area recorded by the Census for all holdings, totalling 107 million hectares. In terms of occupation (including family members and their employees), family farming absorbed, in 2006, 13,040,000 people, i.e. 78.75% of the total workforce in the field – Table 11.3. Thus, it may be said that the socioeconomic importance of Brazilian family farmers, revealed in 1996, was reconfirmed 10 years later, by the data of the 2006 Census.

In fact, the maintenance (or slight decrease) of the participation of family farming in agricultural production, in a period of strong expansion of the agricultural sector, confirms its economic importance. However, this scenario can only be explained by the presence of a subgroup of farmers that has shown enough capacity to develop a modern and entrepreneurial agriculture, increasing the scale of production, innovating and thus being able to capture

Table 11.3 Evolution of the participation of the main variables of family farming in Brazil, 1996 and 2006

Variable	1996	2006
% of Family farmers establishments/ total number	85.17	87.95
% of area of family farmers establishments/total area	30.48	32.00
% of Gross Value of Production / total value	37.91	36.11
% of total working force / total work force	76.85	78.75

Source: IBGE (2006a, 2006b) and Guanziroli et al. (2012).

Table 11.4 Number of family farmers in Brazil and variation according to type, 1996 and 2006

Type	1996	%	2006	%	Variation (%)
A	406,291	9.8	452,750	9.9	11.4
B	993,751	24.0	964,140	21.2	-3.0
C	823,547	19.9	574,961	12.6	-30.2
D	1,915,780	46.3	2,560,274	56.2	33.6
TOTAL	4,139,369	100.0	4,551,855	100.0	11.9

Source: Guanziroli et al. (2012).

some benefits through the articulation with the major agribusiness value chains (soybean complex, fruticulture, dairy, etc.). They are similar to the American family farm (Guanziroli and Di Sabbato, 2014). Other producers, within the family farm sector, in greater numbers, have also contributed to the supply of staples to the domestic market, but have shown no signs of progress and without support are more likely to fall to the lower stratum of poor farmers. Moreover, there are also those more impoverished and also more numerous, exploring tiny plots, with limited capacity to produce surplus to the market, closer to subsistence production, whose survival has depended more on income generated outside the plots in non-agricultural activities, remittances of relatives living in cities, retirements/pensions and income transfers by social programmes.

Guanziroli et al. (2012) compared the evolution of the four subgroups defined in the original work of the FAO/INCRA agreement – Tables 11.4 and 11.5.

The number of holdings of group A, which makes up the elite of the Family Farm sector, represented in 1996 little less than 10% of the total number of family farmers. On the other hand, this group accounted for 50.6% of the gross value of agricultural production (GVAP). The number of establishments of group A grew 11.4% between the two periods and the participation in the GVAP generation rose 19%, a growth of 37%. Group B maintained its numerical participation, but the participation in the GVAP fell from 29.3 to 15.7%, while group C decreased numerically and had its contribution reduced by 50%. The group D, which includes most of the land reform settlers and the

Table 11.5 Participation in the gross value of production by type of income from family farming in Brazil, 1996 and 2006

Type	1996	2006
A	50.6	69.5
B	29.3	15.7
C	9.4	4.7
D	10.7	10.1
TOTAL	100.0	100.0

Source: Guanziroli et al. (2012).

Table 11.6 Annual net monetary income per Brazilian farmer type in Brazil in 1996 and 2006

Type	Annual net monetary income (R$)*	
	1996	2006
Family farms Tipo A	30,333.00	53,236.00
Family farms Tipo B	5,537.00	3,725.00
Family farms Tipo C	1,820.00	1,499.00
Family farms Tipo D	−265.14	255.00
Employer (patronal)		70,903.00

Source: Guanziroli et al. (2012).

* Discounted production costs, but not discounted depreciation.
1996 values updated by IGP-DI.

poorest farmers, grew from 1.9 to 2.5 million establishments and maintained a 10% participation in the product of family farming. Table 11.6 shows that the changes in the values produced obviously generate changes in the average income obtained by the establishments of each group.

The differences of income levels between the groups is large and, in addition, increased between 1996 and 2006. Group A, which consists of approximately 400,000 producers, generates the highest net annual average income, which is equivalent to almost R$4,500 per month (U$1,200). Considering that in rural areas producers usually have access to other non-agricultural incomes and quasi-incomes (such as self-consumption) and that they do not pay rents for housing, this income is equivalent to the earnings of an urban middle-class family. Table 11.7 shows the characteristics of this segment which in some ways resembles the American family farm, French *paysans* or the *familienbetriebe* from Germany.

Examples of group A can be found within producers of soybean, wheat, maize and poultry from the Southern region of the country, milk producers from the state of Minas Gerais (Southeast) and fruit producers from the Northeast region.

This scenario suggests that the concentration process has also occurred within the family farming sector. While some producers have grown, innovated

Table 11.7 Profile of efficient family farming in Brazil – Group A

Total Number Group A	452,700 family farmers (8.70% do total)
Share of total agricultural output Brazil	25.1% (69.5% of 36.11%)
Annual net monetary income (nominal value 2006)	R$ 53,326
Average area per farm	48 hectares
Specialization in production (main product exceeding 65% of total output)	72% are specialized

Source: Guanziroli and Di Sabbato (2014).

and harnessed the opportunities in the international market and the growth outbreaks of the Brazilian economy, others, corresponding to the vast majority of rural producers, have not been able to engage dynamic market activities, neither in the main agribusiness value-chains and thus had to rely on rather ineffective public policies to remedy their most basic development needs (Buainain et al., 2013).

The size of many of the Brazilian family farms as well as poor organization and lack of secondary road networks end up making it difficult to incorporate the necessary technologies to increase production and income. For instance, a number of equipment is expensive and technically unviable to use in a small plot. Moreover, the economic viability of many of them requires long-term investments and financing, which is not customary and easily accessible to this group. Geographic dispersion and spatial isolation require organizational solutions and infrastructure investments, which are not simple initiatives (Buainain and Garcia, 2013). Efforts to strengthen producers' organizations and increase its effectiveness have been undermined by mixing up in the same organization the qualitatively different roles traditionally assigned to the economic and partisan organizations.

Despite this fact, some aspects related to the adoption of technologies were incorporated by expressive portions of family farming between 1996 and 2006, particularly with regard to the access to electricity, which more than doubled in the period of analysis and the use of mechanization with progressive abandonment of traditional 'hoe' farming. This advance can be analysed in Table 11.8.

Table 11.8 also shows that these advances were not necessarily due to the influence of technical assistance, which evolved from 16.67% only to 20.88% between 1996 and 2006 (IBGE, 2006b). It may be that for this reason no advances were recorded in the use of fertilizers and in the associativity process, which would be two strong axes that would justify the demand for a process of technical assistance.

However, in some regions a significant effort to increase the assistance to family was undertaken by the government. In the Northern and Northeast

Table 11.8 Proportion of family farmers in Brazil using components related to the modernization of agriculture – 1996 and 2006

Selected variables	1996 (%)	2006 (%)
Technical assistance	16.67	20.88
Cooperative association	12.63	4.18
Electric power	36.63	74.1
Animal force	22.67	38.75
Mechanical power	27.5	30.21
Manual force	49.83	31.04
Irrigation	4.92	6.23
Fertilizers and corrective	36.73	37.79

Source: IBGE (2006a, 2006b) and Guanziroli et al. (2012).

regions, where in 1996 only between 3% and 6% of farmers, respectively, had access to technical assistance and rural extension, there was an important breakthrough. In 2006, a group of approximately 9% had accessed this service in the Northern and on average 18% in the Northeast. The greatest progress was made in the use of electricity, which was boosted by the programme 'Light for All' (created in 2003 with the objective of bringing electricity to rural regions and to houses with have no access to it), especially in the Northeast. In addition, the adoption of mechanized traction over manual traction was also increased. This technology was encouraged by the 'Moderfrota' (modernization programme for buying machinery) and by PRONAF itself.

In addition to the access to energy, technology and the possibilities of inserting themselves into markets, it is also necessary to consider other dimensions of the transformations through which family farming has passed. A prominent issue in this regard is education. Of the 11 million family farmers and relatives, almost seven million – that is, the majority – knew how to read and write (63%) (IBGE, 2006b). Nevertheless, the agricultural census of 2006 indicates that there were just over four million people who declared not knowing how to read and write. In addition, only 170,000 farmers stated that they have professional qualifications. Although many young people have access to study and the school attendance of women is higher than that of men, Brazil is still among the Latin American countries with the worst indicators of rural education. As Belik (2015) points out, rural citizens enter late at school and abandon it prematurely: from the age of 13 abandonment and few rural young people go to high school. With 16 or 17 years, the difference between urban and rural reaches 10% in school attendance and at 17 years of age 35% of the rural youth do not attend school.

The factors related to the level of education impact on access to public policies, technologies and the use of agricultural pesticides. The school education of rural young people contributes decisively to their insertion (at times in precarious ways) in the labour market. Many of the young people who are part of the better off family farmers group (in cases where the property generates

Table 11.9 Participation of age groups in the Brazilian Agricultural activity (2006–2017)

Age groups	Share of agricultural output	
	2006	*2017*
Less than 25	3.3	2.03
From 25 to 35	13.56	9.49
From 35 to less than 45	21.93	18.29
From 45 to less than 55	23.34	24.77
From 55 to less than 65	20.35	24.01
65 and more	17.52	21.41

Source: IBGE (2006a, 2006b, 2018c).

income far above the average or presents advanced production infrastructure) have access to higher education and most often follow a career unrelated to agriculture, not returning to the countryside to live (Kiyota and Perondi, 2014). Family farming is an inherited and labour-intensive activity, so the succession process between generations can be regarded as one of the most critical stages in the development of the production unit.

In addition to the migration to cities in search of better conditions of living, it can also be noticed a change in the profile of families, which decreased in size due to the decrease in fecundity. Leone et al. (2010, p. 65) claim that 'The most evident manifestation of the decline in fecundity in Brazil was the reduction in the size of families, which went from 4.3 to 3.1 people between 1981 and 2006'. Moreover, the aging of the population also contributed to the change in the structure of Brazilian families (see Chapter 9). Preliminary Census data from 2017 points to this fact, which can be observed in Table 11.9.

Table 11.9 also shows a reduction in the participation of smaller age groups, while the groups older than 45 years increased their share. In 2017, there were 15,036,978 people employed in agricultural establishments, which represent a decrease of 1.5 million people, including producers, their families, temporary and permanent workers.

The previous discussion shows that even in the context of family farming it is possible to notice a process of agrarian development very heterogeneous, relying on capitalized farmers, producing a diversity of products and integrated into dynamic markets, but also involving producers who face the most diverse socio-economic bottlenecks. While a group of more than 400,000 producers is increasingly integrated into the markets, most family producers are still largely in the margins of this development process. The 2017 census data may show the worsening of this profile.

6 Conclusions

Family farming in Brazil has resisted the transformations – somehow aggressive – ensued by the so-called modernization of Brazilian agriculture. In spite of historical and contemporary difficulties, family farming sector still plays an important economic role in the supply of food stuff to the domestic market and also to international market. It was possible to observe that the heterogeneity of Brazilian family agriculture has the following economic profile: a) a highly productive and efficient segment of family farmers, whose competitiveness is closely associated with the competitiveness of the value chains and their capacity to respond to the continuous changes in the markets demands; b) an intermediate segment, more vulnerable, whose survival is continuously threatened by the reduction of family labour due to migration, aging of the remaining family, difficulties to innovate and to respond to general market requirements, including sanitary standards; and c) a segment of poor and very poor family farmers, with low productivity, producing mostly for self-consumption, with occasional commercialization of surplus in local markets, living in the holding or in the peripheries of urban areas and increasingly depending on non-agricultural income and or income transfers either from family members or government. Although the decision to migrate is tied to the opportunity cost to do it, which is low, growing numbers are still leaving the countryside searching for better opportunities in the cities.

Brazilian family farming has undoubtedly undergone a series of transformations since its recognition as a target public of public policies by the Brazilian State. Enough to survive but not enough to ensure the survival of the majority above poverty levels. The future of family farming is still highly dependent upon support from well-designed public policies, targeted to qualify farmers to respond to the transformations of society and in particular to changes in the food markets. Consumers increasingly demand quality products, with certificates of origin and guarantee of animal and plant health. To the same extent, the engagement of family farming in increasingly demanding markets requires much more than rural credit. It requires development of innovation capacities and conditions, management capacity, provision of adequate infrastructure, supply of public goods and continuously and consistent support from the public sector. Access to institutional markets is crucial, but in addition producers must be empowered to face the fierce competition in the markets in general. As said, not a trivial challenge!

Notes

1 It was also determined a regional maximum area as a limit for the total area of family establishments, so that the clipping did not capture large latifundia.
2 Over time, the group legally recognized as family farmer expanded and, from 2006 onwards, the so-called traditional populations, such as the indigenous and *Quilombolas*, as well as foresters and fishermen, became "family farmers" entitled to special assistance provided by Pronaf.
3 The MDA, from an institutional reform, was extinguishing in 2016. All the responsibilities of this structure were transferred to a Special Secretariat for Family Agriculture and Agrarian Development.
4 These parameters define the clipping for targeting the target public in Brazilian public policies aimed at family farming. This delimitation, however, is the target of many

criticisms, due to its limiting nature, which does not recognize the reality of Brazilian family farming, characterized by its heterogeneity. In this sense, in the academic context, the debate on the concept of family farming, which is multidisciplinary, is extensive and is far from reaching a consensus.

5 In 2011, the Brazilian government disclosed that family farming would be responsible for producing 70% of the country's food. Hoffmann (2014) contested the official estimates, showing that family farming could be responsible for 21.4% of the total expenses of Brazilian households with food. Still, this is a high percentage, which values the role of family farming.

12 Structural heterogeneity in rural Brazil

Three regional cases[1]

Alfredo Kingo Oyama Homma, João Ricardo Ferreira de Lima and Pedro Abel Vieira

1 Introduction

The purpose of this chapter is to explore the broad economic-productive and spatial transformations that have occurred in Brazilian rural regions throughout the last five decades. In order to achieve this objective, we will use 'case studies', investigating the major socioeconomic changes presented in three emblematic sub-national contexts. Each analysis is significant and revealing per se, not only in terms of their notable territorial extension and social magnitude, but also in relation to the economic and productive determinants related to the changes there developed.

The first case succinctly scrutinizes several profound transformations in the second largest Brazilian state, Pará, located within the great Amazon region. It is a mammoth state that has been being rapidly transformed because of manifold pressures on its immense remaining forested area in recent decades. Different forces have been employed in this area, which are related to the expansion of agriculture and illegal logging, mineral exploration and major infrastructure works and land settlement reform policies. The main message here is: Pará, due to the expansion of agriculture, has been increasingly ceasing to be an intrinsic part of the 'Amazon controversies' history and is turning into a state now dedicated to various economic endeavours, particularly focused on soybean, livestock and mining. This fact brings up a dramatic array of future implications, not only because it is a process that may expand, threatening the rest of the Amazon forest, but, above all, due to the uninterrupted deforestation, which affects the rainfall regime of most of the country (Nobre, 2014).

The second case refers to the contemporary social and economic occupation of the central region of Brazil – the Centre-West – and its multifaceted impacts on the local main biome, the Cerrado. Curiously enough, the region was considered inadequate for agriculture until the end of the 1950s, but was radically transformed over the last 25 years and is nowadays rapidly becoming the country's main grain and meat producing area. The main argument here is to highlight the remarkable spatial change in land use for agriculture and cattle ranching. This region, which was relatively abandoned and showed no significant productive use until a few decades ago, is the one that presents the most intense 'economic dynamics' nowadays, compared to the other rural regions of Brazil. The empirical evidence is indisputable: at present, the 20 municipalities that account for the largest and most valued agricultural production in the country are all located in this central part of Brazil.

Finally, the third case presented refers to the semiarid region, which is the largest internal part of the rural Northeast, a region that concentrates Brazil's highest density of rural poverty and artificial oasis (the irrigated zone). It also stands out as an important producer of fruit and wine for both domestic and external markets. This section discusses the rural Northeast and, more specifically, the semiarid region, one of the first areas of the country occupied by settlers from the coast during the Portuguese colonization of Brazil, the original cradle of sugarcane crops and of some long-lasting socio-cultural elements of the country. In addition to being affected by periodic droughts, this region is also marked by striking internal differences, from the birth and growth of modern irrigated fruit trees around the São Francisco river basin to the existence of the poorest region of Brazil. In addition, with the expansion of transport and communication structures, persistent movements of out-migration are observed, resulting in rural communities now aged and masculinized.

The trajectories of these three regions over the last five decades have been strongly distinct among themselves, but also when each one is compared to its not-too-distant-past. These are regional histories that emerged after erratic and conflicting connections between the economic modernization ignited in the country's central states (particularly São Paulo) in the 1950s and the dire social and economic typical aspects of the vast backlands – so brilliantly narrated, as an illustration, in the landmark essay *Os sertões*, by Euclides da Cunha (1901). In addition, the cases studies presented here surely have specific and emblematic starting points as well. The evolutions of the state of Pará and of the Centre-West region find their clear connections with the more modernized Southern region after the establishment of the new capital, Brasília, in 1960, located in the geographic centre of the country. With respect to the case of Pará, another factor should be taken into account: the construction of a legendary long road (spanning 1,800 miles) linking the new Brazilian capital to Belém, the capital of the state. The case of the semiarid, in turn, has arguably taken off after the launching of SUDENE (the organism in charge of promoting development in the region) in 1959 and its programme to combat regular droughts that have historically plagued the region. This programme had as its symbol the construction of large dams and attempts to multiply access to irrigation projects, most of them always presented as a 'redemption' for rural producers and bringer of prosperity to the semiarid.

Overall, the cases materialize, in different magnitudes, almost all the main changes that have been the trademarks of the Brazilian rural world in the period – from the expansion and intensification of production and the ensuing increase of productivity (or its lack, in the case of the semiarid region), to environmental impacts and social, economic and cultural processes, as well as governmental actions and the emergence of a new institutional governance.

However, each region also presents singular aspects that make them cases marked by impressive particularities. The Amazon region, for example, is the largest forest in the world and its rich biodiversity is extraordinary. The region encompasses one-tenth of all plant species on the planet, one quarter of all species of butterflies and a tenth of all species of birds and 3,000 species of bees (also one-tenth of the world total), among other impressive indicators (Pivetta, 2013). The region is home to a total of ten times more fish species than any region in Europe. Therefore, debates about the sustainability of the Amazon region do not directly concern Brazilians alone, but humanity as a whole. The Centre-West, on the other hand, whose flat land – once the soil is 'rebuilt' with the application of available technology – offers ideal conditions for large-scale agriculture. Besides, the region is the main source of water for three large rivers that cut the Brazilian territory – Paraná, Paraguay and São Francisco. And the Northeast, 150 years after Emperor D. Pedro II (1825–1891) built the first large dam to minimize the impacts of regular droughts, is still struggling with the lack of water, either for human consumption or for productive purposes, such as irrigation.

2 Pará: the emergence of an agricultural, livestock and mining state

The state of Pará is one of nine northern states that form the region generically entitled 'Amazon'. As it is the largest macro region of the country, each one of these states presents numerous specificities and, in particular, a tremendous diversity of ecosystems. Only one of these states, Amazonas, has an area equivalent to Alaska – see maps in the Introduction of this book. If it were a unique country, the Amazon would be the seventh largest in the world, bigger than the European Union. With the presence of the Amazon river (around 4,000 miles long), the state of Amazonas concentrates one fifth of the volume of fresh water and the largest tropical forest on the planet. Approximately 19% of its original forest area has already been deforested, a total that is superior to the joint surface of Japan and Germany. Although the group of nine states maintains a low demographic density, 13.4% of the Brazilian population (25.5 million inhabitants) currently live in this region – a total population that is bigger than the specific population of 148 countries. As the rate of population growth has been declining and the region has not been the destination of significant internal migrations, the population indicators are expected to remain relatively stable in the near future. The degree of urbanization is higher than 70% and, thus, the Amazon is, curiously, a region of agricultural frontier where an 'urbanized forest' predominates.

Several studies have investigated the Amazon region. The work of Irwin and Goodland (1975), *Amazon Jungle: Green Hell to Red Desert?*, is an important reference. The publication caused broad repercussions and sparked a heated international debate about the theme of deforestation and the recurrent phenomenon of burning induced by the expansion of cattle ranching, an activity that had been strongly advancing in the region due to the opening of roads. Subsequently, the Stockholm Conference in 1972 and, two decades later, the Rio 92 Summit placed the preservation of the Amazon on the world agenda and since then criticisms of deforestation and forest fires have been regularly voiced in all international forums.

Despite the economic possibilities stemming from its immense biodiversity, abundant natural and mineral resources, hydroelectric potentials and contributions (positive or otherwise) to the very essence of the planet's climate, the Amazon is one of the most backward regions in the country. It has widespread pockets of poverty that reach almost three million inhabitants, most of them dependent on government transfer programmes. The region has an indigenous population of approximately 250,000 people, representing 55% of all Brazilian indigenous people. It is estimated that, in the territory later to be the Brazilian Amazon, during pre-Columbian times, one million natives lived in *várzeas* (lowlands) along the rivers and 900,000 in *terra firme* (upland areas). Contrary to the common usage of the expression 'forest peoples', there is currently a high rate of urbanization and there is a clear tendency to develop a depopulated forest in the future, induced by rural–urban migration and by the low profitability of initiatives based on forest products.

The state of Pará is situated at the mouth of the Amazon River and its area is twice the surface of France. It is the second largest Brazilian state, with the oldest and most populous occupation of the Amazon, besides having significant economic activities since when it was a colony of Portugal. It has experienced a great migratory flow in the past, in addition to a long history of land conflicts. Its area already deforested corresponds to a share of 22% of the total area of the state.

Over the four centuries of its history, Pará underwent several relevant moments of rural change, taking as its starting point the foundation of the capital, Belém, in 1616. For most of the time, extractivism has been the dominant driver, taking advantage of the limitless natural resources, a state of affairs that still prevails, to some extent, today. Rubber extractivism, as an illustration, was once the third product of Brazilian exports, between 1887 and 1917, after coffee and cotton, although it never consolidated a model of stable economy.

Pará is characterized by abundant mineral wealth, being the second richest state in mining resources. The Carajás iron ore reserves, estimated in 18 billion tons, correspond to the biggest concentration of high content ore already located in the world. Amazingly, it is a capacity that guarantees extraction for more than a century. Ore exports represent 88% of the state's exports and a third of the Brazilian production. Another important facet is the sheer potential of its great rivers in energy production. The Belo Monte hydroelectric dam on the Xingu River will be the third largest on the planet once completed, while another large hydroelectric plant, Tucuruí, on the Tocantins River, is the fifth largest of the world. It must be emphasized, however, that these strategic sources of energy and huge exports of minerals benefit mainly the richer states of central Brazil. On the other hand, regionally, these enormous projects and respective social and economic dynamics generate, in particular, environmental difficulties and a multitude of social conflicts.

From the earliest Paleo-Indian groups that occupied the region, *toco* agriculture (shifting cultivation) predominated, coupled with the use of patches inside the dense forest or secondary vegetation for the cultivation of cassava. In contemporary times, it has been expanded by small producers of cassava, rice, corn and black beans for self-consumption. Even more recently, with the gradual production of scattered surplus in different parts of the state, the first inroads towards merchant relations have been made. Depending on their location, whether in the *várzeas* (lowlands) or *terra firme* (uplands), most of these producers usually combine a host of activities that articulates vegetal extractivism, hunting and fishing.

From the 1930s onwards, the first typical 'agricultural phase' began, with Japanese immigration introducing jute plantations in the *várzeas* and black pepper in *terra firme*, inaugurating the initial stages of future modernized activities. As referred to earlier, the opening of the Belém-Brasília highway, in 1960, pioneered a terrestrial connection of the Amazon region with the Centre and Southern of the country, previously dependent on ships. In addition, the Transamazon highway (1972), cutting through the rainforest horizontally, linked the region to the Northeast and facilitated the intense entry of northeastern migrants after successive migratory waves.

With these two long and consequential roads, the 'civilization by the rivers' gradually was converted into an 'upland civilization', located on the lands by the sides of the open roads. Cattle ranching was soon introduced and rapidly became the largest form of land use in the Amazon, along with illegal logging (and deforestation) and the large influx of migrants. As a result, the economic and productive interdependence linking the Amazon and the rest of the domestic economy slowly developed. Later on, it was also articulated with the world economy. During this longer period starting in the 1960s, social tensions and major environmental impacts deepened and produced worldwide repercussions. For example, the assassination of the rubber tappers' trade union leader in the state of Acre, Chico Mendes (1944–1988), served as a watershed moment of the development model then on course in the region. Interregional migratory flows reached their zenith during the 1970s and 1980s, exacerbating land conflicts and land invasions. Between 1985 and 2017, 37% of the total number of murders of rural workers and their leaders occurred in Pará, especially in the south of the state.

The number of rural settlements increased exponentially from the end of the 1980s onwards, according to the annual surveys prepared by the Pastoral Land Commission of the Catholic Church. In the state of Pará, the total contingent of settlers is concentrated in more than 1,000 state-sponsored colonization projects that accommodate 225,000 small farmers mainly focused on subsistence production. More than a quarter of these families rely on government transfers to ensure their survival.

At the end of the 1980s, with mounting national and international environmental pressures, cattle ranching and logging gave way to a second cycle of agricultural growth under which six activities expanded their corresponding total area of cultivation (around 200,000 hectares each): soybean, reforestation, cacao, oil palm, corn and fruit trees (Homma, 2017; Cohn et al., 2016). The cultivation of cassava, which had always occupied the largest area and had been grown for several centuries, lost its primacy to soybean in 2015. Nowadays, pastures account for the highest area of land use, with more than 16 million hectares, plus an additional five million hectares of degraded pastures. The total bovine herd has shown signs of stabilization after 2015. Slowly, under pressure from society and markets, the rationale of cattle ranching in the Amazon region is changing and extensive growth is leading to investments aimed at intensifying and increasing productivity. Under such changes, degraded pasture areas and smallholder farms are losing their spaces to modern and more profitable mechanized agriculture.

Small producers, in their turn, who previously engaged in traditional farming production such as cassava, rice, corn and beans, began to lose competitiveness in relation to local or other regions' mechanized agriculture. Extractive products, which were previously supplied by small producers, have been facing growing pressure to secure access to markets (such as cacao, rubber, guaraná, among others).

3 The Cerrado in the centre-west

The Cerrado biome covers an area that represents 22% of the national territory. Although located mainly in the Centre-West region (the states of Goiás, Mato Grosso, Mato Grosso do Sul and the Federal District), the Cerrado also extends to parts of the Southeast (Minas Gerais and São Paulo), Northeast (Bahia, Maranhão and Piauí), besides the Northern (Amapá, Roraima, Amazonas, Rondônia and Tocantins) – see Figures 0.1 and 0.2 in Introduction. It is the largest biome in the country and it contains the sources of the three largest hydrographic basins in South America: the Amazon and the basins of the São Francisco and Prata rivers, which result in a high aquifer potential. The biome is also extremely important in view of its biodiversity, as it shelters more than 10,000 species of native plants already catalogued and about 200 species of mammals, as well as hundreds of species of fish, reptiles and amphibians (Sano et al., 2008).

In addition to crucial environmental aspects, the Cerrado region nowadays plays a decisive economic, social and political importance in the national context. It has been the main frontier of agricultural expansion in the last four decades. Over this time, it has housed substantive population contingents, who have settled there and given rise to urban centres growing above the national average. Besides that, a significant proportion of the biome's population survives from its natural resources, including indigenous peoples, *quilombolas*, *raizeiros* and other communities. These are traditional social groups who accumulated very dense cultural knowledge – some of them with economic implications, such as the case of about 200 plants with medicinal properties or more than 400 plants that can be used in the recovery of degraded soils (Sano et al., 2008).

The dominant pattern of land use suggests that agriculture is the main economic activity in the region. In the last three decades, it has experienced a strong anthropogenic action, in particular in its central part, formally known as the Centre-West. This historical fact places the region, alongside Mata Atlântica, as the two biomes mostly transformed by human action – see Figure 0.2 in Introduction. It is estimated that one fifth of native species no longer exist in protected areas and that at least 140 animal species are threatened with extinction (Sano, 2005; Giustina, 2013).

Due to its rapid and almost chaotic occupation, the Cerrado currently suffers severe environmental damages. A survey carried out with its 1,154 municipalities demonstrated that a bit more than three million hectares are experiencing hydric threats in their permanent protection areas. According to the Brazilian Corporation for Agricultural Research (Embrapa), this deficit may be aggravated by the uncontrolled use of water for irrigation and the loss of biodiversity associated with the expansion of intensive agriculture. Although wide attention usually focuses more on the case of the Amazon, the Cerrado has a significant responsibility in this general picture of national degradation (Assad, 2018).

The Centre-West, when compared to other regions and biomes, displays a high number of hours under solar radiation and appropriate temperatures that qualify it as an ideal terrain for agricultural production throughout the year. The rainfall regime indicates precipitations between 1,200–2,000 mm, thus demarcating two distinct seasons – dry and rainy. The latter one, extending from October to March, registers monthly precipitations around 250 mm and this average, coupled with monthly evaporations of less than 120 mm, usually contributes to an agricultural production without the need of irrigation. Over the rest of the year, the dry season prevails; monthly precipitations are close to zero and evaporations are above 300 mm, a situation of intense water deficit. It is in this period that irrigation is strongly recommended (Sano, 2005).

Being such an enormous biome, its geographical contours are highly varied, its soils are old, deep and well drained, so that in most of its sub-regions the Cerrado is suitable for intensive agriculture. The low natural fertility of the soils was corrected by a practice called 'soil construction'. This technique consists in a gradual improvement of soils by a succession of less demanding crops (for example, rice), then followed by more demanding crops (such as soybeans), to the final cultivation of highly demanding crops (such as cotton, vegetables and fruits). It should be noted, in passing, that the region is adequate for the production of the main agricultural commodities traded in the world. This potential soon transformed the region into the country's main agricultural and cattle-raising frontier after the 1980s.

The gradual occupation of the region was noticeable in the 1930s and consolidated in the 1970s, with the region becoming the country's agricultural frontier and pole of absorption of surplus population after the inauguration of the new capital, Brasília, in 1960. As recent as 2016, the GDP attributed to the municipalities located in the Centre-West (and part of the Northeast that also comprise the Cerrado) accounted for just over 13% of the country's total GDP. This wealth was due, in particular, to the participation in the total production of soybean, corn, cotton and the overall results of cattle ranching and the beef industry. Still in 2016, the same region was home of more than 17 million people, presenting a population growth rate higher than the national one (IBGE, 2018c).

Although some indicators – such as the ratio between the GDP per capita of the Cerrado region and the national one, which is 120% bigger in the biome – show an overall progress, rural poverty is still persistent.

Social inequality in the Cerrado is even more stark when considering the municipal indicators organized under the Firjan Municipal Development Index (IFDM). As an example, one could compare Lucas do Rio Verde and Campinápolis, municipalities located in Mato Grosso. While Lucas do Rio Verde ranks number 58 in the national list of municipalities, and its indicator is 0.8584 (very close to the first city in the national ranking), Campinápolis appears in the 5,443th position, with a lower index (0.4092) than the average found in the Northern (0.5490) and in the Northeast (0.5613). In general, the amplitude between the groups of more and less developed municipalities in the region increased from 2005 to 2015, a fact that accentuates a growing economic and social asymmetry in the states of the Centre-West (Firjan, 2018).

Agriculture was undoubtedly the great driver that has transformed the Cerrado in recent decades. Relying on the spectacular performance of agriculture, the region's GDP grew more than fourfold from 2002 to 2015. The share of agriculture accounts for 10% of the regional GDP and close to 5% of the national GDP (IBGE, 2018c). The broad implications of these changes leave no doubt about the decisive importance of agriculture (and cattle ranching, as a matter of fact) for the future pattern of regional development. In the present century, there has been a robust rate of growth in the industrial and service sectors, most of which is clearly related to the ebullient economic performance of farming endeavours. Although this movement is strong, it must be noted, however, that the growth is unevenly distributed, with concentration in some regional poles. As a consequence, the region is becoming internally heterogeneous and deepening new social and economic asymmetries.

However, when focusing specifically on the intensive production of grains – soybean, corn and black bean and cotton, besides cattle ranching – one observes a relatively homogeneous agriculture. Annual crops used 15 million hectares in the region, while pastures occupied 60 million hectares and permanent crops used around 4 million hectares, leaving more than 60 million hectares under the original vegetation of the biome. Studies carried out by Embrapa suggest that, in keeping with the current technology, the potential for expansion of the agricultural and livestock area in the Cerrado does not exceed 5% of the current total area (Assad, 2018).

Despite the crucial economic importance of grain production and cattle ranching, the development of a more diversified sector has been observed, in face of the expansion of new value-added commodities, such as fruits and vegetables. This might suggest the existence of several agricultural sub-regions in the near future, with distinct socioeconomic and productive configurations and certainly showing differences in relation to the dominant model of intensive large-scale farming (Assad, 2018).

While the total area used for agriculture in the region doubled from 9 million hectares in 1988 to 18.5 million hectares in 2016, the total value of its output rose more than threefold. This increase in value was due to productivity gains and diversification. Agricultural yields increased at rates close to 2% per year between 1988 and 2016, especially bean and corn, which increased by 4.7% and 2.6% per year in the same period, respectively. Notwithstanding these positive indicators, the evolution of total factor productivity (TFP) seems to be cooling down, appearing to be stagnant in this century, according to official data. The TFP indicators from 2005 onwards were not worse due to rising labour productivity resulting from intensive agriculture (the productivity parameters for land and capital factors presented a slight decline in the same period). It must be noted that the 'environmentally adjusted' TFP, which is measured by the ratio between production and the corresponding emission of greenhouse gases, grew more than 4% per year over the last decade and this performance indicates that agriculture in the region clearly pursues the path of environmental sustainability. It is also important to emphasize that, for technological formats called 'integrated production', especially those combining agriculture, cattle ranching and forests, the result might be an increase of food production equivalent to 40 million hectares without any deforestation (Arias et al., 2017).

The diversification of agriculture also contributed to growth when higher value-added products were incorporated, such as cotton and, more recently, fruits and vegetables. As an example, the area cultivated with cotton grew 521% from 1988 to 2016, while the areas with rice, cassava and soybean grew 10%, 96% and 350%, respectively, in the same period. Regional production compared to the national production of high value products also expanded, such as the case of tomatoes (24% of the national production in 2016), potatoes (6%), onions (8%) and garlic (26%) (IBGE, 2018c).

In short, the growth of agriculture in the region occurred after three vectors were materialized: the expansion of the cultivated area, a factor that accounted for about 30% of the increase in production; productivity gains (which accounted for about 60%) and, lastly, the recent diversification of production, which contributed with about 10% of the added value of the production (IBGE, 2018c).

Agricultural production and its expansion in the Cerrado confront several environmental challenges. Given the territorial limits of the agricultural frontier, the growth of agriculture will necessarily depend on intensification, either obtained through productivity or by diversification, both depending on even more use of water resources. Intensification implies more sophisticated techno-logical formats, and, in many contexts, it saves natural resources and deepens sustainability. Conversely, it also has relevant environmental implications, par-ticularly in tropical agriculture environments – for example, intensification may require a greater demand of agrochemicals, which translate not only into increasing production costs but also additional environmental costs, which are sometimes unacceptable for some social segments.

Another important aspect for the development of agriculture in the region is the production of bioenergy. One example is the expansion of the area cultivated with sugarcane, which jumped from mere 230 hectares to 1,800,000 hectares between 1988 and 2016 – see Chapter 7. In addition to sugarcane, the production of water-efficient oilseeds, such as castor bean and safflower, may boost agriculture in savannahs with lower impacts on natural resources, as well as generate new business, such as 'green chemistry'.

The facets of agricultural growth in the region were basically anchored on the large-scale production of commodities, such as rice, soybean, corn, and, more recently, cotton. Although large scale has predominated, this productive and eco-nomic dynamic has also favoured a good number of medium properties (IBGE, 2018c). This context developed an extremely competitive structure, albeit one with many asymmetries among economic agents, thus raising and transcending traditional agricultural risks. The agricultural sector of the Cerrado is a complex system nowadays, requiring much more sophisticated risk management.

However, even if large-scale and capital-intensive agriculture is growingly dominant, it does not mean that the contribution of small farmers is negligible. Apart from being numerous and spread throughout all corners of the region, these farms have significant participation in several products, compared to the country's totals, such as cassava (12%), beans (10%), corn (30%), rice (26%), milk (61%), beef (34%) and pork (37%) (IBGE, 2018c). But it must be noted that part of the small-scale units is embedded in a system dedicated to the production of technology- and capital-intensive commodities, which makes the competitive environment even more difficult for small farmers.

4 The Northeastern semiarid: a new duality

The semiarid region (or Caatinga) is one of the largest Brazilian biomes and home to 1,262 municipalities located in nine states (Maranhão, Piauí, Rio Grande do Norte, Paraíba, Pernambuco, Alagoas, Sergipe, Bahia and Minas Gerais) – see Figures 0.1 and 0.2 in Introduction. Some basic indicators define the region: average annual rainfall of 800 mm or less, Thornthwaite moisture index of 0.50 or less and daily water deficit of 60% or more, considering all days of the year (SUDENE, 2018). The semiarid covers an area of around one million square kilometres, which makes up nearly 12% of the national territory. Its typ-ical vegetation is the Caatinga, but this biome has been threatened by wide-spread desertification. In four states, Piauí, Ceará, Rio Grande do Norte and Paraíba, this phenomenon already comprises more than 95% of their total area.

In the present century, the region has undergone unexpected but positive changes, due to its economic growth rates, which have been higher than the national average. They result from a greater economic expansion and to the new (and also unexpected) forces developed in the region to resist periodic droughts. However, these promising indicators are relative, since the initial level for comparison is very low *vis-à-vis* the rest of Brazil. Several factors influenced the evolution of this region. It started during a time when supermarkets were looted, jobs on 'emergency fronts' were created and dramatic indicators of malnutrition and hunger were usually associated with prolonged periods of insufficient rainfall.

Another revealing tendency, which has become more intense since the 1990s, is the unstoppable movement of urbanization in the region. According to Alves and Souza (2015), its total population grows in parallel with the rates verified in urban areas, despite the reduction in the total rural population. Rural out-migration has been intense, but nowadays the population does not abandon the countryside towards other regions of the country (notably the centre of Brazil), as they used to do from the 1950s to the 1970s; these migrants are moving to the largest cities in the semiarid itself. The reasons that explain these population movements are a combination of an arguably good road system with better means of transportation – either public transportation or motorcycles, as a result of higher family income –, coupled with the demand for work in those cities due to the expansion of civil construction, major infrastructure works in the region and new industrial installations. People decide to migrate mainly between 18 and 40 years old, precisely the population who are mostly affected by lack of employment and income opportunities in the rural settings of the semiarid.

Most specialists agree that the main reason explaining out-migration and the current trend of urbanization in the region is the very low monetary gains of most of those who remain in the countryside, because their agricultural efforts result in dire levels of income. The region is also (possibly) the most populous semiarid region in the world and where most of the country's rural poverty is concentrated, both facets strongly contributing to develop a typical underdeveloped context that squeezes incomes and wages (Buanain and Garcia, 2013). The most urgent social need by far is accessing to water for human consumption. In addition, immediate and pressing actions need to be taken (related to, for example, infrastructure and security) by local authorities, given the emerging and fast pace of urbanization in the semiarid.

4.1 The dual semiarid region

The rural semiarid is strongly demarcated by two distinct social realities: the irrigated and the non-irrigated (or rainfall-dependent) areas. The irrigated areas inevitably stand out for much stronger economic dynamism, higher productivity and intensive production. The non-irrigated areas, on the other hand, have embodied an age-old opposite history: stagnation, low productivity and insufficient production, all aspects resulting in high and permanent levels of rural poverty. It is not analytically possible to understand the semiarid as a whole, since the economic trajectory of irrigated and non-irrigated areas are completely different. Consequently, the nature and goals of public policies implemented in the region are diverse.

(i) Irrigated perimeters: a group of oases in the middle of the semiarid

Irrigated agriculture was developed by public investments, with the installation of 'irrigated perimeters' controlled by DNOCS (the National Department for Works to Combat Droughts) and by CODEVASF (the São Francisco and Parnaíba Valley Development Company). These two federal bodies control all perimeters that exist in the semiarid states, with a total irrigated (or subject of irrigation) area of over 255,000 hectares (DNOCS, 2018; CODEVASF, 2018). However, there are many areas outside these perimeters which are still waiting for these projects. According to FAO/Aquastat (2018), the irrigation potential in the Northeast would be approximately one million hectares. Considering that the Caatinga comprises around 84 million hectares, the total of one million hectares represents approximately 1.2%. That is, a very small proportion of the overall total could be irrigated.

However, this almost negligible percentage has great impact from an economic and social point of view. As an illustration, the combination of natural resources related to the climate and water available through irrigation materialized ideal conditions for the São Francisco Valley sub-region to produce over the entire year. As a result, the sub-region, the most important irrigated area of the Semiarid specialized in fruit production, earned more than 270 million dollars with the export of mangos and grapes in 2017. The whole exported production of fine table grape in Brazil is located in the São Francisco Valley, as well as 85% of exported mangos. Despite the great importance of external markets, the largest consumer of fruit production from the Valley is the domestic market, since only 10% of grapes and 23% of the mango production is exported (Comex Stat, 2018; IBGE, 2018c). Thus, the region also contributes to ensure access to year-round affordable, high-quality, healthy food for the rest of the country.

The various activities of viticulture and mango farming are extremely labour intensive. But there are notable differences in the productive management of these products: viticulture requires women's work more intensely, but mango production is the opposite, with the predominance of men. In the packing houses, women comprise the majority of the workforce in both cases. During the harvest period, usually in the second half of each year, only the Rural Workers' Trade Union (STR) of Petrolina, in Pernambuco, has 49,000 registered workers. This high labour demand occurs in an extremely poor area, a context in which, if it were not for irrigated agriculture, these unskilled workers would probably not be able to find alternative jobs. Thus, irrigated agriculture, in a nutshell, is directly responsible for generating employment, income and foreign exchange.

From the environmental point of view, irrigated fruit production is guided by international standards of quality and is supposed to take into consideration accepted norms of food safety and respect for the environment and for workers' rights. This activity is carried out in such a way that producers struggle to obtain the various types of certificates (Tesco, HACCP, Rainforest Alliance, GlobalGAP, Albert Heijn, BSCI, among others) in order to guarantee access to external markets. However, in the case of small producers, this is a process that demands yet more attention, standing as one of the most acute problems in irrigated agriculture. Although only the rosy aspects are usually shown, there are several difficulties within irrigated agriculture, related to poor management, inefficiency in marketing and lack of an organizational culture. However, these problems are totally different from those faced by non-irrigated agriculture.

(ii) Rain-dependent semiarid sub-regions

Non-irrigated agriculture relies entirely on the vicissitudes of rainfall in the region and irrigation is not used at all. This is the dramatic reality of a vast part of the semiarid, where precipitations are erratic and droughts are cyclically recurrent. Numerous studies have insisted on how to maximize the efficiency of scarce water use and there have been numerous practical attempts seeking strategies to capture, store and use rainwater, through barriers, cisterns or underground dams and other possible solutions.

In most of the region, rainfall reaches average values of less than 500 mm per year. The more a geographical location is in the centre of the region, the less precipitation occurs. Besides being too low, rainfall is usually irregularly distributed over time, generating the 'green drought' phenomenon, which has serious consequences for agricultural production (Silva et al., 2010). As an example, from 2011 to 2017, in the area around the city of Petrolina (located in the Pernambuco state), an average of 228.7 mm per year was registered and the lowest value occurred in 2012, with only 93 mm of precipitation during the year. In addition, all estimated scenarios suggest higher temperatures and lower precipitations not only in this specific city, but for virtually all the semiarid.

A serious social barrier to diminish this problem is the incorrect storage of rainwater by the population, unlike other countries with dry regions that can 'store each drop'. The region has a large number of reservoirs that can be considered 'shallow', whilst smaller collectors with great depth would be more appropriate. The current format contributes to much more intense evaporation, due to the high temperatures that prevail in the region. Thus, in few months within a year, a reservoir can reach its maximum load capacity but also waste much of the water due to evaporation.

Although a necessary condition for agricultural production, water is not the only required resource. About 80% of the semiarid presents soils with low productive potential for several reasons (Silva et al., 2010). A large expanse of land is usually formed by various sub-types of soil, which resemble a large patchwork, with different sub-groups and qualities, although generally poor (hard, shallow and rocky) due to the geological 'founding factor' of the area, with 70% of it being on crystalline shields (Silva et al., 2010). The combined problem of lack of water and poor soil is compounded by serious problems related to the skewed agrarian structure and a large number of unskilled poor small producers with no technical assistance and access to credit and technology. In short, the whole picture presents a set of 'multiple needs' (Aquino et al., 2014).

All these deficiencies in production lead, in particular, to low agricultural productivity in most of the entire semiarid region. Alves and Souza (2015), based on data extracted from the 2006 Census, show that farms with less than 100 hectares, despite representing 87.82% of the total number of farms, are very poor and account for only 18% of the total gross income generated by agriculture in the region. Even the units that are larger than 100 hectares have low gross income per hectare. These figures indicate that access to land is not enough, since soil quality, water for irrigation and access to technology are also equally necessary to obtain sufficient income from agricultural activities in the semiarid.

5 What are the solutions?

The three regional cases summarized here demonstrate, in particular, two main facets worth mentioning. On the one hand, the enormous list of specificities in each case described justifies the need of more in-depth studies about them, in order to devise solutions and paths to development that are also specific and in line with those regional particularities. On the other hand, these cases clearly uncover a picture of social asymmetries that have been deepening with the passing of time, thus bringing to the fore the growing obstacles faced by the vast majority of rural farmers. On top of their immediate need for higher income, any proposed action or policy must take into consideration the possibilities for job-creation, environmental requirements and several other constraints as well. It is for these reasons that answers are not at all trivial – they are not merely technical but involve conflicting interests that can only be overcome through complex exercises of social negotiation.

In the case of the vast Amazon region, here represented by the recent trajectory of Pará, it is likely that the forest will persist 'burning' for a long time if these technological options do not emerge. The solution is not what international organizations commonly defend, such as strategies like 'returning to the forest', living off extractivism, selling carbon credits, or offering environmental services with the creation of extractive reserves or sustainable development reserves. There is a widespread (and misguided) belief that various forms of foreign aid will save the Amazon. The fact is that the environmental dimensions of the region have led to visions and proposals that – when rigorously analysed – are eventually translated into positions which are indeed against agriculture, take an antidevelopment stance and are in favour of an underdevelopment that has historically affected local populations. Countless initiatives, supposedly in favour of extractivists, *quilombolas*, native and riverside populations and small producers, actually conceal embedded productive and technological paradoxes. Their implementation cannot guarantee employment and income for most of the local population, especially its poorest layers. Products stemming from extractivism are offered in still untested markets, such as the sale of carbon credits and environmental services and may fall victim to their occasional success.

In the case of the Cerrado, the challenges are not minor. The region lacks major transport infrastructure to benefit both small and even medium-sized rural properties and the complex needs of various production chains. Despite the growing diversification of production, the regional economy is still fundamentally dependent on the production and trade of four commodities: soybean, corn, cotton and meat. It is particularly vulnerable to climate risks and commodity price volatility in international markets, in addition to increasing environmental impacts (Vieira Junior et al., 2006).

The semiarid region is also under threat from several corners. On the one hand, the devastating drought during the 2012–2017 period, exacerbated by the national economic crisis after 2015, reversed the previous dynamism and reduced the prospects of growth based on the service sector and transfers of income from the federal government. On the other hand, the long period of drought disclosed the vulnerability of the irrigated activity itself. In many areas, irrigation projects, which were developed using a substantial financial investment, were interrupted by lack of water. The rise in water consumption by the urban population, agriculture and energy production seems to be incompatible with the existing local water supply sources, mainly from the São Francisco River (its natural average flow has been gradually decreasing due to deforestation and erosion). Over 70% of the semiarid municipalities suffer permanent water shortages and are supplied by water tank trucks, reproducing the same historical context in which the dependence of water placed the population at the mercy of favour by local elites.

Given these caveats, it is a logical fact that solutions must be different according to each region. The Forest Code approved in 2012 can generate new opportunities for sustainable development. For the Amazon region, the Code establishes the use of mere 20% of the private property and the corresponding obligation to preserve the remaining 80%, while outside the Amazon region the norm is the opposite. In the part of the Cerrado located in the Amazonia states, legal impositions establish the protection of 35% of each property and 65% may be used for productive purposes, which amounts to deforestation of this part. As a consequence of the approval of the new Code by the Congress, an unavoidable reality will gradually be imposed, whether in the Amazon or elsewhere. This new juncture presupposes, in fact, two paths that are not necessarily mutually exclusive: either raising the productivity of the land or seizing regional advantages to maintain the competitiveness and sustainability of productive activities (Tritsch and Arvor, 2016). Another challenge is the reduction of the potential area for production, with the transfer of cattle ranching and cultivated areas to other locations in order to recover the environmental liabilities of deforestation that occurred in the past.

A new agricultural model needs to be developed in Pará (and in the Amazon region as a whole), based on the planting and cultivation of native flora and fauna, with low or no competition with other regions. There is a productive route potentially interested in medicinal, aromatic and cosmetic uses, natural dye and insecticide plants, as well as in health benefits, but still needs more of a proven technological framework. Amazonian agriculture has been based mainly on exotic biodiversity so far (jute, black pepper, soybean, cattle, buffalo, oil palm, coffee, eucalyptus, among others). Such a proposed agriculture based on regional native plants – such as cassava, cacao, guarana, chestnut, açai, cupuaçu, peach palm, only to name some of the most important ones – could combine production with greater sustainability if more advanced technological frames are developed. However, the far-reaching revolution the region could potentially envisage is a serious effort in aquaculture, taking advantage of the nearly limitless availability of water. The production of Amazonian fishes could replace cattle ranching as a source of protein with far less environmental impacts.

It is still unknown when the forest transition in the Amazon will occur[2]: it can happen five or 20 years from now. In most European countries and in many North-American states, the transition occurred when the forests had already been reduced to less than half, sometimes even completely deforested. 19% of the Amazon has been deforested so far and if the present rate is maintained, the deforested area shall increase to 20% or 21% until reversal and stabilization are developed. Empirically, each percentage point in deforestation means the subtraction of five million hectares of forest or secondary vegetation (an area equivalent to the size of Denmark). There is a deforested area limit that needs to be opened in order to give way to agricultural, industrial and mineral activities, cities, road, hydroelectric and port infrastructure, among others, comprising basically around 15% of the total area, with 85% remaining with forest cover, once the process is stabilized.

The development of tropical agriculture is technically possible, both with native or exotic species, but sustainability will depend on the technological pattern adopted. The low accumulated stock of local technology with concrete solutions has been the most challenging issue in the occupation of the Amazon. In fact, cheaper unsustainable practices, in addition to poor technical and monitoring assistance, have been the cause of the systematic destruction of natural resources.

As a consequence, one observes a curious tendency towards an anti-Schumpeterian 'destructive destruction' by the actions of the government itself. There is a lack of sensible government support for research institutions and greater consequence in the management of public affairs, leading to a 'tragedy of communal spaces' in the Amazon. Current legislation on access to biodiversity resources added to the existing legislation on the protection of forest resources but have developed an unattractive complex context in terms of planting, processing and technology generation. There is no broader social agreement on the proposals for the development of the Amazon yet. Those interested in preservation and those motivated by 'destruction' (or production) are, in fact, struggling to survive or serve larger market interests. The protracted impact of many proposals preaching the defence of extractivism tends to harm producers in their search for productive alternatives and also hamper consumers' access to cheaper and better products.

The situation and perspectives of agriculture and cattle ranching in the Cerrado region are quite different. This is a successful example of an agricultural frontier, in which dynamism has been based on productivity gains through innovation to counterbalance the infrastructure deficit. This model of development has led to the relative homogenization of the productive format of modern agriculture, based on the production of grains, fibres and meat. It is true that some of the challenges encountered by the first generation of farmers when they arrived in the region, such as logistics, storage and energy, still persist. The challenge of transportation is not minor either, since the initial transport infrastructure emphasized national integration, with São Paulo as the dynamic centre. The current production, nevertheless, requires an international transport network. Despite the official propaganda, the overcoming of transport obstacles in the region have been being driven mainly by initiatives of farmers and other entrepreneurs or efforts by companies themselves instead of actions promoted by the government.

The second group of challenges is associated with the diversification of agriculture in the Cerrado, with the central purpose of reducing the vulnerability of some commodities. From a strategic point of view, it would be a matter of creating a robust model of diversified agriculture in the region. Perhaps the biggest obstacle relates to the management of natural resources, especially the reduction of deforestation and the best possible technical usage of water resources. This requires a productive intensification of agriculture (irrigation and diversification of production) and new modalities of cattle ranching (integrated systems), as well as a better use of genetic resources and traditional knowledge. Given the attractive profitability of soybean production, stimulating these changes in land use and technological models is a very complex challenge.

In the semiarid region, in turn, when irrigation is unavailable, the survival of most producers depends heavily on government income transfers, such as direct monetary forms of aid, pensions or some payment for environmental services, as a sort of 'guardians of the Caatinga'. Forms of pluri-activity performed by members of the family are also crucial to raise income. Given the recent boom in motorcycle use by poorer families, these multiple forms of labour – rural and urban – have grown visibly in recent times.

In this vast region, the great challenge of increasing productivity as a possible driver to materialize higher income remains. Since the mid-1950s, studies by the Working Group for the Development of the Northeast (GTDN) had already indicated the serious problem of sustaining a low-productivity economy (GTDN, 1997). After more than 50 years, this structural obstacle persists with an aggravating factor: productivity has not grown, but the population has increased fourfold. Agriculture practiced outside irrigated areas is still lagging behind, with very low productivity and it is unable to generate the surplus needed to ensure that families live on an income above the poverty line. The official motto that has guided many public policies has been to promote the 'coexistence' with regular droughts in the semiarid. However, it should be noted that young people living in the region are no longer prepared to 'live' with the droughts. They want to thrive and have purchasing power that allows them to access markets and services.

In the three cases synthesized here, a major challenge is to successfully promote the economic inclusion of small farmers in the markets, enabling the generation of enough income to overcome poverty in a sustainable way and reduce social inequalities. This major challenge depends crucially on consistent and persistent public policies focused on development rather than the short-term view that has guided most of the actions implemented by the Brazilian State. In most experiences, for example, the rationale of these government interventions does not seriously assume that solid technical assistance and various forms of good educational initiatives are essential conditions for real development in these regions.

6 Conclusions

The Brazilian agricultural expansion over the last 50 years, particularly in the last 25 years, has faced several structural transformations of evident economic and productive importance. For the purposes of this chapter, two major changes stand out. First, compared with an earlier historical period – the immediate postwar period – the structural heterogeneity found in the vast rural territory of the country has deepened remarkably. The distances among Brazilian regions, of all natures (economic-financial, productive, technological or, *lato sensu*, organizational), widened and, thus, regional inequalities became an even more typical phenomenon of rural Brazil. It is not a matter of revisiting a past classic, *Os dois Brasis* (1957) by the Frenchman Jacques Lambert, but perhaps insisting on the development format of production that would suggest the structural existence of 'several Brazils' in different regions. The rural world has become a highly differentiated mosaic of economic dynamics, with intense social repercussions, nearly radically restructuring, for example, the rural labour market, now practically unified throughout the territory. There are, therefore, profound changes in diverse scopes of the economy and society that demand renewed efforts of interpretation and understanding.

The second change worth mentioning is that in all cases briefly discussed in this chapter the emergence and consolidation of a new pattern of production is observed, one no longer based on the extensive and unproductive exploitation of natural resources and abundant and cheap labour. On the contrary, its new foundations lie in the intensification of capital, in the increase of productivity caused by technology and in impressive organizational innovations. The heterogeneity is accentuated by the detachment and consolidation of this new structural pattern, which is not accessible to most producers under present Brazilian conditions.

This chapter intended to offer general views on three regional contexts that are paradigmatic of this broad transformation process now on course in Brazilian rural regions. These are different situations, although interdependent, due to the relations of some types of markets, such as labour and basic foods, for example, as well as the financial markets (investments of firms in different regions), among other possibilities that have been brought to fruition in increasing magnitude. The chapter also suggests the need to expand studies that relate the whole and its interpretation to specific sub-territorial situations as the only analytical path that will explain the economic and productive possibilities of globalized rural Brazil in the coming years. This expansion is also imperative because it is the only way to foresee the social, institutional and political consequences of this course of transformation, which will probably close a chapter of the Brazilian history in its innumerable rural shades.

Notes

1 Each section of this chapter results from previous longer and detailed preliminary unpublished internal reports by one of the three authors. Alfredo Homma wrote about the case of Pará, João Ricardo Lima about the particularities of the semiarid region in the rural Northeast and Pedro Abel Vieira about the pattern of agrarian development in the Centre-west.

2 The forest transition occurs when the balance of deforestation is offset by reforestation and recovery of forest liabilities induced by the new Brazilian legislation (Chazdon et al., 2016; Veríssimo and Nussbaum, 2011; Barbier et al., 2017).

13 Challenges of current land governance in Brazil

Beyond the historical, political and social demands for land reform

Bastiaan Philip Reydon

1 Introduction

Brazil is a country with one of the largest areas of arable farmland in the world. However, it has one of the highest rates of concentration of land ownership and cases of land-focused conflict, both in urban and rural areas. The main reason for this scenario is the absence of a system of land administration capable of effectively controling the use of and access to land ownership. Its absence and the existence of a myriad of laws and organizations that do not interact with each other have mainly served the interests of large landowners, who were able, over time, to take possession of free public land, speculate and dispose of it without any constraint and control from the State (Reydon et al., 2015).

Primarily, from the beginning of the 1950s, the main policy proposed to address the predominance of largescale, inefficient ownership, both internationally and in Brazil, was the implementation of agrarian reform.[1] The agrarian reform proposed to strip latifundia into smaller rural enterprise units, and in various countries it was sold as a panacea for two different, but convergent problems: the inefficiency of traditional agriculture and the concentration of power of land aristocracy.

In Brazil, the proposal to implement an agrarian reform was on the political, economic and social agenda for many decades, until the end of the 1990s. The country undertook significant and costly agrarian reform between 1985 and 2010, benefiting around one million families, but no economic, social or political impacts had been felt.[2] The Landless Movement (MST, in Portuguese), the main catalyst in this process, which has never accepted the legitimacy of this agrarian reform, lost much of its political clout and has continued to propose a massive agrarian reform as an important way to move forward towards socialism.

On the other hand, the agriculture and livestock sector in Brazil has, over the course of the last 50 years, seen an extraordinary evolution, with increased production and productivity, thus completely fulfilling its role of producing food, raw materials, foreign exchange and energy. However, this process has further concentrated production in large land properties, marginalizing family farming reducing occupation in rural areas, stimulating exodus from the countryside and exacerbating environmental contradictions (Buainain et al., 2014).

The problems associated with land ownership/tenure affect the vast majority of families in Brazil,[3] and have their origin in the historic process of occupation of Brazilian territory (Silva, 1996) and the creation of land legislation and rules that were always patchy, unenforced and unintegrated (Reydon et al., 2017). However, the mounting contradictions regarding land use, social conflicts in rural areas and environment conservation point to the need of having clearer rules on the use and occupation of the rural and urban soil.

The definition of preservation areas of nature is essential for assuring the provision of the so-called ecological services and the rich biodiversity, especially of tropical forests. The absence of limits or regulation on land access reduces incentive to use the soil in more efficient ways vis-à-vis the maintenance of low-productivity production systems based on the abundance of low-cost land.

Regarding land conflicts, violence continues to claim hundreds of victims in the countryside and fatalities abound on both sides, among farmers and their foremen and also landless people. In cities, repossession orders in occupied areas, conflicts over ownership, false filing in land registry offices and various types of irregularity with land registration and transactions are numerous, usually involving expensive and protracted legal resolution.

In this chapter the key issue of land distribution and the agrarian situation in Brazil is analysed through the lens of land governance, positing that the country requires more than agrarian reform, as has been historically demanded by social movements. It requires a rather significant improvement in land governance strategy and policies, which would provide the means to reconcile seemingly contradictory objectives, such as social justice in rural areas, environmental protection and sustainable expansion of agricultural production.

2 The agrarian situation in Brazil

The land-ownership problem in Brazil persists even in the twenty-first century. At a time when Brazil is striding boldly towards becoming one of the global food power, various aspects of its agrarian context are still a matter of concern. The country continues to appear in foreign news broadcasts with four serious dysfunctions associated with land tenure and land conflicts, involving human casualties; an extremely high concentration of land ownership, land-grabbing[4] and deforestation of the Amazon Forest. In addition, land speculation aggravates these problems and further distorts the allocation of resources and the use of land, especially free land owned by the State. As noted by Reydon and Fernandes (2017), successful land speculation is part of the economic mindset in Brazil. This speculation occurs in different ways, ranging from valid investments and local development to the less unethical methods, such as those resulting from deforestation and the unlawfully transformation of rural land into urban developments.

2.1 Agrarian conflict[5]

Table 13.1 shows that, throughout the first decade of this century, the number of disputes over land, some of which involve violence and significant human costs, remains at a high level. The number of conflicts stands at around one thousand per year, with over 300,000 people involved during the last three decades.

It is undeniable, therefore, that an agrarian issue related to violence in the countryside does exist. This conflict, however, is fundamentally the result of the disorderly pattern of land occupation and the absence of effective mechanisms that guarantee rights to land tenure or ownership in the country.[6]

2.2 Evidence of fraud and falsification involving land in Brazil

As land in Brazil was usually occupied without any payment, as required by the Land Law, regularization of land has always been a source of fraud and falsification of documents are an aggravating factor to this process. In other words, some occupants, given the lenient and permissive nature of land governance, resorted to fraud and falsification in order to obtain their registration and thereby make their ownership official. The commonest subterfuge, however, are falsifications and frauds involving land that is already occupied by various types of traditional populations and small farmers, who end up being, therefore, a common from these areas.

Fraud is, therefore, a common process of grabbing land from public heritage and registering it as legal private property. These well-known practices were systematized in the report entitled White Paper on Land Grabbing in Brazil, INCRA (1999:2):

Table 13.1 Some numbers on conflict in the countryside, Brazil, 2003–2016

	Number of conflicts	Murders	People involved	Area involved (ha)
2003	1,690	73	1,190,578	3,831,405
2004	1,801	39	975,987	5,069,399
2005	1,881	38	1,021,355	11,487,072
2006	1,657	39	783,801	5,051,348
2007	1,538	28	795,341	8,420,083
2008	1,170	28	502,390	6,568,755
2009	1,184	26	628,009	15,116,590
2010	1,186	34	559,401	13,312,343
2011	1,363	29	600,925	14,410,626
2012	1,364	36	648,515	13,181,570
2013	1,266	34	573,118	6,228,667
2014	1,286	36	817,102	8,134,241
2015	1,217	50	816,837	21,387,160
2016	1,536	61	909,843	23,697,019

Source: Pastoral Land Commission, Countryside Conflicts – several years.

In a survey which is the first of its kind, INCRA is mapping the country's land structure in order to identify, one by one, cases of fraud and falsification of land ownership title. Land grabbing is one of the most powerful domain and land concentration tools in the rural milieu of Brazil. Across the whole country, the total area of land suspected of being the object of land grab is approximately 100 million hectares, or four times the area of the state of São Paulo or the area of Central America plus Mexico. In the Northern region, the numbers are alarming: of the total area of the state of Amazonas, 157 million hectares, it is suspected that no less than 55 million are the result of land grabbing, corresponding to three times the territory of Paraná. In the state of Pará, a 'ghost' sold approximately nine million hectares of public land to dozens of successors.

The same report, published by INCRA (1999:15), preliminarily points to the causes of these problems when it states:

> Fraud was historically facilitated by certain institutional loopholes such as the lack of a single cadaster. The land agencies at the three levels (federal, state and municipal), are not connected to each other. In Brazil, unlike other countries, there are no special, specific records for large areas. Federal and state cadasters are not cross-checked and the federal registration, under current legislation, is declaratory. The supervision of registry offices leaves much to be desired.

In 2001, the legislative House conducted an exhaustive survey of the land-ownership situation by way of a Parliamentary Commission of Inquiry whose focus was Land Grabbing[7] in the Amazon. The report showed that the acquisition of land in Brazil takes place by maintaining its exclusionary, concentrated character, through the absence of adequate management of public land, the lack of an overall mapped cadaster and a flawed system of registration. Despite the fact that frauds occur more frequently in the Northern region of Brazil, the types of fraud described below occur frequently all over the national territory.[8] The main ones are:

1) *Registration without the corresponding title deed or previous registration, (...).*
2) *Duplicate property registration, (...)*
3) *Acceptance of the property registrations contained in property division rulings, which did not present the corresponding proof of title (...).*
4) *Recording of annotations or the opening of new enrollments, corresponding to demarcations of tracts of land, without legal authorization or that of INCRA(...).*
5) *Registration of deeds of purchase and sale and other supposed title deeds issued with an age of 20 years or more (...)*

As a result of surveys conducted by the Federal Government, the courts brought a number of legal actions to cancel various titles filed by the land registry offices. At the beginning of the twenty-first century, according to Lima (2002), in 14 judicial districts of the state of Amazonas (see Figure 0.1 in the Introduction of the book), the equivalent of 48.5 million hectares of properties registered with the respective land registry offices were cancelled. In 2009, the National Council of Justice (CNJ) cancelled 410 million hectares in respect of 5,500 rural property registrations in registry offices in the state of Pará (Rodriguez et al., 2013).

In short, despite the existence of a wealth of constitutional, agrarian, environmental and planning laws, as well as laws involving civil property, they are amalgamated into the three spheres that govern land relations in Brazil. In an attempt to implement the establishment and regularization of land-ownership rights, registration, documentation and other associated processes, the mechanics are leaving a lot to be desired and permit various forms of land-ownership fraud, which reinforces the processes of land concentration and frequently leads to conflict over land ownership.

2.3 Concentration of land ownership

One of the features of the land situation in Brazil is the land-ownership concentration distribution, as shown in Table 13.2. Brazil has possibly one of the highest rates of land concentration in the world.

The Gini coefficient of ownership continues at a high level of 0.85 and shows no sign of decreasing despite efforts at democratization/distribution via agrarian reform. The share of the total area of the smallest 50% of agriculture and livestock establishments continues at around 2.3%, while the largest 5% of establishments add up to over 69.3% of the total land. The extensive agrarian reform, has not altered the Brazil's agrarian structure, as the settlers have still not received title, meaning that the expropriated properties remain intact.

High concentration of land ownership is one of the main sources of the country's large social and economic inequalities and of rural poverty,[9] inasmuch as the poorest do not have access to the land.

Table 13.2 Land structure of agriculture & livestock establishments in Brazil

	1975	1985	1995/6	2006	2017
No. establishments (million)	5.0	5.7	4.8	5.12	5.0
Total area in ha (million)	323.9	369.6	353.6	333.0	350.2
Mean area (ha)	64.9	71.7	72.8	67.1	70.1
Gini Coefficient	0.855	0.859	0.857	0.856	–
Area of smallest 50% (%)	2.5	2.4	2.3	2.3	2.3
Area of largest 5% (%)	68.7	69.7	68.8	69.3	69.4

Source: IBGE (2018c).

The dysfunctional pattern of urban land occupation itself also has its origins in the high concentration of rural land, which feeds the processes of social exclusion and urban poverty.

An example of poor incentives to invest in the intensification of production is the idleness and/or low degree of utilization of agricultural land, expressed in the low average rate of beef cattle capacity in the country, which is a little over one animal per hectare. Another dimension of the high concentration of land in the country is the largescale acquisition of land via illegal means, including by foreigners.

2.4 Deforestation of the Amazon rainforest

The persistently high levels of deforestation in the Amazon region are also related to the lack of an answer to the agrarian question in Brazil, particularly the regulation of land ownership. Figure 13.1, based on satellite images, demonstrates that the deforestation in the Amazon, in recent years, is ranging from 6.4 to 7.4 million hectares, dropping to less than 5,000 km^2 in 2012, which represents a substantial improvement. However, it is still a high level of deforestation for a biome with the characteristics of the Amazon region, which plays strategic roles for the sustainability of Brazilian agriculture – the rain forest is one of the major sources of rainfall in the Cerrados and in the Southeast regions – and for the stabilization of climate in the world.

Numerous studies[10] have evaluated the causes of deforestation in the Brazilian Amazon. One such study, by Moutinho et al. (2016), lists the six main factors: a) the Growth Acceleration Plan (PAC) and infrastructure works; b) growth in the demand for commodities (meat and grain); c) unsustainable policy on rural

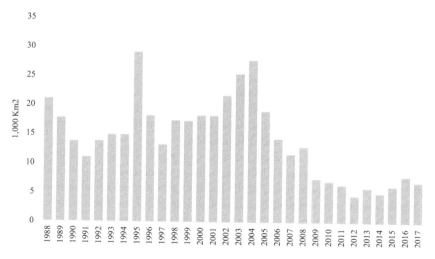

Figure 13.1 Annual deforestation in the Legal Amazon (Km2 a year). Source: PRODES[11] (2017).

settlements (agrarian reform); d) inadequate application of the Forestry Code; e) lobbying by Agribusiness in the National Congress and f) land-ownership ambiguities and the existence of undesignated public forests. Margulis (2004), in more general terms, states that the main drivers of deforestation are: a) increase in profits linked to the use of land in the Amazon region; b) accessibility of public policies and loans for the region; c) installation of infrastructure for access to frontier areas; d) phases of GDP growth.

Reydon (2011), while not disagreeing with the aforementioned conclusions, stresses that the mechanism of Amazon deforestation is the product of the traditional form of continuous expansion of the agricultural frontier in Brazil, with the occupation of (private or public) virgin lands, the legal extraction of timber, the introduction of extensive livestock farming[12] and, subsequently, the development of a more modern agriculture and livestock sector. These economic activities are the primary source of income for new poor settlers, thus legitimizing the occupation of land by this group. However, this land is latter transferred, by various means, to land grabbers and large farmers and entrepreneurs.[13] In the long run, the land is used to more intensive livestock farming or, if there is demand, converted to cultivating grain or other economic activities.

However, what is important for occupation or deforestation is the existence of an expectation that there will be demand for this land at some point in the future, causing its price to rise significantly.[14] The closer it is to being used productively, the higher the appreciation of these lands.

3 From agrarian reform to adequate land governance

The land ownership situation in Brazil, with its disputes over land in both the countryside and cities, the concentration of land ownership, land speculation, fraud and deforestation, goes unscathed and the main policy implemented to curb these problems was agrarian reform. This is certainly due to political pressure and the diagnosis that it would resolve the land problem in the country. As part of this policy, over 1.4 million families were resettled across an area of almost 92 million hectares, as shown in Table 13.3. This was one of the largest agrarian reforms undertaken anywhere in the world.[15] As mentioned, there is no evidences that the agrarian reform has contributed to reduce land concentration[16] in the country; neither to solve the other problems, such as fraud and land appropriation, conflicts and deforestation.

For De Janvry (1981), the main function of agrarian reforms, whether related to the transition from semi-feudal to capitalist or socialist systems, is to shift political power out from the hands of the traditional landed elite. Agrarian reform in Brazil, despite the impressive numbers, did not fulfil the function proposed by Janvry, nor did it create the conditions for the construction of a fairer society.

Defenders of agrarian reform in Brazil, such as Robles (2018: 29), understand that there is no place at the present time for the pursuit of agrarian reform along the lines of a more profound social transition:

Table 13.3 Brazilian Land Reform – Official Beneficiaries, 1964–2013

Period of Military and Democratic Regimes	No. of Families Settled	Set Target	Total area (Million hectares)	No. of Families Settled – Average Per year
Military (1964–1984)	77,465	N/A	13.8	3,873
Sarney (1985–1990)	89,950	1.4 million	4.5	17,990
Collor and Franco (1990–1994)	60,188	N/A	2.3	15,049
Cardoso (1995–2002)	540,704	N/A	20.8	67,588
Lula (2003–2010)	614,088	400,000	47.9	76,761
Rousseff (2011–2013)	75,335		2.5	25,111
Total	1,457.730		91.8	
Total (1985–2013)	1,380.265		78.0	

Sources: Data collected from the following sources: 'Agrarian Reform: Commitment of everyone'. Department of Social Communication, Presidency of the Republic, 1997; INCRA, Summary of INCRA Activities, 1985–1994; MDA, Summary 2003–2006: Agrarian development as a strategy; and INCRA Journal, Summary 2003, 2010 and 2014.

Notes: 1. Most of these families received land titles via colonization and settlement projects. Although during the 1995–2010 period there was a substantial increase in the granting of land titles, the total number fell short of the 1.4-million target set in 1985.

Indigenous and landless rural worker movements cannot, by themselves, defend and advance their interests within the present socioeconomic context. The correlations of political forces are not in their favor. Therefore, these movements need to rethink, reshape and reorient their visions, strategies and objectives to reinvigorate the struggle for the defense of their cultures and livelihoods. Certainly, this requires building more organic links with urban-based movements. Perhaps, a more organized and concerted rural–urban political alliance – built on a strong class consciousness, identity and solidarity – would be capable of advancing far-reaching structural changes in the Brazilian countryside. Without radical agrarian reform, Brazil is likely to remain one of the most unequal societies in the world.

The management or administration of tenure and the use of land remains a topic that has been neglected by policy-makers and scholars of the agriculture and livestock sector in Brazil, despite its considerable importance. The apparent indifference is due, on the one hand, to the weight exerted by the interest aroused by the processes of agrarian reform and distribution of land, while on the other hand, through the legal and institutional framework of Brazil, which has always approached the topic in a segmented, unintegrated fashion (Reydon et al., 2017).

Despite resistance, this topic has increasingly aroused the interest of international cooperation agencies, financial institutions and also the Brazilian government. Among these agencies, the involvement of the United Nations FAO may be highlighted, which published 'The Voluntary Guidelines on Responsible Governance of Tenure of Land, Fisheries and Forests in the Context of National Food Security' (VGGT), approved at the thirty-eighth extraordinary session of the Committee on World Food Security (CFS), in May 2012.

Figure 13.2 presents the main elements for structuring an effective land governance mechanism: a good cadaster with the mapping of all the land and its respective identifiers. Combined with this cadaster, the management of land markets through legal ownership guarantees and the values associated with it, for the purposes of taxation, *inter alia*. On the other hand, for the efficient management of land, there must be policies on the use of land and its development. With this complete picture, it is possible to achieve sustainable development.

4 Land governance in Brazil: recent progress

In Brazil, the institutional and legal framework for the administration of land is mostly to blame for the critical land situation in the country, inasmuch as the agencies behave in a competitive and disconnected manner (Reydon et al., 2017).

According to the World Bank (2014), all of these problems relate to the fact that the country has a set of rules tied to land ownership that do not allow

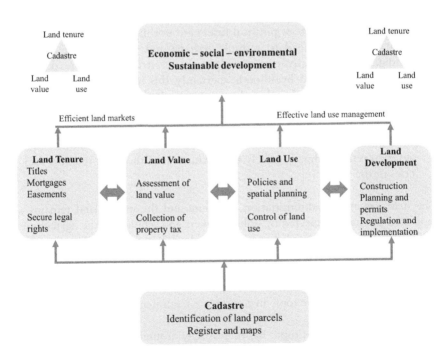

Figure 13.2 Land governance schematic. Source: Williamsom et al. (2010).

for proper regulation, resulting from the: a) lack of a cadaster; b) possibility of taking possession of and regularizing land; c) absence of taxes on the land, ending up with d) the possibility of continual land speculation.

Law 10.267/2001 is probably the key element in the transformations which can be observed in the governance of land in Brazil since the end of the 1990s, especially through the creation of the National Registry of Rural Properties (CNIR).[17] The CNIR brings together information from the land and thematic cadasters since, besides INCRA and the Internal Revenue Service, all the other Public Federal Administration agencies must be producers, suppliers and users of its information database (§3, article 7, of Decree n. 4449/2002).

The CNIR is being developed in a way that both tenure and ownership can coexist without overlapping, by means of the basic parcel unit that has been adopted. The implementation of the cadaster begun in 2005, using the following tools: The National Property Certification System (SNCI) and the Land Management System (SIGEF), which will be addressed below.

The main point that should be highlighted in respect of the construction of the CNIR is that it establishes the integration of land and thematic cadasters, having the SNCR and CAFIR databases at its core. Comprising the CNIR, the rural property certification service was created in 2003, permitting the tracking, monitoring and control over all the processes of rural property certification. This system is being supplanted by the SIGEF, which was implemented at the end of 2013, by digitizing all the information.

4.1 The Land Management System (SIGEF)

SIGEF, as part of the SNCI, is an electronic tool developed by the National Institute for Colonization and Agrarian Reform (INCRA) and the now defunct Ministry of Agrarian Development (MDA), to provide supporting information on land governance across national territory. It is composed of a digital platform into which the receipt, validation, organization, regularization and provision of georeferenced information on rural, public and private properties is input. The aim is to speed up the implementation of the Cadaster with all the country's georeferenced properties. The system has been up and running since November 2013 and is interconnected with, among others, the following public stakeholders: FUNAI, ICMBio, SPU.[18]

The area already input to the system, in the form of raw data, equates to 75.7% of the country's total surface area – Table 13.4. After eliminating overlaps, mainly with government areas such as conservation units, settlements, etc., we come to a total of 522.3 million hectares, equivalent to 61.3% of the total area of Brazil. It is undeniably an extraordinary result obtained, considering the SIGEF has only been in existence for four years.

Table 13.4. also shows that certified private properties number just 263,000, occupying an area of 178 million hectares which, when compared to the non-digital SNCR cadaster, with five million properties and 643 million hectares,

Table 13.4 Occupied area and the number of geo-referenced properties in the INCRA cadaster (CNIR/SIGEF) in 2017

Consolidated INCRA CNIR

INCRA own information

Type	Properties	Area (ha)	%
Settlements projects	7,796	76,907,385.5915	22.1
Traditional people's land – *Quilombola*	312	2,323,928.4275	0.7
Certified Public Properties – Number / Area	9,800	86,554,346.3380	24.8
Certified Private Properties – Number / Area	263,038	178,342,807.0506	51.2
Land Regularization Agreements	107,853	4,335,993.9629	1.2
Subtotal	**388,799**	**348,464,461.3705**	

Base access of partner entities

Type	Properties	Area (ha)	%
Indigenous people's land	588	116,625,185.0128	**18.1**
Conservation Units – Area	1,481	152,029,511.1307	23.6
Georeferenced Polygons – Dept. Agrarian Reorganization (SRA)	80,041	3,254,260.6942	0.5
Georeferenced Polygons – Legal Land Programme	148,969	23,976,310.1240	3.7
Subtotal	**231,079**	**295,885,266.9617**	45.9
Grand Total	**619,878**	**644,349,728.3322**	
Net area per the archives		**522,397,153.3900**	61.3
Net area (257.5 million) plus certified (264.8 million) Total Area of Brazil		**851,576,700.0000**	

Source: INCRA land archives.

shows there is still a large discrepancy. This is a result of the fact that not all properties were obliged to carry out georeferencing. Those with less than four modules, who were not obliged, still remain, signifying a big number with a small area.

The area of Indigenous Land, settlements and Conservation Units amounts to 345,562,081.74 hectares, equivalent to a rather substantial 40.6% of the national territory. In addition to all of these, which will complete the cadaster in the next few years, the large number of tenures is also a significant component to be regularized in the country and with the new law 13465/2017, significant progress will be made, as we shall demonstrate in the next section. Still on the subject of the cadaster, we must also highlight the efforts that some agencies are making with regard to the construction of the new cadaster (SINTER), which will bring together all existing cadasters, even the urban ones.

4.2 SINTER – National System of Territorial Information Management

The new cadaster which will unify all the others will be the SINTER (Decree no. 8.764/2016), coming under the responsibility of the Internal Revenue Service in Brazil. The new system is being created so as to benefit from the potential of existing modern technology, such as the electronic registry of the Land Registry Offices and the georeferencing/certification performed by INCRA, in order to meet the Brazilian State's requirements for efficiency and create an information platform that can be used by various agencies in the different spheres of government, organizing territorial data.

SINTER is a public management tool with cadastral and geospatial data of urban and rural properties registered in the Federal Union, the states, municipalities and the Federal District of Brasília (Article 1, Decree no. 8.764/2016) – Figure 13.3.

Each property will have an identifier unique to the national domain, with a structure that is specified in the Operational Manual. The information related to the valuation of properties will be consolidated in SINTER, including to provide support for the calculation of the Property Price Index (§2, Article 8, Decree no. 8.764/2016). Statistical, cyclical and structural information related to the securities and property markets and the information relating to the guarantees attached to loan transactions, shall be processed by SINTER in accordance with the data submitted by the public registries. This will enable the Brazilian Central Bank to perform unified queries across national territory of information relating to the loan and access to the information required for it to perform its duties (Article 14, Decree no. 8.764/2016).

In addition, SINTER will be a national territory management database with a multipurpose concept, an official and systematic inventory of national territory developed with appropriate technology, bringing together the electronic registration from the Land Registry Offices and the CNIR geo-referencing

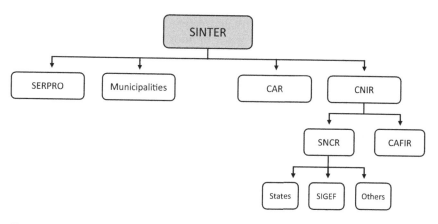

Figure 13.3 Proposed structure of SINTER.

data, including other cadasters produced by agencies, states and municipalities, which will be superimposed on the land ownership cadaster. It will be an information platform that can be used by the various agencies in different spheres of government, organizing territorial data.

The system will enable database queries to be performed by bodies such as the Internal Revenue Service, the Office of the Attorney General for the National Treasury (PGFN), Federal Police, Office of the Comptroller-General, Federal Assets Department (SPU), among others within Public Federal Administration and the Judiciary Branch, which will be able to use the data in their respective applications and create their own layers of viewing. SINTER will be able to check the overlapping of areas automatically and even alert the registrar to the fact, all of which will fully comply with the constitutional framework and the responsibilities reserved for the registrars. SINTER is the means through which the weaknesses of land governance will be addressed, bearing in mind that it will promote the integration and transparency of information.

Another distinctive aspect of SINTER is that it will enable integration with other thematic cadasters and particularly with the recently created Rural Environmental Registry (CAR), a result of negotiations for the approval of the Forestry Code.

5 Rural Environmental Registry (CAR) and National Rural Environmental Registry (SICAR)

Since the beginning of the 1990s, an important debate on environment-related issues has mobilized social movements, farmers, scientists, government and non-governmental agents, which eventually came to a significant agreement between landowners and environmentalists, the approval of the Forestry Code (see Chapter 8) and the creation of the CAR. The CAR maps up the use of land, but doesn't address legal aspects of land ownership. Decree n. 7.8300/ 2012 established that the CAR should include data on the owner, rural landholder or individual directly responsible for the rural property, the respective georeferenced layout of the property perimeter, the areas of interest to society in general and the areas of public use, with information concerning the location of native vegetation remains, Areas of Permanent Preservation, Areas of Restricted Use, consolidated areas and the location of the Legal Reserves (article 5).

The intention of this tool is to help with the process of environmental regularization of rural properties and tenure, plotting a digital map from which the area values are calculated for environmental diagnosis. It is a declaratory and mandatory electronic registration. The declarants are not obliged to submit supporting documents, but the pertinent agency may at any time request the submission of documents, which may be submitted electronically (§4 of article 7 of Decree no. 7.860/2012).

The recording of the rural property in the CAR should preferably be made with the municipal or state environmental agency which, under the terms of the regulations, will request the following from the rural owner or landholder: i) identification of the rural owner or landholder; ii) proof of ownership or tenure; iii) identification of the property by way of a plan and specifications containing an indication of the geographic coordinates with at least one definition point of the property perimeter, informing the location of the remains of native vegetation, the Areas of Permanent Preservation, Areas of Restricted Use, consolidated areas and, if available, also the location of the Legal Reserve.

The benefits that CAR registration may bring include: possibility of the regularization of the Areas of Permanent Preservation and/or Legal Reserve; suspension of sanctions; acquisition of agricultural credit; purchase of agricultural insurance; deductions for areas of Permanent Preservation, Legal Reserves and restricted use; financing; exemption from taxes for the principal inputs and equipment. Information on tenure, ownership or any other type of relationship between the declarant and the property, is self-declaratory. This has meant that close to 100% of properties in some states in the country have already been registered.

The declarant has access to the application, completes the survey and submits it to SICAR, then this submission generates a protocol which is not an enrolment but rather a registration number (this number is supplied by SICAR) which is exhibited at the foot of the database and the status of the property appears according to the information declared (asset pending or cancelled). To be enrolled in the SICAR does not mean that the property is environmentally conformant. There will be filtering analyses and assessments by technicians for regularization, similar to the Income Tax declaration.

Accordingly, other outcomes additional to its primary function have also become possible, such as the mapping of all the springs (that are located on private property), the mapping/sizing of existent ecological corridors, the possibility of integrating these areas/information with the public conservation units, etc. Not to mention the priority results already defined for the mapping and sizing of Legal Reserves, Areas of Permanent Preservation, waterways and other bodies of water, on all properties in the country.

6 Land regularization: from the Terra Legal programme to Law 13.465/2017

The Legal Amazon is composed of seven states in the Northern region of Brazil, namely Acre, Amapá, Amazonas, Pará, Rondônia, Roraima and Tocantins, as well as a part of the states of Mato Grosso and Maranhão, totalling 521,742,300 hectares – see Figure 0.1 in Introduction. Thus, 59% of the Brazilian territory makes up the Legal Amazon. However, the region houses just 12.34% of the country's population. This enormous territory suffers from poor land governance leading to a lack of control over the private expropriation of public land, lack of security over the right of land ownership, deforestation, conflict and unbridled land speculation.

To a large degree, the insecurity of ownership rights is caused by the existence of tenure, in parallel with the right of ownership and with the possibility of transforming tenure into ownership.

The size of the territory and the variety of forms of occupation sometimes overlap, occasioning a series of problems that make it impossible to exercise good land governance. The *Terra Legal* programme, created by Law 11.952 of 2009, was designed precisely to deal with these problems, focusing on land regularization of federal tracts of land in the Legal Amazon. It primarily starts with the transfer of public land that has no specific purpose, in the form of tracts of land already set aside for the municipalities or federal agencies, taking into consideration the regularization of urban plots, indigenous lands, conservation units, agrarian reform settlements, *quilombola* (traditional populations) territories and private squatters. To this end, the aforementioned law created the Extraordinary Office for Land Title Regularization in the Legal Amazon (SERFAL), reporting to the now defunct Ministry of Agrarian Development (MDA).

The main proposal of Law 11.952 was the regularization and entitlement of tenures of up to 15 fiscal modules (which vary according to municipality, the largest fiscal module measuring 110 hectares – for a maximum of 1,650 hectares, in the case of 15 modules of 110 ha). The basic requirement to receive the title is that the squatter may not have any other title and must be working the land for production.

The programme carries out the georeferencing of the plots and the cost of regularization depends on the number of fiscal modules regularized. Thus, regularization prices vary under the *Terra Legal* programme: up to one fiscal module, regularization is free of charge; between one and four modules, the cost depends on the market price; and for more than four modules, the cost is directly based on market price minus subsidies. In any case, it is possible to pay in cash with a discount of 20% or in instalments over 20 years.

The federal government possesses an area of approximately 120 million hectares in public tracts of land without specific purpose in the Legal Amazon, 57 million hectares of which are the focus of the programme. By 2017, 18.3 million hectares were set aside for other agencies, 38.6 million hectares are under review for future allocation – Table 13.5.

Table 13.5 Scope of the *Terra Legal* Programme

Total Area of Legal Amazon (501,600,000 hectares)	Hectares	%
Public Federal Land, earmarked	120,567,000	
Public Federal Land, allocated (*affected area*)	63,567,000	
Scope of *Terra Legal* programme	**57,000,000**	**100**
Areas assigned (MMA, FUNAI, INCRA, SPU, federal states)	18,313,784	32
Issuance of rural and urban titles		
Land to be earmarked through the *Terra Legal* programme	38,686,216	68

Source: MDA (2017).

The good news about the *Terra Legal* programme, on the one hand, is that it had georeferenced around 60.1 million hectares and earmarked 13.4 million hectares by June 2017, principally for new public usage: Indigenous Land, Conservation Units and settlements. However, the results regarding the regularization of squatters are as yet not very representative: 29,000 titles and 155,000 plots geo-referenced. This is fundamentally due to the low capacity and inflow of funds for this purpose.

The important thing, however and what the critics of the *Terra Legal* programme fail to see, is that the programme has achieved its objective of fundamentally looking after the smaller stakeholders. According to official data, the vast majority of beneficiaries are smallholding farmers, with less than 100 hectares.

It is true that the results fall short of the initial forecasts, but do point the way and demonstrate the potential of the solution provided by the enhanced rules for land regularization introduced the new legislation (Law 13465/2017), including the extension of the scope of the *Terra Legal* to other regions and urban areas.

The proclamation of Law 13.465 of July 2017 on the regularization of land (both rural and urban), will possibly have a big impact on the situation of weak land governance in the country. In rural areas, it will roll out the regularization mechanisms of the Rural Land programme, which was only in operation in the Amazon, to the country as a whole. In urban areas, the possibility of simple, objective regularization, with the effective participation of municipal administrations, could be the main mechanism for resolving the situation of numerous Brazilian households that find themselves in legal limbo. There are not reliable data on the number of fragile and irregular rural landownership titles, but preliminary assessment on the INCRA Rural Property Registration (CI-INCRA), carried out by Reydon et al. (2017), points for an expressive number of properties to be regularized in Brazil. The legal framework already in place is adequate to enhance land ownership governance and ensure land property rights. What is needed for land registration to take off in Brazil is political will, training, consistent provision of funds and inter-institutional integration. Not an easy task in the Brazilian political scenery.

7 Conclusions

After nearly 20 years of democratic governments committed to helping the less-favoured populations, which have implemented one of the biggest agrarian reforms in the world, the agrarian issue continues to be one of the main bottlenecks of Brazilian reality, both urban and rural.

There continues to be land conflict, large owners taking possession of free lands, deforestation in the Amazon, numerous squatters without any guarantees for their lands, land registries registering nonexistent properties, foreigners acquiring land without any control, amongst other problems.

At the same time, Brazilian agriculture has put in an exemplary perform-ance, with growth in food production, energy and foreign currency, greater international inclusion, among others. The security associated with land own-ership, however, continues to be a significant Achilles heel for both rural and urban areas.

Indications are that, despite the continuing weak land governance in the country, there have been significant improvements, for instance, with the rural cadaster, the CNIR and its operator, the SIGEF, as it has already georeferenced more than 70% of the territory. One of the goals of the rural land agency, INCRA, is better land governance, showing that there has been a clear shift of emphasis. Certainly, the approval of Law 13.465/2017, which sets out the possibility of more simplified regularization processes for land-grabs and other informality associated with the land, has meant that agrarian reform has ceased to be the most important of the land policies and the regularization and granting of titles to settlers and with public federal lands have become priority policies.

This, however, is part of a broader process of expansion of land governance in the country, in which a complete cadaster is essential. This has to start with a process of entitlement that reconciles property information based on satel-lite images[19] with a survey of properties with owners and legitimate squatters (uncontested possession). Only with effective land governance, particularly the creation of a modern, self-contained cadaster will it be possible to: a) guarantee the rights of private ownership for different ends: purchase and sale, leasing, loan guarantees, granting of payments for environmental services, amongst others; b) identify public land, including lands belonging to the federal states, assuring adequate use for: the creation of Conservation Units, Indigenous Land, settlements, colonization or other aspects; c) establish with greater security sundry other land policies: agrarian reform, agrarian credit, land taxes; d) regu-late the processes of land purchase in order to limit access to foreigners, to land-owners already with large tracts of land, or specific regions; e) zone the use of land – establish and regulate by imposing limits, through zoning, on agriculture and livestock production in specific regions; f) regulate the processes of agricul-tural land conversion into urban land; g) keep cadasters up-to-date in order to enable correct, effective and fair charging of taxes on rural territory (ITR) and taxes on urban property (IPTU);

Changes are required to accommodate the needs of the twenty-first cen-tury for electronic data processing. These technological innovations also permit improvements that will revolutionize the property registration system, which consists of the use of three dimensions. In addition, the right to own-ership is becoming more complex as the result of the greater flow of infor-mation and higher volume of economic interests associated with ownership. Certain rights and restrictions, particularly those relating to environmental protection, are sometimes applied to all properties and other times, only to some of them.

Information on zoning, environmental protection, soil, vegetation, agricultural production, use of land, among others, can be made available with the use of information technology. On the web, using SIG, information from different sources is available in the form of layered maps with all the necessary information. This option is preferable to the current practice of trying to store and update all information in the cadaster by property, which, due to the volume of properties and information involved, is impossible to achieve.

The ideal situation would be full integration between all the main land-related institutions. The paths to this integration are political and administrative in nature and will have to be defined as they go along. The institutions can stay as they are, but information will have to be integrated and shared. This is referred to in the literature as 'Polycentric Governance' and requires the commitment of all agencies so that they will work together to follow established rules.

Of course, achieving full integration will take some time and the need for improvement is immediate. Therefore, the institutions will have to work in an integrated manner and the information systems will have to be automatically updated. The land registry offices will certainly continue with their role directly linked to the Judiciary.

However, to get to this point of integration, there is a need to build, in the near future, a joint commitment with the government that the management of the territory is fundamental for all the other policies to work in harmony. To this end, there has to be an effective commitment by the presidency of the republic to take charge of the process of construction of effective land governance in the country, by linking together the various aspects: cadaster, registration, regularization, collection of all land-related taxes, values and soil use.

Interests that oppose proper land governance remain on both sides: a) those who do not accept that the present agrarian situation, the product of a historical process, should be consolidated or who crave an agrarian reform that will transform the reality in Brazil and b) those who can still benefit from weak land governance through taking possession of vacant land, the seizure of protected land (Conservation Units, Indigenous Lands and others) and land speculation, the aim of which is always to obtain direct economic gains from the land.

Later on, when land governance is consolidated, the cadaster and possibly part of the governance, should be transferred to appropriately qualified municipal government. The idea is that, gradually, municipalities, as they acquire more resources, more structure and more trained personnel, can take over the cadasters and all the other activities involving the use and regulation of the soil, under the supervision of state and federal governments. This should include the collection of IPTU and ITR taxes. Only in this way will we be able to have a territory with adequate use for economic, social and environmental ends, satisfying the needs of the population as a whole.

Notes

1 For a review of international literature on the importance of Agrarian Reform, see Biswanger et al. (2009), and for domestic literature, Kageyama (1993).

2 Robles (2018: 28) says that

after three decades of agrarian reform, Brazil remains a country with a very high level of land inequality. Over 1.3 million (INCRA figures), or 1 million (DATALUTA figures), landless peasants were settled during this period, mostly in public lands, far away from main economic hubs.

3 Rural and urban families are affected by high land prices, high cost of registering land, legal insecurity of land, among other factors.

4 Land-grabbing signifies using false documents to certify ownership, usually usurped from public lands. It may take place with the consent of the registrar or it may have been done previously.

5 In spite of the Pastoral Land Commission (CPT), which has been conducting surveys of land conflicts in Brazil for some years and is a competent institution, it should be stressed that differentiating between agrarian and non-agrarian conflict is not evident, so these statistics should be read with some discretion.

6 See Silva (1997) and Reydon (2007), among others, who demonstrate that the pattern of land occupation in Brazil occurred through the taking of possession which, for those with less power, did not always come with guarantees.

7 Brasil. National Congress. Chamber of Deputies. Parliamentary Commission of Inquiry Designed to Investigate the Occupation of Public Land in the Amazon Region. *Occupation of public land in the Amazon region: report of the Parliamentary Commission of Inquiry* No. 187. Documentation and Information Center, Coordination of Publications, 2002.

8 See Bueno (2018) for the case of the Barueri region which presents numerous instances of land ownership problems.

9 Biswanger et al. (2009), Deininger (2003) and Lipton (2009) have shown, based on numerous international experiences with distinct arguments, that the democratization of land access is the primary policy for minimizing rural poverty and generating a more inclusive and participative development model.

10 Moutinho et al. (2016) observe:

A vast body of literature discusses the principal drivers of deforestation in the Brazilian Amazon (…). There is still, however, no consensus concerning which intervention was the most effective in prompting the dramatic reduction in deforestation in the region since 2005.

11 PRODES is a basin restoration program launched by the Brazilian federal government to finance wastewater treatment plants while providing financial incentives to properly operate and maintain the plants.

12 Reydon (2011) shows that the main driver of the transformation to livestock farming is, on the one hand, the existence of a lot of vacant land capable of being expropriated, linked to the possibility of introducing livestock, at low cost, rendering deforestation an unbeatable capital appreciation strategy. A survey conducted by the National Institute for Space Research (INPE) showed that 62.2% of the near 720,000 km^2 clearance of forest was occupied by pastureland.

13 It is frequently these same occupiers who make use of slave labor.

14 This is the result of increases in the price of beef, soy or even of reports that Brazil is going to be the largest alcohol producer in the world. In recent times, these factors have

converged, causing the demand for land to grow even more, as well as its price, encouraging deforestation.

15 According to De Janvry (1981), there are three types of agrarian reform: semi-feudal, capitalist and socialist modes of production. He demonstrates that the first and the last of these are usually the most successful, since the redistribution of land fulfils a decisive role in the process of socio-economic and political transition, while in the capitalist mode, results fluctuate greatly.

16 One of the reasons why it is not known if it affected land structure is that the social movements that argued for agrarian reform were against the granting of titles out of a reluctance to see a further concentration of the land. With Law 13465/2017, this process will be much easier. Moreover, the Census methodology for surveying agriculture and livestock establishments does not allow for this verification, in spite of the fact that 13% of establishments declared they had received land under the agrarian reform programme.

17 For this, this law made significant changes in all land legislation: Law no. 4.947/66 (Brasil, 1966) – Establishes Norms under Agrarian Law (CCIR); Law no. 5.868/72 (Brasil, 1972) – Creates National Rural Credit System – SNCR; Law no. 6.015/73 (Brasil, 1973b) – Provisions concerning public registration; Law no. 6.739/79 (BRASIL, 1979) – Provisions concerning Enrollment and Registration of Property and Law no. 9.393/96 (BRASIL, 1996) – Provisions concerning Tax on Rural Territory (ITR).

18 National Indian Foundation; Chico Mendes Institute for Biodiversity Conservation; Department of Heritage, respectively.

19 Technological innovations in the capture of information by satellite, according to Deininger et al. (2010), permit advances that can revolutionize existing property registration systems.

14 Intellectual trajectories about the Brazilian agrarian transition[1]

Zander Navarro

1 Introduction

This chapter requires an initial comment in order to rigorously circumscribe its interpretative scope. Even being a somewhat obvious facet when one refers to the field of social sciences, the author does not expect to reap any wide agreement in relation to the arguments here set forth. It is so because there are no consolidated analytical efforts so far in Brazil addressing the intellectual *history of ideas* centred on 'the rural'. The chapter is thus looking for possible trails inside a *quasi*-pristine forest.[2] It is well known that social sciences are a multidisciplinary scientific field fractured by intense disagreements. Therefore, this chapter may only delineate an idiosyncratic reading without much hope of being an interpretation accepted even by some of the authors who collaborate in this collection of papers.

In addition, the chapter is desperately short, which further limits its ambitions in the face of the five decades under analysis, the far-reaching transformations of agricultural production and, particularly, the sheer geographic dimensions of rural Brazil reflected in numerous social, economic and regional differences. Since the general subject here scrutinized is highly complex, there is a long list of subjects (and controversies) to be considered. As an illustration, it would be quite revealing to evaluate the body of interpretations accumulated by Brazilian social sciences after being bathed by the lights of foreign influences. The enormous abyss of analytical impacts is certainly surprising, when comparing the magnitude of arguments and models produced by French literature *vis-à-vis* its 'competing narratives', either from other European putative influences or the scant contact with North American authors or ideas. The French stamp on sociology and anthropology research has been intense and profound, although much less so on economic studies.

Thus, this chapter is neither aimed at being a sort of synthesis of *the theory* or framework that would support the analysis of the authors' in the companion pieces, nor is it an all-encompassing and complete description of conceptual notions influencing rural studies over a period of five decades. That would be a task requiring an extensive and different book. As a result, this chapter has two main objectives. First, to submit a broad overview about some of the *main vicissitudes* of intellectual trajectories worth mentioning coupled with a few anecdotal facts as far as Brazilian rural changes are concerned. Secondly, to argue that the period covered by the book (half a century) was characterized by a process of continuous agricultural growth (especially intense in the last twenty years) and this productive background is the real battlefield of ideas fighting to explain the *essence* of historical agrarian development.

Without space constraints, the narrative could be richly illustrated by events, authors, controversies, references, or even acid ideological disputes, thus guaranteeing a denser capacity to explain these vast intellectual journeys. As a result, *three important caveats* are demanded at this point, apart from emphasizing, once more, that the time frame covered in the analysis covers only the last five decades. *Firstly*, in face of the fact that Brazil is so huge, there are vast regions with specific and rich rural narratives that were scrutinized over time by a long list of studies and influential analysts. One only needs to consider, as illustrations, the cases of the Amazon region and the Northeast. The first one embedded into the mysteries of the dense forest and its indigenous peoples, a fascinating complexity that has attracted dozens of scientists, Brazilians and foreigners alike. The Northeastern region, on its side, has had a deep incidence on numerous facets of the social and economic history of the country, since the onset of the Portuguese colonization. For the same reason, most of the native intellectuals, in different periods, were attracted to the particularities of that region, thus resulting in an enormous collection of books and texts exclusively dedicated to the vicissitudes of social development in the Northeast. It is unfortunate that this chapter is unable to deal with these regional specificities.

Secondly, except for a brief mention later on, no further details will be cited in relation to the institutionalization of conventional initiatives promoted by the different disciplines of social sciences that focus on 'the rural' – for example, established graduate programmes, specialized journals, regular scientific meetings, academic societies and so on and so forth.[3] *Thirdly*, the same space limitations do not allow to name and discuss distinct efforts under the sub-theme of 'academic formation'. Surely various intellectual narratives were strongly reinforced after individual efforts during many years under the guidance of leading academics and researchers. Many of them, however, were (and have been) brilliant teachers or supervisors, but with rare published output of significance or broader repercussions. In consequence, these are rather influential colleagues but with no tangible footprints of their real contribution. It would be thus impossible to list them as legitimate bearers of specific academic traditions if no concrete proofs are available. As such, names and published pieces here referred to are mere examples of especial moments that surfaced over the period when specific arguments or debates did materialize for some time. In view of such particularities and their nuances, what is being proposed in this chapter most probably shall find more critical reception than swift acceptance. It is a piece to be understood as a preliminary effort of interpretation with a view to fostering future new corresponding initiatives.

The article is divided into three sections and the first one concisely suggests that the rural contexts often had a place deeply rooted within the social conscience of Brazilians *qua* 'forceful ideas' as a direct result of the infamously aspects of our history. These themes, however, as a rule were object of speculative overviews or lacked theoretical rigor and empirical evidence, at least until the mid-1970s. On that occasion two main foundations galvanized the pioneering essayists: first, the '(social) weight of large rural estates' – so-called *latifundia* – historically born out of a very asymmetric distribution of land. The second pillar, as a consequence, was the resulting 'narrowness of the domestic markets'. These angles contributed to develop two theoretical lineages hostile to one another regarding the role of agriculture and rural regions and their populations when structuring capitalism and Brazilian society. That is, following the economists' jargon: *the role of agriculture in capital accumulation* and the mechanisms through which the surplus could contribute to secure industrialization and economic expansion at large.

The first perspective could be called an 'agrarian view', since it predominantly enlisted social and cultural themes and emphasized the 'burden of the concentration of land', thus stressing the economic and political power of large landowners, also discussing the dramatic conditions affecting rural labour and widespread conflicts in rural regions – in short, the agrarian question *lato sensu*. The second lineage has focused mainly on the economic and financial aspects and, therefore, has been associated with themes such as production and technological modernization, being an 'agricultural view' of changes occurring in the rural regions. When examined from a transition of five decades, the two approaches have been competing for the primacy over available interpretations and the agrarian view prevailed until recently. The accelerated economic expansion of the agricultural sector, however, led to the current supremacy of the second perspective, gradually discarding all previous (agrarian) debates and opinions on the subject. At the same time, the intertwined relations between the disciplines of social sciences interested in rural studies have also changed, because a good number of sociologists and anthropologists is gradually abandoning this field of studies, assuring *pari passu* the dominance of mainstream economists.

The second section mulls over the so-called 'golden years' of the scientific production analysing the Brazilian rural world, covering *grosso modo* the second half of the 1970s and the 1980s, albeit changing the essence and somehow beginning to languish by the late 1990s. This intermediate period lasting approximately two decades saw a rise in the number of researchers and the expansion of scientific output. In a nutshell, the period reflected the definitive institutionalization of the social sciences leading with rural matters having as a backdrop the relatively slow (though unstoppable) transition between an 'agrarian Brazil' anchored in the past and the emergence of a country increasingly overwhelmed by urban social life (as discussed in Chapter 2). Even so, and despite the continued growth of an increasingly modern agricultural economy, the agrarian interpretations prevailed during this period, certainly boosted by the impacts of the democratization that followed the end of the military regime in 1985.

The third section analyses the last 20 years and suggests that we may be undergoing a time of gradual erosion of interest about rural studies. In particular, these years have been noted by broader theoretical perplexities, fragmentation and, notably, excessive ideological overtones – especially among sociologists. The field of rural economics, however, has firmly anchored a relative hegemony of neoclassical or alternative mainstream explanatory models in tandem with the spectacular growth of the Brazilian agricultural economy in this century. As a result, because of the unanswerable assertion of a mode of globalized accumulation typical of capitalism in rural areas, there has been a clear inversion of those mentioned intellectual trajectories, for the agrarian tradition has been rapidly losing ground.

2 Contextual roots

Various characteristics of the period immediately prior to the 1970s help understand the following 50 years, which is the time interval limiting the scientific route analysed in this paper. The deeply rooted capillarity of several structural processes anteceding our timeframe prevailed along time and actually is still currently helping to shape an array of tendencies.

Rural themes were ostensibly ingrained in the public agenda in the 1950s and 1960s. One must bring to mind the fact that in those years most Brazilians lived in rural areas and under a dominant agricultural economy, centred mostly on coffee production (whose epicentre was the state of São Paulo) with a second orbit around the Northeastern sugarcane regions. The country, however, was on the verge of a major transformation. In slightly more than a generation – from 1940 to 1980 – a majority left the countryside and moved to the urban areas. While 70% of the population lived in rural regions in 1940, the same proportion inhabited towns and cities by 1980. Nowadays 86% of the total population lives in urban contexts.

The literature on rural topics was scarce, however, and also poorly constructed from a theoretical and methodological point of view, with few exceptions. One of them was Raymundo Faoro's *Os donos do poder* (1958), a brilliant innovative study that introduced Weberian categories in order to uncover the formation of the country's social strata based on the private appropriation of the land since colonial times. Another masterpiece was *Os parceiros do Rio Bonito* (1964), by Antonio Cândido, a book that could be taken as the pioneering landmark of scientific rural studies in Brazil. It is a rigorous empirical investigation, close to a typical anthropological one, which studies the 'peasant (*caipira*) mode of life' then common in rural regions, founded on poor families of renters or sharecroppers subordinated to large landowners. This was a rural society that gradually disappeared after out-migrations, industrialization and the arrival of mass culture – in recent years also associated with the direct impacts of globalization. But it was a mode of life that was anchored on a pre-capitalist form of production (sharecropping) later made incompatible with capitalist modernization.

The ample collection of outstanding studies by an iconic economist, Celso Furtado, devoted much attention to agricultural issues related to the Brazilian economy. In *Perspectivas da economia brasileira* (1958), for example, Furtado wrote:

> ... the lack of a modern agriculture based on capitalism and founded on the domestic market is largely responsible for the permanent internal imbalance observed in the country... [As a result] the inability of agriculture to respond to the growing demand for food in urban areas constitutes a veritable obstacle to industrial development.
>
> (*apud* CASTRO, 1969, p. 88)[4]

But most works published during those years were insufficiently grounded and their conclusions were usually based on scant empirical evidence.

Although being an oversimplified argument, it would be possible to synthesize the existing 'views on rural social life and production' prior to 1970 into two major modes of enquiry, in which the effort of explaining was seldom separated from political ambitions and ideological choices by the authors. There were no clear divisions between the disciplines of social sciences and the result was thus a set of efforts by essayists discussing rather broadly on Brazil, many times close to rhetorical arguments. Most of them invariably analysed history stressing that the deleterious effects of the country's social development had a known cause – land concentration structured in the very earliest time of colonization. Included in this group of authors are even distant and classical authors who wrote in the nineteenth century, such as Joaquim Nabuco, for example, who analysed the themes of slavery and the need to reform land structure in *O abolicionismo* (1883).

Consequently, the studies that emphasized the 'curse of the land' prevailed from the 1950s and many years after the military coup of April 1964. These were issues tied to the public agenda, particularly in the years immediately prior to the institutional rupture, when the so-called 'agrarian question' and related demands for land reform came to the forefront. Additional factors that at the time contributed were the political visibility resulting from the emergence of the Peasant Leagues in the Northeast and the drive to organize trade unions promoted by the former Brazilian Communist Party (PCB in the Portuguese acronym) in regions with higher incidence of wage earners. The best article about social struggles in the rural areas covering these issues is still 'Peasants and politics in Brazil' (Martins, 1981, first chapter). Nevertheless, the debate was conducted mainly by intellectuals, most of whom were political activists attached to the Marxist canon (Marighela et al., 1980), although many non-partisan researchers also expressed their view under the same theoretical vein (see the collection of articles organized by Stédile, 1994).

This debate, including the then widely accepted social demand for land reform, was so intense that the first president enthroned after the military coup signed the Land Statute in November 1964. The document legally set up the procedures in all their minutiae for the implementation of a national programme of land redistribution, had the government had any desire to do so. An example of the political turbulence of that period was the great strike led by sugarcane workers in the Northeast in 1963, which persist being the largest walkout by salaried employees ever in the rural history of Brazil. On the subject, Raimundo Santos' studies on the Marx-inspired authors are outstanding (see Santos, 2007). A related debate during the same period focused on the nature of labour relations prevailing in the rural areas at the time. Were they feudal in nature or disguisedly capitalist? Moacir Palmeira analysed that topic in his famous, albeit unpublished, PhD thesis (Palmeira, 1971). In passing, it must be noted that most of these intellectuals were *caiopradistas*, a reference to Caio Prado Júnior, the influential Marxist attached to the former Brazilian Communist Party. He studied agrarian development in the country and argued for a typical capitalist path of transformation, thus establishing a Marxist orthodox tradition of reading events in the countryside. Some of his most relevant articles on the subject were published before the military coup of 1964 (see Prado Jr., 1979).[5]

This first view on agrarian development is extremely relevant from the analytical standpoint, although beyond the core objectives of this chapter. Brazil materialized one of the most skewed land distribution systems in the world over time. The historical continuity of that structure stimulated numerous critical interpretations stressing a non-democratic access to land, but also – and particularly – regarding the economic impacts of such concentration. The classical reference book on the matter was *Quatro séculos de latifúndio* (1968) by Alberto Passos Guimarães. The literature on the 'rural world' under that specific perspective has always contemplated the effects of the asymmetrical distribution of land ownership (Hoffmann and Ney, 2010). It is somewhat odd, as a consequence, that the recent land reform programme has transferred approximately 90 million hectares of land (three times the total area of Italy) from large landowners to a million new small landowners since 1995. This impressive performance, however, hardly altered the Gini index for land concentration in the last five decades, given the size of the country.

In addition, as extensively argued elsewhere, the issue of land distribution was gradually made marginal – from the social and political point of view – by the remarkable transformation of production and productivity, especially in this century. When one considers that the demographic rarefaction still trends towards a shrinking of the total rural population *throughout the country* and the resulting lack of social demand for redistribution, land structure in Brazil will certainly continue to strongly concentrate in the hands of the few in the next decades, perhaps forever. Nevertheless, the literature focusing on the 'burden of the land in the hands of a few' produced by intellectuals or politically motivated commentators led to the creation of an 'agrarian axis' of interpretation of production and rural social life. Combining the unequal land distribution and the countless social iniquities which have always characterized daily life in rural areas (particularly the lack of legal rights) and the resultant aberrant social inequality that has prevailed, these agrarian interpretations emphasizing the existence of *latifundia* and social exploitation have been an influential view, although rapidly losing its sway in this century.

The second major theme of interest until the 1960s, especially among economists, was the 'narrow limits of the domestic market'. In other words, this view referred to the impossible expansion of capitalism (or industrialization) because of the very low proportion of consumers. It was so because most Brazilians still lived in rural areas, either surviving on extremely low wages or producing food mainly for their own consumption. This view fits well with the previous one, since the only way out of that structural obstacle, scholars argued, was a massive land reform policy. It was a curious period when conservative analysts held the same position of Marxists, who also defended land reform, albeit through the much more ambitious perspective of 'developing the productive forces to overthrow the contradictions of capitalism'. In the intellectual history of Brazilian social scientists, the first model of interpretation ('agrarian') mobilized, in particular, most sociologists and anthropologists, as well as Marxist economists, while the second perspective ('agricultural') engaged neoclassical economists in particular.

Antônio Barros de Castro's influential article from that period summarized some of the existing interpretations. It was published in his famous book *Sete ensaios sobre a economia brasileira* (1969). Although relatively short, chapter 2 of that book, entitled 'Agriculture and development in Brazil', is a correct introduction to the points of view prevailing at the time. The first part of that chapter covers the 'conflicting positions', emphasizing the theses defended by the various authors involved, while the second part of the text analysed the expected 'functions of agriculture' and their performance (Castro, 1969, pp. 79–146). It is important to mention that Castro was already raising some of the difficulties in interpreting rural history, namely, the 'unprecedented nature of our problems in agriculture'. Castro also remarked that thus far agriculture had placed no 'obstacles to Brazilian industrialization' and concluded by saying that the dominant criticisms at that time – particularly those who claimed to be Marxist authors proposing land reform – were either 'wrong or not critical of agriculture but, rather, stemmed from the socioeconomic system in which we live' (Castro, 1969, p. 79). Years later, Ignácio Rangel, a well-known Marxist economist from that period, would recognize the original sin of most left-leaning analysis:

> Contrary to what we, revolutionaries of the 1930s, believed, the industrialization of Brazil would be possible, even without land reform – in the sense of transforming large landholdings into small family farms. The Prussian or Junker way, 'mutatis mutandis', which replaces the feudal old large estate with the capitalist large scale rural property, not only enabled the industrialization of the country, but also gave said industrialization an extraordinary thrust.
>
> (Rangel, I., 'Fim de linha', in: Folha de São Paulo, 16 November 1988)

In short, the period immediately preceding the 1970s had various important characteristics. The existing analyses were rather poor from their *empirical* standpoint, because they were speculative in nature. They offered many interpretations that were largely wrong, as time would show. Also, national databases, such as the censuses, were not comprehensive enough for weightier analytical study. Furthermore, the social sciences community was still too small and lacked adequate scientific training.

A curious aspect of those years is worth mentioning, which was born out of a frequent overgeneralization. The views and interpretations claimed to be 'national' were actually regional and commonly even specific to São Paulo, the only state with more robust academic and research activities on those years. Thus, the interpretations about 'the country', meaning a national rural Brazil, were, in fact, analyses of social processes in the rural areas of São Paulo, with the resulting conclusions generalized to the rest of the country. This statement is neither an exaggeration nor a meaningless critique since there were several groundbreaking initiatives at the University of São Paulo regarding social research on the rural regions and their populations, especially concentrated in the Center for Rural and Urban Studies. One of founders of those initiatives who fostered intellectual activities deserves to be mentioned: Maria Isaura Pereira de Queiróz.[6] A suggestive example at the time was a book by Maria Conceição D'Incao e Mello, *O boia-fria: acumulação e miséria*, which resulted from her doctoral research carried out in the early 1970s in rural areas of the so-called Alta Sorocabana, in São Paulo. The book studied the emergence of seasonal wage earners known as 'bóia-fria' as the culmination of a process of labour exploitation. According to the author, the growth

> … of the production relations in rural areas resulting from the expansion of commercial agriculture at the expense of subsistence agriculture is accompanied, on the one hand, by the concentration of land property, and, on the other, by substituting forms of exploitation of the labour force with total or partial remuneration *in natura* (sharecropping, renters, or household subordinate workers), by monetary remuneration (salaried workers).
>
> (Mello, 1975, p. 148)

The book was much praised and its theses were considered an 'irreversible trend' which would rapidly change Brazilian agricultural development.[7]

All these advances and blockages of various types were visible toward the end of the 1960s, before another phase began, initially in parallel to the years of economic expansion known as 'the Brazilian miracle'. The book that symbolically marked the birth of a new chapter in the scientific research on the social processes taking place in the Brazilian rural regions was *Vida rural e mudança social*, published in 1972, which included some acclaimed articles by foreign authors and, in the second part, nine articles by the most important Brazilian social scientists who wrote about rural topics (Szmrecsányi and Queda, 1972). If political economy is considered, it is also important to emphasize a research report that, to a certain extent, explained the 'transition' between those two phases and brought many repercussions. It was a survey carried out in rural regions by a group of scholars whose intent was to explain 'rural Brazil'. The report entitled *Posse e uso da terra e desenvolvimento socioeconômico do setor agrícola* involved a large multidisciplinary research team who delved deeply, on the one side, into regional analyses mobilizing the arsenal of tools then available in the field of social sciences. On the other side, the document also warned about the social and political problems caused by land concentration. In fact, it reacted to the Cuban Revolution, trying to propose reforms in the rural areas that would prevent new revolutions in the continent (CIDA, 1966).

3 The golden years

The most exuberant period of rural studies probably flourished from the mid-1970s to the end of the 1990s and spans approximately two decades. Seen in retrospect, those were *the most promising years of the social sciences' research on rural themes in Brazil*. It seems paradoxical, because one would expect a continuous evolution of knowledge and a capacity for analysis of rural social processes *after those years* and entering into the current century. That was not the case, however, as discussed below.

The reasons those activities prospered during that mentioned period perhaps are straightforward to identify. Firstly, whether from an economic angle or deriving from social and political causes, the 'rural weight' *was still too strong* on social conscience and, therefore, attracted most scholars at the time. It was inevitable that the new opportunities open to young researchers pointed to the 'rural world' as their starting point. Roughly a decade later some of those social scientists changed their research interests and migrated to other subjects. Some examples: among the sociologists, mention must be made of Juarez Rubens Brandão Lopes, author of *Do latifúndio à empresa. Unidade e diversidade do capitalismo no campo* (1981), as well as an extremely interesting piece on the capitalist expansion of agriculture in the state of São Paulo, published at the legendary journal *Estudos Cebrap* (Lopes, 1982). Therein, he was one of the first to set aside Marxist rhetoric and tried to calculate an empirical indicator to evaluate the rate of surplus value corresponding to the transformation of agriculture in São Paulo. Maria Rita Loureiro was influential with her books discussing 'petty production', also in São Paulo (Loureiro, 1977, 1987). Another example was José Vicente Tavares dos Santos, whose book *Os colonos do vinho* was the first effort to apply Chayanov's theoretical arsenal to a concrete rural case, empirically demonstrating the mechanisms of commercial subordination of small farmers to the emerging agri-industrial complex in the wine regions of Rio Grande do Sul (Santos, 1978). Santos' book was the first but also the last attempt to introduced Chayanov to Brazilian social sciences, for no other similar scientific effort was ever made again.

Among economists, following opposite theoretical orientations, mention must be made of Sérgio Silva (Silva, 1976, 1981) and Geraldo Muller (Muller,

1981, 1989), the latter a creative contributor to the debate on 'agri-industrial complexes' that emerged in the 1980s. The noteworthy contribution of José Roberto Mendonça de Barros, an exceptionally capable economist and prolific author, who later became one of the most influential analysts of the Brazilian economy (Barros, 1979 and Barros et al., 1983), must also be pointed out.[8] All these scholars were active in the field of 'rural' studies, with significant scientific output and intellectual ascendancy, but later moved to other fields of research.

The second reason for the growth of said studies during the aforementioned period derived from the institutionalization of the multidisciplinary field of the social sciences devoted to the 'rural social processes', which actually occurred during the years of the 'Brazilian miracle' and under an authoritarian political regime. Particularly in the 1970s, research funds grew and the federal universities made many new positions available in these areas of specialization. Also, graduate training was encouraged – mainly abroad – because there were few master's degree programmes and practically no doctoral studies available in the country. In Rio de Janeiro, for example, the creation of graduate courses in 'Agriculture and Development' (CPDA) and in Social Anthropology at the Museu Nacional were extremely important. These courses, which readily recruited and trained dozens of new researchers, had the critical support of the Ford Foundation. In the case of the CPDA, that support gave rise to an exciting academic collaboration that lasted from the late 1970s and went through a good part of the 1980s: namely, the Exchange Program in Social Research about Agriculture (PIPSA), possibly the most remarkable moment in the intellectual history of rural studies in Brazil. Initially, the CPDA researchers participated in the project Recent Evolution and current situation of Brazilian Agriculture, which resulted in a thought-provoking evaluation of the debates prevailing from 1950 to 1970 (Castro, 1979). In regard to the Museu Nacional, the financial support of the Ford Foundation made it possible to mobilize one of the most solid research teams ever constituted in the country. Primarily inspired by Anthropology, this group produced several seminal publications (Garcia, 2003).

The third reason for the growth of rural studies during those years was probably related to the political changes in Brazil beginning in 1985, when the military regime collapsed. At that time, there came to the fore various deplorable social themes always associated with Brazilian rural history, such as social exploitation, poverty, the absence of legal rights and the concentration of land ownership (and its countervailing demand, land reform). It was when those themes could surface more freely and became part of the public agenda. The intense debates that led to a new Constitution in October 1988 strongly contributed to bringing the rural themes into a broader public debate – especially the issues of land reform and social legal rights in the rural areas. The so-called 'agrarian perspective' was thus reinforced and reappeared with new strength on that occasion and was predominant during the next decade and even after that, in the current century. By the end of the 1980s, the Landless Movement (MST), formally created in 1983, had gained growing political clout and gradually amassed more muscles to fight for changes. It must be remembered that the National Confederation of Rural Workers (CONTAG) had been another political force trumpeting the same themes since the 1970. After the political transition towards a democratic regime, some forms of organization of the agrarian bourgeoisie emerged and during some years they were solely studied by Regina Bruno, who launched outstanding publications about these groups (Bruno, 1997).

However, by far the main driving force that could explain the renewed interest and training of a generation of social scientists devoted to rural studies was the remarkable expansion of Brazilian agriculture beginning in the late 1960s until, at least, the macroeconomic crisis that exploded in the early 1980s (Martine and Garcia, 1987; Delgado, 1985). The intense growth of the agricultural economy ignored the perverse social characteristics of the country's rural history, giving rise to the expression 'conservative modernization' proposed by a Marxist author (Silva, 1982). In other words, it meant that there was a capitalist change in rural regions, but the existing land structure remained untouched, a fact that buried the former mentioned thesis of a 'narrow domestic market' (caused by land concentration).

Given space limitations, there is no possibility here of specifying events taking place in shorter periods, when a research project, a book, or some events disseminated a 'new sub-theme', which would attract new discussions for a while. A good example is the topic of pluri-activity: from the end of the 1980s to the mid-1990s, this was a topic that attracted some researchers, produced important results and showed an empirical facet of analytical relevance (Schneider, 2003). This subject studied the emergence of non-agricultural work in rural areas and later it was expanded to show the increasing numbers of non-agricultural jobs articulated with the production chains. It was a timely discussion, because these initiatives provided empirical evidence that the agricultural production sector, as well as the rural regions, were undergoing a deep economic transformation and diversifying their economic structure.

Nevertheless, it is also relevant to mention a series of new trends, processes and changes that occurred in those years. In the face of the degradation of natural resources, for example, one of the most striking facets of the agricultural expansion installed in the 1970s, the 'environmental dimension' emerged as one of the most dramatic themes and, throughout the 1980s, awakened growing interest among researchers. Along that line, a groundbreaking book must be mentioned: namely, *Questão agrária e ecologia*, by Francisco Graziano Neto, who has since been an active participant in the debates regarding the rural world (Graziano Neto, 1982). Especially from the 1990s onwards, environmental topics became a permanent subject of social disputes and fell under the scrutiny of several studies – check Chapter 8 for a detailed analysis.

Many examples from this phase could be cited. While it is not possible to offer a detailed analysis, four well-defined situations that were characteristic of these academic initiatives on the ongoing processes taking place in the Brazilian agricultural regions can be referenced. Firstly, the most fascinating of all examples from the point of view of its theoretical complexity and the sophistication of the arguments put forward, which generated intense debates, is the theme of 'the social *locus* of the small agricultural production in capitalism'.[9] This analytical challenge had long historical roots, going back to the foundational works of the disciplines that studied these issues. In the case of Brazil, a possible focus had its roots in the Marxist controversies of the 1960s, but gained three main contributors in this 'new phase'. Francisco Sá Jr., who discussed the role of impoverished farming in the rural Northeastern region (Sá Jr., 1973); José de Souza Martins, who investigated the place of family farming and its relations with the agricultural modernization in São Paulo (Martins, 1975); and especially, the famous article by Francisco de Oliveira, 'The Brazilian economy: a critique of the dualist reason' (Oliveira, 1972).

These authors, each in their own framework, discussed the ECLA-inspired argument that since the 1950s had proposed a dualist vision to explain underdevelopment in Latin American. This was an extremely pervasive thesis for many years throughout the continent. These authors tried to demonstrate that, in fact, there existed an 'umbilical relation' between the forms of rural poverty of low or no commercial content, their mode of agricultural production and the dynamics of the capitalist economy. To simplify: the authors insisted that there was a direct relation between rural poverty and the production of food sold at low prices, for those staple crops were primarily destined to the social reproduction of the rural farming families in particular. This was a link that actually facilitated the process of capital accumulation, since cheap food assured equally low wages, or so these authors argued. In so doing, however, they ran into the reaction of their critics, who identify them as proponents of a 'functional view' of agricultural/agrarian development and economic expansion, a reading that gave rise to countless criticisms that lasted until the first half of the 1980s.

At the turn of the 1970s, however, a relevant initiative was the international project entitled 'Multinationals and Agriculture', coordinated from Paris by Gonzalo Arroyo. It mobilized various Latin-American researchers and, in fact, developed a Political Economy-inspired alternative to orthodox Marxism, centred mainly on empirical research and also under the impacts of the intense agricultural modernization in some regions of Brazil. A small group of active Brazilian social scientists was involved and their findings eventually developed a new framework (from a left angle) to the strong Marxist orthodoxy then prevailing – so-called 'agri-industrial paradigm'. Gradually it became a model based on the paradigm of economic institutionalism (and its variants later to be developed), a framework that interpreted small farmers as potentially virtuous participants of processes of capitalist expansion in the countryside – in opposition of established arguments about the 'inevitable proletarianization' defended by the old left circles. Two examples of these emergent studies were published by Bernardo Sorj (Sorj, 1980) and Geraldo Muller (Muller, 1981). John Wilkinson has written an illuminating discussion about these theoretical confrontations (Wilkinson, 1986, pp. 11–86). Additionally, conventional dichotomies such as rural versus urban; domestic markets versus exports and even the 'historical need' of land reform were made relatively obsolete after the emergence of this new framework.

However, maybe it was the doctoral thesis of Guilherme Delgado that effect-ively launched a second wave of studies by inspiring numerous researchers to start diverse but related projects on these themes. Delgado, an economist, carried out a thought-provoking analysis about the impressive growth of agriculture and its resulting transformation in the 1970s in Brazil. He was among the first scholars to place due emphasis on the dominant role played by financial cap-ital. Delgado's Marxist analysis was published in book form in 1985 (Delgado, 1985), followed immediately thereafter by other authors who wrote about the logical 'next theoretical step' after that framework proposed by Delgado, namely the emergence of agri-industrial complexes, particularly at the University of Campinas, the collective endeavour coordinated by José Graziano da Silva and Ângela Kageyama (Muller, 1989; Kageyama, 1990). Nevertheless, these efforts gradually lost pace and, by the early 1990s, were left out of the more gen-eral debates – remarkably, in view of the analytical importance of the effort. Fortunately, studies about production chains were not entirely interrupted but experienced a fruitful continuity under the initiatives carried out at the University of São Paulo through the 'Program Pensa' and under the intellec-tual brilliance of Décio Zylbersztajn and Elizabeth Farina.[10] This was a research initiative that introduced a third way to analyse relations between agriculture and industry, this time influenced by the original agribusiness programme established at Harvard by Ray Goldberg in 1955. In short: over the 1980s, three frameworks were disputing interpretations about the economic and productive transformations in Brazilian rural regions. Two of them claimed to be 'on the left', one based on orthodox Marxism, a second inspired in novel contributions then offered by Political Economy at large and opened to new authors and proposals, making strong attempts to understand the emergence of a multi-tude of relations linking agricultural transformations and agri-industries. The third one, centred on the University of São Paulo and the 'Pensa' programme of research introduced analysis of agri-chains inspired in models developed by Goldberg and his associates.

Another special moment was the project 'Characterization of the new Brazilian rural, 1981/95 (Project "Rurbano")', also coordinated by José Graziano da Silva, which mobilized a large number of researchers from eleven states. The project aimed at 'analyzing the transformation of the rural-urban relations in Brazil beginning in 1981 based on the micro data from the PNADs [household surveys]' (Silva, 1999b, p. xii). The analysed period was the 1990s in particular and the project resulted in several papers, some focusing on spe-cific regions, trying to identify the formation of the 'new rurality' supposedly arising in various regions of the country. The author emphasized that this new historical moment was characterized by the expansion of a 'modern agriculture' linked to agri-industries, but also a 'subsistence sector' whose role would be, in typical Marxist jargon, to maintain 'a relative overpopulation and reserve army of landless workers in the rural regions' (*Ibid*), thus ignoring the possibility of poor families abandoning the countryside, actually an empirical fact that was intensified in this century.

In another relevant research development, albeit restricted to sociology in particular, the period also witnessed the proliferation of mainly descriptive research projects on 'rural settlements'. The MST was then undergoing a gradual expansion with frequent invasions of private landholdings and the slow formation of new settlements. Several sociologists who were inspired by clearly ideological readings about rural realities tried to perceive, in their corresponding fieldworks, the emergence of 'forms of resistance' (to capitalism) by settlers arising in many of those reformed areas. In the 1990s, in particular, such research initiatives, frequently resulting from dissertations or theses, grew almost exponentially. It was actually a dismaying moment in the history of rural sociology, since the vast majority of these studies were openly naïve when calling attention to social actions by settlers that, in fact, were nonexistent.

In a risky simplified retrospective covering the last 50 years, and within a synthesis that prevents giving emphasis to some notable exceptions that certainly marked this phase, the trajectory of sociology centred on rural areas, for the most part and at different times was guided mostly by ideological motivations. Broadly speaking, it was a discipline that walked through the initial analyses regarding the 'social need for land reform' to the later merely descriptive texts about rural settlements and conflicts in the rural areas and, in the 1990s, an almost magical exaltation of 'family agriculture'. More recently, sociological research has focused on another field and minted a conceptually empty term, namely 'agroecology' (Navarro, 2013).[11] Undaunted, many sociologists have frequently emphasized that, *in most circumstances,* they have been able to uncover anti-capitalist intentions moving poor families.[12]

Finally, as an aside and to mention a notable exception compared to the previous comments, it is important to emphasize the brilliant academic career of a fabled sociologist and author from the University of São Paulo (USP), José de Souza Martins. He probably responds for the largest scientific production among sociologists with 37 books published as of August 2018. It is indeed an exceptional career inspired by a sociology 'of the Brazilian society', even if empirically focused particularly on rural environments in most of his field research. After joining USP in the late 1960, Martins has had a prolific and all-encompassing production for more than fifty years. He is probably the only Brazilian sociologist to develop an innovative sociological theory. It is impossible, however, to provide even a contour of his production given the space limitations of this chapter. An initial approach to Martins' sociology is found in the recently published *festschrift* (Frehse, 2018).

4 Recent trends

The literature on rural processes here discussed has revealed some distorting characteristics that over the years were self-defeating in their search for more robust results. From the point of view of the different disciplines, for example, the contributions of the various scientific branches have been utterly hetero-geneous. It is surprising that political science has not shown much interest in carrying out research on the existing political structures and modes of human interaction that still prevail in rural regions. In fact, political science professionals have only rarely studied the Brazilian countryside with any degree of con-tinuity. The body of categories, concepts and theories typical of the discipline has been studied, in particular, by sociologists and anthropologists, sometimes causing a loss of analytical depth.[13]

Anthropology, in its turn, after the fruitful period mentioned previously and usually under the inspiration of researchers associated with the Museu Nacional, seems either to be running out of steam in this century or addressing other themes separate from the rural contexts. It should be emphasized, however, that most fieldworks under the auspices of the Museu were carried out in rural areas of the Northeastern region. Only rarely did anthropological endeavours take place in other regions, but exceptions are the books by Margarida Maria Moura, whose studies focused on central Brazil (Moura, 1978, 1988).

Lastly, a brief review of the contributions of economists shows that their dis-cipline has evolved very differently from the previously discussed fields of know-ledge. Generally speaking, research efforts about rural processes by economists in the last fifty years have followed a very specific course. In the 1970s, the dominant theoretical approaches were influenced by either orthodox Marxism or a structuralist stance under the tenets of ECLA. The role of neoclassical economists was less influential in those earlier years. But the expansion of new academic courses and research as a whole, as well as the growth of the agricul-tural economy, slowly changed those choices of theoretical approaches. During the expansion years briefly surveyed in the previous section the models of the economists associated with the neoclassical tradition gradually grew and their position became consolidated in several research institutions.[14] They slowly set aside the structuralist position (and its different shades) and, particularly, held the Marxist tradition at bay. Beginning in the early 1990s, after the fall of the Berlin wall, but especially early this century, with the spectacular growth of the agricultural economy (Navarro and Buainain, 2017), mainstream (neoclassical or other schools) views became hegemonic, to the extent that various graduate courses in 'agribusiness' have been established. Such seem to be the irreversible trends in the field of economics devoted to rural matters.

It must be noted, however, that this reversion should acknowledge add-itional factors. Among them the relevant contributions developed in the Federal University of Viçosa, in the University of São Paulo (in its campus of Piracicaba – ESALQ) and also the role of the Getúlio Vargas Foundation, in Rio de Janeiro (in particular the exceptionally fruitful contribution of Mauro de Rezende Lopes and Ignez Vidigal Lopes). However, another traditional research institution, IPEA, located in the capital Brasília, has gone on a contrary course. In the past this government organization was instrumental when stimulating economic research on rural subjects but in this century this field is becoming irrelevant in its research agenda.

A close look at the evolving themes among the disciplines under the umbrella of the social sciences would probably reveal a gradual general decrease of interest in rural issues, in particular among sociologists and anthropologists. Many are the reasons: the demographic exodus observed in the countryside, the political cooling down of former explosive themes, the end of government interventions to promote land reform and also because rural social movements have drastically lost their visibility, thus reducing the preferred objects of analysis of those disciplines. Under a distinct rationale, the interest of economists for the same topics has also diminished, as in the past and these specialists have been concentrating on exclusively economic and financial topics, since the sector has become increasingly decisive for the Brazilian economy. Equally, the research typical of historians only rarely focused on these topics in the last fifty years and, consequently, 'historical' readings only exist because of the efforts of other social scientists, such as Edmar Bacha, who brilliantly wrote about the coffee sector (Bacha, 1992) and several pieces by the well-known sociologist José de Souza Martins, on various periods of rural history (see, as an example, Martins, 1979).

These brief remarks are intended to clarify that the scientific output on social rural processes in this multidisciplinary field, as a result, has been fragmented and irregular. Only exceptionally particular efforts have been maintained for a longer period in an attempt to consolidate knowledge accrued by cumulative efforts. As a rule, the opposite has occurred, with researchers erratically choosing their preferred topics along time.

Other contributing facts affect the overall performance as well. Most social scientists in Brazil pay little attention to international debates and, surprisingly, little reflection on various publications by their own Brazilian colleagues. Benchmark books like *From Farming to Biotechnology. A Theory of Agri-industrial Development* (Blackwell, 1987), translated into Portuguese (1990) and whose three authors have direct links to Brazilian rural themes[15]; *State and Countryside. Development Policy and Agrarian Politics in Latin America* (Johns Hopkins University Press, 1986) by Merilee Grindle; or *The Agrarian Question and Reformism in Latin America* (Johns Hopkins University Press, 1981) by the influential Alain de Janvry, exerted very little influence on Brazilian authors. The books were sometimes dismissed *in limine*, as in the case of the first book cited, which was rapidly rated a mere manifestation of 'technological determinism' (Silva, 1992).

Even books by reputed Brazilian scholars, in some cases, did not result in any debate worth the name. As an illustration of this complacency, two situations are paradigmatic. Firstly, the book *O desenvolvimento agrícola. Uma visão histórica* (1991), by José Eli da Veiga. It is an excellent comparative study of several national experiences in agrarian development where forms of family farming did prosper. Veiga analyses the historical reasons that could explain the fact and the book illuminates several social and economic processes that might be seen as universal (Veiga, 1991). Soon after, another landmark book, *Paradigmas do capitalism agrário em questão* (1992), by Ricardo Abramovay, was published. Most probably, for various reasons, it is the single most important book on agrarian development ever written by a Brazilian social scientist. It is a book of very dense analysis about several core aspects of agrarian development and a seminal contribution for the field (Abramovay, 1992). Both books, however, did not cause relevant repercussions and debates among the community of social scientists. It is possible to insist that the book by Abramovay, in particular, if duly studied, would represent a genuine turning point to sustain more creative analyses about agrarian development in the country.

Lastly, the agricultural transformation experienced in this century has introduced a new and pressing fact, namely the need to interpret rural development as 'a totality'. Different trends and processes, from the unification of labour markets that are linking various regions and the rural and urban labour markets; the increasing difficulty to secure investments in agriculture in order to assure the continuous growth of agricultural productivity; the participation of new firms, including international corporations, in the now-globalized agricultural sector; the recent reduction of the labour supply; the difficulties arising in some regions with the management of water resources, among many other challenges, all of them suggesting the need for an interpretation of rural regions as a totality (and their imbrications with the national determinants). Thus, the tradition of studies focusing on regions, sectors, or specific issues, which was always the main characteristic of this field of research, may be inappropriate from now on. These events are beginning to encourage new efforts to analyse agriculture under different and newer lenses. Fabio Chaddad's recent study was the pioneering effort in that direction. His goal was to achieve a broad view of the types of entrepreneurship and organization of value chains, including the various types of farmer organizations. The study focuses on the most dynamic regions of the agricultural economy, particularly as regards the relation between the southern states and the Center-West region, where a substantial part of the agricultural production takes place (Chaddad, 2016).

Driven by this concern, mention should also be made of an ambitious recent research initiative, in which several of the authors of this book also participated. It was entitled 'the seven theses project' because the starting point was an article published in 2013 under the same heading (Buainain et al., 2013). The article proposed a radical reinterpretation of the development of Brazilian agriculture on the basis of which a comprehensive research project was developed and carried out that spawned, already in the following year, a very long collection entitled *O mundo rural no Brasil do século 21* (Buainain et al., 2014). The texts proposed an offhand renovation of the traditional interpretation of rural Brazil, to be considered hence as a totality, rather than a set of constituent parts, on the basis of the fundamental premise that there has been, in the last 20 years, a profound change in the rationale of capital accumulation in agriculture, a sector increasingly captured by forms of global financial capital. The book was published rather recently, so that the impact of those various theses submitted by the authors are just beginning to be discussed by Brazilian social scientists.

Once these trends are analysed as a set of interconnected propositions and coming back to the initial considerations of this chapter, it is inevitable to

conclude that the 'battle of ideas and arguments' has followed a curious evolution, pitting two opposite readings about the development of capitalism in
rural areas of Brazil and, within the scope of said transformation, the role of
production and the future of rural life. The first reformist interpretation, titled
'agrarian', which involved intellectual narratives aligned with structuralism and
Marxism (*lato sensu*, with political economy). This reading especially mobilized
sociologists and anthropologists, as well as part of the economist pertaining to
the left and was dominant for a long time within the fifty year time period
of this study. In the light of the tragic story of rural Brazil, that interpretation
mobilized more resources for research and potent initiatives to create knowledge in order to interpret agrarian development. It was the most influential
vision until, *grosso modo*, the turn of the century. Nevertheless, the growth of the
agricultural economy, which took root during the 1970s and has been slowly
building up ever since, expanded vigorously at the turn of the century and, consequently, the 'agricultural' (economic) outlook recently became more vigorous
and dominant. There does not seem to be a place, in view of this inversion, for
the former agrarian perspective to resuscitate and, thus, the dispute of ideas and
arguments that prevailed in the last five decades may be fading.

5 Conclusions

Fifty years of continuous growth of the agricultural sector and the recent emergence of Brazil as one of the most important food producing countries has been
insufficient among the community of social scientists to generate a set of solid
research agendas organized around a consistent analytical logic. Considering
the various fields of social sciences, the evaluation of intellectual narratives
demonstrates a path that is usually erratic, affected by political constraints, international fads and the personal preferences of researchers thus strongly reflecting
idiosyncrasies sometimes distant from the realities if considering production
and the social life prevailing in rural regions.

Even more damaging is the fact that these specific disciplines have been analyzing social processes in rural areas in an extremely heterogeneous manner. In
practical terms, political science has contributed practically nothing to interpret
those issues, while sociology many times has been subservient to ideological
influences, easily adhering to initiatives with little scientific content. Thus, the
overall knowledge resulting from the efforts of social scientists has brilliantly
moved forward in some specific sub-topics, while no researchers have been
interested in many other themes.

In the face of the significant economic and financial expansion of the agricultural sector in this century, the processes amenable to analysis using economic models are increasingly consolidated and this fact, together with the
relative demographic shrinkage of the countryside, leads to a lack of interest
on the part of the other disciplines. Consequently, it would not be surprising
if, soon enough, the research communities interested in the social and economic processes coming about in rural areas were limited to mainstream

economists. The properly social themes typical of sociology, as well as the cultural phenomena and political processes that usually constitute the efforts of anthropologists and political scientists, seem to be increasingly absent from the list of topics object of ongoing research in Brazil.

Notes

1 Many thanks are sincerely due for Alberto R. Cavalcanti, Alfredo Homma, Anita Brumer, John Wilkinson and Ryan Nehring, who read an earlier version of this chapter and offered very valuable comments. Needless to say, any remaining shortcomings are my exclusive responsibility.

2 It is surprising that the best analysis about the establishment of rural sociology in Brazil, for example, was published in 1971, but no similar effort has been undertaken ever since. Please refer to the excellent report by José Arthur Rios, one of the pioneers of the field in Brazil (Rios, 1971).

3 As an additional feature, the author of this chapter was the organizer of the only series of books on 'rural studies' that currently exists in Brazil and was responsible for the first 20 published books. His successors secured its academic strength and this series has now published 54 books. Check at: www.ufrgs.br/pgdr/publicacoes/livros/serie-estudos-rurais-pgdr

4 The author's most specific analysis on the theme is to be found in 'The agrarian structure in the Brazilian underdevelopment' published in the book *Análise do Modelo Brasileiro* (Rio de Janeiro: Civilização Brasileira, 1972, pp. 91–120).

5 It is also necessary to mention the contributions of Ignácio Rangel from 1950 to the 1970s. His work frequently addressed agrarian issues and related themes, such as land structure and land reform. Ignácio Rangel is an extremely original and emblematic representative of the field of political economy, as well as a heterodox and controversial author. He left a vast body of work that cannot be scrutinized in this chapter. To that end, see Rangel (2005) and Jabbour (2017).

6 See the pioneer study entitled 'Sociology in Brazil' (1956) by Antônio Cândido. The study shows a series of academic and scientific initiatives, particularly in São Paulo, which prove the intellectual primacy of the activities in the field of sociology in that state. (Cândido, 2006).

7 Although of lesser impact, another example of undue generalization regarding changes observed in a given region (São Paulo) to the rest of the country was the doctoral thesis by an influential author, José Graziano da Silva, which was later published as a book (Silva, 1981). In his research he also pointed to the emergence of seasonal labour in agriculture in São Paulo as a sure sign of the immediate future of Brazilian agriculture.

8 Other benchmark authors would be Fernando Homem de Melo, whose book *O problema alimentar no Brasil: a importância dos desequilíbrios tecnológicos* (Paz e Terra, 1981) was highly influential at that time. Also, José Eli da Veiga, with an impressive scientific production on rural themes, albeit attracted, since the 1990s, to a socio-environmental focus, economic growth topics and others separate from the more circumscribed 'rural' field.

9 It is rather dismaying that the national debate in the field of rural studies has ignored most of the international discussions – especially those in the English-spoken sphere. It was the case, for example, of all literature inspired in the acclaimed article by Susan Mann and Charles Dickinson originally published in 1978. Ten years later it was translated into Portuguese (Mann and Dickinson, 1987). Most probably the dominant Marxist

orthodoxy in rural studies in Brazil vetoed any discussion on those proposed ideas about capitalist development in agriculture.

10 See http://pensa.org.br/.

11 In passing, it must be noted that especially in the 1980s, following an international tendency, 'social movements' (or 'conflicts') also attracted many sociologists as a theme of research. The rural face of these subjects was extensively studied by Ilse Scherer-Warren who has been the author of a long list of publications about the subject (for an example, Scherer-Warren, 1989).

12 It must be emphasized that, for some years now, there have not been any sociologists focusing on the scientific investigation of the social processes in rural areas in the two largest and most important Brazilian universities (USP and Unicamp, both located in São Paulo).

13 In the last two decades or so, there emerged numerous efforts to investigate rural 'public policies'. Although a risky generalization, perhaps it would not be unfair to emphasize that the vast majority of these efforts produced mainly descriptions but not proper analysis of those policies, in particular because a serious understanding about 'the State' in Brazil is still to be materialized.

14 As an example of typical neoclassical analysis in Economics, check the vast scientific production of Eliseu Alves (Alves, 2006).

15 David Goodman was the CEO of the Brazilian office of Ford Foundation from the late 1970s to the mid-1980s. He is the author of several important analyses about Brazilian agricultural development (Goodman, 1977; Goodman and Redclift, 1981). First in London and later at the University of California he wrote extensively in the field. Bernardo Sorj is a Peruvian who has lived in Brazil since his youth and is one of the rare political scientists with a scientific production on rural themes, albeit rather short (SORJ, 1980). John Wilkinson is a British sociologist also living in Brazil since concluding his PhD; he also has an important scientific production (Wilkinson, 1986, 2008).

References

Abramovay, R. (1992). *Paradigmas do capitalismo agrário em questão*. São Paulo: Editora da Unicamp.

Adami, M., Rudorff, B. F., Freitas, R. M., Aguiar, D. A., Sugawara, L. M., & Mello, M. P. (2012). Remote sensing time series to evaluate direct land use change of recent expanded sugarcane crop in Brazil. *Sustainability*, 4(4), 574–585. doi: 10.3390/su4040574.

Albuquerque, A. C. S., & Silva, A. G. (2008a). *Agricultura tropical: Quatro décadas de inovações tecnológicas, institucionais e políticas*, volume 1. Brasília-DF: Embrapa Informação Tecnológica.

Albuquerque, A. C. S., & Silva, A. G. (2008b). *Agricultura tropical: Quatro décadas de inovações tecnológicas, institucionais e políticas*, volume 2. Brasília-DF: Embrapa Informação Tecnológica.

Alkimim, A., Sparovek, G., & Clarke, K. C. (2015). Converting Brazil's pastures to cropland: An alternative way to meet sugarcane demand and to spare forestlands. *Applied Geography*, 62, 75–84. doi: 10.1016/j.apgeog.2015.04.008.

Almeida, A. M. (2014). The Minimum Price Guarantee Policy and the actions of the National Food Supply Company in the period subsequent to the raising of commercial trade barriers: an institutional shift and new instruments. Doctoral thesis, Escola Superior de Agricultura Luiz de Queiroz, University of São Paulo, Piracicaba. doi: 10.11606/T.11.2014.tde-05052014-105819.

Almeida, E. S., Perobelli, F. S., Ferreira, P. G. C. (2008). Existe convergência espacial da produtividade agrícola no Brasil? *Revista de Economia e Sociologia Rural*, 46(1), 31–52. doi: 10.1590/S0103-20032008000100002.

Alves, E. (1979). *A produtividade da agricultura*. Brasília, DF. Retrieved November 25, 2018, from: http://ainfo.cnptia.embrapa.br/digital/bitstream/item/150520/1/A-produtividade-da-agricultura-Alves.pdf

Alves, E. (2006). *Migração rural-urbana, agricultura familiar e novas tecnologias*. Coletânea de artigos revistos. Brasília-DF: Embrapa Informação Tecnológica.

Alves, E. (2010). Embrapa: A successful case of institutional innovation. *Revista de Política Agrícola*, 19, 64–72.

Alves, E., Contini, E., & Gasques, J. G. (2008). Evolução da produção e da produtividade da agricultura brasileira. In: Albuquerque, A. C. S., & Silva, A. G. (Eds.). *Agricultura tropical: quatro décadas de inovações tecnológicas, institucionais e políticas*, volume 1. Brasília, DF: Embrapa Informação Tecnológica, pp. 67–98.

Alves, E., & Oliveira, A. J. (2005). O orçamento da Embrapa. *Revista de Política Agrícola*, 14(4), 73–85.

Alves, E., & Pastore, A. C. (1980). A política agrícola do Brasil e a hipótese da inovação induzida. In: Alves, E., Pastore, J., & Pastore, A. C. *Coletânea de trabalhos sobre a Embrapa*. Brasília, DF: Embrapa-DID, pp. 9–14.

Alves, E. & Rocha, D. P. (2010). Ganhar tempo é possível? In: Gasques, J. G., Vieira Filho, J. E. R., & Navarro, Z. *A agricultura brasileira: desempenho recente, desafios e perspectivas*. Brasília-DF: Ipea/Mapa, pp. 275–290.

Alves, E., & Souza, G. S. (2015). O semiárido segundo o Censo Agropecuário 2006 e os censos de população 1991, 2000 e 2010. *Revista de Política Agrícola*, 24(1), 74–85.

Alves, E., Souza, G. S., & Rocha, D. P. (2012). Lucratividade da agricultura. *Revista de Política Agrícola*, 21(2), 45–63.

Alves, F. J. C., & Almeida, L. M. M. C. (2000). Novas formas de contratação de mão-de-obra rural na nova configuração do complexo agroindustrial citrícola paulista. *Informações Econômicas*, 30(12), 7–19.

ANDA – Brazilian Fertilizer Association (2011). Investimentos no Brasil. Retrieved November 25, 2018, from: http://anda.org.br/multimidia/investimentos.pdf

ANFAVEA – Brazilian Automotive Vehicle Manufacturers Association (2018). *Estatísticas: Séries Históricas*. Retrieved November 25, 2018, from: www.anfavea.com.br/

ANP – National Agency of Petroleum, Natural Gas and Biofuels (2018). Capacidade instalada de biodiesel (B100) segundo unidades produtoras. Retrieved November 25, 2018, from: www.anp.gov.br/publicacoes/anuario-estatistico

Aquino, J. R., Radomsky, G. F. W., Spohr G., Peñafiel, A. P. P., & Radomsky, C. W. (2014). Dimensão e características do público potencial do grupo B do Pronaf na região Nordeste e no estado de Minas Gerais. In: Schneider, S., Ferreira, B., & Alves, F. (Eds.). *Aspectos multidimensionais da agricultura brasileira*: diferentes visões do Censo Agropecuário 2006. Brasília-DF: Institute of Applied Economic Research (IPEA), pp. 77–105.

Araújo, J. A., & Vieira Filho, J. E. R. (2018). *Análise dos impactos do Pronaf na agricultura do Brasil no período de 2007 a 2016*. Discussion Paper 2412. Rio de Janeiro: IPEA.

Araújo, P. F. C., & Meyer, R. L. (1979). Política de crédito agrícola no Brasil: objetivos e resultados. In: Veiga, A. (Coord.). *Ensaios sobre política agrícola brasileira*. São Paulo: Secretaria da Agricultura, pp. 137–162.

Arbache, J. (2011). Transformação demográfica e competitividade internacional da economia brasileira. *Revista do BNDES*, 36(42), 365–392.

Arias, D., Vieira, P. A., Contini, E., Farinelli, N. & Morris, M. (2017). *Agriculture productivity growth in Brazil: Recent trends and future prospects*. Washington, DC: World Bank Group.

Arruda, N. M., Maia, A. G., & Alves, L. C. (2018). Desigualdade no acesso à saúde entre as áreas urbanas e rurais do Brasil: uma decomposição de fatores entre 1998 a 2008. *Caderno de Saúde Pública*, 34(6), e0032816. https://doi.org/10.1590/0102-311x00213816

Assad, E. (2018). Agricultura sustentável: bioma cerrado. Unpublished work. Brasília-DF.

BACEN – Brazilian Central Bank (2018a). Matriz de dados do crédito rural. Retrieved December 21, 2018, from: https://dadosabertos.bcb.gov.br/dataset/matrizdadoscreditorural

BACEN – Brazilian Central Bank (2018b). FAQ Programa Nacional de Fortalecimento da Agricultura Familiar – Pronaf. 2017. Retrieved November 25, 2018, from: www.bcb.gov.br/pre/bc_atende/port/PRONAF.asp

Bacha, E. L. (1992). Política brasileira do café: Uma avaliação centenária. In: Martins M., & Johnston E. (Eds.). *150 anos de café*. Rio de Janeiro: Marcelino Martins & E. Johnston Exportadores, pp. 15–136.

Bacha, E. L., & Bonelli R. (2012). *Accounting for the rise and fall of post-WW-II Brazil's growth*. Working paper. Institute for Economic Policy Studies/Casa das Garças. Retrieved November 25, 2018, from: http://iepecdg.com.br/wp-content/uploads/2016/03/120630BachaBonelli.pdf

Bacha, E., & Bolle, M. B. (2013). Introdução. In: Bacha, E., & de Bolle, M. B. (Orgs.). *O futuro da indústria no Brasil – desindustrialização em debate*. Rio de Janeiro: Civilização Brasileira, pp. 13–22.

Baeninger, R. (2012). Rotatividade migratória: um novo olhar para as migrações internas no Brasil. *REMHU: Revista Interdisciplinar da Mobilidade Humana*, 20(39), 77–100. doi: 10.1590/S1980-85852012000200005.

Baer, W. (1984). Industrialization in Latin America: Successes and failures. *Journal of Economic Education*, 15(2), 124–135. doi: 10.1080/00220485.1984.10845060.

Baer, W. (2008) *The Brazilian economy: Growth and development*, 6th ed. London: Lynne Rienner.

Balestro, M. V., & Lourenço, L. C. B. (2014). Notas para uma análise da financeirização do agronegócio: além da volatilidade dos preços das commodities. In: Buainain, A. M., Alves, E., Silveira, J. M., & Navarro, Z. (Orgs.). *O mundo rural no Brasil do século 21*. Brasília, DF: Embrapa, pp. 241–265.

Balsadi, O. V., Borin, M. R., Silva, J. G., & Belik, W. (2002). Transformações tecnológicas e a força de trabalho na agricultura brasileira no período 1990–2000. *Agricultura em São Paulo*, 49(1), 23–40.

Barbier, E. B., Delacote, P., & Wolfersberger, J. (2017) The economic analysis of the forest transition: A review. *Journal of Forest Economics*, 27, 10–17. doi: 10.1016/j.jfe.2017.02.003.

Barros, G. S. C. (2000). A transição na política agrícola brasileira. In: Montoya, A., & Parré, J. L. (Orgs.). *O Agronegócio Brasileiro no Final do Século XX*, volume 1. Passo Fundo-RS: UPF Editora, pp. 57–71.

Barros, G. S. C. (2010). Política Agrícola no Brasil: subsídios e investimentos. In Gasques, J. G., Vieira Filho, J. E. R., & Navarro, Z. (Orgs.). *A Agricultura Brasileira. Desempenho, Desafios e Perspectivas* . Brasília: IPEA, pp. 237–258.

Barros, G. S. C. (2014). Agricultura e indústria no desenvolvimento brasileiro. In: Buainain, A. M., Alves, E., Silveira, J. M., & Navarro, Z. (Orgs.). *O mundo rural no Brasil do século 21*. Brasília, DF: Embrapa, pp. 79–116.

Barros, G. S. C. (2016). Medindo o crescimento do agronegócio: Bonança externa e preços relativos. In: Vieira Filho, J. E. R., & Gasques, J. G. (Orgs.). *Agricultura, Transformação Produtiva e Sustentabilidade*. Brasília-DF: Institute of Applied Economic Research (IPEA), pp. 219–249.

Barros, G. S. C., Castro, N. R., Gilio, L., & Almeida, A. N. (2016). O mercado de trabalho do agronegócio brasileiro – estrutura e perfil. In: *54º Congresso da Sociedade Brasileira de Economia*, Administração e Sociologia Rural, Maceió.

Barros, J. R. M. (1979). Política e desenvolvimento agrícola no Brasil. In: Veiga, A. (Coord.). *Ensaios sobre política agrícola brasileira*. São Paulo: Secretaria da Agricultura, pp. 8–17.

Barros, J. R. M., Pastore, A. F., & Rizzieri, J. A. B. (1983). A evolução recente da agricultura brasileira até 1970. In: Araújo, P. F. C., & Schuh, G. E. *Desenvolvimento da agricultura: estudos de casos*, volume 5. São Paulo: Pioneira, pp. 257–77.

Barros, R. P., Foguel, M. N., & Ulyssea, G. (2007). *Desigualdade de renda no Brasil: uma análise da queda recente*. Brasília-DF: Institute of Applied Economic Research (IPEA).

Barros, R. P., Henriques, R., & Mendonça, R. (2001). *A estabilidade inaceitável*: Desigualdade e pobreza no Brasil. Text for Discussion, 800. Rio de Janeiro-RJ: Institute of Applied Economic Research (IPEA).

Baumann, R. (2000) O Brasil nos anos 1990: uma economia em transição. In: Baumann, R. (Org.). *Brasil – uma década em transição*. Rio de Janeiro: Editora Campus, pp. 11–53.

Belik, W. (2015). A heterogeneidade e suas implicações para as políticas públicas no rural brasileiro. *Revista de Economia e Sociologia Rural*, 53(1), 9–30. doi: 10.1590/ 1234-56781806-9479005301001.

Beltrão, K. I., Camarano, A. A., & Mello, J. L. E. (2005). *Mudanças nas condições de vida dos idosos rurais brasileiros*: resultados não esperados dos avanços da seguridade rural. Text for Discussion, 1066. Rio de Janeiro-RJ, Institute of Applied Economic Research – IPEA.

Benatti. G. S. S. (2018). *State capabilities and public policies: an analysis based on the experience of the National Program to Strengthen Family Farming (Pronaf) from 1996 to 2016.* Master Thesis, Instituto de Economia, Universidade Estadual de Campinas.

Bertzky, M., Kapos, V., & Scharlemann, J. P. W (2011). Indirect land use change from biofuels production: implications for biodiversity. JNCC Report, No. 456.

Bianchini, V. (2015). *20 anos do Pronaf, 1995–2015: avanços e desafios.* Brasília: SAF/MDA, p. 113.

Bielschowsky, R. (2009). Sesenta años de la Cepal: Estructutarismo y neoestructuralismo. *Revista Cepal*, 97, pp. 173–194.

Binswanger-Mkhize, Hans P., Bourguignon, C., & Brink, R. van den. 2009. Agricultural land redistribution: toward greater consensus. Agriculture and Rural Development, World Bank. Retrieved from: https://openknowledge.worldbank.org/handle/10986/2653 License: CC BY 3.0 IGO.

BNDES & CGEE – National Bank for Economic and Social Development and Center for Management and Strategic Studies (2008). *Bioetanol de cana-de-açúcar: energia para o desenvolvimento sustentável*, 1st ed. Rio de Janeiro: Banco Nacional de Desenvolvimento Econômico e Social, p. 314.

Bonelli, R. (2006). Nível de atividade e mudança estrutural. In: *Estatísticas do século XX*. Rio de Janeiro: IBGE, pp. 317–412.

Botelho, E. P. (2016). Role of CAMPO in PRODECER: A successful "coordination" model for agricultural development. In: Hosono, A., Rocha, C. M. C., & Hongo, Y. (Eds.). *Development for sustainable agriculture: The Brazilian Cerrado*. London: Palgrave Macmillan UK, pp. 235–249. doi: 10.1057/9781137431356_11.

Boteon, M., Cappello, F. P., Gomes, F. G., & Vianna, M. M. (2013). Citros – É viável continuar na citricultura? *Revista Hortifruti Brasil*, 123, 12–13.

Bragagnolo, C., & Barros, G. S. C. (2015). Impactos dinâmicos dos fatores de produção e da produtividade sobre a função de produção agrícola. *Revista de Economia e Sociologia Rural*, 53(1), 31–50. doi: 10.1590/1234-56781806-9479005301002.

Brancalion, P. H. S., Garcia, L. C., Loyola, R., Rodrigues, R. R., Pillar, V. D., & Lewinsohn, T. M. (2016). A critical analysis of the Native Vegetation Protection Law of Brazil (2012). Updates and ongoing initiatives. *Natureza & Conservação*, 14, 1–15. https://doi.org/10.1016/j.ncon.2016.03.003.

Brandão, A. S. P. (1989). Efeitos de políticas setoriais e macroeconômicas sobre os incentivos agrícolas. In: XXVII Congresso Brasileiro de Economia e Sociologia Rural.

Brandão, A. S. P, & Carvalho, J. L. (1991). *Trade, exchange rate, and agricultural pricing policies in Brazil:* The country study. World Bank Comparative Studies: The Political Economy of Agricultural Pricing Policy. Washington-DC: The World Bank.

Brandão, A. S. P., Rezende, G. C., & Marques, R. C. (2005). *Agricultural growth in Brazil in the period 1999–2004: Outburst of soybeans and livestock and its impact on the environment. Text for Discussion, 1.103.* Rio de Janeiro-RJ: Institute of Applied Economic Research (IPEA).

Brasil (1966). Law n. 4.947, 6th April 1966. Establishes Norms under Agrarian Law. Brasília-DF: Presidência da República – Casa Civil.

Brasil (1972). Law n. 5.868, 12th November 1972. Creates National Rural Registration System. Brasília-DF: Presidência da República – Casa Civil.

Brasil (1973). Law n. 6.015, 31th December 1973. Provisions concerning public registration. Brasília-DF: Presidência da República – Casa Civil.

Brasil (1979). Law n. 6.739, 05th December 1979. Provisions concerning enrollment and registration of property. Brasília-DF: Presidência da República – Casa Civil.

Brasil (1996). Law n. 9.393, 19th December 1996. Provisions concerning Tax on Rural Territory (ITR). Brasília-DF: Presidência da República – Casa Civil.

Brasil (2006). Law n. 11.326, of 24 July 2016. It establishes the guidelines for the formulation of the National Policy of Family Agriculture and Rural Family Enterprises.

Brasil (2012a). Law n. 12.651, 25th May 2012. Protection of native vegetation. Brasília-DF: Presidência da República – Casa Civil.

Brasil (2012b). Decree n. 7.830, 17th October 2012. Rural Environmental Registry (CAR). Brasília-DF: Presidência da República – Casa Civil.

Brasil (2014a). *Conheça as linhas de crédito do Pronaf.* Brasília-DF: Secretaria Especial de Agricultura Familiar e do Desenvolvimento Agrário. Retrieved October 17, 2018, from: www.mda.gov.br/sitemda/secretaria/saf-creditorural/linhas-de-cr%C3%A9dito

Brasil (2014b). *Programa de Garantia de Preços para a Agricultura Familiar – PGPAF.* 2013/2014. Brasília-DF: Ministério do Desenvolvimento Agrário. Retrieved November 25, 2018, from: www.mda.gov.br/sitemda/sites/sitemda/files/user_img_19/PGPAF.pdf

Brasil (2016a). *Relatório de levantamento operacional no Sistema Nacional de Crédito Rural.* Fiscalização 202/2016. Tribunal de Contas da União. Secretaria-Geral de Controle Externo Secretaria de Controle Externo de Agricultura e Meio Ambiente.

Brasil (2016b). *Aquisição de produtos da agricultura familiar para a alimentação escolar.* Presidência da República, Ministério da Educação, Fundo Nacional de Desenvolvimento da Educação, Diretoria de Ações Educacionais, Coordenação-Geral do Programa Nacional de Alimentação Escolar. Brasília, 2ª edição. CD/FNDE nº 04/2015.

Brasil, Ministry of Agriculture, Livestock and Food Supply (2017). *PROAGRO.* Retrieved October 17, 2018, from: www.agricultura.gov.br/assuntos/riscos-seguro/risco-agropecuario/proagro

Brasil (2018). Sicar – National Rural Environmental Registry. Retrieved March 1, 2018, from: www.car.gov.br/#/.

Bruno, R. A. L. (1997). *Senhores da terra, senhores da guerra: a nova face política das elites agroindustriais no Brasil.* Rio de Janeiro: Forense Universitária/Editora da UFRRJ.

Bryan, G., Chowdhury, S., & Mobarak, A. M. (2014). Underinvestment in a profitable technology: The case of seasonal migration in Bangladesh. *Econometrica*, 82(5), 1671–1748. doi: 10.3982/ECTA10489.

Bryceson, D. F., & Jamal, V. (Eds.) (1997). *Farewell to farms: De-agrarianization and employment in Africa.* Aldershot: Ashgate.

Buainain, A. M. (1999). Trajetória recente da política agrícola brasileira. PhD thesis, Instituto de Economia, Universidade de Campinas, Campinas.

Buainain, A. M., Alves, E., Silveira, J. M., & Navarro, Z. (Orgs.) (2014). *O mundo rural no Brasil do século 21.* Brasília-DF: Embrapa.

Buainain, A. M., Alves, E., Silveira, J. M., & Navarro, Z. (2013). Sete teses sobre o mundo rural brasileiro. *Revista de Política Agrícola*, 22(2), 105–121.

Buainain, A. M., & Dedecca, C. S. (2008). *Emprego e trabalho na agricultura brasileira*, 1a. ed. Brasília-DF: Instituto Interamericano de Cooperação para a Agricultura (IICA).

Buainain, A. M., & Garcia, J. R. (2013). Contextos locais ou regionais: importância para a viabilidade econômica dos pequenos produtores. In: Navarro, Z., & Campos, S. K. (Orgs.). *A pequena produção rural e as tendências do desenvolvimento agrário brasileiro*: ganhar tempo é possível? Brasília-DF: CGEE, pp. 133–176.

Buainain, A. M., & Garcia, J. R. (2015). Recent development patterns and challenges of Brazilian agriculture. In: Shome, P., & Sharma, P. (Eds.). *Emerging economies: Food and energy security, and technology and innovation.* New Delhi: Springer-Verlag, pp. 41–66.

Buainain, A. M., Neder, H. D., & Garcia, J. R. (2014). Social inclusion in rural Brazil under Lula. In: De Castro F., Koonings, K., & Wiesebron, M. (Eds.). *Brazil under the workers' party.* London: Palgrave Macmillan. doi: 10.1057/9781137273819.

Bueno, A. P. S. (2018). Causes of legal insecurity of land ownership in Brazil: The case study of Santana de Parnaíba/SP. Master thesis, Instituto de Economia, Universidade Estadual de Campinas, p. 145.

Camarano, A. A. (Org.) (2014). *Novo regime demográfico: uma nova relação entre população e desenvolvimento.* Rio de Janeiro-RJ: Institute of Applied Economic Research (IPEA).

Cândido, A. (2006). A sociologia no Brasil. *Tempo Social,* 18(1), 271–301. doi: 10.1590/S0103-20702006000100015.

Cano, W. (1998). *Raízes da concentração industrial em São Paulo,* 4a ed. Campinas: Editora da Unicampp, p. 322.

Cardoso, F. H. (1960). O café e a industrialização da cidade de São Paulo. *Revista de História,* 20(42). doi: 10.11606/issn.2316–9141.rh.1960.119977.

Carneiro, F. F., Augusto, L. G. S., Rigotto, R. M., Friedrich, K., & Búrigo, A. C. (2015). *Dossiê ABRASCO: um alerta sobre os impactos dos agrotóxicos na saúde.* Rio de Janeiro: EPSJV; São Paulo: Expressão Popular, p. 624.

Carvalho Filho, I. E. (2008). Old-age benefits and retirement decisions of rural elderly in Brazil. *Journal of Development Economics,* 86(1), 129–146. doi: 10.1016/j.jdeveco.2007.10.007.

Castro, A. B. (1969). *Sete ensaios sobre a economia brasileira.* Rio de Janeiro: Forense.

Castro, A. C. (Org.) (1979). *Evolução recente e situação atual da agricultura brasileira.* Coleção "Estudos sobre o desenvolvimento agrícola". Brasília-DF: BINAGRI, 268 p.

Castro, A. S., & Rossi Júnior, J. L. (2000). *Modelos de previsão para a exportação das principais commodities brasileiras.* Text for Discussion, 716. Rio de Janeiro-RJ: Institute of Applied Economic Research (IPEA).

Castro, J. (1946). *A geografia da fome. A fome no Brasil.* Rio de Janeiro: Empresa Gráfica O Cruzeiro.

Cattaneo, A. (2002). *Balancing agricultural development and deforestation in the Brazilian Amazon.* Research Report. Washington, DC: International Food Policy Research Institute. doi: 10.2499/0896291308rr129.

Caume, D. J. (2009). Agricultura familiar e agronegócio: falsas antinomias. *REDES,* 14(1), 26–44.

CECAFÉ – Brazilian Coffee Exporters Council (2017). Monthly export statistics – December 2017. Retrieved November 25, 2018, from: www.cecafe.com.br/en/statistics/monthly-exports/

CEPALSTAT (2018). Bases de datos y publicaciones estadísticas. Comisión Económica para América Latina y el Caribe. Retrieved November 25, 2018, from: estadisticas.cepal.org/cepalstat/Portada.html

CEPEA – Center for Advanced Studies on Applied Economics (2018). *Brazilian agribusiness GDP.* Retrieved November 25, 2018, from: www.cepea.esalq.usp.br/en/brazilian-agribusiness-gdp.aspx

CFP – Production Financing Company (1989). *Reformas necessárias na política de garantia de preços mínimos.* Informativo Mensal. Brasília-DF: CFP.

CGEE – Center for Management and Strategic Studies (2006). *Estudo sobre o papel das organizações estaduais de pesquisa agrícola.* Brasília-DF: CGEE, 180 p.

CGEE – Center for Management and Strategic Studies (2009). *Bioetanol combustível: uma oportunidade para o Brasil.* Brasília- DF: CGEE, 536 p.

Chaddad, F. R. (2016). *The economics and organization of Brazilian agriculture: Recent evolution and productivity gains.* New York, NY: Elsevier.

Chaddad, F. R., & Boland, M. (2009). Strategy-structure alignment in the world coffee industry: The case of Cooxupe. *Review of Agricultural Economics*, 31(3), 653–665.

Chazdon, R. L., Brancalion, P. H. S., Laestadius, L., Bennett-Curry, A., Buckingham, K., Kumar, C., Moll-Rocek, J., Vieira, I. C., & Wilson, S. J. (2016). When is a forest a forest? Forest concepts and definitions in the era of forest and landscape restoration. *Ambio*, 45(5), 538–550. doi: 10.1007/s13280-016-0772-y.

CIDA – Inter-American Committee for Agricultural Development (1966). *Posse e uso da terra e desenvolvimento sócio-econômico do setor agrícola.* Washington, DC: CIDA/OEA, p. 649.

Cline, W. R. (1970). *Economic consequences of land reform in Brazil.* Amsterdam: North-Holland Publishing.

CODEVASF – Companhia de Desenvolvimento dos Vales do São Francisco e do Parnaíba (2018). Elenco de projetos. Retrieved November 25, 2018, from: www.codevasf.gov.br/ principal/perimetros-irrigados/elenco-de-projetos

Coelho, C. N. (2001). 70 anos de política agrícola no Brasil (1931–2001). *Revista de Política Agrícola*, 10(3), 3–58.

Cohn, A. S., Gil, J., Toledo, C., & Berger, T. (2016). Patterns and processes of pasture to crop conversion in Brazil: Evidence from Mato Grosso State. *Land Use Policy*, 55, 108–120. doi: 10.1016/j.landusepol.2016.03.005.

Colsera, L. L. (1993) A política de garantia de preços mínimos e os valores básicos de custeio. *Revista de Política Agrícola*, 2(3), 13–15.

Comex Stat (2018). Análise das Informações do Comércio Exterior. Retrieved March 2, 2018, from: http://comexstat.mdic.gov.br/pt/home/

Conab – National Food Supply Company (2013). *Programa de Aquisição de Alimentos – PAA: Resultados das ações da Conab em 2012.* Brasília-DF: Conab. Retrieved October 18, 2018, from: www.conab.gov.br/agricultura-familiar/execucao-do-paa

Conab – National Food Supply Company (2018a). *Boletins de safra.* Brasília-DF: Conab. Retrieved November 25, 2018, from: www.conab.gov.br/

Conab – National Food Supply Company (2018b). *Programa de Aquisição de Alimentos – PAA: Resultados das Ações da Conab em 2017*, volume 13. Brasília-DF: Compêndio de estudos Conab.

Correa, P., & Schmidt. C. (2014). Public research organizations and agricultural development in Brazil: How did Embrapa get it right? *Economic Premise*, 145, 1–10.

Cruz Costa, J. (1967). *Contribuição à história das ideias no Brasil*, 2nd ed. Rio de Janeiro: Editora Civilização Brasileira.

Cunha, J. M. P., & Baeninger, R. (2001). A migração nos estados brasileiros no período recente: principais tendências e mudanças. *Bahia Análise & Dados*, 10(4), 79–106.

Da Costa, F. L, & Miano, V. Y. (2013). Estatização e desestatização no Brasil: o papel das empresas estatais nos ciclos de intervenção governamental no domínio econômico. *Revista de Gestion Publica*, 2(1), 145–181.

De Grammont, H. C. (2017). Notas sobre el uso del concepto de desagrarización hecho por diferentes autores. Unpublished manuscript, México City.

Deininger, K. (2003). *Land policies for growth and poverty reduction.* Washington, DC: World Bank and Oxford University Press.

Deininger, K., Selod, H., & Burns, T. (2010). The land governance framework: methodology and early lessons from country pilots. In: Deininger, K., Augustinus, C., Enemark, S., & Munro-Faure, P. *Innovations in land rights recognition, administration and governance.* Washington, DC: World Bank, GLTN, FIG and FAO, pp. 188–203.

De Janvry, A. (1981). The role of land reform in economic development: Policies and politics. *American Journal of Agricultural Economics*, 63(2), 384–392.

De Janvry, A. (1983). Why governments do what they do? The case of food price policy. In: Johnson, G, & Schuh, G. E. (Eds.). *The role of markets in the world food economy.* Boulder: Westview, pp. 185–212.

Delgado, G. C. (1985). *Capital financeiro e agricultura no Brasil 1965–1985.* São Paulo: Ícone.

Dias, G. L. S., & Amaral, C. M. (2000). Mudanças estruturais na agricultura brasileira, 1981–1998. In: Baumann, R. (Org.). *Brasil: Uma década em transição.* Rio de Janeiro: Cepal, Campus, pp. 223–253.

Dias, G. L. S., & Amaral, C. M. (2010). Mudanças estruturais na agricultura brasileira, 1981–1998. In: Baumann, R. (Org.). *Brasil - Uma Década em Transição.* Rio de Janeiro: Cepal, Campus, pp. 223–253.

Dias-Filho, M. B. (2016). *Uso de pastagens para a produção de bovinos de corte no Brasil: passado, presente e futuro.* Belém, PA: Embrapa Amazônia Oriental, 42 p.

DNOCS – National Department for Works to Combat Droughts (2018). Parâmetros públicos de irrigação. Retrieved March 2, 2018, from: www.dnocs.gov.br/~dnocs/doc/canais/perimetros_irrigados

Dosi, G. (1984). *Technical change and industrial transformation: The theory and an application to the semiconductor industry.* London: Palgrave Macmillan UK, 338 p. doi: 10.1007/978-1-349-17521-5.

Duncan, K., Rutledge, I., & Harding, C. (1978). *Land and labour in Latin America: Essays on the development of agrarian capitalism in the nineteenth and twentieth centuries.* Cambridge: Cambridge University Press.

Embrapa (2002). *Pesquisa agropecuária e qualidade de vida:* a história da Embrapa. Brasília-DF: Embrapa.

Embrapa (2018a). *Visão 2030. O futuro da agricultura brasileira.* Brasília-DF: Embrapa. Retrieved November 26, 2018, from: www.embrapa.br/en/visao/trajetoria-da-agricultura-brasileira

Embrapa (2018b). *Biological nitrogen fixation.* Brasília-DF: Embrapa. Retrieved November 26, 2018, from: www.embrapa.br/en/tema-fixacao-biologica-de-nitrogenio/nota-tecnica

EPE – Energy Research Office (2018). *Brazilian Energy Balance 2018: Year 2017.* Rio de Janeiro-RJ: Empresa de Pesquisa Energética.

Evenson, R. E., & Gollin, D. (2003). Assessing the impact of the green revolution, 1960 to 2000. *Science,* 300(5620), 758–762. doi: 10.1126/science.1078710.

Evenson, R. E., & Kislev, Y. (1975). *Agricultural research and productivity.* New Haven, CT: Yale University Press.

FAO – Food and Agricultural Organization of the United Nations (2014). *Feeding the world, caring for the Earth.* Rome: FAO, p. 41.

FAO/AQUASTAT (2018). Food and Agriculture Organization of the United Nations. Retrieved November 26, 2018, from: www.fao.org/nr/water/aquastat/main/index.stm

FAO & INCRA. (1994). *Diretrizes de política agrária e desenvolvimento sustentável.* Brasília-DF: FAO/INCRA, p. 24.

FAO & INCRA (2000). *Novo retrato da agricultura familiar: o Brasil redescoberto.* Brasília-DF: Projeto de Cooperação Técnica FAO/INCRA, p. 74.

FAOSTAT (2018). Food and agriculture data. Retrieved August 25, 2017, from: www.fao.org/faostat/en/#home

FEBRAPDP – Federação Brasileira de Plantio Direto e Irrigação (2018). Área do Sistema Plantio Direto. Retrieved October 30, 2018, from: https://febrapdp.org.br/area-de-pd

Ferraro, A. R. (2012). Alfabetização rural no Brasil na perspectiva das relações campo-cidade e de gênero. *Educação e Realidade,* 37(3), 943–967.

Figueiredo, A. C., & Limongi, F. M. P. (2007). Instituições políticas e governabilidade: desempenho do governo e apoio legislativo na democracia brasileira. In: Melo, C. R., & Saez, M. A. *A democracia brasileira: balanço e perspectivas para o século 21*. Belo Horizonte: UFMG, pp. 25–32.

Figueiredo, A. M., Souza Filho, H. M., & Paullilo, L. F. O. (2013). Análise das margens e transmissão de preços no sistema agroindustrial do suco de laranja no Brasil. *Revista de Economia e Sociologia Rural*, 51(2), 331–350. doi: 10.1590/S0103-20032013000200007.

FIRJAN – Federação das Indústrias do Rio de Janeiro (2018). *Índice Firjan de desenvolvimento municipal*. Retrieved October 30, 2018, from: www.firjan.com.br/ifdm/

Frehse, F. (Org.) (2018). *A sociologia enraizada de José de Souza Martins*. São Paulo: Com-Arte.

Fuglie, K. O. (2010). Total factor productivity in the global agricultural economy: Evidence from FAO Data. In: Alston, J. M., Babcock, B. A., & Pardey, P. G. *The shifting patterns of agricultural production and productivity worldwide*. Ames: Iowa State University, pp. 63–95.

Furtado, C. (1989). *Formação econômica do Brasil*. São Paulo: Editora Nacional.

Garcia, A. (2003). A sociologia rural no Brasil: entre escravos do passado e parceiros do futuro. *Sociologias*, 10, 154–189. doi: 10.1590/S1517-45222003000200006.

Garcia, J. R. (2007). The National Program of production and use of biodiesel in Brazil and the family farm in the Northeast Region. MSc dissertation, Campinas, UNICAMP. Retrieved from: www.repositorio.unicamp.br/handle/REPOSIP/285464

Gasques, J. G. (2015). *Gastos Públicos na Agricultura*. Unpublished work, Brasília-DF.

Gasques, J. G. (2017). *Nota sobre gastos públicos na agricultura*. Brasília-DF: DCEE/CGEA.

Gasques, J. G., Bacchi, M. R. P., & Bastos, E. T. (2018). Crescimento e produtividade da agricultura brasileira de 1975 a 2016. *Carta de Conjuntura IPEA*, 38, 1–9.

Gasques, J. G., Bacchi, M. R. P., Rodrigues, L., Bastos, E. T., & Valdes, C. (2016a). Produtividade da agricultura brasileira: a hipótese da desaceleração. In: Vieira Filho, J. E. R. & Gasques, J. G. (Orgs.). *Agricultura, transformação produtiva e sustentabilidade*. Brasília-DF: Abag/Ipea, pp. 143–163.

Gasques, J. G., Bacchi, M. R. P., Rodrigues, L., Bastos, E. T., & Valdes, C. (2016b). *A produtividade total dos fatores na agricultura – uma análise de quebra estrutural*. Maceió-AL: 54º Congresso SOBER.

Gasques, J. G., & Bastos, E. T. (2009). *Gastos públicos na agricultura brasileira. Revista de Política Agrícola*, 18(2), 18–29.

Gasques, J. G., & Bastos, E. T. (2014) Gastos públicos e o desenvolvimento da agropecuária brasileira. In: Buainain, A. M., Alves, E., Silveira, J. M., & Navarro, Z. (Orgs.). *O mundo rural no Brasil do século 21*. Brasília-DF: Embrapa.

Gasques, J. G., Bastos, E. T., Bacchi, M. R. P, & Valdes, C. (2010b). *Produtividade total dos fatores e transformações da agricultura brasileira: análise dos dados dos Censos Agropecuários*. Campo Grande-MS: 48º Congresso SOBER.

Gasques, J. G., Bastos, E. T., Bacchi, M. R. P., & Valdes, C. (2012b). Produtividade da agricultura brasileira e os efeitos de algumas políticas. *Revista de Política Agrícola*, 21(3), 83–92.

Gasques, J. G., Bastos, E. T., Valdes, C., & Bacchi, M. R. P. (2012a). Total factor productivity in Brazilian agriculture. In: Fuglie. K. O., Wang, S. L., & Ball, V. E. (Eds.). *Productivity growth in agriculture: An international perspective*. Oxfordshire: CAB International, pp. 145–162.

Gasques, J. G., & Verde, C. M. V. (1990). *Crescimento da agricultura brasileira e política agrícola nos anos oitenta*. Text for Discussion, 204. Brasília-DF: Institute of Applied Economic Research (IPEA).

Gasques, J. G., Verde, C. M. V., & Bastos, E. T. (2006). *Gasto público em agricultura: retrospectiva e prioridades*. Text for Discussion, 1225. Brasília-DF: Institute of Applied Economic Research (IPEA).

Gasques, J. G., Vieira Filho, J. E. R., & Navarro, Z. (2010a). *A agricultura brasileira: desempenho recente, desafios e perspectivas*. Brasília-DF: IPEA/MAPA.

Giustina, C. C. D. (2013). Degradação e conservação do cerrado: uma história ambiental do estado de Goiás. PhD thesis – Programa de Pós-Graduação em Desenvolvimento Sustentável da Universidade de Brasília, Brasília, 206 p.

Gollnow, F., & Lakes, T. (2014). Policy change, land use, and agriculture: The case of soy production and cattle ranching in Brazil, 2001–2012. *Applied Geography*, 55, 203–211. doi: 10.1016/j.apgeog.2014.09.003.

Goodland, R. J., & Irwin, H. S. (1975). *Amazon jungle: Green hell to red desert?* Amsterdam: Elsevier, p. 155.

Goodman, D. (1977). Rural structure, surplus mobilization, and modes of production in a peripheral region: The Brazilian Northeast. *Journal of Peasant Studies*, 5(1), 3–32. doi: 10.1080/03066157708438035.

Goodman, D., & Redclift, M. R. (1981). *From peasant to proletariat: Capitalist development and agrarian transition*. Oxford: Blackwell.

Graziano Neto, F. (1982). *Questão agrária e ecologia*. São Paulo: Brasiliense.

Graziano Neto, F. (2016). *Desenvolvimento e democracia no campo*. São Paulo: Editora Baraúna.

Graziano Neto, F., & Navarro, Z. (2015). *Novo mundo rural: a antiga questão agrária e os caminhos futuros da agropecuária no Brasil*. São Paulo: Editora UNESP.

GTDN – Working Group for the Development of the Northeast (1997). Uma política de desenvolvimento econômico para o Nordeste. *Revista Econômica do Nordeste*, 28(4), 387–432.

Guanziroli, C. E. (2007). PRONAF dez anos depois: resultados e perspectivas para o desenvolvimento rural. *Revista de Economia e Sociologia Rural*, 45(2), 301–328. doi: 10.1590/S0103-20032007000200004.

Guanziroli, C. E., Buainain, A. M., & Di Sabbato, A. (2012). Dez anos de evolução da agricultura familiar no Brasil: (1996 e 2006). *Revista de Economia e Sociologia Rural*, 50(2), 351–370. doi: 10.1590/S0103-20032012000200009.

Guanziroli, C. E., & Di Sabbato, A. (2014). Existe na agricultura brasileira um setor que corresponde ao "family farming" americano? *Revista de Economia e Sociologia Rural*, 52(Suppl. 1), 85–104. doi: 10.1590/S0103-20032014000600005.

Hare, D. (1999). 'Push' versus 'pull' factors in migration outflows and returns: Determinants of migration status and spell duration among China's rural population. *Journal of Development Studies*, 35(3), 45–72. doi: 10.1080/00220389908422573.

Hayami, Y., & Ruttan, V. (1985). *Agricultural development: An international perspective*, 2nd ed. London: Johns Hopkins University Press.

Helfand, S. M. (1999). The political economy of agricultural policy in Brazil: Decision making and influence from 1964 to 1992. *Latin American Research Review*, 34(2), 3–41.

Helfand, S. M. (2001). The distribution of subsidized agricultural credit in Brazil: Do interest groups matter? *Development and Change*, 32(3). doi: 10.1111/1467-7660.00213.

Helfand, S. M., Rocha, R., & Vinhais, H. E. F. (2009). Pobreza e desigualdade de renda no Brasil rural: uma análise da queda recente. *Pesquisa e Planejamento Econômico*, 39(1), 59–80.

Heredia, B., Medeiros, L., Palmeira, M., Cintrão, R., & Leite, S. P. (2002). Análise dos impactos regionais da reforma agrária no Brasil. *Estudos Sociedade e Agricultura*, 10(18), 73–111.

Hoffmann, R. (2014). A agricultura familiar produz 70% dos alimentos consumidos no Brasil? *Segurança Alimentar e Nutricional*, 21(1), 417–421.

Hoffmann, R., & Ney, M. G. (2010). Evolução recente da estrutura fundiária e propriedade rural no Brasil. In: Gasques, J. G., Vieira Filho, J. E. R. & Navarro, Z. *A agricultura brasileira: desempenho recente, desafios e perspectivas*. Brasília-DF: IPEA/MAPA, pp. 45–64.

Homma, A. K. O. (2017). A terceira natureza da Amazônia. *Revista Paranaense de Desenvolvimento*, 38(132), 27–42.

Horie, L. (2012). Política econômica, dinâmica setorial e a questão ocupacional no Brasil. Master thesis, Instituto de Economia, Universidade Estadual de Campinas.

IBAMA (2018a). PMDBBS – Projeto de Monitoramento do Desmatamento dos Biomas Brasileiros por Satélite. Retrieved June 1, 2018, from: http://siscom.ibama.gov.br/monitora_biomas/index.htm

IBAMA (2018b). *Vendas de Ingredientes Ativos por Unidade da Federação – 2014*. Brasília-DF: IBGE. Retrieved June 1, 2018, from: https://ibama.gov.br/phocadownload/qualidadeambiental/relatorios/2014/vendas_ingredientes_ativos_uf_2014.xls

IBGE – Brazilian Institute of Statistics and Geography (2006a). *Estatísticas do Século XX*. Brasília-DF: IBGE. Retrieved April 4, 2018, from: https://biblioteca.ibge.gov.br/visualizacao/livros/liv37312.pdf

IBGE – Brazilian Institute of Statistics and Geography (2006b). *Brazilian Agricultural Census 2006*. Brasília-DF: IBGE.

IBGE – Brazilian Institute of Statistics and Geography (2016). *SIDRA – Sistema IBGE de Recuperação Automática*. Brasília-DF: IBGE.

IBGE – Brazilian Institute of Statistics and Geography (2018a). *Sistema IBGE de Recuperação Automática – SIDRA*. Brasília-DF: IBGE. Retrieved March 3, 2018, from: https://sidra.ibge.gov.br/home/scnt/brasil

IBGE – Brazilian Institute of Statistics and Geography (2018b). *Municipal agricultural production*. Brasília-DF: IBGE.

IBGE – Brazilian Institute of Statistics and Geography (2018c). *Brazilian Agricultural Census*. Brasília-DF: IBGE.

ICO – International Coffee Organization (2018). Trade statistics table. Retrieved November 26, 2018, from: www.ico.org/trade_statistics.asp?section=Statistics

IMEA – Institute of Agricultural Economics of Mato Grosso (2017). *Composição do funding do custeio da soja para safra 2016/17 em Mato Grosso*. Retrieved November 26, 2018, from: www.imea.com.br/imea-site/relatorios-mercado

INCRA – Institute National Colonization and Agrarian Reform (1999). *Livro Branco da grilagem de terras no Brasil*. Brasília-DF: INCRA.

INCRA – Institute National Colonization and Agrarian Reform (2015). *Números da Reforma Agrária*. Retrieved March 17, 2016, from: www.incra.gov.br/

INCRA – Institute National Colonization and Agrarian Reform (2016). Famílias Assentadas – histórico até 2016. Retrieved October 29, 2018, from: www.incra.gov.br/tree/info/file/11934

INCRA – Institute National Colonization and Agrarian Reform (2017). Área incorporada ao programa de Reforma Agrária – histórico até 2016. Retrieved October 29, 2018, from: www.incra.gov.br/tree/info/file/11933

INPE – National Institute of Spatial Research (2018a). *PRODES – Projeto de Monitoramento do Desmatamento na Amazônia Legal por Satélite*. Retrieved March 14, 2018, from: www.obt.inpe.br/prodes/dashboard/prodes-rates.html

INPE – National Institute of Spatial Research. PRODES Cerrado (2018b). *INPE divulga dados sobre o desmatamento do bioma Cerrado*. Retrieved September 01, 2018, from: www.obt.inpe.br/OBT/noticias/inpe-divulga-dados-sobre-o-desmatamento-do-bioma-cerrado

IPEA – Institute of Applied Economic Research (2018). Ipea data social. Brasilia-DF: IPEA. Retrieved December 15, 2018, from: www.ipeadata.gov.br

IPEADATA (2018). *Base de dados socioeconômicos*. Brasília-DF: IPEA.

Jabbour, E. (2017). O marxismo e outras influências sobre o pensamento de Ignacio Rangel. *Economia e Sociedade*, 26(3), 561–583. doi: 10.1590/1982–3533.2017v26n3art2.

Kageyama, A. (1990). O novo padrão agrícola brasileiro: do complexo rural aos complexos agroindustriais. In: Delgado, G. C. (Org.). *Agricultura e políticas públicas*. Brasília-DF: Institute of Applied Economic Research (IPEA), pp. 113–234 .

Kageyama, A. (1993). A questão agrária brasileira: interpretações clássicas. *Revista da ABRA*, 23(3), 5–16.

Kageyama, A., & Silva, J. G. (1983). Os resultados da modernização agrícola dos anos 70. *Estudos Econômicos*, 13(3), 537–559.

Kiyota, N., & Perondi, M. A. (2014). Sucessão geracional na agricultura familiar: uma questão de renda? In: Buainain, A. M., Alves, E., Silveira, J. M., & Navarro, Z. (Orgs.). *O mundo rural no Brasil do século 21*. Brasília-DF: Embrapa.

Knothe, G., Gerpen, J.V., Krahl, J., & Ramos, L. P. (2006). *Manual de Biodiesel*. São Paulo: Editora Edgard Blucher.

Krein, J. D., & Stravinsk, B. (2008). Relações de trabalho, regulação e conflitos. In: Buainain, A. M., & Dedecca, C. (Eds.). *Emprego e trabalho na Agricultura brasileira*. Brasília-DF: Instituto Interamericano de Cooperação para a Agricultura (IICA), pp. 357–388.

Lago, A. C. L., Bonomi, A., Cavalett, O., Cunha, M. P. C., & Lima, M. A. P. (2012). Sugarcane as a carbon source: The Brazilian case. *Biomass and Bioenergy* 46, 5–12.

Lamarche, H. (Coord.) (1993). *Agricultura familiar: comparação internacional – uma realidade multiforme*. Campinas: Editora Unicamp.

Lapola, D. M., Schaldach, R., Alcamo, J., Bondeau, A., Koch, J., Koelking, C., & Priess, J. A. (2010). Indirect land-use changes can overcome carbon savings from biofuels in Brazil. *Proceedings of the National Academy of Sciences*, 107(8), 3388–3399. doi: 10.1073/pnas.0907318107.

Lathuillière, M. J., Miranda, E. J., Bullec, C., Couto, E. G., & Johnson, M. S. (2017). Land occupation and transformation impacts of soybean production in Southern Amazonia, Brazil. *Journal of Cleaner Production*, 149, 680–689. doi: 10.1016/j.jclepro.2017.02.120.

Lazzarini, S. G., & Nunes, R. (1998). Competitividade do sistema agroindustrial da soja. In: Farina, E. M. M. Q., & Zylbersztajn, D. (Coord.). *Competitividade no agribusiness brasileiro*. São Paulo: PENSA/USP/IPEA, pp. 194–420.

Lee, E. S. (1966). A theory of migration. *Demography*, 3(1), 47–57.

Leite, R. C. C., Leal, M. R. L.V., Cortez, L. A. B., Griffin, W. M., & Scandiffio, M. I. G. (2009). Can Brazil replace 5% of the 2025 gasoline world demand with ethanol? *Energy*, 34(5), 655–661. doi: 10.1016/j.energy.2008.11.001.

Leme, M. F. P., & Zylbersztajn, D. (2008). Determinantes da escolha de arranjos institucionais: evidências na Comercialização de Fertilizantes para Soja. *Revista de Economia e Sociologia Rural*, 46(2), 517–546. doi: 10.1590/S0103-20032008000200009.

Leone, E. T., Maia, A. G., & Baltar, P. E. (2010) Mudanças na composição das famílias e impactos sobre a redução da pobreza no Brasil. *Economia e Sociedade*, 19(1), 59–77. doi: 10.1590/S0104-06182010000100003.

Libera, A. A. D. (2016). Technological dynamics in agriculture of the Cerrado of Mato Grosso: An agent-based approach. PhD thesis, Instituto de Economia, Universidade de Campinas, Campinas.

Lima, M. C. M. (2002). *Relatório das Correições Extraordinárias nos Registros de Terras Rurais no Estado do Amazonas*. Manaus: Governo do Estado do Amazonas, Secretaria da Cultura do Estado do Amazonas (SEC), 440 p.

Lipton, M. (2009). *Land reform in developing countries property rights and wrongs*. London and New York: Routledge, p. 456.

Lopes, I. G. V. (1992). Política de intervenção do governo na agricultura. *Revista de Política Agrícola*, 1(1), 7–8.

Lopes, I.V., & Lopes, M. R. (2010). O fim das cinco décadas de tributação da agricultura no Brasil. *Revista de Política Agrícola*, 19, 31–41.

Lopes, I.V., Lopes, M.R., & Barcelos, F.C. (2007). Da substituição da importação à agricultura moderna. *Revista Conjuntura Econômica*, 61(11), 56–66.

Lopes, J. R. L. (1982). Empresas e pequenos produtores no desenvolvimento do capitalismo agrário em São Paulo (1940–1970). *Estudos Cebrap*, 22, 41–110.

Lopes, M. R. (1986). *A intervenção do governo nos mercados agrícolas no Brasil: o sistema de regras de intervenção no mecanismo de preços*. Brasília-DF: CFP, Coleção Análise e Pesquisa.

Loureiro, M. R. (1977). *Parceria e capitalismo*. Rio de Janeiro: Zahar.

Loureiro, M. R. (1987). *Terra, família e capital: formação e expansão da pequena burguesia rural em São Paulo*. Petrópolis: Vozes.

Lowder, S. K., Skoet, J., & Singh, S. (2014). What do we really know about the number and distribution of farms and family farms worldwide? Background paper for The State of Food and Agriculture. *ESA Working Paper*, 14(2), 1–38.

Lundvall, B.-Å. (Ed.) (1992). *National systems of innovation: Towards a theory of innovation and interactive learning*. London: Pinter.

Luz, N.V. (1978). *A luta pela industrialização do Brasil*. São Paulo: Editora Alfa Omega.

Machado-da-Silva, C. L., & Graeff, J. F. (2008). Desenvolvimento e institucionalização de práticas em espaços sócio territoriais: a região dos Campos Gerais. *Organizações & Sociedade*, 15(45), 233–252.

Maia, A. G. (2010). A contribuição das fontes de rendimento na dinâmica da distribuição espacial de renda no Brasil. *Nova Economia*, 20(3), 461–490. doi: 10.1590/S0103-63512010000300003.

Maia, A. G. (2013). Estrutura de ocupações e distribuição de rendimentos: uma análise da experiência brasileira nos anos 2000. *Revista de Economia Contemporânea*, 17(2), 276–301. doi: 10.1590/S1415-98482013000200004.

Maia, A. G. (2016). A gravity model analysis of the rural exodus in Brazil. In: *Annals of the X World Conference – Spatial Econometrics Association*, Rome, Italy.

Maia, A. G., & Buainain, A. M. (2015). O novo mapa da população rural brasileiro. *Confins*, 25, 1–26.

Maia, A. G., & Menezes, E. (2014). Economic growth, labor and productivity in Brazil and the United States: A comparative analysis. *Brazilian Journal of Political Economy*, 34(2), 212–229. doi: 10.1590/S0101-31572014000200003.

Maia, A. G., & Sakamoto, C. S. (2014). A nova configuração do mercado de trabalho agrícola brasileiro. In: Buainain, A. M., Alves, E., Silveira, J. M., & Navarro, Z. (Orgs.). *O mundo rural no Brasil do século 21*. Brasília, DF: Embrapa, pp. 591–620.

Maia, A. G., & Sakamoto, C. S. (2016). The impacts of rapid demographic transition on family structure and income inequality in Brazil, 1981–2011. *Population Studies*, 70(3), 293–309. doi: 10.1080/00324728.2016.1201588.

Malerba, F., & Orsenigo, L. (1996). Schumpeterian patterns of innovation are technology-specific. *Research Policy*, 25(3), 451–478. doi: 10.1016/0048-7333(95)00840-3.

Mann, S., & Dickinson, C. (1987). Obstáculos ao desenvolvimento da agricultura capitalista. *Literatura Econômica*, 9(1), 7–26.

Manzatto, C.V., Assad, E. D., Baca, J. F. M., Zaroni, M. J., & Pereira, S. E. M. (2009). *Zoneamento agroecológico da cana-de-açúcar: Expandir a produção, preservar a vida, garantir o futuro*. Rio de Janeiro-RJ: Embrapa Solos.

MAPA – Ministry of Agriculture, Livestock and Food Supply (2018a). *Agrostat: estatísticas de comércio exterior do agronegócio brasileiro*. Brasília-DF: MAPA.

MAPA – Ministry of Agriculture, Livestock and Food Supply (2018b). Plano ABC – Agricultura de Baixa Emissão de Carbono. Retrieved March 14, 2018, from: www.agricultura.gov.br/assuntos/sustentabilidade/plano-abc

Mapbiomas (2018). Mudanças de cobertura e uso: Mapbiomas v. 3.0. Mapbiomas. Retrieved November 27, 2018, from: http://mapbiomas.org/map#transitions

Margulis, S. (2004). *Causes of deforestation of the Brazilian Amazon*. World Bank Working Paper, n. 22. Washington, DC: World Bank.

Marighela, C. et al. (1980). *A questão agrária no Brasil: textos dos anos sessenta*. São Paulo: Editora Brasil Debates.

Martine, G., Camarano, A. A., Neupert, R., & Beltrão, K. (1988). A urbanização no Brasil: retrospectivas, componentes e perspectivas. In: ABEP (Ed.), Anais do 4° Encontro Nacional de Estudos Populacionais, Olinda, Olinda, PE, pp. 19–65.

Martine, G., & Garcia, R. G. (1987) *Os impactos sociais da modernização agrícola*. São Paulo: Editora Caetés.

Martinelli, L. A., Naylor, R., Vitousek, P. M., & Moutinho, P. (2010). Agriculture in Brazil: Impacts, costs, and opportunities for a sustainable future. *Current Opinion in Environmental Sustainability*, 2(5–6), 431–438. doi: 10.1016/j.cosust.2010.09.008.

Martins, J. S. (1975). *Capitalismo e tradicionalismo*. São Paulo: Pioneira.

Martins, J. S. (1979). *O cativeiro da terra*. São Paulo: Hucitec.

Martins, J. S. (1994). *O poder do atraso. Ensaios de Sociologia da história lenta*. São Paulo: Hucitec.

Martins, J. S. (1981). *Os camponeses e a política no Brasil*. Petrópolis: Vozes.

Mattos F. L., & Silveira R. L. F. (2018). The expansion of the Brazilian winter corn crop and its impact on price transmission. *International Journal of Financial Studies*, 6(2), 1–17. doi: 10.3390/ijfs6020045.

Mattos, E., & Ponczek, V. (2009). Estigma, oferta de trabalho e formação de capital humano: evidências para beneficiários de programas de transferência no Brasil. *Pesquisa e Planejamento Econômico*, 39(2), 309–340.

McNeill, J. R. (1986). Agriculture, forests, and ecological history: Brazil, 1500–1984. *Environmental Review*, 10(2), 123–133. doi: 10.2307/3984562.

MDA – Ministry of Agrarian Development (2016). *O que é o Programa Nacional de Produção e Uso do Biodiesel (PNPB)*. Secretaria Especial de Agricultura Familiar e do Desenvolvimento Agrário. Brasília-DF: MDA.

MDA – Ministry of Agrarian Development (2017). *Sistema de Acesso a Informações do Programa Terra Legal*. Brasília-DF: MDA.

Medeiros, L. S. (1989). *História dos movimentos sociais no campo*. Rio de Janeiro: FASE.

Mello, M. C. I. (1975). *O boia-fria: Acumulação e miséria*. Petrópolis: Vozes

Mello, N. G. R., Artaxo, P., Mello, N. G. R., & Artaxo, P. (2017). Evolução do plano de ação para prevenção e controle do desmatamento na Amazônia legal. *Revista do Instituto de Estudos Brasileiros*, 66, 108. doi: 10.11606/issn.2316-901x.v0i66p108-129.

Melo, F. B. H. (1982). Disponibilidade de alimentos e efeitos distributivos: Brasil, 1967/79. *Pesquisa e Planejamento Econômico*, 12(2), 343–398.

Melo, F. H. (1991). A questão da política de preços para produtos agrícolas domésticos. *Revista Brasileira de Economia*, 45(3), 385–396.

Ménard, C., Saes, M. S. M., Silva, V. L. S., & Raynaud, E. (2014). *Challenges to economic organization: Plural forms*. São Paulo: Atlas.

Menezes Filho, N., Campos, G., & Komatsu, B. (2014). *A evolução da produtividade no Brasil. Policy Paper, 12*. São Paulo: Centro de Políticas Públicas, INSPER.

Milanez, A. Y. (2007). Os fundos setoriais são instituições adequadas para promover o desenvolvimento industrial do Brasil? *Revista do BNDES*, 14(27), 123–140.

MMA – Ministry of the Environment (2011). *Plano de ação para prevenção e controle do desmatamento e das queimadas no cerrado*. Brasília-DF: MMA. Retrieved November 27, 2018, from: www.mma.gov.br/estruturas/201/_arquivos/ppcerrado_201.pdf

MMA – Ministry of the Environment (2016). *Planos de ação para a prevenção e o controle do desmatamento – documento base: contexto e análises (versão preliminar)*. Brasília-DF: MMA.

MMA – Ministry of the Environment (2017). *Plano Nacional de Recuperação da Vegetação Nativa*. Brasília-DF: MMA.

MMA – Ministry of the Environment (2018). *CAR – Boletim Informativo: dados até 16 de fevereiro de 2018*. Brasília-DF: MMA. Retrieved November 27, 2018, from: www.florestal. gov.br/documentos/car/boletim-do-car/3294-boletim-informativo-janeiro-de-2018/file

MME – Ministry of Mines and Energy (2018). Brasília-DF: MME. Retrieved November 27, 2018, from: www.mme.gov.br/web/guest/secretarias/petroleo-gas-natural-e-combustiveis-renovaveis/programas/renovabio/principal

Montoya, M. A. Bertussi. L. A. S., & Lopes, R. L. (2017). A cadeia soja no Brasil: uma abordagem Insumo-Produto do PIB, emprego, consumo de energia e emissões de CO2 no período de 2000 a 2014. Text for Discussion. Núcleo de Economia Regional e Urbana da Universidade de São Paulo.

Moreira, C. F., Fernandes, E. A. N., & Vian, C. E. F. (2011). Características da certificação na cafeicultura brasileira. *Organizações Rurais & Agroindustriais*, 13(3), 344–351.

Moreira, G. C., & Teixeira, E. C. (2014). Política pública de pesquisa agropecuária no Brasil. *Revista de Política Agrícola*, 23(3), pp. 5–17.

Moreira, J. R., & Goldemberg, J. (1999) The alcohol program. *Energy Policy*, 27(4), 229–245. doi: 10.1016/S0301-4215(99)00005-1.

Moreira, M., Nassar A, Antoniazzi, L., Bachion, L. C., & Harfuch L. (2012). Direct and indirect land use change assessment. In: Poppe M. K., & Cortez L.A. B. (Eds.). *Sustainability of Sugarcane Bioenergy*. Brasília, Brazil: Center for Strategic Studies and Management, pp. 183–213.

Moura, M. M. (1978) *Os herdeiros da terra*: Parentesco e herança numa área rural. São Paulo: Hucitec.

Moura, M. M. (1988) *Os deserdados da terra*. Rio de Janeiro: Bertrand Brasil.

Moutinho, P., Guerra, R., & Azevedo-Ramos, C. (2016). Achieving zero deforestation in the Brazilian Amazon: What is missing? *Elementa of the Science Anthropocene*, 4. doi: 10.12952/journal.elementa.000125.

MTE – Ministry of Labor and Employment (2018). Data. Brasília-DF: MTE.

Mueller, C. C., & Martine, G. (1997). Modernização da agropecuária, emprego agrícola e êxodo rural no Brasil – A década de 1980. *Revista de Economia Política*, 17(3), 85–104.

Muller, G. (1981). *O complexo agroindustrial brasileiro*. São Paulo: Fundação Getúlio Vargas.

Muller, G. (1989). *Complexo agroindustrial e modernização agrária*. São Paulo: Hucitec.

Navarro, Z. (2010). The Brazilian Landless Movement (MST): Critical times. *Redes*, 15(1), 196–223.

Navarro, Z. (2013). Agroecologia: as coisas em seu lugar (A Agronomia brasileira visita a terra dos duendes). *Colóquio*, 10(1), 11–45. doi: 10.26767/coloquio.v10i1.23.

Navarro, Z. (2016). O mundo rural no novo século (Um ensaio de interpretação). In: Gasques, J. G. & Vieira Filho, J. E. (Orgs.). *Agricultura, transformação produtiva e sustentabilidade*. Brasília-DF: Institute of Applied Economic Research (IPEA), pp. 25–64.

Navarro, Z., & Buainain, A. M. (2017). The global driving of Brazilian agrarian development in the new century. In: Buainain, A. M., et al. (Eds.). *Globalization and agriculture: Redefining unequal development*. Lanham, MD: Lexington Books, pp. 9–30.

Navarro, Z., & Campos, S. K. (2013). A 'pequena produção rural' no Brasil. In: Campos, S. K., & Navarro, Z. (Eds.). *A pequena produção rural e as tendências do desenvolvimento agrário brasileiro: ganhar tempo é possível?* Brasília-DF: CGEE, p. 268.

Neri, M. (2011). *Pobreza e nova classe média no campo*. Rio de Janeiro: Centro de Políticas Públicas e Sociais, FGV/IICA.

Neri, M. (2012). A década inclusiva (2001–2011): *Desigualdade, pobreza e políticas de renda*. Comunicado do Ipea, 155. Brasília-DF: Institute of Applied Economic Research (IPEA).

Neves, M. F. (Coord.), Trombin, V. G., Milan, P., Lopes, F. F., Cressoni, F., Kalaki, R. (2010). *O retrato da citricultura brasileira*. Ribeirão Preto: Editora Markestrat, p. 137.

Nobre, A. D. (2014). *O futuro climático da Amazônia: Relatório de avaliação científica*. São José dos Campos: ARA; CCST-INPE; INPA.

Nogueira, L. A., Capaz, R. S., Souza, S. P., & Seabra, J. E. (2016). Biodiesel program in Brazil: Learning curve over ten years (2005–2015). *Biofuels, Bioproducts and Biorefining*, 10(6), 728–737. doi: 10.1002/bbb.1718.

Novacana (2018). *As usinas de açúcar e etanol do Brasil*. Retrieved November 27, 2018, from: www.novacana.com/usinas_brasil

OECD – Organization for Economic Co-operation and Development (2005). *OECD Review of Agricultural Policies – Brazil*. Paris: OECD.

OECD – Organization for Economic Co-operation and Development (2018). OECD PSE/CSE database. Retrieved November 27, 2018, from: www.oecd.org/agriculture/agricultural-policies/producerandconsumersupportestimatesdatabase.htm

OECD/FAO (2015). *OECD-FAO Agricultural Outlook 2015*. Paris: OECD Publishing. doi: 10.1787/agr_outlook-2015-en.

OCDE/FAO (2018). *Agricultural Outlook 2018–2027*. Paris/Rome: OECD Publishing. doi: 10.1787/agr_outlook-2018-en.

Olinger, G. (1996). *Ascenção e decadência da extensão rural no Brasil*. Florianópolis: EPAGRI.

Oliveira, F. (1972). A economia brasileira: crítica à razão dualista. *Estudos Cebrap*, 2, 5–82.

Oliveira, F. E. B., Beltrão, K. I., & Ferreira, M. G. (1997). *Reforma da previdência*. Text for Discussion, 75. Brasília-DF: Institute of Applied Economic Research (IPEA).

Oliveira, J. C. (1977). *Política de preços mínimos no Brasil*, volume 1. Coleção Análise e Pesquisa. Brasília: Comissão de Financiamento da Produção.

Oliveira, J. C. (1984). Incidência da taxação implícita sobre produtos agrícolas no Brasil. *Pesquisa e Planejamento Econômico*, 14(2), 399–452.

Oliveira, K. F., & Jannuzzi, P. M. (2005). Motivos para migração no Brasil e retorno ao nordeste: padrões etários, por sexo e origem/destino. *São Paulo em Perspectiva*, 19(4), 134–143. doi: 10.1590/S0102-88392005000400009.

Orair, R. O., & Gobetti, S. W. (2011). Governo gastador ou transferidor? Um macrodiagnóstico das despesas federais (2001–2011). In: *Brasil em desenvolvimento: Estado, planejamento e políticas públicas*. Brasília-DF: Institute of Applied Economic Research (IPEA).

Paige, J. (1975). *Agrarian revolution: Social movements and export agriculture in the underdeveloped world*. New York: Free Press.

Palmeira, M. (1971). Latifundium et capitalisme: lecture critique d'un débat. PhD thesis, EHESS, Paris.

Paschoal, A. D. (1979). *Pragas, praguicidas e a crise ambiental*: problemas e soluções (1a ed.). Rio de Janeiro: Fundação Getúlio Vargas.

Pastore, A. C., Alves, E. R. A., & Rizzieri, J. A. B. (1974). *A Inovação induzida e os limites à modernização da agricultura brasileira*. São Paulo: FIPE/USP.

Patrick, G. (1975). Fontes de crescimento na agricultura brasileira. In: Contador, C. R. (Org.). *Tecnologia e desenvolvimento agrícola*. Rio de Janeiro: IPEA/INPES, pp. 89–110.

Pavitt, K. (1984). Sectoral patterns of technical change: Towards a taxonomy and a theory. *Research Policy*, 13(6), 343–373. doi: 10.1016/0048-7333(84)90018-0.

Peixoto, M. (2008). *Extensão rural no Brasil – uma abordagem histórica da legislação*. Centro de Estudos. Text for Discussion, 48. Brasília-DF: Consultoria Legislativa do Senado Federal.

Perz, S. G. (2000). The rural exodus in the context of economic crisis, globalization and reform in Brazil. *International Migration Review*, 34(3), 842–881. doi: 10.2307/2675947.

Pingali, P. L. (2012). Green revolution: Impacts, limits, and the path ahead. *Proceedings of the National Academy of Sciences*, 109(31), 12302–12308. doi: 10.1073/pnas.0912953109.

Pinto, L. C. G. (1980) *Notas sobre política agrícola e crédito rural*. Campinas, São Paulo: NA.

Pivetta, M. (2013). Novas aves da Amazônia. *Pesquisa Fapesp*, 207, 18–23.

PNA – Plano Nacional de Agroenergia 2006–2011 (2006). Ministério da Agricultura, Pecuária e Abastecimento. Secretaria de Produção e Agroenergia. 2nd ed. rev. Brasília-DF: Embrapa Informação Tecnológica.

Prado Jr, C. (1979). *A questão agrária no Brasil*. São Paulo, Editora Brasiliense.

Prebisch, R. (1964). *Dinâmica do desenvolvimento Latino Americano*. Rio de Janeiro: Fundo de Cultura.

PRODES (2017).Taxas de Desmatamento Da Amazônia Legal. Projeto PRODES. Ministério da Ciência e Tecnologia, IBAMA, Ministério do Meio Ambiente, INPE. Retrieved May 05, 2018, from: www.obt.inpe.br/prodes/prodes_1988_2010.htm

Ramos, P. (2014) Uma história sem fim: a persistência da questão agrária no Brasil contemporâneo. In: Buainain, A. M., Alves, E., Silveira, J. M., & Navarro, Z. (Orgs.). *O mundo rural no Brasil do século 21*. Brasília-DF: Embrapa.

Rangel, I. (2005). *Obras reu nidas*. Rio de Janeiro: Contraponto.

Reydon, B. P. (2007) A regulação institucional da propriedade da terra no Brasil: uma necessidade urgente. In: Ramos, P. *Dimensões do Agronegócio Brasileiro: Políticas, Instituições e Perspectivas*. Brasília: MDA.

Reydon, B. P. (2011). O desmatamento da floresta Amazônica: causas e soluções. *Revista Política Ambiental*, 8, 143–155.

Reydon, B. P., & Fernandes, V. B. (2017). Financialization, land prices and land grab: A study based on the Brazilian reality. *Economia e Sociedade*, 26, 1149–1179. doi: 10.1590/1982-3533.2017v26n4art12.

Reydon, B., Fernandes, V. B., Bueno, A. P. S., & Siqueira, G. P. (2017). *Governança de terras: da teoria à realidade brasileira*. Brasília-DF: FAO.

Reydon, B. P., Fernandes, V. B., & Telles, T. S. (2015). Land tenure in Brazil: The question of regulation and governance. *Land Use Policy*, 42, 509–516. doi: doi.org/10.1016/j.landusepol.2014.09.007.

Rezende, G. C. (2002). *A política de preços mínimos e o desenvolvimento agrícola da região Centro-Oeste*. Text for discussion, 870. Brasília-DF: Institute of Applied Economic Research (IPEA).

Rezende, G. C. (2006). Políticas trabalhista, fundiária e de crédito agrícola no Brasil: uma avaliação crítica. *Revista de Economia e Sociologia Rural*, 44(1), 47–78. doi: 10.1590/S0103-20032006000100003.

Ribeiro, R. P. (1985). *O sistema brasileiro de assistência técnica e extensão rural – uma análise retrospectiva*. Leituras Selecionadas, 17. Brasília-DF: Empresa Brasileira de Assistência Técnica e Extensão Rural (EMBRATER).

Rios, J. A. (1971). *A sociologia rural no Brasil: Sua evolução, principais problemas e situação atual*. Rio de Janeiro-RJ: SPLAN.

Robles, W. (2018). Revisiting agrarian reform in Brazil, 1985–2016. *Journal of Developing Societies*, 34(1), 1–34. doi: 10.1177/0169796X17749658.

Rocha, S. (2006). Pobreza e indigência no Brasil: algumas evidências empíricas com base na PNAD 2004. *Nova Economia*, 16(2), 265–299. doi: 10.1590/S0103-63512006000200003.

Rocha, S. (2013). *Pobreza no Brasil: A evolução de longo prazo (1970–2011)*. Estudos e Pesquisas No. 492. Rio de Janeiro-RJ: INAE – Instituto Nacional de Altos Estudos.

Rodriguez, J. R., Treccani. G. D., Benatti, J. H., Oliveira, A. U., Loureiro, V. R., Sá, J. D. M., Alves, A. C. P., Faria, C. S., Hollanda, T. P. B., Hirata, A., Minuici, G., Nascimento, M. S., Selders, M. C. N., & Machado, G. C. (2013) *Registros Públicos e Recuperação de Terras Públicas*. Série Repensando o Direito, 48. Brasília-DF: Ministério da Justiça.

Romeiro, A. R. (2014). O agronegócio será ecológico. In: Buainain, A. M., Alves, E., Silveira, J. M., & Navarro, Z. (Orgs.). *O mundo rural no Brasil do século 21*. Brasília-DF: Embrapa.

Romeiro, A. R., & Abrantes, F. J. (1981). Meio Ambiente e Modernização Agrícola. *Revista Brasileira de Geografia*, 43(1), 3–46.

Rossi, F. R. (2017). Determinantes da adoção de irrigação por citricultores da região centro-norte do Estado de São Paulo. PhD thesis, Programa de Pós-graduação em Engenharia de Produção, Universidade Federal de São Carlos, UFSCar, São Carlos.

Sá Jr., F. (1973). O desenvolvimento da agricultura nordestina e as funções das atividades de subsistência. *Estudos Cebrap*, 3, 87–148.

Sabourin, E. (2007). Que política pública para a agricultura familiar no segundo governo Lula? *Sociedade e Estado*, 22(3), 715–751. doi: 10.1590/S0102-69922007000300009.

Saes, M. S. M. (2010). *Strategies for differentiation and quake-rent appropriation in agriculture: the small-scale production*. São Paulo: Editora Annablume, p. 184.

Saes, M. S. M., & Farina, E. M. M. Q. (1999). *O Agribusiness do Café do Brasil*. São Paulo: Editora Miilkbizz.

Sakamoto, C. S., & Maia, A. G. (2012). Dinâmica do mercado de trabalho agrícola e impactos sobre a distribuição de rendimentos nos anos 2000. *ABET*, 11(2), 11–31.

Salomão, K. (2016). Quais foram as 40 maiores exportadoras até setembro. Exame, Negócios. Retrieved December 17, 2018, from: https://exame.abril.com.br/negocios/quais-foram-as-40-maiores-exportadoras-ate-setembro/

Sampaio, R. M. (2017). Biodiesel no Brasil: capacidades estatais, P&D e inovação na Petrobras Biocombustível. PhD thesis, Instituto de Geociências, Universidade Estadual de Campinas, SP.

Sano, E. E. (2005). Monitoramento semidetalhado (escala de 1:250.000) de ocupação de solos do Cerrado: considerações e proposta metodológica. In: *Anais do XII Simpósio Brasileiro de Sensoriamento Remoto*. Goiânia, Brasil: INPE, pp. 3309–3316.

Sano, S. M., Almeida, S. P., & Ribeiro, J. F. (Eds.) (2008). *Cerrado: ecologia e flora*. Brasília-DF: Embrapa Informação Tecnológica, p. 279.

Santana, C. A., Silva, F. P., Garcia, J. R., Buainain, A. M., Loyola P. (2014). O tripé da política agrícola brasileira: crédito rural, seguro e Pronaf. In: Buainain, A. M., Alves, E., Silveira, J. M., & Navarro, Z. (Orgs.). *O mundo rural no Brasil do século 21*. Brasília-DF: Embrapa, pp. 827–864.

Santos, J. V. (1978). Os colonos do vinho. *Estudo sobre a subordinação do trabalho camponês ao capital*. São Paulo: Hucitec.

Santos, R. (2007). *Agraristas políticos brasileiros*. Brasília-DF: Fundação Astrojildo Pereira.

Scherer-Warren, I. (1989). *Movimentos sociais*. Florianópolis: Editora da UFSC.

Schiff, M., & Valdes, A. (1992). *The political economy of agricultural pricing policy, Volume 4: A synthesis of the economics in developing countries*. Baltimore: Johns Hopkins University Press for the World Bank.

Schneider, S. (2003). *A pluriatividade na agricultura familiar*. Porto Alegre: UFRGS Editora.

Schuh, G. E. (1974). A modernização da agricultura brasileira. In: *Alternativas de desenvolvimento para grupos de baixa renda na agricultura brasileira*. São Paulo: IPE/USP, pp. 120–184.

Schultz, T. W. (1964). *Transforming traditional agriculture*. New Haven and London: Yale University Press.

Seguy, L., Bouzinac, S., Trentini, A. & Côrtes, N. A. (1998). Brazilian frontier agriculture. *Agriculture et Developpement*, Special Issue, 2–63.

Shirota, R. (1988). Crédito rural no Brasil: subsídio, distribuição e fatores associados à oferta. Master thesis, ESALQ/USP, Piracicaba-SP.

Silva, A. C. (1995). De Vargas a Itamar: políticas e programas de alimentação e nutrição. *Estudos Avançados*, 9(23), 87–107. doi: 10.1590/S0103-40141995000100007.

Silva, F. P. (2012). Financiamento da cadeia de grãos no Brasil: o papel das tradings e fornecedores de insumos. Master thesis, Universidade Estadual de Campinas, Campinas.

Silva, J. G. (1981). *Progresso técnico e relações de trabalho na agricultura*. São Paulo: Hucitec.

Silva, J. G. (1982). *A modernização dolorosa: Estrutura agrária, fronteira agrária e trabalhadores rurais no Brasil*. Rio de Janeiro: Zahar.

Silva, J. G. (1992). Fim do 'agribusiness' ou emergência da biotecnologia? *Economia e Sociedade*, 1(1), 163–167.

Silva, J. G. (1999a). *Tecnologia e agricultura familiar*, 2nd ed. Porto Alegre: UFRGS editora.

Silva, J. G. (1999b). *O novo rural brasileiro*. Coleção "Pesquisas". Campinas: Instituto de Economia da Unicamp.

Silva, L. O. (1996). *Terras devolutas e latifúndio: efeitos da lei de 1850*. Campinas: Editora da Unicam, p. 373.

Silva, L. O. (1997). As leis agrárias e o latifúndio improdutivo. *São Paulo em Perspectiva*, 11(2), 15–25.

Silva, N. M., Angeoletto, F., Santos, J. W. M. C., Paranhos Filho, A. C., Vacchiano, M. C., Bohrer, J. F. C., & Cândido, A. K. A. A. (2017). The negative influences of the new Brazilian forest code on the conservation of riparian forests. *European Journal of Ecology*, 3(2), 116–122. doi: 10.1515/eje-2017-0019.

Silva, P. C. G., Moura, M. S. B., Kill, L. H. P., Brito, L. T. L., Pereira, L. A., As, I. B., Correia, R. C., Teixeira, A. H. C., Cunha, T. J. F., & Guimarães Filho, C. (2010). Caracterização do semiárido brasileiro: fatores naturais e humanos. In: Bezerra Sá, & Silva, P. C. G. (eds.). *Semiárido brasileiro: pesquisa, desenvolvimento e inovação*. Petrolina: Embrapa Semiárido, pp. 17–48.

Silva, S. S. (1976). *Expansão cafeeira e origens da indústria no Brasil*. São Paulo: Alfa-Ômega.

Silva, S. S. (1981) *Valor e renda da terra: o movimento do capital no campo*. São Paulo: Polis.

Smith, G. W. (1969). Brazilian agricultural policy: 1950–1967. In: Ellis, H. S. (Ed.). *The economy of Brazil*. Berkeley: University of California Press.

Soares, F. V., Ribas, R. P., & Osório, R. G. (2016). Evaluating the impact of Brazil's Bolsa Família: Cash transfers in comparative perspective. *Latin American Research Review*, 45(2), 173–190.

Soares-Filho, B., Rajão, R., Macedo, M., Carneiro, A., Costa, W., Coe, M., Rodrigues, H., & Alencar, A. (2014). Cracking Brazil's Forest Code. *Science*, 344(6182), 363–364. doi: 10.1126/science.1246663.

Sorj, B. (1980) *Estado e classes sociais na agricultura brasileira*. Rio de Janeiro: Zahar.

SOSMA – SOS Mata Atlântica (2018). Atlas da Mata Atlântica. Retrieved September 5, 2017, from: www.sosma.org.br/projeto/atlas-da-mata-atlantica/dados-mais-recentes/

Souza, D. C., & Oyama, M. D. (2011). Climatic consequences of gradual desertification in the semi-arid area of Northeast Brazil. *Theoretical and Applied Climatology*, 103(3–4), 345–357. doi: 10.1007/s00704-010-0302-y.

Souza, M. M. C (1999). O analfabetismo no brasil sob enfoque demográfico. *Cadernos de Pesquisa*, 107, 169–186. doi: 10.1590/S0100-15741999000200007.

Souza, S. P., Seabra, J. E., & Nogueira, L. A. H. (2017). Feedstocks for biodiesel production: Brazilian and global perspectives. *Biofuels*, 9(4), 1–24. doi: 10.1080/17597269.2017.1278931.

Souza, S. S., & Silva, E. A. (2012). Reforma agrária e planejamento regional: Uma proposição Estado – Mercado. *Planejamento e Políticas Públicas*, 38, 237–262.

Staduto, J. A. R., Rocha Jr., Weimar F., & Bitencourt, Mayra B. (2004). Contratos no mercado de trabalho agrícola: o caso das cooperativas de trabalhadores rurais. *Revista de Economia e Sociologia Rural*, 42(4), 637–661. doi: 10.1590/S0103-20032004000400006.

Stédile, J. P. (Org.) (1994). *A questão agrária hoje*. Porto Alegre: Editora da Universidade.

SUDENE – Superintendency for the Development of the Northeast (2018). *Planejamento Regional SUDENE*. Retrieved March 02, 2018, from: http://sudene.gov.br/planejamento-regional/delimitacao-do-semiarido

Suzigan, W. (1971). A industrialização de São Paulo: 1930–1945. *Revista Brasileira de Economia*, 25(2), 89–111.

Suzigan, W. (1988). Estado e industrialização no Brasil. In: *XIV Congresso Internacional da Associação de Estudos da América Latina*, New Orleans.

Szmrecsányi, T., & Queda, O. (1972). *Vida rural e mudança social*. São Paulo: Editora Nacional.

Tavares, P. A. (2010). Efeito do Programa Bolsa Família sobre a oferta de trabalho das mães. *Economia e Sociedade*, 19(3), 613–635. doi: 10.1590/S0104-06182010000300008.

Teixeira, E. C., Clemente, F., & Braga, M. J. (2013). A contribuição das universidades para o desenvolvimento da agricultura no Brasil. In: *XXV Seminário Internacional de Política Econômica*, Viçosa-MG.

Todaro, M. P. (1969). A model of labor migration and urban unemployment in less developed countries. *American Economic Review*, 59(1), 138–148. doi: 10.2307/1811100.

Trigueirinho, F., Minelli, J. C., & Tokarski, D. (2016). *Biodiesel: oportunidades e desafios no longo prazo*. Brasília-DF: ABIOVE/APROBIO/Ubrabio.

Tritsch, I., & Arvor, D. (2016). Transition in environmental governance in the Brazilian Amazon: emergence of a new pattern of socioeconomic development and deforestation. *Land Use Policy*, 59, 446–455.

Tyson, L., & Spence, M. (2017). Exploring the effects of technology on income and wealth inequality. In: Boushey, H., DeLong, J. B., & Steinbaum, M. (eds.). *After Piketty: The Agenda for Economics and Inequality*. Cambridge, MA: Harvard University Press, pp. 170–208.

UBRARIO – Brazilian Union of Biodiesel and Biojetfuel (2018). Programa Nacional de Produção e Uso de Biodiesel, PNPB. Retrieved October 16, 2018, from: https://ubrabio.com.br/pnpb

UN – United Nations (2018a). United Nations International Statistics Database (UN Comtrade Data). Retrieved December 15, 2018, from: https://comtrade.un.org/

UN – United Nations (2018b). Convention documents, UNFCCC. Retrieved August 16, 2018, from: https://unfccc.int/process/the-convention/history-of-the-convention/convention-documents

UNICA – Brazilian Sugarcane Industry Association. Unicadata. Retrieved September 16, 2018, from: www.unicadata.com.br

USDA – United States Department of Agriculture (2018a). Citrus: World Markets and Trade. Retrieved December 20, 2018, from: www.fas.usda.gov/data/citrus-world-markets-and-trade

USDA – United States Department of Agriculture (2018b). Global Agriculture Trade System, Foreign Agricultural Service. Retrieved December 20, 2018, from: www.fas.usda.gov/databases/global-agricultural-trade-system-gats

Valdés, A. (1996). *Surveillance of agricultural price and trade policy in Latin America during major reforms*. World Bank Technical Paper. Washington, DC: World Bank Group.

Vasconcelos, F. A. G. (2008). Josué de Castro e a Geografia da Fome no Brasil. *Cadernos de Saúde Pública*, 24(11), 2710–2717. doi: 10.1590/S0102-311X2008001100027.

Veiga, J. E. (1991) *O desenvolvimento agrícola*: uma visão histórica. São Paulo: HUCITEC.

Veiga, J. E. (2000). Pobreza rural, distribuição da riqueza e crescimento: a experiência brasileira. In: Tófilo, E., Veiga, J. E. Da, Stiglitz, J., Hoff, K., Squire, L., Lundberg, M., Birdsall, N., Olinto, P., & Tanzi, V. (Eds.). *Distribuição de Riqueza e Crescimento Econômico*. Brasília-DF: Núcleo de Estudos Agrários e Desenvolvimento Rural, p. 200.

Veiga, J. E. (2001). O Brasil rural ainda não encontrou seu eixo de desenvolvimento. *Estudos Avançados*, 15(43), 101–119. doi: 10.1590/S0103-40142001000300010.

Veloso, F. (2013). *Dinâmica recente da produtividade no Brasil*. Conferência do Desenvolvimento 2013. Rio de Janeiro: IBRE/FGV.

Verdi, L. (2018). Moratória da soja conserva a Amazônia. Retrieved December 16, 2018, from: http://noticias.ambientebrasil.com.br/clipping/2018/01/11/141165-moratoria-da-soja-conserva-amazonia.html

Veríssimo, A., & Nussbaum, R. (2011) *Um resumo do status das florestas em países selecionados – Nota Técnica*. São Paulo: Greenpeace, p. 54.

Versiani, F., & Suzigan, W. (1990). O processo brasileiro de industrialização: Uma visão geral. In: *X Congresso Internacional de História Econômica*, Louvain.

Vieira Filho, J. E. R. (2012). *Políticas públicas de inovação tecnológica*. Discussion Paper 1722. Brasília-DF: Institute of Applied Economic Research (IPEA).

Vieira Filho, J. E. R. (2014). *Difusão biotecnológica: a adoção dos transgênicos na agricultura*. Text for discussion, 1937. Brasília-DF: Institute of Applied Economic Research (IPEA).

Vieira Filho, J. E. R. (2018). *Efeito poupa-terra e ganhos de produção no setor agropecuário brasileiro*. Text for discussion, 2386. Brasília-DF: Institute of Applied Economic Research (IPEA).

Vieira Filho, J. E. R., & Fishlow. A. (2017). *Agricultura e indústria no Brasil*: inovação e competitividade. Brasília-DF: Institute of Applied Economic Research (IPEA).

Vieira Filho, J. E. R., & Fornazier. A. (2016). Productividad agropecuaria: reducción de la brecha estructural entre el Brasil y los Estados Unidos de América. *Revista CEPAL*, 118, 215–233.

Vieira Filho, J. E. R., & Silveira, J. M. F. J. (2012). Mudança tecnológica na agricultura: uma revisão crítica da literatura e o papel das economias de aprendizado. *Revista de Economia e Sociologia Rural*, 50(4), 721–742. doi: 10.1590/S0103-20032012000400008.

Vieira Filho, J. E. R., & Vieira. A. C. P. (2013). *A inovação na agricultura brasileira: uma reflexão a partir da análise dos certificados de proteção de cultivares*. Text for discussion, 1866. Brasília-DF: Institute of Applied Economic Research (IPEA).

Vieira Junior, P. A., Vieira, A. C. P., & Buainain, A. M. (2006). O Centro-Oeste brasileiro como fronteira agrícola. In: *VII Congreso de la Asociación Latinoamericana de Sociología Rural*, Quito, Peru.

Villarreal, A., & Hamilton, E. R. (2012). Rush to the border? Market liberalization and urban- and rural-origin internal migration in Mexico. *Social Science Research*, 41(5), 1275–1291. doi: 10.1016/j.ssresearch.2012.02.007.

Walter, A., Galdos, M. V., Scarpare, F. V., Leal, M. R. L. V., Seabra, J. E. A., Cunha, M. P., Picoli, M. C. A., & Oliveira, C. O. F. (2014). Brazilian sugarcane ethanol: Developments so far and challenges for the future. *WIREs Energy and Environment*, 3, 70–92. doi: 10.1002/wene.87.

Wanderley, M. N. B. (1999) Raízes históricas do campesinato brasileiro. In: Tedesco, J. C. (Org.). *Agricultura familiar: realidades e perspectivas*. Passo Fundo: EDIUPF.

Wang, P., Poe, G. L., & Wolf, S. A. (2017). Payments for ecosystem services and wealth distribution. *Ecological Economics*, 132, 63–68. doi: 10.1016/j.ecolecon.2016.10.009.

Wedekin, I. (2017). *Economia da pecuária de corte – fundamentos e o ciclo de preços*. São Paulo: Wedekin Consultores, p. 180.

Wilkinson, J. (1986) *Estado, agroindústria e a pequena produção*. São Paulo: Hucitec.

Wilkinson, J. (2008). *Mercados, redes e valores*. Porto Alegre: UFGRS Editora.

Williamson, I., Enemark, S., Wllace, J., & Rajabifard, A. (2010). *Land administration for sustainable development*. Readlands, CA: ESRI Press Academic.

World Bank (2014). *Brazil land governance assessment*. World Bank Report no. 89239. Washington, DC: World Bank Group.

World Bank (2017). *World development indicators*. Retrieved December 20, 2018, from: https://datacatalog.worldbank.org/dataset/world-development-indicators

World Bank (2018a). *World Bank Open Data*. Retrieved August 23, 2017, from: http://data.worldbank.org/

World Bank (2018b). World Integrated Trade Solution. Retrieved December 21, 2018, from: https://wits.worldbank.org/

World Commission on Environment and Development (1987). *Our common future*. New York: Oxford University Press.

Zylbersztajn, D. (2014). Coordenação e governança de sistemas agroindustriais. In: Buainain, A. M., Alves, E., Silveira, J. M., & Navarro, Z. (Orgs.). *O mundo rural no Brasil do século 21*. Brasília, DF: Embrapa, pp. 267–294.

Index

For Product Safety Concerns and Information please contact our EU
representative GPSR@taylorandfrancis.com Taylor & Francis Verlag GmbH,
Kaufingerstraße 24, 80331 München, Germany

Printed and bound by CPI Group (UK) Ltd, Croydon, CR0 4YY

01/05/2025

01858414-0006